Second-Generation Reforms in Infrastructure Services

Federico Basañes
and Robert Willig
Editors

Published by the Inter-American Development Bank
Distributed by The Johns Hopkins University Press

Washington, D.C.
2002

1300 New York Avenue, N.W.
Washington, D.C. 20577

Produced by the IDB Publications Section.

To order this book, contact:
IDB Bookstore
Tel: 1-877-PUBS IDB/(202) 623-1753
Fax: (202) 623-1709
E-mail: idb-books@iadb.org
www.iadb.org/pub

Cataloging-in-Publication data provided by the
Inter-American Development Bank
Felipe Herrera Library

Second-generation reforms in infrastructure services / edited by Federico Basañes and Robert Willig.

p. cm.
Includes bibliographical references.
ISBN:1931003017

1. Infrastructure (Economics)—Latin America. 2. Infrastructure (Economics)—Law and legislation—Latin America. 3. Competition—Latin America. 4. Telecommunications—Latin America. 5. Electric utilities—Latin America. I. Basañes Federico. II. Willig, Robert D., 1947-. III. Inter-American Development Bank.

363.6 S24—dc21 LCCN: 2001097985

Table of Contents

CHAPTER 1

Introduction

Federico Basañes

During the past two decades, Latin American countries have made pioneering efforts in the design and implementation of reform schemes in infrastructure services. In addition to widespread privatization, the so-called first-generation of reforms encompassed deregulation and restructuring in the provision of energy, water, telecommunications, and transport services. As a consequence of these reforms, the conflicting roles of governments as owners, operators, and regulators were reallocated, with private agents and independent regulators undertaking important parts of these functions. Vertical restructuring of the industries allowed generation, transmission, distribution, and retail to operate as separate activities. Horizontal restructuring fostered entry and rivalry among incumbents and new entrants. Regulation aimed at introducing competition in potentially competitive industry segments, such as generation and retail, has been put in place.

These reforms have proved successful as a means to shape suitable environments for attracting private investment. At the same time, the outcomes have been somewhat mixed in terms of increased efficiency, coverage, and enhanced consumer welfare. However, there is widespread agreement regarding the potentially pivotal role of these reforms in paving the way for economic and social modernization. Some general observations on the dynamics of reform might shed light on the unraveling of protracted reform processes in some countries.

Reforms take place amid the interaction of existing and emerging special interests. It is useful to describe the reform process as evolving in two steps (Dixit 1999): the design of the rules (rulemaking) and the operation of the new institutions in place (policymaking). With this format in mind, a few regularities can be anticipated. Small countries with weak institutions could be tempted to identify reform with privatization of infrastructure assets and with few restrictions on market structure and conduct. If reform takes place in this environment, it is no surprise that the first step may be the phenomenon known as *state capture* (Hellman, Jones, and Kaufmann 2000). Powerful firms could shape the rules of the game to their own advantage at a high social cost.

Captor firms are likely to be *de novo* private firms facing a vague delineation of property rights ex ante. They will try to hedge against this poor definition and take advantage of their bargaining strength vis-à-vis the government. In network utilities, this could result in vertical or horizontal integration, increased end-customer prices, or the provision of contract clauses transferring all risks to the state, yet yielding handsome profits. The political pressure exerted by groups that have lost in the reform may then induce the government to renegotiate the rules of the game. This is a difficult and costly process in which captor firms ask for compensation, measured against expected income under the rules of the game that they helped to devise.

In some countries, the incumbent firms are large, reform has left the property structure untouched, and the courts do not have a strong tradition of enforcing property rights. In these cases, the use of influence—relationships with politicians and the state bureaucracy—yields a process of continuous bargaining with the regulator in the policymaking arena and capture is unlikely. In addition, in most countries, a multi-principal governance structure oversees the regulatory body. Therefore, the reform could produce erratic results and low-powered incentives.

Reform creates and redistributes property rights. However, the ex post situation cannot outperform the initial state of affairs if special interest groups are powerful enough (either by capture or influence) to exacerbate the problem of multiple principals in the regulatory process, or if the institutions are weak. Successful reform requires consensus on how to approach the present set of challenges, the second-generation issues leading to the consolidation or reorientation of initial reforms. As the effects of the initial reforms have unfolded, a new set of challenges has become apparent, especially in countries where the reform process began earliest. This explains why most of the case studies in this book deal with experiences in the initial years after privatization in Argentina, Chile, and Colombia.

This book contributes to the ongoing debate on how to meet these challenges. Renowned experts from academia, industry, regulatory agencies, and international organizations deal with post-privatization dispute settlement mechanisms, access arrangements to network industries, and inroads aimed at achieving effective competition in the reformed industries. There are complex issues at stake and wide differences of approach, rendering the need for further reflection and debate all the more apparent.

Part I. Post-Privatization Disputes and Renegotiations

In general, the sectors involved in the reforms have been characterized to some degree by economies of scale and scope, which in turn have required the direct regulation of the private firms. The reforming countries lacked a regulatory tradition and had weak legal and institutional frameworks. Therefore, they had to use a number of specific instruments to establish the way in which tariffs, quality, investment, or exclusivity would be determined and would evolve over time. Yet, some degree of discretion was also permitted to allow the newly created regulatory bodies to adjust to unforeseen developments, such as changes in technology or demand. In addition, the economic context in which the initial reforms were carried out did not allow the time needed to refine terms, and many loopholes remained. Naturally, those unforeseen events did occur, calling for the use of discretion by regulatory agencies. In some cases, this led to renegotiations and disputes regarding the method for adjusting tariffs, the extent of exclusivity, or the character of investment and expansion. In many cases, the demands made during the dispute process were beyond the authority of the regulatory agencies to fulfill, causing the intervention of public officials.

The studies in this part evaluate a set of contractual adjustments resulting from renegotiations and disputes that took place in the initial years after the reform process began. They also focus on the origin of the disputes, the procedures used to settle them, and the consequences of the solutions with regard to economic efficiency, financial equilibrium, and transfers among different agents.

In chapter 2, Artana, Navajas, and Urbiztondo analyze the regulation and contractual adaptation of public utilities in Argentina in 1991-97. They look at cases of contractual adjustments, renegotiations, and disputes in energy, water, telecommunications, and transportation. These cases provide varied lessons. For instance, deficient contract design paves the way for renegotiations, putting more pressure on the regulatory task. Similar effects produce poorly designed cross subsidies or insufficient competition in the award process. By contrast, highly visible sectors, in which consumers feel the impact of the regulatory measure immediately, yield an environment in which regulatory adjustment of the contract is more balanced.

Overall, the decisions included in this study show some bias toward the objectives of the regulated firms; exceptions are mostly concentrated in the more autonomous regulatory agencies in the energy sectors. The implementation of regulation in the public utility sectors of Argentina seems to have been more problematic in terms of assuring the selection of the best offer in the auctions for the privatized public firms and services given in concession. Problems have also arisen in adequately protecting the interests of captive users. The authors compare different levels of government and show that expropriating behavior is more apparent at provincial levels, and tends to affect firms that extract natural resources.

New instances of contractual renegotiations appear to have a common bias against consumers and to favor the regulated firms. Firms are forgiven for not having reached the previously contracted obligations, and the chapter describes a wave of noncompeted renegotiations. At the same time, the firms must meet the demand for faster expansion and higher investments, perhaps because public officials have some degree of anxiety about increasing investment. It is also interesting to note that none of these decisions were debated publicly, a practice which might have provided an effective mechanism for achieving contractual stability.

In chapter 3, Basañes, Saavedra, and Soto examine a series of post-privatization disputes and renegotiations that took place in the power sector in Chile after the privatization process. This chapter also assesses how that experience was internalized in the design of the regulatory framework for highway concessions. The cases reviewed suggest that conflict has stemmed from three main sources: vertical integration, ambiguities in the regulatory framework, and the institutional weaknesses of regulatory bodies. Chile's experience with private sector participation in the electricity sector provides ample evidence of the importance of adequately designing the structure of the post-privatization market, implementing the appropriate regulatory framework, and developing the institutional capabilities to enforce the regulation.

Several lessons stemming from the regulation of the electricity sector have been implemented in the highway-franchising program. In particular, the experience in the electricity sector has positively influenced institutional and regulatory design. The authorities have reacted quickly in response to perceived wrongdoing or regulatory weaknesses, refusing to change franchise conditions on grounds that a bidder in a concession must accept the risks and that renegotiating is costly and hampers the government's reputation. The government has been careful to avoid the creation of a large and politically powerful holding. By imposing restrictions on the number of franchises a firm can hold, the government signaled its commitment to setting up a competitive industry and to limiting the potential for a large concessionaire to have political power. Lastly, taking into account the limitations of the judiciary system when dealing with disputes in the electricity sector, the government created specific entities to deal with contract disputes between highway concessionaires and the authorities.

In chapter 4, Benavides and Fainboim address conflicts and disputes in telecommunications, energy, and highway concessions in Colombia. The bargaining strength of domestic industrial groups, which tried to seize expected high profits in the cellular phone business, explains the dynamics of the telecommunications sector. It had been state owned and managed for many years, and the government badly needed the political support of those industrial groups (already in the media business). The terms of the concessions and the way the disputes have been handled are favorable to the concessionaires.

In the energy sector, the country recorded the first and largest attempt to change the new market rules by a coalition of senators. The coalition had interests in the coal industry and had influence on the management of fuel-fired generation firms before the reform. The coalition tried to force the entry of a substantial amount of coal-fired plants (to be treated as must-run, base-load plants in the market, bypassing the bidding process into the pool). The transaction and search costs implied by the electoral rules explain the difficulties that the coalition had in reaching a majority agreement in the senate. The chapter also discusses the successful injection of capital to Energía Eléctrica de Bogotá, which is a good example of how to handle institutional constraints in the presence of entrenched interests (such as unions or old-guard politicians).

The authors show that the highway sector is an example of muddling through in contract design by the government. There are numerous examples of strategic behavior and conceptual mistakes, including the format for granting concessions and the risk allocation process. The government undertook risks that the concessionaire could have handled better. Early termination clauses were not clearly stated as different from *force majeure* considerations. Therefore, the analyzed concession contracts tended to impede efficient breaching.

In chapter 5, Legisa describes two of the most important disputes that have taken place in the energy sector in Argentina. The detailed story telling approach provides in-depth information from the point of view of the regulator on practical ways to cope with such significant incidents. The first case refers to a distribution outage that left the city of Buenos Aires in the dark for 10 days. The regulatory agency's quick reaction, the exemplary significance of the contractual penalties imposed, and the subsequent rebuttal of the distributor's appeal set important landmarks in the history of efficient dispute resolution. The second case has to do with the transmission concessionaire company's request for revised remuneration. Thorough examination of the request enabled the regulator to revise the method of calculation provided for in the concession contract. A new resolution was issued, assigning connection and capacity payments among users.

Part II. Promoting Competition in the Provision of Public Services: Access Arrangements to Network Industries

Deregulation efforts have successfully expanded the scope of competition in a number of sectors with network characteristics. In most cases, the competing activities still need to use the existing network to provide the service. That is, for competition to be effective, access to the natural monopoly part of the industry is required. Regulating access to the network therefore becomes crucial for competition to be harnessed for the efficient functioning of these industries. Policymakers must create proper conditions for entry into the competitive segment. At the same time, they must not induce excessive entry, expropriate previous investments, discourage future investment in the monopolized part of the industry, or generate inefficient bypass. Developing and transition economies in particular need access pricing rules that are easy to implement because of severe measurement problems and lack of technical expertise.

This part presents a sample of experiences regarding access arrangements to networks in the electricity, natural gas, potable water, and telecommunications sectors, as well as the role of governments and regulatory authorities vis-à-vis the private sector. The studies analyze the legislation and regulatory actions in each case. Principles and results of the theoretical and analytical work on access pricing are translated into a set of tractable rules and procedures. The chapters present an operationally useful approach to the definition and implementation of access and interconnection rules in network industries. This practical guidance shows policymakers in the region how to ensure the access of competitors to essential network facilities on terms that are consistent with efficient competition and that afford the owners of such facilities a fair opportunity to recover their prudently incurred costs.

In chapter 6, Ordover and Willig set forth a series of practical rules for pricing access in telecommunications, with some relevance to other network industries. The rules aim to meet the policy challenges derived from an incumbent's monopoly control over access. Such control creates the ability and incentives for the incumbent to overprice the service and to unfairly compete with new entrants. The regulator is thus confronted with two alternatives: implementing tight regulation of access, thus enhancing incentives to inefficient bypass, or resorting to relaxed regulation that would encourage entry of competitors that are less efficient than the incumbent. Access rates should provide the incumbent with the correct incentives to efficiently invest in the network.

In chapter 7, Laffont discusses efficient network access pricing rules for developing and transition economies. His recommendations focus mainly on the optimal use of the network when cost recovery is a constraint. First, the type of accounting information available is crucial for assessing the workability of cost-based access pricing rules. In the absence of such data, price cap regulation and international benchmarking are the only possible options. Second, the rules should depend on the other types of instruments available. Often, access pricing rules are also used for accommodating entry. It seems that with fixed costs of entry there is no simple solution to this problem and one should not use access prices for this purpose. Multiple objectives are detrimental to good governance; other instruments should be used if entry in the services is to be encouraged. Third, the main entry problem in developing countries is entry in infrastructure. Access rules should make sure and credible that investors in infrastructure can recover their costs. Generous access rules may be needed for this purpose. From this point of view, the obsession with long-run incremental cost goes in the wrong direction. Fourth, nonprice conditions for interconnection are as important as pricing for efficient liberalization. Regulatory attention should also be paid to these conditions.

In chapter 8, Díaz and Soto concentrate on the Chilean experience in regulating access to networks in electricity and telecommunications. The study offers an insightful comparative analysis of developments in both sectors up to 1999, and of the reasons for differences in reform outcomes. Although regulation in the electricity sector was once considered pioneering, it has not adapted to market evolution and is now to a large extent outdated. By contrast, in the telecommunications sector, regulation was initially weak and incomplete, but it has steadily progressed and adapted to changes in the industry. Ambiguities and limitations in the regulatory framework regarding the practical application of the open-access principle led to substantial distortions in the functioning of the electricity sector, while vertical integration deepened the adverse effects of poor regulation. In the telecommunications sector, implementing open-access provisions has demanded a substantial effort on the side of regulators to overcome both the limitations of regulation and the economic and political power of telephone service incumbents.

The evolution of regulation in the Chilean telecommunications and electricity sectors offers an interesting contrast regarding the role of the authorities in overcoming the limitations imposed by regulatory ambiguities and inefficient privatization outcomes. In the telecommunications industry, the authorities have pursued an active stance of attacking the sources of monopoly power and introducing competition policies in local and long-distance telephone service markets. In the electricity sector, lack of regulation has led to substantial litigation over monopoly power, over-investment in transmission facilities, and friction among competitors in the generation market. Developments in the Chilean power sector illustrate the significance of designing an adequate time frame for the correct implementation of reforms in utility sectors. Since developing a competitive market when there is a dominant operator is a costly and long-term process, schemes for reducing market power should be put in place before the divestiture of the industry, and restrictions on vertical integration should be introduced during the privatization process.

In chapter 9, Urbiztondo, Auguste, and Basañes deal with open access, interconnection, and competition in the electricity, natural gas, and telecommunications sectors in Argentina in the initial years after the privatization. The authors address five main issues: how access is determined; the kind and degree of competition; regulatory measures that have affected access and competition; desirable and likely regulatory measures; and future developments. A thorough examination of these issues leads to highly encouraging considerations. Compared with the experiences in other countries, there is significant room for advancing deregulation and competition in the industries analyzed in Argentina.

Strong competition is developing in all three sectors, but it has been delayed by natural learning and attempts to maintain cross subsidies. Although there is insufficient advancement of principles on access prices to guide regulation and arbitration in the future, the current default tariffs make this of secondary importance. Indeed, in addition to the pricing of access, issues such as unbundling, the degree of deregulation, provision of incentives to expand the networks, confidentiality of arrangement (including the possibility of price discrimination), the general structure of tariffs, and the existence of cross subsidies should also be taken into consideration regarding the extent of competition in regulated industries.

Part III. Highlights of Second-Generation Reforms in Energy Sectors in Latin America and around the World

This part conveys a forward-looking, global vision of second-generation reforms under way in energy markets around the world. It puts forward the economic and technological rationale for completing the reform process in the electricity and gas sectors. The chapters present a thorough analysis of the issues involved in the introduction of retail competition in electricity provision, the liberalization of gas sectors, and the functioning and evolution of power exchanges. Cutting-edge schemes from Australia, Europe, Latin America, New Zealand, and the United States provide illustrations. One common lesson emerges from the three studies in terms of what could be the main pending issue for the next wave of reforms: unless there is an adequate market structure in place with a sufficient number of rival firms competing, the benefits of reforms will be unlikely to reach consumers.

In chapter 10, Millán offers an update of the multifaceted reform processes that power exchanges have undergone around the world, two decades after the launching of the pioneering experiments in Chile and the United Kingdom. This chapter shows that imported power exchange models need to be adapted to each country's circumstances. However, despite efficiency issues, first-generation reforms were pivotal in developing competitive electricity markets. The experiment has not failed in any country so far. Current adjustments to the systems aim at improving competition, rather than returning to centralized systems. Millán draws a number of important lessons from second-generation reforms of power exchanges, including the need for flexibility when designing new power markets, and the requirements for preventing abuses of dominance, among others.

In chapter 11, Beato and Fuente introduce the idea of the ability to choose for all electricity consumers, or giving "power to the people," as the last step in completing the process of liberalization of power sectors. In fact, the establishment of free choice for customers purchasing electricity services is at the heart of second-generation regulatory reform. Therefore, the fortunes of electricity retailers will largely be determined by how well they understand their customers and respond to their needs and preferences in terms of prices, services, products, and expectations. The process in which retailers strive to develop new services and products in accordance with the new environment will mark a historic transition away from consumers that are captives of monopolies, toward a competitive, market-driven approach to servicing regular contestable customers.

In chapter 12, Beato and Fuente tackle reform developments under way in the gas industry in Latin America. In the past decade, environmental concerns and increased demand for energy have led to intensified exploitation and discovery of gas fields. At present, Latin America is self-sufficient in natural gas, with Argentina, Mexico, and Venezuela accounting for about 75 percent of total natural gas production. Bolivia and Colombia are also significant producers. An intense wave of reform has swept most of these countries. Privatization, free entry to exploration and production, and wellhead price deregulation shaped first-generation reforms. The set of second-generation reforms under way encompasses free entry in the transportation and distribution segments; full separation of transportation, distribution, and supply; and the establishment of secondary markets for transportation rights. The authors demonstrate that, in spite of the significant progress achieved by the reform process, the market power of large incumbents at the exploration and production stages hampers further inroads.

References

Dixit, A. K. 1999. *Some Lessons from Transaction-cost Politics for Less-developed Countries.* Working Paper no. 1.01. Princeton University, Princeton, N.J.

Hellman, J. S., G. Jones, and D. Kaufmann. 2000. *Seize the State, Seize the Day. State Capture, Corruption and Influence in Transition.* Policy Research Working Paper no. 2444. The World Bank, Washington, D.C.

Part I. Post-Privatization Disputes and Renegotiations

CHAPTER 2

The Regulation and Contractual Adaptation of Public Utilities in Argentina

Daniel Artana, Fernando Navajas, and Santiago Urbiztondo

Since 1990, Argentina has experienced an unprecedented process of transfer of services and publicly owned firms to the private sector, both by selling assets and by contractual agreements (concessions) with or without exclusivity. In general, but not always, the sectors involved have been characterized to some degree by economies of scale and scope, which, in turn, require the direct regulation of the private firms. Because of the weak reputation and institutional background of public policy in Argentina, the contracts are specific about the way in which tariffs, quality, investment, and exclusivity are to evolve over time. Yet, some discretion has been left to the newly created regulatory bodies to adjust those contracts according to unforeseen developments.

Nevertheless, the economic context in which the initial privatizations were carried out did not allow the time to refine terms and many loopholes remained. Naturally, those unforeseen events have come to pass and regulatory agencies have had to use their discretionary powers. In some cases, the alleged modifications in the environment have given rise to renegotiations regarding the method of adjustment of tariffs, the extent of exclusivity, and the character of investment and expansion. Some modifications have gone beyond the authority of the regulatory agencies, causing the intervention of public officials.

In this chapter we evaluate a set of contractual adjustments, renegotiations, and disputes that have taken place in Argentina since 1991.[1] First, we consider whether the decisions analyzed are inside the initial contract or represent a modification of it (that is, whether they are outside the initial contract). Second, we discuss whether the events were motivated by unexpected shocks (which

[1] For a wider range of examples, see Artana, Navajas, and Urbiztondo (1998).

were very difficult or even impossible to foresee), loopholes in the initial contracts (ambiguities) that should not have existed, or a contractual failure to respect the initial contract (a holdup by one of the parties). Third, we describe the actors involved in the disputes and the "production" of these innovations, that is, the regulatory agencies, ministries, legislators, industry associations, regulated firms, consumer representatives, and advocates. Fourth, we describe how these disputes were resolved. Fifth, we evaluate the solutions in three dimensions: (1) the degree of respect given to the letter and spirit of the existing contract; (2) their effect on static and dynamic efficiency (in terms of welfare); and (3) the transfers between users and regulated firms, on the one hand, and among different types of users, on the other hand.

The chapter summarizes cases in natural gas, electricity, water and sewerage, telecommunications, and railways. Some of the cases constitute renegotiations of the original contracts, others represent contractual interpretations by the regulatory bodies. The common feature is that discretion was used in each of the decisions, calling for an evaluation and explanation regarding their characteristics. These cases differ in terms of the sectors and technical characteristics involved, the impact and visibility in the press, the direction of the final decisions, the reactions by the owners of the regulated firms, and the jurisdictional level of the authorities involved.

The Natural Gas Sector

Since the privatization of Gas del Estado S.A. in 1993, eight private distribution companies have provided natural gas in Argentina.[2] Three main production areas in the country (Norte, Neuquina, and Austral) and two different pipelines (north and south) supply the eight distribution companies. The industry was vertically separated to favor the development of competition wherever it was technologically and economically feasible. In particular, large industrial users may buy gas directly (through brokers) from producers, bypassing the distribution companies, either commercially or physically.

Despite this regional separation at the distribution level, regulation of transportation and distribution is centralized at the federal level, and it is carried out by the Ente Nacional Regulador del Gas (ENARGAS), an autarkic entity created at the time of privatization. ENARGAS's decisions are constrained and guided by the regulatory framework and operation licenses. Upstream, that is, at

[2] Soon there will be nine distribution companies, as the provision of natural gas will be available in the Mesopotamia region.

the production fields, prices are set competitively by various producers. The most important producer, REPSOL-YPF (Yacimientos Petrolíferos Fiscales), has a majority of the market, raising some concerns about the degree of actual competition taking place. In accordance with Law 24.076 and Presidential Decree 1732/92, ENARGAS is responsible for approving tariffs (that is, margins) for transportation, tariffs for final users, and the pass-through of gas costs. It also verifies safety and quality requirements and environmental conditions. Other federal and provincial agencies regulate upstream activities. The executive (of the federal government) grants transportation and distribution licenses that are valid for 35 years and renewable for 10 additional years. At the end of that period, a new auction will have to be carried out to determine which private entities will continue to provide transportation and distribution services.

Case I. Retained Gas

Retained gas is the percentage of transported fluid used as an input to transport gas from the fields to the city limits.[3] Since 1994 the market price of natural gas in the fields in Argentina has increased faster than the index of international prices used as a reference to adjust the price cap for distribution companies.[4] As a result, the distribution companies have asked ENARGAS for an increase in tariffs to final users in order to compensate them for the higher-than-expected cost of retained gas. The percentage of retained gas in total gas transported has admittedly remained constant, and thus the claim is only due to the change in relative prices. At the time Gas del Estado was privatized, prices were set by public authorities and were judged to be too low. Given the initial conditions in the production fields, it could be argued that the faster increase in the price of gas had to be anticipated at the time of the privatization. The case has been managed so far within the scope of bilateral relations between the distribution companies and the regulator, without the involvement of external parties to the sector (such as the ombudsman, political representatives, or consumer groups), mainly because ENARGAS rejected the petition of the distribution companies.

The conflict in this case arises from a difference between the distribution companies and the regulator regarding an issue that is not explicit in the regulatory framework. That is, the issue was part of the initial contract, but there was a

[3] That is, transportation companies rent their pipelines to distribution companies. Only 97.5 percent of the natural gas purchased from producers is actually sold to final users, the difference being computed as a cost of transportation. The distribution companies pay for this cost. Therefore, the transportation companies are not affected by the percentage of "retained gas" or by its price.

[4] Distribution companies buy most of their gas on a long-term basis and therefore the significance of the spot market is only relative. Nevertheless, we refer to the market price of gas in order to simplify the exposition of the problem.

dispute about its interpretation. In effect, the contract does not mention the index to be used in order to adjust the cost of retained gas. However, the transportation licenses establish explicitly that the tariff for transportation will be adjusted according to changes in the U.S. producer price index (PPI). The distribution companies demanded that the price of retained gas be adjusted by the actual price paid for this input, and ENARGAS authorized only an increase equivalent to observed changes in the PPI (which were smaller).

It is debatable whether retained gas is a transportation input that should be adjusted by the PPI, or a commercial gas that should be adjusted according to changes in its own prices. The regulatory framework supports both alternatives. The distribution companies highlight the second paragraph of article 41 of Law 24.076, which says that, "transportation and distribution companies will be allowed to reduce totally or partially the profitability contemplated in their maximum tariffs, but they have to recover their costs in any case." This, in turn, allows them to ask for tariff adjustments due to objective, justified, not repeating, and not previously anticipated reasons (following article 46 of Law 24.076 and accompanying legislation).[5]

By contrast, Law 24.076 (article 37) specifies that tariffs for gas consumed by final users are the sum of the price of gas paid to producers, the transportation margin, and the distribution margin. The application of this legislation (by Decree 1738/92) defines the transportation margin as the remuneration of that service in its different alternatives regardless of who contracts it (that is, it includes the distribution companies). In turn, the licenses for transportation indicate that these tariffs will be adjusted every six months according to observed changes in the PPI, and every five years according to efficiency and investment parameters. However, in no case is it established that the price of gas is an element of judgment to be considered in such an adjustment. In other words, the cost of transportation is defined as independent of the price of natural gas in the fields. Finally, the distribution licenses establish that adjustments for the variation in the price of gas purchased have to be computed in relation to the number of cubic meters consumed (point 9.2.2.2). Accordingly, changes in the cost of the gas purchased by the distribution companies are passed through to the final tariffs only on the basis of the final consumption of it. This leads to the conclusion that the difference between the volumes of gas purchased and sold is implicitly defined as a transportation input whose periodic adjustment responds to changes in the PPI and not to changes in the price of gas in the fields, thus supporting the position adopted by ENARGAS.[6]

---

[5] It could be argued that, since the problem could emerge in subsequent periods, it would be repetitive and therefore the distribution companies would not have the right to petition for an adjustment in tariffs. However, it should be understood that once this decision is made, there would be no further need to modify the (conceptual) regulation in the future, and then it should be considered as nonrepetitive.

[6] However, the transportation companies do not intervene by purchasing gas from producers to use it in the transportation process as retained gas.

In principle, the conflicting arguments demand an analysis. However, the position defended by the distribution companies has an important weakness: if an index other than the PPI is used for a transportation input, then it would be possible to question whether other inputs (different from gas) should be effectively adjusted by the PPI. For example, it would be admissible to adjust the cost of some construction materials by the price of steel, or to adjust the cost of labor by a wage index. This would be a violation of the price-cap rules. The contract opted for the adjustment of tariffs according to the PPI (avoiding the information and incentive problems of cost-of-service regulation), without distinguishing among the different inputs to the process. Therefore, it is not appropriate to differentiate among the inputs when this proves to be convenient for one of the parties. Furthermore, regarding the second paragraph of article 41 of Law 24.076, it has not been established that tariffs have to allow for item-by-item cost coverage. Therefore, the law can be interpreted as a requirement over global costs. Thus, economic arguments support ENARGAS's rejection of the petition by the distribution companies.

From the regulatory point of view, it is admissible for the distribution companies to petition for an adjustment in the regulatory practice, but the economic arguments do not support their position. The decision adopted by ENARGAS was to refuse the change in the formulas for adjustment of the final tariffs by indexing retained gas to the price of gas in the fields. This decision respected the existing contract, while avoiding undue transfers from users to regulated firms or among different users. It respected the price-cap spirit of the contract at the same time that it reduced the scope for future demand for contract renegotiations when market conditions are unfavorable to the regulated firms.

This decision by ENARGAS can be explained by three factors. First, the relative (economic) magnitude of the conflict explains the decision because the adjustment clause refers to an input that represents approximately 2.5 percent of total gas costs, preventing strong participation by interest groups. Second, the opposite decision would have meant a change in existing practices that was not supported by economic considerations. Third, the characteristics of the industry and the design of the regulatory agency, as described in Urbiztondo, Artana, and Navajas (1997), do not introduce incentives for ENARGAS to bias its objectives toward those of the regulated firms.

The Electricity Sector

To take advantage of the potential competition in generation, privatization of Argentina's electricity sector included a ban on vertical integration. Distribution in the greater Buenos Aires metropolitan area (which includes the city of Buenos

Aires and 14 municipalities of the province of Buenos Aires), previously in the hands of the federal government, was awarded to two private concessionaires in 1992. Many provincial governments followed the same strategy when privatizing local distribution companies. Transmission of the interconnected grid was given in concession to a private firm (Transener), also in 1992, under an open-access rule.[7]

Transmission represents only about 10 percent of the total value added of the sector, but it is crucial for competition in generation. The costs of transmission include capital costs for the construction of new lines, operation and maintenance costs, and the power losses between exporting and importing points (estimated at 3 to 5 percent of the amount of electricity transmitted).

The revenues of transmission firms are not clearly related to costs. About 55 percent of Transener's revenues are related to power losses and 45 percent to capacity costs. In fact, Transener does not set the quantity of electricity it sells or the price it charges. It can decide only whether it participates in a new project and its effort to operate the grid. Moreover, generators and the distribution companies usually pay for power losses and as energy losses increase, the transmission company receives more income. Although there are penalties for reductions in the quality of service, asymmetric information between the firm and the regulator introduces an incentive problem.[8]

Problems in financing new investments in transmission lines are a common occurrence in other countries as well. Potential solutions to these problems are vertical integration (used in Argentina when the electricity sector was publicly owned), cooperative agreements (like those used in Scandinavia, only feasible with few participants), and decision rules (used in Argentina, Chile, and the United Kingdom).

In Argentina, a group of users (generators) or a new transmission company can propose a project for the expansion of the transmission grid. The proposal may be vetoed in a public hearing if more than 30 percent of the users of the system reject it. If it is accepted, the project is auctioned for construction. The firm that bids the lowest construction cost estimate wins the bid. Users pay the investment charges based on the estimate of the benefits they will receive from the new line. Transener supervises the construction and operation of the new

[7] There are five regional transmission companies. New firms are allowed to build and operate new transmission lines under the technical supervision of Transener.

[8] Penalties paid by Transener during 1995 increased by $8.1 million, while its total revenues increased by $2.6 million. During 1996, penalties paid were $1.5 million higher than in 1995, while revenues were $3.1 million higher. This suggests that during 1995 the marginal penalty might have been higher than the marginal revenue from lost energy, but the opposite happened during 1996. Since these penalties might arise for various reasons and available data are for revenue from all sources (not only for the 55 percent related to power losses), incentive problems could still be relevant.

line. Electricity generating companies can also agree to pay the capacity cost to a construction company. However, given the open-access rule, they are forced to allow any other user access to the line, paying only the operation and maintenance costs. Therefore, this alternative has an obvious free-rider problem regarding who pays for the capacity costs.

The expansion of capacity also has financing problems that are exacerbated in the case of an interconnected system with open access. As electricity flows according to the resistance of the line, in interconnected systems there are unintentional power flows that affect users other than those connected through one of the transmission lines (a typical externality). Although open access may have advantages in that it fosters competition, it introduces public good problems.[9] In the Argentine case there are three additional problems: (1) Transener has an incentive to postpone new investments if the additional revenue it perceives through an increase in power losses is higher than the penalties it has to pay for a deterioration in the quality of the service; (2) not all beneficiaries (especially future ones) are able to participate in the process of deciding to expand capacity; and (3) users pay the capacity costs through an estimate of benefits that does not reflect true economic benefits.

Finally, the public hearing process is expected to create delays in the expansion of capacity.[10] Since the investment charge is not proportional to the benefits that each user receives, those users who may be negatively affected in the estimate of benefits are encouraged to veto the project. Some benefits, for instance the improvement in the reliability of the grid when it has less congested lines, are not even counted. Transener may have an incentive to postpone new investments to avoid reductions in power losses that reduce its revenues.

Case II. Construction of a New Electricity Transmission Line

Transener operates three transmission lines that link the Comahue region (an exporting area rich in natural gas with many power plants, both hydroelectric and thermal) to the city of Buenos Aires. New investment in generation in the Comahue region created an excess supply and led to congestion in the three transmission lines, which would induce a reduction in local prices for final users. When this happens the regulatory framework in Argentina does not allow the price paid by users in the Comahue region to fall. Purchasers of energy continue

[9] For example, a user that did not pay for the construction of a new line may use the open-access principle to be served by that line. In Argentina, that user might even be served before those who paid for the construction of the line. This creates an obvious incentive for not revealing true preferences if charges for investments are based on the revealed preference of each firm.

[10] See Gasparini (1997).

paying the spot price and energy generators have to place the difference in prices (between the average spot price for the country and the estimated market price for the Comahue region) in a special account to raise funds to finance the construction of a new line. Electricity generating companies in Comahue have an incentive to propose a new project to the extent that the investment charges they have to pay are lower than the higher revenues they will obtain when the price they receive is the full spot price.

A group of generating companies in Comahue proposed a project to build a fourth transmission line in 1994, but the project was voted down. (Some Comahue generating companies were among those who voted against the project.) In 1996 the entire region's generating companies proposed a project to build a fourth line. This suggests that they entered negotiations to solve the externalities inside the group. Another factor may have encouraged cooperation: the special account raised about $100 million (the cost of the fourth line was estimated at about $250 million).[11] This created an incentive for opportunistic behavior in the government to use the money for purposes other than construction of the line. There was some opposition at the time the project was debated, but it represented less than the required 30 percent to force a veto. [12]

After the project was approved by the regulatory agency Ente Nacional Regulador de la Electricidad (ENRE), there were further delays caused by debates about the details of the technical and economic conditions for the bid.[13] Finally, in 1997 the bid was called and Transener won with an annual investment charge of $24.5 million for 15 years.[14] It took about three years to complete the process of deciding whether it was necessary to construct a fourth line, where it would be constructed, and who would be responsible for building it.

Procedures for expanding electricity transmission capacity were included in the regulatory framework, but they were flawed and encouraged a long negotiation process. The actors involved were the regulatory agency and the users of the system. There was some politicization of the discussion, especially when the builders had a dispute about their different status concerning the value-added tax.

---

[11] Amounts are in U.S. dollars.

[12] At that time, ESEBA was a generation and distribution company in the province of Buenos Aires. It voted against the project because it had no problems selling its energy, but, being a generator, it would have to pay for the capacity costs of the fourth line.

[13] For example, the operator of the fourth line will use some facilities owned by Transener. This requires the calculation of an access charge. Protest also arose because a newly created society for the construction of the fourth line faces a higher financial cost than preexisting firms (like Transener and other interested firms) due to differential tax treatment.

[14] The offers made by the other three participants ranged from $24.9 million to $39 million.

The construction of the fourth line was approved and auctioned following the steps included in the regulatory framework, but with long delays, as the economic analysis of the rules suggested would happen. The solution reached obeyed the letter and spirit of the original contract, but did little to solve the incentive problems that encourage delays in the investment in new capacity. Although there is no way to solve all the incentive problems that arise because of the public good characteristics and the externalities involved in the transmission of electricity, existing regulations could be improved. In fact, ENRE is working on a new regulation to govern private agreements between generators and builders (that is, an alternative to the public hearing process) that will assure privileged access to the line for those generators paying for it. Other generating companies will be allowed to use the line (paying the operation and maintenance costs) only if there is excess capacity.

The public hearing alternative could be improved. For example, Gasparini (1997) suggests that: (1) the veto should be abolished; (2) the estimate of the benefits of each user should be better matched to economic benefits (this is possible given the information available); (3) all beneficiaries should be included (not only those within the region, also recognizing the limitation for new users to be represented); and (4) discussion of more than one project at the same time should be encouraged.

As a general lesson, a poor definition of property rights created more problems than expected. Matters could be improved while maintaining the open-access rule, although a more flexible application of it would help reduce the free-rider problem that appears when decisions have to be made regarding new investments.

The Water and Sewerage Sector

Provincial governments are responsible for the provision and regulation of water and sewerage. Provision is still typically in the hands of public companies, although many provinces (Corrientes, Santa Fe, Tucumán, Neuquén, Córdoba, Formosa, and Mendoza) have recently awarded the provision to private companies that are subject to provincial regulation. Provincial regulation is sometimes delegated to an autarkic agency created to that effect and in other cases performed by an already existing public agency. In the Buenos Aires metropolitan area, the service previously supplied by a federal public enterprise named Obras Sanitarias de la Nación was given in concession in 1993 to Aguas Argentinas, a private firm managed by a French operator. Regulation was delegated to Ente Tripartito de Obras y Servicios Sanitarios (ETOSS), which was created at the time of the concession, and whose board of directors includes an equal number of representatives from national, provincial, and municipal government.

Among ETOSS's responsibilities are the approval of tariffs, supervision and approval of infrastructure and expansion works, and supervision of the firm's relationships with its customers. The tariff structure is very complex, based on several characteristics of the properties served. Metering is mandatory for commercial and industrial users, but optional for residential consumers.[15] When the service is metered, the fixed charge based on the property value is reduced by 50 percent. Furthermore, since the initial coverage was very deficient in the province of Buenos Aires, the concession determined a mandatory expansion plan for the first five years, recalculated every five years until the end of the concession (which is for 30 years).

Case III. Determination of Infrastructure Charges in Buenos Aires, 1994

The 1993 concession contract set the "referential" infrastructure charges for the expansion of the residential network for both water and sewerage. All new users would have to pay the same tariff for having pipes pass in front of their properties. These values were increased by 42 percent in 1994, but still continued to be called referential. Accordingly, ETOSS proceeded (Resolution 83/95) to determine definite charges (as opposed to referential ones) for water service (sewerage charges were not modified as there were no new expansion projects in this service).[16] It linked charges directly to the surface of the land owned by the new user and to the degree of improvements in the affected streets and sidewalks. In that sense, the decision could be considered to be inside the initial contract, as the previous tariffs were defined as referential, and implicitly subject to changes anticipated in the same contract.

The sole formal participant was the regulator, as the Resolution does not mention any previous interaction with other parties. There have been no debates in the press (to our knowledge at least) about this issue, not even a discussion about its justifications.

According to an article appearing in the press after the implementation of the resolution by ETOSS, the infrastructure charge ranged between $400 and $600 (*Clarín* 1996a). This suggests that the charge might be greater than the $450 referential charges set in 1994. Other estimates in the press tend to confirm this when they refer to a 1996 range between $450 and $600. This level looks particularly high following a 10-percent reduction in infrastructure tariffs that

---

[15] The option to meter a residential property can be requested by any of the parties (at the requesting party's cost), but actual metering in this segment of users is currently very low.

[16] Although the Ministry of the Economy and Public Works must approve tariff adjustments, the resolution by ETOSS apparently did not comply with this mandatory step.

Aguas Argentinas implemented in 1996. That corresponded to the reduction in labor taxes, which, by contractual agreement, had to be passed on to consumers (see *Ambito Financiero* 1996a, 1996b).[17]

In interviews with Aguas Argentinas staff, we confirmed that this hypothesis is correct. On average, each user, except for the owners of very small properties, faces a higher charge for infrastructure. The position of Aguas Argentinas is that the referential value specified in the contract was derived by estimating the cost of the connection for a whole new project, and assuming that the density of properties would be relatively high (say, 40 properties of 250 square meters per hectare). However, the actual density observed in the expansion zone turned out to be lower (that is, the typical property turned out to be larger than 250 square meters). Thus, the higher infrastructure fee levied on each new connection as a consequence of Resolution 83/95 generates the same total revenue to the firm as that anticipated with the referential charge (corresponding to a higher expected density).

It should be noted that the firm should have foreseen the lower density of properties in the expansion zone and included it in the calculations for bidding on the concession rights. Accordingly, ETOSS could have argued that the average charge for new users could not vary. The lower revenues generated by the lower-than-expected density fall under commercial risk. Clearly, the lack of guidance regarding the principle to apply for the adjustment of the referential charges is a loophole in the initial contract.

The initial evaluation of the renegotiation is negative, even considering that the new structure of the infrastructure charges promoted efficiency in the sense of linking charges to infrastructure costs, sending better signals and incentives for expansion, and reducing the need for monitoring and the tendency for renegotiations.[18] First, the changes to the contract did not respond in the spirit of the concession contract (in the sense that the regulatory scheme cannot be defined as cost-based),[19] and thus the difference in density from the one expected could be considered a sunk cost for the concessionaire (that is, a commercial risk). Second, the contract keeps a regressive cross subsidy between properties

[17] In any case, the following exercise is illustrative. A typical property with 400 square meters of surface, with the lowest installation cost (unpaved road and no sidewalk improvement), and using the smallest connection pipe size has to pay $476.7, a figure higher than the previous $450.

[18] Although the elasticity of demand is minimal, reducing the importance of efficiency considerations, the introduction of a direct relationship between charges and costs reduces cross subsidies from properties with no improvements toward users with properties with access to more public infrastructure.

[19] The concession allows for an adjustment of tariffs when input costs increase above 7 percent, but this is not related to the issue considered here or to the general criterion of price-cap regulation governing the contract.

included in the same expansion project.[20] Third, there is no evidence that any user improved its situation because even those with the lowest costs of new infrastructure have to pay a higher charge than the referential one, representing, in fact, a transfer from new users to the regulated firm.

Thus, as the contract did not foresee any modifications of the referential charge within a given period, and although we lack the additional information necessary for a final judgment (that is, the average surface of properties of new users, average characteristics of the land, and improvements in the expansion zone), ETOSS's decision seems to have unilaterally favored the regulated firm.

As a lesson to be learned from this case, it should be noted that this decision might have been facilitated by its low visibility at the time of enactment (together with other factors). However, its actual application proved to be very troublesome as it became visible (that is, the higher infrastructure charges had to be paid by the new users) in a less favorable economic context (that is, high unemployment in 1995 and 1996, and better-organized consumer groups).

The Telecommunications Sector

The telecommunications sector was one of the first and most important privatizations in Argentina. The industry was privatized in 1990, at the beginning of the first term of the current administration, when the country had not yet recovered from the severe macroeconomic conditions of the 1980s. The sector was made up of two firms (Telefónica de Argentina and Telecom Argentina) that provided urban and interurban domestic services. One firm provided service to the northern part of Argentina, while the other did so for southern Argentina. Both firms shared the Buenos Aires metropolitan area in equal parts. They shared the provision of international services in a joint enterprise, and owned one of the three main mobile telephone companies. They also owned one of the three (leading) data transmission companies and entered the cable-TV business only recently.

Thus, the situation at the time of privatization was one of monopoly in local, domestic long-distance, and international services along with limited competition in the other segments, where both firms had important interests. Competitive pressures were therefore supposed to be negligible during the licensing period. That period was a seven-year concession of exclusivity rights in

[20] Since the cost of expansion considered for the infrastructure charges is that of the average property in the area included in the expansion project, and assuming that the public infrastructure the properties have access to is positively correlated with the wealth of property owners, then there is a subsidy within the area of expansion from those who do not enjoy public infrastructure to those who do. Note that the infrastructure charge increases with the average cost of expansion in the area of the project.

all voice transmission services (except for the mobile segment). The concession was under CPI-X price regulation (where CPI is the consumer price index and X was set at 2 percent per year), along with quantitative targets dealing with the expansion of lines. The exclusivity of the license could be extended in 1997 for three years, with an increase in X to 4 percent per year, only if the investment targets were met.

The institutional regulatory framework was defined immediately after the bidding process with the creation of the Comisión Nacional de Telecomunicaciones (CNT). Commission members were appointed by the executive without an open call or contest for the posts. During the first year, CNT was an autonomous body. This changed in 1991 when the executive intervened in CNT after the creation of the position of Undersecretary of Telecommunications (within the scope of the Ministry of the Economy and Public Works and Services). Since then, CNT has remained under the control of the executive,[21] particularly since 1996 when the Undersecretary of Telecommunications was removed from the Ministry of the Economy and upgraded to Secretary of State in the office of the president. This summarizes the evolution of the most unstable and politically dependent regulatory agency in Argentina following privatization. CNT neither was captured by dominant firms nor remained an independent body; in fact, it became a direct responsibility of the executive.

Since it was an early privatization, telecommunications was perhaps affected by many "imperfections" of institutional design. However, one of the major or more visible differences between this and later privatizations (such as natural gas and electricity) was that the tariff structure (based on pervasive cross subsidization that had a clear distribution purpose) was transferred to the new setting. In fact, at the time of the privatization, cross subsidies were even more severe than what had been customary in Argentina.[22] This, in turn, transferred into the future institutional setting all the tensions associated with a heavily cross-subsidized price structure. Therefore, it is not surprising that the undoing of this price structure and the administration or governance of the tariff rebalancing process became the central regulatory issues in telecommunications in Argentina.

[21] Late in 1993 the positions on the board of directors were filled by contest, but in 1995 a new intervention changed the board.

[22] Since the end of the Second World War, when Argentina nationalized most of its public utilities, prices have been set following more or less politically or distributionally motivated patterns depending on the administration, and thus generating cycles in the price levels and structures (Porto and Navajas 1989). However, at the end of the 1980s, when the country was in the grip of hyperinflation, the structure of cross subsidies in favor of residential customers (and against businesses) was exaggerated. The government had decided to protect low-income customers (defined as urban or low consumption) from the sharp decline in real earnings (see, for example, Navajas and Porto 1990). This exaggeration of cross subsidies was corrected before privatization in gas and electricity (for example, natural gas residential tariffs per cubic meter were one-third of the industrial tariff, a relation symmetrically reversed at the time of privatization).

Case IV. Tariff Adjustment, 1991–97

The time span of this case is the longest of all regulatory conflicts; it started in 1991 and has not yet been resolved and no agreements have been reached. For this reason, we have divided this overview into five parts or phases that correspond to historical developments. It should be noted from the outset that the modification of the structure of tariffs being discussed (a reduction in the price of long-distance calls and an increment in short-distance tariffs and rentals) admits both static and dynamic efficiency gains (if properly designed). However, it also means there is a redistribution of income from some residential callers (mostly residents of the Greater Buenos Aires area) to other types of users (residential users in the interior of the country and commercial and industrial users). This feature makes the modification politically unappealing (a characteristic that has been singled out as a major cause for the historic cross subsidies that have existed in this industry in both developed and developing countries).

Phase 1. Deindexation and Adjustment of Rates

An almost unique feature of the privatization of telecommunications in Argentina was that it preceded the macroeconomic stabilization of prices. This is particularly important for the contractual conflict analyzed here because in April 1991 Argentina anchored its exchange rate to the dollar in a one-to-one convertibility scheme, and prohibited price indexation in the private sector to ease the adjustment of expectations (influenced by a long history of inflation and unsustainable price freezes) to new macro fundamentals. Following deindexation, the Ministry of the Economy decided that prices of public services should not be adjusted by the (more than) 20-percent CPI increase registered in February 1991. This was the end of the CPI-X formula as stated in the telecommunications license, and the start of a conflict/negotiation pattern between the government and telecommunications firms. Under the circumstances, CNT, which was superseded by the Ministry of the Economy in a regulatory decision, started to lose power.

In fact, the Ministry started to negotiate a way out of the CPI-X system directly with the firms. The solution reached was to modify the formula from pesos to U.S. dollars, without modifying the X. That is, all tariffs were now expressed in dollars and, therefore, supposedly protected from devaluation. Prices would be adjusted each semester according to changes in the U.S. PPI. Of course, the firms took this as a violation of their licenses and began legal actions (unsuccessfully) in an attempt to get the cumulative difference according to the old formula.[23]

[23] Domestic inflation did not converge to international standards until the second half of 1992, and cumulative inflation since the beginning of convertibility (April 1991) has been 62.2 percent.

During the negotiating process, the firms demanded compensation in the form of permission to readjust tariff rates, as was specified in their licenses. Apparently, this was not the concern of the Ministry of the Economy insofar as the adjustment could be delayed because it did not interfere with the Ministry's major short-term concern of no price increases. The firms did not get a written acceptance of the adjustment until November 1991, when Presidential Decree No. 2585, designed by the Ministry of the Economy, established the "dollarization" of tariffs, the new adjusted formula adapted to U.S. inflation, and the guidelines for adjusting the tariff structure. The main guideline was to determine that the adjustment should be neutral for the firms, as defined by the invariability of revenues before and after the adjustment. The decree also announced that the adjustment would be undertaken shortly (within six months).

In December 1991, the Ministry took over CNT, creating the Under-secretariat of Telecommunications to which CNT was annexed. This direct intervention remained for almost two years without any major development, a fact that reflected the reluctance of the Ministry to change what had been achieved in 1991.[24] The new CNT officials recruited in October 1993 also followed this strategy; they were reluctant to make substantive modifications (many of the members of the new board of directors had a negative opinion of Decree No. 2585).

Phase 2. Toward the Public Hearing of 1994

In 1993 the development of call-back competition in international calls made existing rates unsustainable, and the firms began to lose outgoing traffic.[25] Until then, the closed monopoly nature of the Argentine market could sustain heavy cross subsidies. Development of call-back was the first signal that the preprivatization price structure was going to be difficult to sustain.[26]

---

[24] Between December 1991 and March 1992, the Ministry proceeded to sell 30 percent of the equity of the two telecommunications companies that had remained under public ownership.

[25] Call-back competition is when callers from Argentina have accounts with a foreign operator abroad and are able to indicate which calls they want to make that are initiated by the foreign operator at a much lower price than it would be if initiated locally.

[26] The extent of call-back penetration was initially constrained to international calls and later (in 1995) was extended to long-distance domestic calls. The limit to call-back penetration was the so-called accountancy charge, which is the transfer price a U.S. or other foreign telecommunications company has to pay the Argentine telecommunications companies for receiving the call. The charge, which is an agreed (reciprocal) transfer or access price, was set in previous agreements at $0.75 per minute. Any call-back tariff then had this figure as a floor on which to price the call. Assuming competition in the call-back market, prices could go as low as this figure plus costs for the activity. By the time the call-back started to hit the companies, average international charges of the two telecommunications companies were well above $2, and long-distance calls were up to $1.6. In the case of interurban calls, since call-back operators need to enter

The companies increased pressure for fulfillment of the rate adjustment agreement of 1991. They presented the call-back case before the courts, arguing that the government should ban it because it violated their exclusivity rights. The courts interpreted the exclusivity issue as a territorial one and found that the provision of international voice transmission from abroad did not go counter to that exclusivity.

Amid this dispute over call-back, the Undersecretary of Telecommunications and the companies agreed to implement a public hearing mechanism (that is common in gas and electricity) on the issue of tariff adjustment. The mechanism is a public meeting in which interested parties express their views on the issue at stake. The results of the meeting could be informative (as was the case in telecommunications) or mandatory. The first hearing (actually there were three meetings) took place in November 1994, and the companies were invited to present their proposal, a fact that was in accordance with the procedures established both in the license and in Decree No. 2585.

The proposal was very unsatisfactory from a welfare point of view and aroused the suspicions of well-informed analysts and the general public.[27] This hearing was the first instance in which a group or implicit coalition opposing the rebalancing expressed itself with some effect on public opinion.

Phase 3. The NERA Report and the Second Round of Public Hearings

The negative experience of the first hearings gave rise to a new takeover of CNT in early 1995. Since then, CNT has remained a mere branch of the Undersecretariat, which took control of the process of adjustment. In fact, the Undersecretariat now fell under the control of the (newly created) Secretariat of Energy and Public Works of the Ministry of the Economy. The Secretariat took direct charge and decided to hire an international consulting firm, which was expected to complete a report on the adjustment issue in six months. This

Argentina twice to contact two calling parties in the country, they had to pay two accountancy charges that added up to $1.5. This led the companies to argue in 1995 that, with the more expensive domestic long-distance call at or below $1.5, the call-back operator should be accused of dumping practices, that is, selling below its costs. However, this argument is flawed by the fact that the cost is established by a transfer or access price that is an international convention between Argentina and the rest of the world, and is above the ones established between most developed countries. The determination of this charge at more normal values could have created a large entry of call-back operators into the domestic market.

[27] In short, the proposal solved the required rebalancing (too-high international and long-distance domestic charges and too-low rental charges and local call rates) with a modest reduction in the former (in relation to what was required according to efficiency criteria), and a similar increase in the latter. However, it disguised a big increase in tariffs by proposing a segmentation of the main metropolitan area (Buenos Aires), whereby local calls would be classified as short-distance domestic calls, that is, reducing the geographical definition of urban area. Once this new zoning was explained in the press, general opinion turned negative. According to the consulting group NERA (1995), approval of this restructuring scheme would have generated an important increase in the profits of the companies, which later questioned this conclusion.

became known as the NERA (1995) report, which produced a technical proposal for adjusting rates with seven different options depending on the constraints that could be included in the adjustment process.

The NERA (1995) report was discussed in a second public hearing, which took place in January 1996 under increasing opposition from three interest groups: one represented by the ombudsman (*Defensor del Pueblo*); the second by consumer groups; and the third by opposition members of parliament. Although the NERA report supported the economic case for an adjustment of rates (within the institutional constraints), it had several flaws, as noted in other studies and reports (for example, Artana and others 1996; Mitchell and Taylor 1995; Yarrow 1995). However, the critique of the interest groups was not of a technical nature. Although the criticisms were all different, they did point to the inconvenience of the adjustment. The groups argued that: (1) the companies had high profits and this called for a reduction in charges for interurban long-distance and international calls without any compensation; (2) prices for international calls were being reduced anyway by the companies in response to competition from call-back firms, and the adjustment would shield the companies from lower prices; (3) information regarding costs and demand was insufficient and unreliable to justify an adjustment exercise; and (4) the restructuring was unfair to many consumers who did not make long-distance or international calls.

These criticisms are not entirely wrong, although they do not make a case for not adjusting telephone rates in Argentina. First, it is true that the firms have been profitable, but this is irrelevant in a (within-period) price-cap regulatory framework. Firms were supposed to maximize profits, and gained from the previous existing organization in the sector. Second, it is true that prices for international calls were being adjusted downward and that the readjustment could protect the firms from this situation yielding undue compensation for these reductions. However, this element could be easily subtracted from the readjustment exercise (as proposed in Artana and others 1996). The call-back was not an effective solution for correcting distortions in interurban calls, particularly short-to-medium-distance calls. Third, it is true that demand and cost estimates are neither abundant nor very robust. However, available estimates coupled with international evidence (Ahumada and others 1996) can give a fair range of values that, given the magnitude of preexisting price distortions, can safely justify an adjustment.[28] Furthermore, even accepting some unreliable

[28] The argument is similar to an exercise in optimal marginal tax reform. If prices (for example, for urban and long-distance interurban calls) are not optimal, then there exists an inverse optimum problem and a direction of marginal reform that can justify the adjustment as a welfare gain. Given the size of the initial relative price distortion, there is a range of values for the basic parameters (price elasticities of demand and marginal costs) that validate the move. One needs only the true parameters to be within the limits (although one does not know the exact values) to justify beginning the adjustment process. This argument is further elaborated in Navajas (1996).

estimates of fixed and variable costs (a common problem in dealing with cost estimates in telecommunications), the move to an efficient regulated price structure may yet be desirable (Urbiztondo 1995). Finally, it is true that the adjustment leaves some consumers worse off, particularly those who had been favored by preexisting distortions. Simple evaluations of the change in consumer welfare before and after the adjustment indicate aggregate gains at the expense of a significant redistribution between urban and interurban consumers (Ahumada and others 1996; Navajas 1996).

Another nontechnical problem with the NERA report is that it could not be taken as a proposal because, according to the existing license, the government cannot fix or change (or even propose a change to) the tariffs. Instead, the proposal should come from the companies, as was the case during the 1994 hearings. The government can only accept or reject the proposal.

To complicate matters, immediately after the second set of public hearings, in February 1996, the Ministry of the Economy issued a ministerial resolution ordering the Secretary of Energy and Public Works to make a decision on the adjustment rates. This occurred after the companies had chosen one of the options of the NERA report. The complication came from the fact that this resolution could be construed as direct government involvement in fixing telephone rates, a legal argument later used by the ombudsman.

However, this decision was not implemented because political changes within the executive (due to a disagreement over control of the post office privatization process) led to the removal of the Undersecretariat of Telecommunications from the Ministry of the Economy. The office was upgraded to Secretariat of State, answering directly to the President of the Republic. CNT was completely enmeshed in this structure, and moved into the orbit of the new Secretariat, which was created in March 1996.

Phase 4. Toward the Third Public Hearing and Decree 92/97

In the second half of 1996, the new Secretariat authorities began a more decided approach to implementing the adjustment, with (according to them) "direct presidential instructions." One of the first things they did was to abolish the ministerial resolution issued in February. The authorities established a new mechanism for the readjustment to take place, which was not much different from what had been established before the NERA report. The new mechanism clearly stated that the government could not propose an adjustment, but instead could evaluate and decide on proposals made by the companies (with the final consent of the firms).

In October 1996, the companies presented a new proposal, which improved on previous ones, such as the 1994 proposal, by taking into account the progress made, particularly after the debate over the NERA report. The

Table 2–1. Tariff Structures in the Rate Adjustment Conflict in Argentina

Service	Original value	FIEL[a] exercise in efficient prices: Value	FIEL[a] exercise in efficient prices: Change (percent)	October 1996 proposal by companies: Value	October 1996 proposal by companies: Change (percent)	Decree 92/97: Value	Decree 92/97: Change (percent)
Rental charge, residential	8.9	22	147	16	80	12.5	40
Rental charge, commercial	35	79	126	35	0	35	0
Free units (in pulses)	75						
Local calls	0.022	0.033	49	0.033	50	0.026	18
Interurban calls							
Short distance	0.26	0.06	-75	0.22	-15	0.2	-23
Medium distance	0.75	0.08	-89	0.54	-28	0.54	-28
Long distance	1.4	0.11	-92	0.58	-59	0.64	-54
International calls	2	0.98	-51	0.90	-55	1	-50
Low-user scheme	No	Yes[b]		Yes[c]		Yes[c]	

Note: Values are approximations and averages. Rentals are in dollars per month; units (pulses) are also monthly (1 unit = $0.044). All call charges are expressed in dollars per minute. "Pulses" (so-called PTFOs) are a metering convention on which the pricing is defined. One pulse costs $0.044 and lasts two minutes for normal urban calls. The pricing is adjusted throughout the relation between pulses and minutes or seconds without changing the value of the pulse.

a. Fundación de Investigaciones Económicas Latinoamericanas.

b. Up to 450 pulses/month, same rental as before and call charge equal to twice the new price.

c. Up to 150 pulses/month, reductions in the rental start with 20 percent (up to 70 pulses) and then drop. This scheme is not well designed, as explained in the text.

proposal had some salient features (see table 2–1). The proposal increased the rental charge by 80 percent and the local call rates by 50 percent. It eliminated the free minutes embodied in the old tariff structure and implemented a low-user scheme to protect low-income consumers. However, it also reduced charges for interurban short-to-long calls by 15 to 59 percent, and for average international calls by 55 percent.

The Secretariat evaluated this proposal and called for a new (the third and most recent) public hearing in December 1996. The interest groups participated in that debate, as did other business organizations and individuals from the interior of the country who were supposed to express their support for the adjustment, given the large drop in the price of interurban communications. To avoid pro-urban pressure, particularly in the large metropolitan area of Buenos Aires, the hearing was scheduled to take place in a provincial capital. The hearing was a reiteration of old arguments by opponents of the adjustment and, therefore, did not add new issues to the debate. The perception from the Secretariat's viewpoint was that the time had come to announce an adjustment modifying the one proposed by the companies. In February 1997, the Secretariat decided to go ahead with the adjustment and, instead of using the (expected) mechanism of a Secretarial Resolution, issued a Presidential Decree (No. 92/97) to signal that the decision had full political support.

The adjustment thus decreed was a modification of the one proposed by the firms in order to make the changes less abrupt (see table 2–1). First, residential rental charges were increased by 40 percent, which was half the amount requested by the firms. Second, the cost for a one-minute local call was allowed to rise by 26 percent (which was the result of an increase of 33 percent in the peak period from 10:00 A.M. to 1:00 P.M., and a change in the normal and reduced-rate periods); the decree also established a poorly designed low-user scheme.[29] Third, the reductions in prices of both interurban and international calls were in general less sharp than proposed by the firms, with the exception of short-distance interurban calls.[30]

After this decision, the Secretariat rapidly found that it had underestimated the capacity of interest and pressure groups to block the adjustment. The counterattack came in the following months through a large number of judicial hearings that led to perhaps the hottest legal dispute in recent history, and to chaos in the legal status of telephone rates in Argentina. Press coverage of the dispute was, in general, favorable to the case against adjustment, with economic arguments being relegated to second place.

Phase 5. Legal Confusion and the Partial Implementation of the Adjustment

In a few weeks, there were dozens of suits that asked (mainly federal) judges to interrupt the adjustment of telephone rates, with few requesting the opposite. The leading or more important judicial decisions can be classified as follows:

- Dr. Bustos Fierro's decision in Córdoba came after lawyers for the industrial association argued that the adjustment should be accepted and implemented. The association lawyers said it represented relief from an unfair situation for the customers in the interior of the country, who used the long-distance service more intensively. This was the only case decided in favor of the adjustment. The Federal Court of Appeals in Córdoba has confirmed the decision.

---

[29] The low-user scheme in the Argentine debate was first suggested by Artana and others (1996) and can be thought of as an optional (self-selected), two-part tariff. The trouble with the decree was that the established scheme did not have conditions of continuity, convexity, and therefore self-selection for the scheme to be Pareto superior a la Willig (1979). Being designed for residential consumers, the nonexistence result of Ordover and Panzar (1980) does not apply to this case.

[30] In particular, for the interior of the country, the Secretariat decided to give some short-distance calls the status of urban calls, yielding big price reductions in calls of up to 30 kilometers. This was to compensate small towns located at distances that are shorter than those of the metropolitan area of Buenos Aires. In fact this reclassification from interurban to urban calls is precisely the opposite of what was proposed in the 1994 hearings.

- Dr. Sarmiento's decision to grant protective action (*amparo*) in Buenos Aires followed the argument brought by the ombudsman (Dr. Maiorano). The argument was that the adjustment could not be held valid because the Secretariat had violated legal procedures by failing to submit the decision to a public hearing. Although this is not a final verdict, it proved effective since it was later accepted by the Court of Appeals of Buenos Aires. The Secretariat appealed the protective action, arguing that there was no case because the adjustment had not changed any tariffs, but rather modified a proposal made by the companies. In addition, the Secretariat argued that the protective action was based on the resolution issued by the Ministry of the Economy in February 1996, which had been superseded in March 1997 and was no longer valid (see the section on phase 4). In August 1997, Dr. Sarmiento ordered the Telecom firms to send bills using the old pre-adjustment tariff structures.
- Dr. Heyland's grant of protective action in Buenos Aires was in response to action brought by a local opposition council member (Mr. Polino) in collaboration with an association of consumer interests. In the judge's opinion, the adjustment went against article 42 of the National Constitution (reformed in 1994) and, therefore, it should be voided. In June, Dr. Heyland got tough with the companies, applying fines for charging the new tariffs. In those parts of the country where the companies were not sending out bills until the situation became clearer (so as to avoid fines), the judge fined them for not sending out the bills.
- Dr. Rodríguez's verdict in Mendoza followed adjustments made by an opposition member of the National Congress (Ms. Zucardi). This was similar to the case in Córdoba and was later confirmed by the Federal Court of Appeals. Among all the legal actions considered, this was the only one that raised economic arguments. One unintentional source of confusion that contributed to the judge's decision was the fact that the National Institute of Statistics (INDEC) had to compute the increase in telephone rates to be included in the CPI. This was based on the 1985-86 expenditure survey, which was, in turn, based on consumption patterns in Buenos Aires, and was based almost exclusively on rental charges and local calls. When INDEC computed the increase, taking into account the elimination of free minutes, it reported an increase in telephone charges or outlays of around 60 percent (press coverage of this had a significant impact on public opinion). Dr. Rodríguez's verdict stated that according to INDEC, which is an official body, the adjustment did not balance rates because only increases were being registered. In addition, in the judge's opinion, the increase violated the peso convertibility law. It was very difficult to explain to the judge that the

INDEC measurement depended on a biased sample, and that there were conceptual flaws in his argument because the convertibility law does not forbid changes in relative prices and, in fact, says nothing about the behavior of prices.

The reaction of the companies to this situation was not uniform. The northern company (Telecom) decided to go ahead with the adjustment, while the southern one (Telefónica) did not send out any bills in Mendoza and Buenos Aires in reaction to the legal actions and possible fines. By the end of September, the situation was rather chaotic and the firms waited for a Supreme Court ruling that was postponed until after the October parliamentary election. Amid speculation that the Supreme Court was reluctant to hear the contradicting cases of Córdoba, Buenos Aires, and Mendoza, the Attorney General was consulted on whether the Supreme Court should resolve the dispute. The Attorney General's reply was not clear and gave rise to a sense of uncertainty. He maintained that the Supreme Court should not intervene in measures of protection such as those presented in Buenos Aires, and that there was, in principle, no contradiction between the Córdoba and Mendoza verdicts. Furthermore, he added that the ombudsman should not participate in cases where some consumers are made worse off and others are made better off.

Summing up, the initial decision analyzed in this long case was made by the government and was not in compliance with the initial contract. Decisions made after the renegotiation of 1991 were in compliance with the (corrected) contract, although there were many institutional uncertainties surrounding the government action. The following events characterize the case:

- The initial decision responded to a macroeconomic stabilization shock that required deindexing contracts. Since the application was of a general nature, it cannot be interpreted as a hold-up decision. The government further proved its initial intention to compensate the companies with a restructuring of tariffs, and it eventually fulfilled this commitment.
- The actors involved in the dispute were the executive (which superseded and practically removed the regulators), the regulated companies, and a coalition of opposing groups formed by the ombudsman, the opposition parties, consumer associations, and many judicial courts.
- The mechanism used to reach a solution in the dispute between the executive and the companies was a nonbinding public hearing with a final decision to be made by the former and agreed to by the companies. The courts did not accept this mechanism.
- The evaluation of the decision made by the Secretariat admits different interpretations. First, it respected the contract as modified in 1991, although politically it was costly to do so. Second, it represented a

move toward both static and dynamic efficiency, as cross subsidies among different services were reduced and the resulting structure was closer to Ramsey principles, giving correct signals for expansion and entry following deregulation and intermodal competition in the future. Last, the adjustment in prices might have favored the regulated firms for not having considered the extent of protection against the penetration of call-back operations and because the reduction in short and medium-distance tariffs was minor (except for areas neighboring large urban centers in the interior of the country), and due to the difficulty in anticipating the full extent of the adjustment (that is, due to the creation of peak-load charges).

- The main lesson to be learned from this case is that the conflict owes a lot to deficiencies in the privatization process, in particular, the maintenance of a highly inefficient and unsustainable pricing structure. This made the debate in telecommunications in Argentina a rather old-fashioned one, where the main topic was how to deal with cross subsidies in a closed monopoly. Other interesting aspects relate to the blocking capacity of interest groups and to the way the weak regulatory agencies lost control in favor of the executive.

The Transportation Sector

This section describes two cases in the transportation sector: railway freight concessions and renegotiations of two concessions of the Port of Buenos Aires.

The national network of railways had been operated by the state-owned company Ferrocarriles Argentinos since 1946. Between 1991 and 1993, the government began to make concessions from the network, in separate units by service and region, although it remained vertically integrated. The maintenance of the network and its operation were assigned to the concessionaires. The railroads were divided into six freight units and seven suburban passenger units; the latter formed the commuter network in the greater Buenos Aires metropolitan area, one of which remained public. The urban passenger services were transferred to the provincial governments.[31] The regulatory jurisdiction remained under federal control.[32] Until 1996, each concession had its own regulatory body. A

[31] An exception was the Buenos Aires-Mar del Plata corridor, which was also concessioned by the federal government. Many of the provinces opted to discontinue service because it required high subsidies to be economically viable.

[32] Currently there is an emerging jurisdictional conflict regarding the commuter network for suburban access to Buenos Aires because the local government wants to participate in the renegotiation of the contracts that are now in the hands of the federal government.

1997 presidential decree merged all the railway and road regulatory agencies into one, which is part of the Secretariat of Transportation and Public Works in the Ministry of Economy and Public Works.

The organization of maritime ports in Argentina is undergoing major changes. In 1992, Law 24.093 established that, with the exception of the country's five main ports, the provinces could request the transfer of management for existing and new commercial and industrial maritime ports. Provincial operation of ports would require federal government approval of location, safety, and environmental considerations, but the federal government would in no way be involved in determining the characteristics of eventual concessions to be organized by the provinces.[33] This legislation was the starting point for a process of decentralization of operations. In many instances, this meant allowing the participation of private operators through concessions. In this changing context, a conflict has emerged regarding the administration of the contract for the port of Buenos Aires, which consists of two areas: Puerto Nuevo and Dock Sud. Control over Dock Sud was transferred to the province of Buenos Aires, which awarded a concession to a private operator in 1995. Puerto Nuevo remains federally owned, but it was also given in concession to a private operator in 1994. This has given rise to strong competition between the two.

Case V. Renegotiation of Railway Freight Concessions, 1997

The key elements of any concession are the requirements the operator must fulfill and the fees it must pay, both of which impact costs and the level and structure of tariffs. Also important, although sometimes forgotten, is the consistency of incentives to carry out all the terms of the contract (either through auditing efforts and penalties or through the use of private incentives to maximize profits). Since an auction tries to match the seller with the best buyer, the design of the concession has to account for the interrelationship among these aspects in a way that effectively induces competition and the selection of the best possible option.

The five existing freight concessions were designed for a 30-year duration with an optional 10-year extension. Competition from trucks sets a limit on tariffs to final users (and thus the regulatory burden does not fall here, although it is reasonable to require approval by the regulatory authority before changes in prices). The key issue is how to combine in an incentive-compatible way the payment, required expansion, quality of service, and employment of the

---

[33] The five ports retained by the federal government are Buenos Aires (located in the city of Buenos Aires), Bahía Blanca and Quequén (in the province of Buenos Aires), and Rosario and Santa Fe (in the province of Santa Fe).

preexisting labor force, and access charge to alternative users of the network (that is, provinces that wish to provide passenger services). Naturally, there are different feasible combinations of fees and requirements according to the objective followed.

In this case, the goal of concessioning the service was to find new sources of funds to expand capacity and improve the efficiency of the operation of the network, because its underdevelopment and poor functioning exerted a heavy burden on the Treasury. Another goal was to increase the use of a less-polluting means of transportation which paradoxically suffers from the effect of public subsidies to roads for automobiles. By contrast, privatization experiences before convertibility and the Brady Plan (in 1990 and 1991, respectively) had stressed financial aspects of privatization. Furthermore, since Ferrocarriles Argentinos was transferring passenger service to the provinces, the objectives included not only the development of freight service, but also passenger service, which would be promoted by lower charges for access to the railway network.

Combining these elements so as not to destroy incentives is not a simple matter. Generally speaking, the concessionaires must find it in their interest to respect the offers made. If this is sufficiently the case, then offers will not be opportunistic and the auction will attract serious investors and at the same time minimize ex post renegotiation of contractual terms. The importance given to all these aspects does not mean that the criterion for selecting the best offer has to combine all of them. The weights given to each would make the selection process very problematic and even arbitrary, increasing the chance of opportunistic offers made just to win the competition but resting on the hope of ex post bilateral renegotiation. Instead, it would be highly advisable to fix two of the three variables, providing some degree of flexibility in the contract, and to organize competition in the third variable. For instance, the quality and expansion requirements of the network could be predefined. Similarly, an access charge consistent with real competition by alternative providers of passenger transportation over the network could also be established. The best offer would then be the one fulfilling these conditions and offering the highest fees for the rental of the assets received.[34]

This choice would certainly be transparent and probably would also be more difficult to modify. Having explicitly combined different conditions to be considered in the offers, the organizer of the concession typically tries to guess about consistency and credibility by analyzing the relationship between the three conditions and projections made by the participants. This facilitates contract

[34] Naturally, if requirements are tighter, the highest fees will be lower. Thus, the establishment of quality requirements while competing on fees is perfectly compatible with different objectives pursued in the privatization process.

modifications when these conditions do not hold. Since the weights attached to each dimension might induce high levels of investment, announced projections must look optimistic, even if actual projections are not and the benefits of the concession reside in different dimensions. If, instead, the requirements of the concession were fixed (or linked in the contract to observed market conditions), there would be no need to require explicit projections of traffic and other market conditions, which would make it more difficult for the firms to claim that "unexpected events" require a renegotiation.[35]

Unfortunately, the auctions for the concessions of freight services and the operation of railways in Argentina determined the selection of the winning bids according to a complex set of weights regarding fees, access charges, and investment plans (in addition to experience, size of the work force, and participation of domestic investors, making matters even worse). Although traffic has increased (62 percent between 1992 and 1994, according to the former Secretariat of Transportation and Public Works),[36] competition from trucks has been strong. In addition, actual demand has failed to reach the projections, inducing concessionaires to lag behind in their investment plans and in the payment of fees. According to the press, the concessionaires have carried out only 50 percent of the investment plans and owe $20 million in fees, which for some concessionaires corresponds to being overdue on more than one year of monthly payments (see *Clarín* 1997). The contracts called for the application of penalties due to these faults, including the termination of the concessions, but they have proven to be difficult to enforce.

The problem with enforcement also stems from the fact that carrying out the initial investment plans would be inefficient and, therefore, the renegotiation would be Pareto-improving.[37] The ex post inefficiency of the investment

[35] The relative ability to renegotiate multidimensional offers and one-dimensional offers is at this point a theoretical conjecture with no formal model to defend it (to our knowledge). Regarding the case of water in Buenos Aires, for instance, renegotiation occurred even with one-dimensional offers in 1994. This also happened, to a certain extent, in the Port of Buenos Aires in 1995. In this case, it was not a renegotiation, but rather the misuse of a clause of the contract. Although the offers were ordered according to the fees only, they had to be explicit regarding the traffic to be assured, which later was argued. Still, the transparency in the selection of the best alternative with one-dimensional offers reduces the scope for opportunistic behavior and, other things equal, should reduce the probability of renegotiation. Naturally, other things must be equal to draw conclusions from different experiences, among them the warranty for the execution of the contract, the structure of final tariffs making incentive-compatible the expansion of the network and the investment plan, the autonomy and technical expertise of the regulatory body, and the concentration and lobbying abilities of providers and users.

[36] Interview by Radio Continental, February 17, 1995; see *Ambito Financiero*, CD-ROM.

[37] The renegotiation would be very transparent if it were competed in the market. In that case, the concessions would be terminated and a new auction would be organized in which the assets added by the private operators could be included in the package at the price requested by the owners (provided that the new participants had the option to reject these assets). If the option is technically impossible, then the valuation

plans justifies some type of renegotiation. However, the fact remains that the method used to select the best offer was quite inefficient. This, in part, reflects the difficulties faced in most auctions, which needed to be repeated to find interested investors; in some cases, there was only one offer presented. And the renegotiation does have its costs. Indeed, a lower access charge together with a lower investment plan would have meant a much better concession outcome, and also probably a more attractive auction with more high-quality offers.

In July 1997, the executive ordered the Secretary of Transportation and Public Works to modify the concession contracts (Presidential Decree 605/97), following the authorization to do so by the Comisión Bicameral de Reforma del Estado (a bicameral regulatory review commission) in April 1996.[38] The reasons for renegotiation alluded to in the decree include "unforeseen changes in conditions, which made contract plans incompatible with the level and composition of the demand," in part due to a "shortfall in actual demand relative to expected demand."

Renegotiation requirements in the decree correctly include four important constraints. First, they do not affect the "economic and financial equation" of the concessions (that is, leaving profits constant as in a rebalancing of tariffs toward a Ramsey structure).[39] Second, they preserve the principle of entrepreneurial risk assumed at the time of competition for the market. Third, they introduce flexibility to formal (or input) requirements but respecting substantial (or output) results. Lastly, the agreement is subject to both internal and external scrutiny by auditors, such as Sindicatura General de la Nación (an internal auditor of the executive), Auditoría General de la Nación (an ex post agency directed by a representative of the first political party in the opposition), and the Bicameral Reform Commission.

of all the assets transferred has to be done by the authorities. New concession requirements should be modified to avoid the inconsistencies of the previous ones (the current operators could participate and continue the operation of the freight services provided that they are the highest bidders). The fact that the government has not adopted this alternative leaves open three possible interpretations. The first is that the government has problems in executing the contract, which would then trigger a problematic lawsuit. The second is that the government believes the transaction costs of this alternative are too high, including running the risk that the services may collapse at some point in time. And the third is that there is simply an inadequate mechanism to defend the interests of taxpayers and users of the service (either due to a lack of capacity on the part of public officials or the lobbying efforts of current operators). Since the contract did not include the government's active participation in the provision of certain inputs or services to the concessionaires, the last two options seem to be the most relevant ones, but distinction among them is rather difficult and therefore not attempted here.

[38] During 1995 the executive was trying to renegotiate the contracts without going through Congress. The Commission opposed these attempts, arguing that the discussion disregarded important issues such as the dispute over access charges involving the provincial operator in Buenos Aires, which had demanded a renegotiation of the $5 per train/kilometer access charge. This charge was, allegedly, 10 times higher than international standards (see *Clarín* 1996b).

[39] Presumably, the renegotiation will include lowering the access charge and the fees, whereas the investment plan will be adapted and the ownership of the assets used will be more flexible.

Given the decision to start a bilateral renegotiation of the contract, the characteristics of the mandate are appropriate ex post, allowing improvements relative to the initial contract. The renegotiation would aim to solve the problems of investments for which there is no effective demand, and the current high access charges that delay the actual development of competition and expansion in the provision of long-distance passenger transportation by alternative providers, such as the provinces. Nevertheless, the renegotiation will be carried out with asymmetries of information and a weakened bargaining position by the Secretary of Transportation and Public Works, making it unlikely that "the financial and economic equations of the contracts remain constant," as mandated in the decree.

Renegotiation is a costly process that should be avoided at the time of the design of the competition for the market. This requires consistency and flexibility in contract clauses, defining the exogenous changes that would lead to changes in the contract and the guiding principles to follow, and avoiding causing opportunistic misconduct by either party. These characteristics in the design of the concessions have not been observed in this case. Thus, although the final details of the decision have not been determined yet, so that a final evaluation must be postponed, these considerations are illustrative and insightful.

Case VI. Renegotiations of the Port of Buenos Aires, 1995

The two concessions of the Port of Buenos Aires have different characteristics. The concessionaires of Puerto Nuevo have to pay a high canon (resulting from the economic offer they made in the auction of the concession contracts), whereas the concessionaire of Dock Sud has to pay a significantly smaller canon.[40] The concessionaire of Dock Sud is the owner of the land used for the operation of the port. Other differences are related to mandatory investments, taxes, and commitment to employ the preexisting labor force. Naturally, the geographical proximity between the two areas of the port has given place to strong competition (not only port-to-port, but also terminal-to-terminal), a result of which has been a significant reduction (50 percent) in the tariffs charged to shippers.

In light of this situation, the operators of Puerto Nuevo have lodged a demand pointing out the asymmetries in the respective concessions and arguing that the characteristics of Dock Sud's concession are a violation of the rights of the Puerto Nuevo operators as they were defined at the time of their participation in the auction. The operators of Puerto Nuevo allege that the rules of the game

---

[40] Formally speaking, the concessionaires of Puerto Nuevo pay the *tasa a las cargas* (that is, a charge for each ton transported), but have to assure a minimum volume of transportation and pay the port authorities for it. Since the guaranteed level of transported merchandise has been well above the actual volume transported, this charge is a fixed cost, and can be interpreted as a canon to be paid regardless of the volume of freight transported.

have been changed. Initially, the volume to be transported was to be distributed among the port terminals, and the operators of Puerto Nuevo took this into account when preparing their bid. Now, however, a new terminal does not pay the canon and does not have obligations with the labor force yet enjoys certain services. Thus, Puerto Nuevo operators argue, there is an important difference compared with the original auction.[41]

The consideration of the reasonableness of these demands has centered on the comparison of costs among terminals in Puerto Nuevo and Dock Sud. However, it should be noted that the comparison is incorrect. It is like discussing whether Coca-Cola and Pepsi-Cola have different costs to level the playing field. Moreover, it will always be possible to construct cost estimates pointing in one or the other direction (for instance, modifying arbitrarily the opportunity cost assigned to the land owned by the concessionaire of Dock Sud, or changing the time preference applicable to investments already sunk versus investments to be carried out in the future). In that sense, the (ex post) asymmetry of the concessions is a weak argument to justify a modification of the contracts. Thus, the evaluation of the conflict has to be ex ante of investments, and according to the relevant legal and information environments.

As soon as this dispute emerged in April 1995, there was a 25 percent reduction in the canon charged by the port authority of Puerto Nuevo, the Administración General de Puertos, AGP, according to Resolution No. 6/95. The analysis of the resolution requires precision in terms of the applicable legal framework. Article 34 of the Pliego de Bases y Condiciones para la Licitación de las Terminales de Puerto Nuevo (the Pliego) says that a new regulatory agency, SAP, will replace the AGP and that the canon paid by the private concessionaires may be adjusted so as to cover the expenses of the administration and common port services. However, article 24 of the Pliego established that the winning bid would be the one with the highest economic offer among qualified participants. Article 35 stated that, "during the first, second and third years of the concession, the canon would be 40 percent, 60 percent and 80 percent of the amount offered in the auction, respectively." The Article anticipated that from the fourth year on the adjustment would follow the global volume of transportation for the entire port relative to the volume at the time of privatization. In other words, the contract made explicit the adjustment mechanism for the canon, anticipating that the magnitude of transported merchandise would grow in the first three years, including some sort of insurance or protection from the fourth year on. At the same time, it allowed the authorities of the port to modify the canon so as to obtain the resources necessary to finance operation of the port.

---

[41] Interview with Mayra Tebot, a member of Intefema (the operator of Terminal 6 of Puerto Nuevo, which went bankrupt less than one year after the beginning of the concession), *El Cronista*, February 22, 1995.

It is possible that the contradiction between the authority given to the SAP in order to modify the canon and its predetermination in the Pliego for the first three years of the concession allow some legal space for having reduced the canon by 25 percent five months after the beginning of the concession in Puerto Nuevo. In fact, the arguments used to justify this decision were that, "as a result of various measures, important economies in the operation of the AGP and significant increases in revenues will result, thereby abiding by the formal requirements for taking such a measure." Nevertheless, leaving aside this legal aspect which we do not intend to solve here, from the economic point of view there is no contradiction. In effect, the 25 percent reduction in the canon paid by the operators of the terminals of Puerto Nuevo cannot be justified, not only because it occurred only five months after the beginning of the concession (invalidating the meaning of the economic offers used to select the winners of the auction),[42] but also because it did not benefit the owner of the port (that is, the federal government, taxpayers, and users of port services). It has to be stressed that there was no authority to reduce the canon based on the degree of competition in the sector.[43]

In any case, regardless of the AGP's interpretation of resolution no. 6/95, the evaluation of the conflict and eventual renegotiations of the contracts are a more general matter. First, the sequence of the division of jurisdictional powers between the federal government and the province of Buenos Aires indicates that the concession of Dock Sud was not a violation of the contractual obligations in Puerto Nuevo. Knowledge of the conditions under which the Dock Sud concessionaire would operate could have been imperfect, but the firms that participated in the bidding for the Puerto Nuevo terminal should have foreseen this.

Second, the competitive nature of the sector, both looking to the future and in terms of the design of the Puerto Nuevo auction, renders improper all renegotiations based on competitive developments occurring after the auction. The 25-percent reduction in the canon for the Puerto Nuevo terminals in April 1995 is an unjustified contractual change for the participants at the auction in

---

42 The inconsistency between article 34 of the Pliego and the auction mechanism used in this case should be noted, as it implies a lack of relationship between the economic offers by potential operators and the budget of the port. The offers lack any meaning if the canon offered is immediately adjusted in order to finance operation expenses. It is like auctioning a painting to the highest bidder and then reducing the payment arguing that the seller does not need so much money. It would have been more appropriate (i) to exclude any reference in the Pliego to the adjustment of the canon according to the budget of the port (which faces the restriction of article 12 of Law 24.093, Ley de Puertos, which requires that port administrators reinvest all their resources), or (ii) auction the contract based on the lowest tariff to shippers (à la Demsetz, fixing the required contribution to finance the operation of the port).

43 The arguments for this decision also state that "the reduction of the canon... will produce effects conducive to increases in the competitiveness of the port of Buenos Aires and its concessionaires," an aspect which should not play any role in the decision to reduce the canon, and which is suggestive of the true reason for adopting this measure.

Puerto Nuevo who offered a lower canon and lost the concessions (to the extent that such a measure did not reflect the true changes of the costs of services provided by the port authority).

Third, as already mentioned, the real competitive variable in Puerto Nuevo was the canon. Therefore an eventual difference between expected and guaranteed traffic (implicit in the canon) is irrelevant as an argument of renegotiations. Furthermore, although the design of the Pliego (regarding flexibility to adjust the canon given to the port authority) and the mechanism chosen to select offers in the auction are inconsistent, the authority to change the canon is not related at all to the development of new competition or to the financial outcome for the firms awarded the concession of the Puerto Nuevo terminals.

Fourth, the correct definition of a "level playing field" is ex ante, and the variable canon adjusts for the different conditions of the concessions and the expectations of ex post competition. This definition emerges from a simple analytical model where it can be easily demonstrated that a sequence of auctions with different ex post conditions is perfectly compatible with normal benefits for those who anticipated developments correctly, which must be presumed to be what happened.[44]

Fifth, the reduction of the canon in Puerto Nuevo is neutral as far as equilibrium is concerned, that is, it does not produce a modification of the tariffs competed. Since the canon is a fixed cost, its reduction does not alter the equilibrium level of charges by the operators of terminals to the shippers (at least in the absence of significant imperfections in the credit market). This means it is a direct transfer from the owner of the port (that is, the federal government and, thus, taxpayers) to the operators of the port. This transfer has no social benefit; if the operators go bankrupt in the current situation, then there could be a new auction in which the canon offered would be lower.

Finally, the renegotiations of the Puerto Nuevo concession contracts could give rise to a tax war between the federal government and the province of Buenos Aires, triggering the renegotiations of the concession of Dock Sud. This jurisdictional competition could have desirable effects in other circumstances, but in this case would lead only to a transfer of rents to the operators of the terminals (if it generates a reduction in fixed costs), or to a subsidy to international commerce (if it involves subsidies linked to the volume transported), or simply to an inefficient tariff structure that does not consider externalities generated by the operation of ports.

On the one hand, the 1995 decision by the AGP to reduce the canon paid by the operators of the Puerto Nuevo terminals by 25 percent was within the bounds of the contract. On the other hand, the province of Buenos Aires

[44] See Urbiztondo, Artana, and Navajas (1997).

had not changed on the contract as of November 1997. The 25-percent reduction was motivated by the lobbying activity of the Puerto Nuevo concessionaires, who claim to have received an unexpected shock (the degree of truth in the claim might be relative, and thus the decision could be described as a contractual failure, that is, an unjustified modification of the contract). Furthermore, there was an inconsistency between the method for selecting offers and the authority given to adjust the canon in the contract that helps to explain the ongoing nature of the conflict itself.

The actors involved in the dispute are the AGP, the concessionaires in Puerto Nuevo, the province of Buenos Aires, and the operator of Dock Sud, whose positions were generally reflected in the press as well (the Bicameral Commission also analyzed the decision ex post, and its participation should be considered relevant for the future of the negotiations). No public hearings or judicial actions have been held so far, although there might be some in the future, as the issue has not yet been put to rest.

The mechanism used to reach the (initial) solution was a resolution by the AGP. The current dispute is characterized by an ongoing debate with joint studies by the AGP and the province of Buenos Aires, whereas the concessionaires of the two ports lobbied actively. The AGP decision respected the letter of the contract but not its spirit. The decision involved the misuse of an instrument that was designed for ends different from the emergence of competition, as it cannot be seriously argued that new economies allowed the AGP to reduce its budget by 25 percent within five months of the beginning of the concessions. The reduction does not contribute to efficiency because it is a reduction of a fixed cost without affecting the equilibrium tariff. It represents a transfer from users (that is, taxpayers who could invest more in the infrastructure of the port) to the concessionaires. Nevertheless, the AGP has avoided taking further measures in this regard in spite of pressures from the concessionaires of the Puerto Nuevo terminals. This might be the result of closer congressional scrutiny.

As a lesson, it should be noted that there are flaws in the design of the competitive environment in Puerto Nuevo that are now being exploited by the concessionaires. In addition, the multiplicity of political jurisdictions allows lobbying efforts directed to different areas. This case shows that it is very hard to grant exclusivity under jurisdictional decentralization of the property of facilities (that is, AGP and the province would have to coordinate the characteristics of their concessions, which is difficult to do).

Conclusion

Table 2-2 summarizes the salient characteristics of the six cases studied in this chapter. The cases provide varied lessons. For instance, deficient contract design paved the way for renegotiations, putting more pressure on the regulatory task. Similar effects produce poorly designed (automatic) cross subsidies or insufficient competition in the award process. By contrast, highly visible sectors, in which consumers feel the impact of the regulatory measure immediately, yield an environment in which regulatory adjustment of the contract is more balanced. Overall, the decisions included in this study and in Artana, Navajas, and Urbiztondo (1998) show some bias toward the objectives of the regulated firms. In this sense, the implementation of regulation in the public utility sectors of Argentina seems to have been more problematic in terms of assuring the selection of the best offer in the auctions for the public firms privatized and services given in concession. It has also been more problematic in terms of adequately protecting the interests of captive users than in terms of political opportunism and "expropriation" by changing the rules.

Since this chapter was first written in December 1997, the country has reached important decisions in the privatization and regulation of infrastructure. One such decision regards the extension of exclusivity and the introduction of managed competition in the telecommunications sector (not particularly in line with what was established in the initial contract). Another is a broad renegotiation of tariffs and obligations in water and sanitation services provided by Aguas Argentinas in Buenos Aires, including stronger environmental requirements and a higher and more easily implementable price structure. The government has increased tariffs for urban public transportation (both motor and rail operations), attempted to modify highway concessions (substituting tolls by a general tax on oil), and made concessions of airports.

These new instances of contractual renegotiation appear to have a common bias against consumers and to favor the regulated firms. At the same time, these cases go together with requirements for faster expansion and higher investments, forgiving firms for not having reached the previously contracted obligations. This is striking because the public positions adopted by members of the governing party have created an atmosphere that anticipates expropriatory behavior (this is even more so at the local level, and particularly with firms extracting natural resources). Perhaps public officials have some degree of anxiety about higher investments (another example of an intertemporal inconsistency of political cycles), or there may be other reasons for this wave of renegotiations. It is also interesting to note that none of these decisions were debated in public audiences, which would appear to offer an effective mechanism for reaching contractual stability.

Table 2–2. Summary

Event	Sector	Type of contractual adjustment	Evaluation of the decisions	Design of contracts and competition	Characteristics of regulatory bodies	Context of operation	Importance of the issue involved	Participation of consumers
1. Retained gas	Natural gas	Resolution	Correct decision (reduced lobbying)	Correct	ENARGAS has formal and real autonomy based on design and context.	Decisions have direct effect on consumers; many firms acting separately.	Relatively low	None, due to the type of decision
2. Construction of a transmission line in the Comahue region	Electricity	Resolution based on public audience which passed veto power	Slow decision, but correct	Relatively correct, but the sector is technologically very complex	ENRE has same properties as ENARGAS	Ditto natural gas, although the issue considered follows individual rules	High	None, only generators and DCs participated in the hearings
3. Modification of infrastructure charges in Buenos Aires	Water and sewerage	Resolution	Incorrect decision: transferred rents to the firm, but improved allocative efficiency	Vague/no guide for modification of referential tariffs			Relatively lower	None

Table 2–2. (Continued)

Event	Sector	Type of contractual adjustment	Evaluation of the decisions	Design of contracts and competition	Characteristics of regulatory bodies	Context of operation	Importance of the issue involved	Participation of consumers
4. Tariff rebalancing	Telecommunications	Presidential decree	Complicated decision, with pros and cons in every dimension	Unbalanced tariff structure aggravated the adjustment of the contract	CNT is taken over by the Secretariat of Communications, i.e., it is not autonomous	Very important and competing interests in place, high visibility of the decision, regional conflict	Extremely high	Very active, in various instances, through different representatives, and press coverage
5. Renegotiation in freight railways	Transportation	Presidential decree	Ex post reasonable decision, following poor design of auction, with negative precedent setting	Bad design in various dimensions (multiple arguments in the offers, etc.)	Regulator is not autonomous by design, not even formally	Various firms that do not compete among themselves	Very high	None, but some publicity was given in the press
6. Adjustment of canon in Puerto Nuevo	Transportation	Resolution	Negative decision, with transfer of rents to concessionaires, following design of the contract	Inconsistent design (adjustable canon, used as the competing variable)	Regulator is not autonomous; its replacement by an autonomous body was designed in the contract but is delayed	Jurisdictional separation of authority, and very indirect impact of final consumers (low visibility)	Very high	None (low visibility and indirect effect)

References

Ahumada, H., W. Cont, F. Navajas, A. Porto, and M. Solanet. 1996. "Elasticidades de demanda y evaluación de distorsiones tarifarias del servicio telefónico." FIEL, Buenos Aires, Argentina.

1996a. "No sólo Bussi tiene problemas con la privatización del Agua." Buenos Aires (February 23).

———. 1996b. "La renegociación del contrato de concesión de Aguas Argentinas." Buenos Aires (November 25).

———. 1994. "Carlos Varelo con Gregorio Díaz Luceró," Radio América CD-ROM (August 9).

Artana, D., R. López Murphy, F. Navajas, and S. Urbiztondo. 1996. *El rebalanceo de las tarifas telefónicas.* Documento de trabajo no. 48. FIEL, Buenos Aires.

Artana, Daniel, Fernando Navajas, and Santiago Urbiztondo. 1998. Regulation and Contractual Adaptation in Public Utilities: the Case of Argentina. Technical Study, No. JFM-115, Inter-American Development Bank, Washington, D.C.

Clarín. 1996a. "Suspenden intimaciones por la conexión de agua," April 24. Buenos Aires.

———. 1996b. April 20. Buenos Aires.

———. 1997. September 28. Buenos Aires.

Gasparini, L. 1997. *La transmisión de energía eléctrica. Incentivos a la provisión eficiente y a la expansión de capacidad.* FIEL, Buenos Aires.

Mitchell, B., and L. Taylor. 1995. "Preliminary Findings Regarding NERA Report." Charles River Associates (Memorandum to Telefónica de Argentina).

Navajas, F. 1996. "Una evaluación cuantitativa del rebalanceo de tarifas telefónicas." FIEL, Buenos Aires.

Navajas, F., and A. Porto. 1990. "La tarifa en dos partes cuasi-optima: Eficiencia, equidad y financiamiento." *El trimestre económico,* Vol. LVII (4), No. 223.

NERA. 1995. "Restructuring of Basic Telephone Services. Final Report for the Ministry of the Economy." National Economic Research Associates, London, UK.

Ordover, J., and J. Panzar. 1980. "On the Nonexistence of Pareto Superior Outlay Schedules." *Bell Journal of Economics* 11.

Porto, A., and F. Navajas. 1989. "Tarifas públicas y distribución del ingreso: Teoría y medición preliminar para la Argentina." *Revista de análisis económico* 4(2).

Urbiztondo, S. 1995. "Confusing Fixed and Variable Costs under Ramsey Regulation." FIEL, Buenos Aires.

Urbiztondo, S., D. Artana, and F. Navajas. 1997. "Competencia y renegociación en el Puerto de Buenos Aires: un análisis económico." FIEL, Buenos Aires.

Willig, R. 1979. "Pareto Superior Nonlinear Outlay Schedules." *Bell Journal of Economics* 9.

Yarrow, G. 1995. "Issues Surrounding the Rebalancing of Basic Telephone Services."

CHAPTER 3

Post-Privatization Renegotiations and Disputes in Chile

Federico Basañes, Eduardo Saavedra, and Raimundo Soto

During the past decade, Latin American countries have accumulated extensive experience in the privatization of infrastructure services and in the institutional and regulatory reforms essential to foster a suitable environment for private investment. Chile has undertaken remarkable reforms and transferred publicly owned utilities to the private sector either by selling the assets or through concession agreements. Because of the reforms, the country has been able to attract private participation to the provision of public services such as energy, transportation, telecommunications, and potable water and sewerage. This has resulted in significant efficiency improvements as well as increased coverage.

The sectors involved in the reforms have usually had natural monopoly characteristics that require direct regulation of private firms and the use of specific instruments (laws or contracts) to establish the way in which tariffs, quality, investment, and exclusivity would be determined and evolve over time. Although the Chilean legal system is specifically designed to limit discretion in the public sector, some degree of discretion was permitted to allow the regulatory bodies to adjust to unforeseen developments, such as changes in technology or demand. Some ambiguities or unspecified areas remain in the design of the new sector structure and the newly created regulatory framework.

Renegotiations and disputes arise frequently when complete long-term contracts cannot be written at the moment of contracting and in the absence of institutions that can credibly enforce those contracts. The consequences of these problems are exacerbated when market design is inadequate or regulation is incomplete. These problems are characteristic of developing countries; as a result, disputes have been a part of the Chilean privatization experience.

The authors are grateful to Kaushik Basu, Michael Klein, and seminar participants at ILADES-Georgetown University and the Inter-American Development Bank for helpful comments, and to Sonia Adriasola for research assistance.

More than a decade after the start of the reform process, unforeseen events have provided evidence of the loopholes in the design of the reform. This has called for the use of discretion by regulatory agencies and, in some cases, has led to renegotiations and disputes beyond the authority of the regulatory agencies, causing the intervention of public officials.

In this chapter, we analyze several post-privatization disputes and renegotiations that have taken place in Chile between 1980 and 1999 in the electricity sector.[1] Privatization of the sector was, to a large extent, completed a decade ago, providing enough time to properly evaluate renegotiations and disputes. The chapter also assesses how the lessons learned in the reform of electricity were internalized in the design of the regulatory framework for highway concessions.

A number of issues that might have played a crucial role in inducing or inhibiting disputes in the two sectors are presented and analyzed. We then examine renegotiations and disputes between regulators and firms, among firms (when they are the result of the privatization process), and between consumers (represented, for example, by the Antitrust Commission) and firms currently working in the industry or potentially interested in participating. The focus is twofold, encompassing the nature of the dispute as well as the roles different agents play in it (firms, consumers, the government, and other institutions such as the judiciary system).

The Electricity Sector in Chile

Until the 1930s, there was little state intervention in the electricity sector in Chile; service was provided by the private sector through domestic and foreign investment in public utility companies and independent generation. The 1930s marked a period of stagnation as a result of the adverse effects of the Great Depression and increasing political intervention in utility tariffs. Empresa Nacional de Electricidad (Endesa), a public corporation, was created in 1944. From the beginning, Endesa was a vertically integrated firm, comprising power generation, transmission, and distribution. It was responsible for strategic planning in the industry, expanding the capacity for generation and transmission, and meeting the needs of isolated areas. Endesa became the dominant firm in the industry by the mid 1950s, with access to important financial resources and concentrating most of the country's generation capacity and transmission lines. During the

[1] The Chilean electricity sector has experienced some changes during 2000, which to some extent reshape the structure of the industry and its regulatory framework. However, our conclusions are robust to those changes.

1950s and 1960s, the industry's main problem was the government's tendency to keep tariff rates too low (for political reasons), which, in turn, did not provide adequate incentives for investment. In the early 1970s, the government nationalized Chilectra (the largest distribution company) and took control of the 51 largest electricity companies in the country, virtually nationalizing the entire industry.

The structure of the industry changed markedly after the coup d'état of 1973. First, the government relinquished its role as a producer and distributor, and committed itself only to regulation and strategic planning activities. To that end, two institutions were created in 1978: the Superintendency of Electricity and Fuels (SEC), a supervisory agency for electricity activities, and the National Energy Commission (CNE), which replaced Endesa in its role as strategic planner. Nevertheless, Endesa retained operational regulatory responsibility until 1982, when CNE's role was enhanced to include regulatory activities. At the same time, a new legal framework was enacted that established norms applicable to all the companies in the sector regardless of ownership. This provided an opportunity for private companies to enter the sector on equal legal ground as state-owned companies. These norms included regulation of production, transportation, distribution, concessions, easements, prices, quality, and safety conditions of facilities, machinery and instruments, and relations of the companies with the state and the private sector.

Separation of the different productive stages was started in 1981 in preparation for privatization. The divestiture of Chilectra resulted in the creation of one generation company (Chilgener, currently Gener) and two distribution companies (Chilquinta in Valparaiso and Chilectra in Santiago). Endesa was broken into five independent distribution companies, three generating complexes (Endesa, Pullinque, and Pilmaiquén), and three independent integrated systems (Edelnor in the north and Edelaysen and Edelmag in the extreme south).

Privatization was carried out according to the notion that electricity generation was a potentially competitive market. Distribution and transmission were considered local and natural monopolies and, therefore, needed to be regulated. Four privatization mechanisms were used: (1) sale of small distribution and generation subsidiaries of Endesa through public bidding (Saesa and Frontel); (2) privatization of large-scale distribution and generation companies by auctioning blocks of shares on the stock exchange;[2] (3) sale of shares to the public in small

[2] In 1986 and 1987, the government auctioned three small hydroelectric generators that belonged to Chilgener and two medium-size hydroelectric generators belonging to Endesa. In 1987, distributors Chilectra and Chilquinta and generator Chilgener were completely privatized. In 1988 and 1989, small distribution subsidiaries of Endesa were privatized.

quantities (a mechanism called "popular capitalism");[3] and (4) divestiture of ownership in two distributors (Chilectra and Chilquinta) through the repayment in shares of the reimbursable financial contribution clients make in order to access the network (start-up investment).

The electricity sector is currently made up of two large, independent, private systems (the Central Integrated System and the Greater Northern Integrated System) and two small, isolated state-owned systems. The Central Integrated System has an installed capacity of 5,300 MW and serves most of the country's central and southern regions, where commercial, industrial, and residential consumption are concentrated. The Greater Northern Integrated System has an installed capacity of 1,300 MW and serves the north, where most mining activities are concentrated. The two publicly owned systems are Edelaysen (23 MW) and Edelmag (48 MW), which serve the southernmost part of the country.

Regulation is designed to support a specific market structure that assumes that some segments of the market (generation and large consumers) can operate competitively and others (distribution and transmission) cannot. This implies that standard antitrust legislation could deal with potential noncompetitive behavior in generation and direct sales to large consumers, but that supervision and regulation are needed for distribution and transmission activities.

Currently, five institutions govern the activities in the electricity industry (excluding the judiciary system):

- The *Antitrust Commission and the National Economic Prosecutor (Fiscal Nacional Económico)* are both devoted to preventing noncompetitive behavior in all markets, including the electricity sector. The National Economic Prosecutor is an independent branch of the government whose role is to investigate noncompetitive practices. The Preventive Commission is a regional, first-instance judiciary body allowed to punish noncompetitive practices. The Resolution Commission is a second-instance court, also allowed to punish wrongdoing. The Supreme Court is the only court of appeal for sanctions applied by the Antitrust Commission.
- The *Ministry of the Economy* has the right to set tariffs (as proposed by CNE) and promote the efficient development of the generation, transmission, and distribution subsectors.

[3] Popular capitalism consisted of selling a limited quota of shares to public employees, at a price lower than the value of the shares on the stock exchange. The purchase of shares could be financed with a portion of the employee retirement funds. Between 1988 and 1990, Endesa and its transmission system were privatized to a large extent using this system.

- The *Superintendency of Electricity and Fuels (SEC)* is an independent supervisory agency (related to the Ministry of the Economy) in charge of monitoring compliance with the law and regulations. It controls the quality of service and safety of facilities, processes applications for concessions, and prepares the information required to set tariff rates.
- The *National Energy Commission (CNE)* is a government advisory agency on all matters related to energy (including electricity, oil, gas, and nuclear power). Its duties include establishing sector policies and development strategies, studying and proposing economic and technical norms, and calculating tariffs and prices. CNE is made up of an Executive Council and an Executive Secretariat. The Council is presided over by a representative of the President of the Republic and composed of a committee of six ministers. The Executive Secretariat is in charge of the administration of the Commission, and the Council delegates compliance with all the tasks for which the agency is responsible to the Secretariat. Most of the proposals for the restructuring of the electricity sector have been prepared by CNE.
- The *Economic Load Dispatching Center (CDEC)* is a coordination entity designed to optimize the operation of the generation system. In the short run, CDEC acts as a clearinghouse in the energy market. In the long run, it is in charge of planning the operation of the combined generation-transmission system. Its main objectives are to preserve the security of service; to guarantee the most efficient operation of the electricity system's facilities as a whole; and to ensure the right of way on transmission systems, as established by concession agreements.[4] There are limitations to participation in the CDEC directory, although all companies can use the system. Only companies with a minimum generating capacity of 60 MW are allowed to participate on the board of directors. CDEC's one-year presidency term rotates among its members and decisions are binding. Dissensions (raised by one or more members) are resolved by the Ministry of the Economy within 120 days of issue.

Consumers that use less than 2 MW of power face *regulated prices*, as it is deemed that their negotiating capacity is limited with regard to the distribution company that operates as a monopoly in its concession area. The regulated price is determined by the regulator as a combination of the *node price* (described below) and a regulated margin, which corresponds to the imputed *value added of distribution*.

---

[4] CDEC performs the following specific tasks: informs electricity companies of current demand and supply conditions; calculates the spot marginal costs; coordinates major preventive maintenance of the generation facilities; verifies compliance with operating and preventive maintenance programs; determines and values transfers of electricity among CDEC members; and coordinates the operation of transmission systems.

Consumers that use more than 2 MW of power are free to negotiate prices, power, and energy directly with generators or distribution companies. Market conditions, in particular long-term contracts, determine the price. It is noteworthy that the regulatory design of the market assigns a prominent role to this "free market" final consumer segment. If the free market operates as expected, the free market price provides an easy and nondisputable reference by which regulated prices can be determined. In fact, the law establishes that in setting the node price, calculations made by the regulators must be compared with free market prices. If the calculated node price is above or below a range of 10 percent, it should be adjusted to coincide with the limits of the range.

Distributors pay the node price to generators, unless they have signed a contract specifying otherwise. Node prices correspond to the sum of the *basic energy and power cost* and a *penalty factor.* The basic energy cost is calculated by weighing medium-term marginal costs at a specific point in the network forecast for the next four years of operation of the Central Integrated System. Costs are obtained using an optimization model that incorporates water supply restrictions and a projection of demand for the next 10 years. The basic price of power is calculated considering a gas-fueled plant, according to a formula that includes the cost of investment in diesel turbines; the cost of investment in transmission lines; fixed operating and maintenance costs; capital recovery factors; a theoretical power reserve margin of the electricity system; and losses on the transmission line. Penalty factors correspond to marginal losses of transmission in the system, and they are determined by considering the distances from every node to the network, as well as the level of tension of the conductors.

Current electricity law defines only the conceptual aspects of determining basic energy costs. In practice, CDEC estimates short-term marginal costs on the basis of the marginal production of power and energy supply in the most important loading center of the system (Santiago). In turn, this implies that producers located at different points in the system should bear all the costs of transportation required to reach the consumption center.

Chilean law assumes that high-voltage transmission is a natural monopoly and posits that tariffs should equal marginal costs, while long-term financing gaps should be covered through tolls charged to users. As a result, the law guarantees the right of passage (easement) for all generators as a way to allow competition on an equal footing between generators. The transmission firm cannot refuse the use of the lines, even if the tariff has not been agreed to in advance. Transmission firms earn income from two sources: the generating companies, which pay a toll fee for the use of the system, and penalty factors. Toll fees, which are a two-part tariff, were established by law as a form of protection provided to the transmission company so that it will not incur losses, since its average operating costs are higher than its marginal costs.

Potential Sources of Conflict in the Electricity Sector

The structure and regulation of the electricity sector might have inhibited or led to disputes. Renegotiations and conflicts arise for a number of reasons, all of which are present with varying intensity in Chile. In some cases, open conflict has occurred in the form of arbitration or lawsuits, while in others the analysis suggests that renegotiations will likely take place in the future.

Market Structure and Ownership

Chile's geography poses peculiar challenges to the electricity industry and suggests areas of potential conflict. The Andes Mountains make hydroelectric power generation optimal in the south, where dams are relatively easy to build and rain is abundant. However, in the desert north, thermoelectric generation is the only viable alternative. In addition, while thermoelectric supply is a determining factor, hydrological risks make hydroelectric supply random. Since thermoelectric and hydroelectric generating companies compete under different operating cost conditions, profitability depends heavily on strategic actions that give rise to several areas of potential conflict. In particular, conflict may arise with regard to the management of water reserves by hydroelectric companies, the allocation of technical risk among firms, the calculation of marginal and operating costs, the order in which each firm's supply is dispatched to consumers, and the terms and structure of contracts among firms. These issues usually arise from the existence of information asymmetries.

The Andes Mountains make importing lower-priced electricity from Argentina economically nonviable because the cost of building transmission lines and transportation losses are extremely high.[5] However, the same is not true of natural gas, for which there are alternative uses (heating, cooking, and industrial). The development of Chile's natural gas industry, while still in its infancy, has contributed to changing the structure of the country's electricity industry. Natural gas affects both thermal and hydroelectric generating companies by altering the optimal mix of technologies in the industry. This explains why, when the government announced that it would grant concessions for the construction and operation of gas pipelines, both thermal and hydroelectric companies rushed to position themselves in this new market.

As expected, conflicts and intense lobbying arose with regard to the location of gas pipelines, the auctioning of long-term contracts, and the regulation of the new market. These led the government to take a strong position on the subject,

---

[5] Although this is true for most of the country, lines are being built in the north to supply the independent Greater Northern Integrated System.

Table 3–1. Participation of Firms in the Main Integrated Electricity Systems in Chile, 1998
(Percent)

	Generation		Transmission lines		Distribution	
Firm	**SIC[a]**	**SING[b]**	**SIC[a]**	**SING[b]**	**SIC[a]**	**SING[b]**
Endesa (controlled by Enersis)	54.8	4.7	12.3	3.6	-	-
Gener Group	26.3	17.5	7.7	8.0	-	-
Colbún	14.7	-	-	-	-	-
Tocopilla	-	40.2	-	31.6	-	-
Edelnor	-	26.3	-	28.9	-	-
Other generators	4.2	11.3	0.5	-	-	-
Transelec (owned by Endesa)	-	-	69.5	-	-	-
Transnet	-	-	6.5	-	-	-
Private transmission lines (mining)	-	-	-	27.9	-	-
Chilectra (controlled by Enersis)	-	-	-	-	37.0	-
Chilquinta	-	-	-	-	11.1	-
CGE	-	-	-	-	16.8	-
Other private distribution companies	-	-	-	-	35.1	-
State companies	-	-	-	-	-	100.0
Total	100.0	100.0	100.0	100.0	100.0	100.0

[a] Central Integrated System.
[b] Greater Northern Integrated System.
Source: National Energy Commission (CNE).

signaling that it dislikes the idea of integration among energy markets and that it would monitor very closely any contract along those lines.

The first main criticism of the reform process in Chile arises from the structure of ownership that emerged from privatization, which is characterized by an important degree of vertical integration. Although the state monopoly was broken up prior to divestiture, the law allowed Endesa to maintain a dominant position when privatized. Until 1999, Endesa produced about 55 percent of power generation in the Central Integrated System (see table 3–1). Lack of restrictions on ownership across segments of the industry had permitted Endesa to keep its virtual monopoly in high-voltage transmission. This is despite the generally accepted opinion that a unique high-voltage transmission line was the only economically viable structure in a country as narrow as Chile. In fact, the reform of the electricity sector was based on the notion that there is a natural monopoly in transmission, but the reform presumed that the monopoly could be duly regulated. In addition, as a result of the privatization of distribution companies, Enersis, which controlled Endesa, held 74 percent of the shares in the main distribution company, Chilectra.

This vertically integrated structure has been the source of a large number of disputes and conflicts. Democratic administrations have claimed repeatedly that Endesa's dominant role in generation and transmission does not allow for fair competition in the sector. A large-scale lawsuit was initiated in 1990 when the National Economic Prosecutor complained to the Antitrust Commission, charging that Chilectra, Endesa, and Transelec engaged in noncompetitive behavior (discriminating against a small producer, Pullinque). The accusation was rejected on an appeal to the Supreme Court. The prosecutor initiated a second procedure against Enersis immediately after the first trial ended. The second trial lasted until June 1997, and again favored Enersis.

A second line of criticism arises from the fact that divestiture led to the creation of several classes of shares with different decision-making power. For example, few preferential shares allow control of Endesa and its affiliates. During most of the 1990s, Enersis controlled Endesa with only 25 percent of the shares.[6]

A third line of criticism arises from the "first-move advantage" that Endesa held at the time of the reform. As the former sole agency responsible for investment plans, it had access to privileged information on new commercial areas, water rights, and reserves management. This information could have been used to discriminate or block entry of potential competitors.

After privatization, it is clear that the government could have imposed tighter ownership controls to prevent one group from holding interests in distribution, transmission, and generation simultaneously. However, ownership would not be the main issue if regulations were correctly enacted and information asymmetries were insignificant. Unfortunately, this is not the case in Chile.

Regulation of the Electricity Sector until 1999

Regulation of the electricity sector is complex, from a technical and an economic point of view. The process is further complicated in Chile, where some important aspects of the regulatory framework have not been specified in sufficient detail. Both elements suggest the existence of several areas that are potential sources of contract renegotiations and disputes.

---

[6] Preferential shares were created to increase incentives for efficient management. Transaction prices for these shares have been considered by critics of privatization as being too low because book values were used (as opposed to market values). A correlated problem is that privatization did not consider clear procedures and a thorough revision of the financial stance of bidders. Thus, it allowed practices that do not lend themselves to the required transparency of the process (for a detailed description, see Sáez 1993).

Energy Dispatch

Only companies with a minimum generating capacity of 60 MW are allowed to participate on the Board of Directors of CDEC. That fact and the concentration of property in generation explain why Endesa and its affiliates have had majority participation in CDEC. Due to the largely technical nature of CDEC's mandate, conflict was practically absent until the 1998–99 drought.

Distribution

Prices for distribution are reviewed every four years. As such, this constitutes a preannounced negotiation, in which strategic behavior is likely. Operators have suggested, for example, that the government engaged in lawsuits precisely when tariffs were to be revised, in an attempt to curtail the bargaining power of large players in the industry. The regulator has claimed that distributors engaged in lobbying through private sector entities during tariff revisions.

The regulatory mechanism requires the government and firms in the industry to agree on a range of inflation-adjusted prices to be charged to consumers for a pre-specified number of years. Prices are established such that an efficient firm obtains a targeted rate of return on assets. Since such a firm does not exist, a simulation model is used as a benchmark. In principle and under symmetric information, the mechanism should provide adequate incentives to firms to reduce costs by forcing them to compete against the simulated optimal firm (this could be considered a form of yardstick competition). Under asymmetric information, however, this mechanism has important shortcomings. One unsolved problem is how the regulator obtains the cost structure of the efficient firm. Experience shows that when information is based on actual market data, costs are strongly influenced by those of the existing monopoly so that, in practice, the mechanism tends to converge to the standard rate-of-return model.

Furthermore, the way in which tariffs are set could also distort prices. Both the regulator and the monopoly make their own cost estimates. If discrepancies remain after negotiation, the final estimated cost of the efficient firm is the weighted average of the estimates provided by the firm and the regulator. In this case, opportunistic behavior clearly arises during renegotiations.

Node Prices

The determination of node prices allows for several areas in which disputes could arise. First, prices are determined on the basis of forecasts of water availability and a safety margin. Since Endesa holds most of the water rights and manages water reserves, small hydroelectric producers have claimed it has an information advantage that hampers competition in generation. At the same time, operators (in particular, thermoelectric firms) dispute safety margins and other technical issues as being too beneficial for hydroelectric companies. Although these disputes do not necessarily reflect the workings of the industry, they point to the potential damaging role that information asymmetry could play in the sector.

A side issue, but a crucial one affecting the industry, is that distributors have the legal right to buy at node prices to serve the regulated market. Thus, distributors can obtain economic quasi-rents by allocating purchases at will. Since short-run marginal costs differ between thermoelectric and hydroelectric producers during the year (because of changing levels of water reserves and weather conditions), a distributor could potentially benefit a particular company by signing contracts for only part of the year. In the long run, this would produce high-profit and low-profit generators, and could eventually drive the latter out of the market.

Transmission Tolls

Chilean regulation guarantees open access to transmission lines. This means that, as long as it has excess capacity, a transmission company cannot refuse to serve any producer interested in dispatching energy to a consumer or to be sold in the spot market. However, the regulation is incomplete in two important areas: new investments required to expand the network and transmission tolls.

The electricity law enacted in 1982 did not establish clear procedures for setting transmission charges. The legal framework was modified in 1990 to establish the price system for the transmission sector. Although the law was passed and it covered the basic lines along which prices are to be set, its corresponding statute (which determines prices in practice) was drafted only in 1998 and is not operative to date. This has been one of the main sources of dispute among private firms.

When capacity is limited or new transmission lines are necessary, the law presumes that interested firms and the transmission company can negotiate an agreement to undertake the required investments. To a large extent, the law does not consider the possible asymmetric bargaining power of firms, in particular when the additional demand is not substantial.

Large mining operations have been able to deal efficiently with this problem through public auctions of their demand for energy. In these cases, the negotiation involves generation and transmission companies. As is usually the case, when a satisfactory offer is not possible, the generating company offers to build its own (dedicated) transmission line. However, this option is limited to customers with a large demand.

Cases of Open Conflict and Renegotiations

In this section, we present eight cases of open conflicts that went through either the judiciary system (Antitrust Commission, Court of Appeals, and Supreme Court) or private arbitration processes. These are not only the most representative cases, but also cover most of the disputes through 1999. The first three cases have to do with market structure issues, and the last five have to do with regulatory failure issues. It is important to bear in mind that each case is unique.

Case 1. Vertical Integration Disputes

The National Economic Prosecutor initiated (and subsequently lost) two major trials in which it tried to order the divestiture of vertical integration between Endesa and Transelec. The first trial (1990–92) followed a complaint to the Antitrust Commission by the small producer Pullinque against Enersis for noncompetitive behavior due to vertical integration. The prosecutor started the process and conducted the investigation. The claim was based on three elements: (1) that participation of Enersis in generation (Endesa), transmission (Endesa), and distribution (Chilectra) hampered competition; (2) a set of allegations by Pullinque of wrongdoing by Endesa; and (3) the fact that a representative of Enersis was elected as chief executive officer of Endesa.

The Resolution Commission voted in favor of Enersis. An appeal to the Supreme Court was also favorable to Enersis, although by a split decision. The Supreme Court declared that no evidence of abuse of power or misconduct accompanied the prosecutor's claim and that imposing sanctions would amount to limiting the constitutional rights of Enersis. The Supreme Court agreed with only the third element of the claim, that election of an Enersis director as chief executive officer of Endesa could negatively affect the transparency necessary for the competitive functioning of the sector. Consequently, the court's decision required that the authorities adopt the necessary measures to ensure and reestablish transparency in the electricity market. As of 1999, no measure has been enacted.

Investigations to support a second claim of vertical integration were initiated in 1992, immediately after the first trial denied the prosecutor's claim. The prosecutor sued Endesa and Transelec on the grounds that vertical integration could potentially hamper economic efficiency by encouraging noncompetitive behavior. The prosecutor's goal was to divest the vertically integrated consortium of Endesa and its transmission subsidiary, Transelec. The original claim did not name Enersis as a defendant, focusing only on Endesa, Transelec, and Chilectra to avoid dismissal of the suit on the basis of double jeopardy. However, Enersis became part of the proceedings when it took control of Endesa in 1994.

Although the judges' verdict in favor of Enersis in the second trial was unanimous, rumors abounded that opinions among the judges were heavily divided. The prosecutor characterized the verdict as "abusive," but refrained from pursuing the issue to the Supreme Court. In addition to the June 1997 verdict, the Antitrust Commission issued the following recommendations for improving performance in the electricity sector:

- The pertinent authorities must issue a statute for the sector (which had been pending since 1990) as soon as possible.
- Because of the existence of information asymmetries, Transelec must become the owner of the assets it manages.
- Given the lack of adequate procedures to ensure the expansion of the transmission network when that becomes necessary, Transelec should open itself up to participation by other interested firms.
- In order to increase transparency, distribution companies should purchase energy and power by means of a public auction, based on nondiscriminatory rules and regulations and readily available public information.

Analysis of this case shows several points. First, the prosecutor had a very weak case. In fact, the claim was presented in terms of fears that Chilectra would grant preferential contracts to other Enersis firms and fears that there could be conflicts of interest within CDEC because the firms were part of the Enersis holding company. The prosecution did not explain how these practices could be implemented or what types of behavior would be consistent with these fears. Second, the prosecution relied on legal arguments, disregarding economic facts, and failed to convince the judges of the need to consider the conditions that could allow for noncompetitive behavior instead of looking for documented proof of such behavior (as required by the Supreme Court in its 1992 decision). Third, potential beneficiaries of the divestiture of Enersis were surprisingly absent from the process.

Case 2. Discrimination against a Generator

This case illustrates how the existence of a vertically integrated conglomerate may discriminate and predate a potentially competitive segment of the industry. The sources of the conflict were a 1989 agreement signed by all members of CDEC regarding prorating sales to distributors, a poorly designed contract between Chilectra and Colbún, and the role played by the arrival of new producers in the generation market. According to the 1989 agreement, at each point in time Chilectra had to buy energy at node prices from Endesa and Gener in an amount proportional to the annual supply of energy contracted by Chilectra with each of them. This clause was imposed by CDEC to avoid noncompetitive practices by Chilectra in favor of other members of the vertically integrated firm Enersis. Colbún had signed a contract to become Chilectra's residual supplier in the market, that is, when its other suppliers (Endesa and Gener) could not meet demand.

In 1991, Pehuenche (an Endesa subsidiary) started operations and began to sell energy to Chilectra without complying with the 1989 agreement. Enersis interpreted the 1989 agreement as binding only for companies that were members of CDEC at the time (that is, Endesa, Gener, and Colbún). Accordingly, a contract was signed allowing Pehuenche to sell energy to Chilectra without respecting the proportionality limits.

In 1992, Colbún sued Chilectra, Endesa, and Pehuenche for discrimination and predatory practices. Colbún claimed that Pehuenche's noncompliance with the 1989 agreement was detrimental to Colbún's interests. Colbún claimed that, as a residual supplier, it was required to provide vast amounts of energy only when marginal costs were above node prices, and very little during the rest of the year. This situation left Pehuenche better off (selling at node prices above marginal costs) to the detriment of Colbún (selling below marginal costs), while Endesa and Chilectra were unaffected. As mentioned by Blanlot (1993), the long-run condition that marginal costs should equate node prices (which is at the basis of the price mechanism) was not met.

Colbún based its allegations on the fact that market discrimination was raising its long-run marginal costs. According to Colbún, this was evidence of predatory behavior on the part of Enersis. The following elements contributed to this dispute:

- The contract signed by Colbún and Chilectra was clearly incomplete and disadvantageous to Colbún, particularly when compared with those signed by Endesa and Gener with Chilectra.
- The relationship of Chilectra, Endesa, and Pehuenche as members of the same holding company increased the potential for discrimination.
- Between April and June 1991, when marginal costs were above node prices, Pehuenche did not sell any energy to Chilectra, so that Colbún had to supply Chilectra at a loss. During the second semester of 1991, when the marginal cost was below node prices, Pehuenche supplied large amounts of energy to Chilectra, forcing Colbún's sales to drop to zero.

When the Minister of the Economy decided in favor of Colbún, Enersis took the case to the Antitrust Commission on the grounds that the minister was not competent to decide the matter. The Resolution Commission studied the dispute without reaching a decision. In September 1992, the parties settled the dispute. Enersis signed an agreement saying it would modify its contracts and compensate Colbún for its losses. Chilectra and Colbún signed a contract for 1992-2001, with characteristics similar to those signed by other suppliers (Endesa and Gener).

Several authors favor Colbún's position, remarking that the crucial factors facilitating discriminatory practices were the existence of a conglomerate in the industry and an ambiguous regulatory framework in the electricity sector in Chile (Bitrán and Saavedra 1993; Blanlot 1993; and Morandé and Sánchez 1992). The discriminatory strategy was profitable only to Chilectra's stockholders that belonged to Enersis.

Case 3. Exclusivity of Concession Areas

This case highlights the role of timely decisions by the authorities to enhance competition between two distributors. Distributors in Chile have been granted concession areas that are, most of the time, exclusive and based on historical (preprivatization) precedents. In fact, concessions are granted immediately upon request, except when the regulator considers it technically unfeasible. Areas of concession can be urban or suburban, facing different legal and regulatory treatment (for example, they face different regulated prices). The regulators can grant concessions without limitations, but have traditionally expressed doubts about allowing overlapping distribution networks. In fact, the head of CNE declared in 1996 that concentration of distribution activities is determined by technical, not economic, factors, and that two distribution networks would be inefficient.

Concession areas in electricity have never been questioned. In fact, they have become the private property of the firms. Nevertheless, conflict arose in Santiago when a large distribution firm (Chilectra) was accused of predatory practices by a rival (Sinel) in an area where concessions overlapped de facto. Chilectra, the main distributor in the Santiago area, usually covers the urban sector. Sinel is a small rural distributor. The electricity law states that tariff rates must be set for customers, not for geographical areas. Hence, when Chilectra began to sell in Sinel's territory, the latter feared that it would be eliminated from the market if cross subsidies from urban to semi-urban consumers were allowed; semi-urban distribution costs are 15 percent higher than urban costs (Paredes, Sánchez, and Fernández 1995). In 1991, Sinel complained to the Antitrust Commission.

The Prevention Commission of the Antitrust Commission ruled that overlapping should not be allowed. The Resolution Commission reversed that decision, stating that concession areas were not exclusive (thus allowing overlaps), but that selling prices to regulated consumers among firms could not differ. Thus, in practice, the higher court favored competition.

Case 4. Lack of Definition of Transmission Tolls

This case illustrates how incomplete regulation (absence of a pricing mechanism for transmission tolls) and the resulting uncertainty can lead to socially inefficient outcomes. Lack of proper definitions of transmission tolls and cost sharing in expansion investments have been the most important areas of conflict and renegotiations in the electricity industry in Chile. The law guarantees open access to the transmission network as long as capacity allows it. When capacity does not permit an additional user, investment in the network and its associated costs should be established freely through negotiations between the user and the owner of the network. The potential user, therefore, has the choice of connecting with the network of the transmission company (avoiding undertaking the investments) or building the lines to satisfy its own requirements and connecting with the network at the points it deems most suitable. An intermediate solution would be to build the lines it needs and connect with the network only for the use of sections that have surplus capacity.

The law also establishes that the company that owns the facilities should calculate the value of the toll, the areas of influence, and the new replacement value and how it should be prorated among firms. Nevertheless, the transmission company should make the replacement values and operating costs for all the sections of the system available to all members of the Central Integrated System. A user who does not agree with the toll calculated by the company has recourse to arbitration.

In 1990, Colbún, then a state-owned firm, began supplying energy to Chilectra. From the beginning, Colbún and Endesa disagreed on transmission tolls and connection fees. By the end of that year, both firms agreed to call in the Arbitrage Commission to settle matters. However, the Commission was unable to determine what the transmission costs should be and the proportion that Colbún should pay. Between 1992 and 1997, Colbún and Endesa-Transelec disagreed on the amount of those tolls. Colbún made annual provisions (tentative payments) of $12 to $13 million until the dispute was resolved.[7]

During 1994, the disagreement between Transelec and Colbún regarding transmission tolls widened. According to a study of transmission costs by Transelec, an annual payment of $21 million was consistent with the proportion of energy sent by Colbún to Santiago (prorated). Colbún rejected this proposal on the grounds that it was arbitrary and monopolistic, and increased pressure on the Arbitrage Commission to resolve the dispute concerning unpaid transmission fees. Fearing it could lose at the arbitration table and face further litigation costs, Colbún began studying an alternative solution to its transmission problem: namely,

[7] Values are in U.S. dollars.

building its own transmission line to Santiago. The study concluded that the line would cost $70 million to build, which represented $7.5 million a year in terms of Colbún's cost of capital. Taking into consideration yearly operating costs of $4 million, the cost of owning its own transmission lines would be, at most, $11.5 million a year.

Once Colbún decided to build a private transmission line, Enersis (which owned Transelec through Endesa) followed two different strategies. The first one was to convince Colbún (and the government) that an independent line was an inefficient solution, not only from a social point of view, but also from a strictly private perspective. Hence, in June 1995, Transelec offered a transmission fee of only $10.5 million a year; by the end of 1995, it reduced the fee to $10.3 million a year. The second strategy consisted of starting conversations with the government in order to reduce or eliminate vertical integration in generation and transmission markets. Despite indications that two transmission firms would be socially inefficient given important scale economies in this segment of the market, the government did not intervene.

In spite of scale economies in transporting electricity, Colbún's annual costs for using its own lines were only $1 million more than under Transelec's final proposal. In addition, building its own line meant that Colbún would be able to avoid litigation costs. Considering the history of conflicts between the Enersis firms and Colbún, it does not seem a high price to pay for independence. Moreover, building only one transmission line and hiring backup service from Transelec, whose fees are not regulated, did not assure Colbún that Transelec would not use its monopoly power to extract rents in the future.

Disputes related to this case did not end after Colbún started building its own lines. The first problem arose as a result of a new Endesa hydroelectric plant, Pangue, which was scheduled to enter into service in March 1997. Transelec requested permission to expand the capacity of its transmission lines to accommodate Pangue's production. CNE responded that an expansion was unnecessary because Colbún's withdrawal as a Transelec client meant that Pangue's needs could be met and delays could be easily avoided. Colbún's new transmission lines were expected to be in service in June of that year. Since the existing lines were insufficient to transport Pangue's energy without considerable losses, Enersis initiated a strong debate in order to obtain compensation from Colbún for delays in the construction of its lines. The firms decided to resolve these problems through a mediator who worked successfully beyond the standard role as arbitrator to devise a technical solution and ease the conflict. Colbún's transmission lines finally entered into operation in August 1997.

Case 5. Tariff Setting in the Regulated Distribution Market

This case shows how legal ambiguities provide scope for opportunistic behavior. After the tariff-setting process was concluded in November 1996, CNE announced the new regulated distribution prices (tariffs) in the electricity sector that would be applicable for the next four years. The tariffs were between 5.8 and 6.4 percent lower than the prevailing values. Immediately after the announcement, three major companies (two of them, Chilectra and Río Maipo, controlled by Enersis) argued that the new tariff scheme was arbitrary. They appealed to the court for protection. The third firm involved was Eléctrica Puente Alto.

The main effect of this appeal (or demand for protection) was to prevent the price change until the court determined whether CNE had the authority to make the price adjustment and whether it had proceeded according to regulations. As a result, until the court came to a conclusion, distribution companies were able to charge the prevailing tariffs.

In order to signal their agreement with the fact that electricity distribution was cheaper than it had been four years before, the three distribution companies reduced fixed charges by between 26 and 42 percent (Chilectra reduced charges by 30 percent). These changes were implemented between November 6 and 11, 1996. A similar reduction was implemented by five other minor distribution companies during the first week of December. However, reductions in fixed charges were negligible compared with the tariff reductions imposed by CNE.

The regulator realized that distribution companies were able to profit by delaying the tariff reduction announced by CNE. This arose from the absence of legislation forcing monopolies to return to consumers any extra payments when the courts determined the need for tariff reductions. Accordingly, on December 4, the government enacted legislation to close this loophole. The legislation went into effect on December 28, 1996.

On January 31, 1997, the Court of Appeals accepted the demands of the companies. Immediately, both the regulator (CNE) and the State Defense Council (which joined the conflict as a consumer representative) appealed to the Supreme Court. The Supreme Court overturned the Court of Appeals' decision and the new regulatory tariffs went into effect on April 28. Extra payments that were made between December 28, 1996 and April 28, 1997 were later returned to consumers. Nevertheless, extra income obtained in the November 4 to December 27, 1996 period was not returned to consumers. Distribution companies realized additional profits of around $7 million as a result of the lawsuit.

Case 6. Regulation of Related Industries

This case illustrates how an inadequate design for the natural gas sector could potentially hamper performance in the electricity market. In July 1990, Chile and Argentina signed an initial agreement to allow the construction of a gas pipeline between the two countries. In August 1991, they signed a protocol to specify detailed conditions for export, including a daily limit of five million cubic meters. In early 1992, ENAP (the Chilean state-owned monopoly oil refinery) signed an agreement to buy gas from YPF (its counterpart in Argentina). The project was to bring gas into Chile by way of a mountain pass located 800 km south of the Santiago main consumption center. The estimated cost of the project was $1 billion. In March 1993, the TransGas holding company was formed.

In November 1993, a Chilean gas distributor (GASCO) began a study of an alternative pipeline through a nearby mountain pass located 200 km southeast of Santiago. GASCO invited Enersis's main rival, Gener, to become its partner in GasAndes. In August 1994, GasAndes obtained permission from the Argentine government to purchase gas. This measure was proposed by Argentina's Finance Minister as a mechanism to reduce the power of the recently privatized oil company, YPF. In June 1995, the governments of Argentina and Chile signed a new protocol eliminating limits on gas exports, allowing GasAndes to compete with TransGas.

In mid 1994, TransGas and GasAndes agreed to name an arbiter to determine the feasibility of merging the two projects. Disagreements started over the person chosen as arbiter, and spread to questions over control of the joint venture. Since the latter question could not be solved, the proposal was abandoned. At the same time, the government hired a consulting firm to evaluate the projects and determine the feasibility of each. The arbiter concluded that the projects were incompatible with each other, while the consulting firm favored GasAndes.

As a result of the failure of the joint venture, the companies entered a brief but fierce price war to sign long-term contracts with clients during May and June of 1995, and to ensure the economic viability of the projects. Final offers were as much as 24 percent lower than initial tariffs and the expected reduction in electricity prices was estimated at 10 percent. In July 1995, GasAndes won the open-season process by offering a tariff that was 1 percent below that of TransGas. Even Endesa, a subsidiary of Enersis, contracted to buy gas from the rival venture. In August 1995, and after Enersis abandoned the project, TransGas withdrew.

Competition of this sort produces an important amount of lobbying and pressure for special treatment. Both holdings pressured CNE through the media (as well as by lobbying politicians and ministers) to gain an exclusive concession. Nevertheless, CNE assumed a neutral role regarding the key issues and, in fact, moved quickly when changes in market design were necessary. Likewise, the Minister of Finance played a neutral role despite the fact that he had been in charge of evaluating the TransGas project long before becoming minister.

CNE played an important role in fostering transparency. First, when the Argentine authorities announced their interest in redesigning the gas protocol to increase competition, CNE seized the opportunity to inhibit Enersis from becoming a mega-monopoly in gas and electricity. CNE formed a team to design the market and sign a new protocol. Second, the government did not play a crucial role in determining the outcome of the confrontation by using its power through Colbún (which was state-owned at the time); the government allowed technical considerations to be the major force behind contractual arrangements. Third, the authorities controlled lobbying within the government by contracting with a private firm to decide which project was socially preferable, maintaining the discussion within technical limits.

Case 7. Allocation of Water Rights

This case highlights how the inadequate allocation of water property rights might deter entry into the electricity generation market. Water property rights are an important source of disputes for three reasons. First, watersheds run from east to west and are not interconnected; thus, they make arbitration unfeasible. Second, since the country is so narrow, water descends from an altitude of 4,000 meters to sea level in less than 100 miles; as a result, the possibilities for locating hydroelectric generating units are limited. Third, the weather tends to be erratic, creating large hydrological risks. Consequently, water rights are crucial for the development of hydroelectric companies.

Shortly before privatizing the electricity sector, the government reformed water rights that were, at the time, the sole property of the government. New regulations retained the property in the hands of the state, but established the right of private parties to request concessions to use water for consumption and other purposes. Any individual or firm could claim water rights at no cost (except in the case of disputes in which the government could auction the rights). In addition, rights would not expire and there were no penalties for holding rights without effective use.

At the time Endesa was privatized, its water rights were transferred to the new proprietor. These water rights largely exceed Endesa's investment plan; in fact, Endesa's water rights were such that if generating plants were built, production could increase by 3,100 MW, which is 75 percent of the current capacity of the Central Integrated System. In addition, Endesa holds water rights for another 2,000 MW in the south, which could potentially be linked to the Central Integrated System at moderate cost. After privatization, Endesa claimed another 79 water rights out of some 280 claims filed by different electricity and industrial companies.

Operators in the market have expressed fears that Endesa could use water rights as an entry deterrence mechanism. The extent to which these water rights can be used as a barrier to market entry depends on the availability of alternative sources for generating electricity. In this sense, imports of natural gas from

Argentina have reduced the value of water rights as a source of monopoly power in generation. Nevertheless, in 1996 the Antitrust Commission recommended that Endesa not be given additional water rights, to avoid noncompetitive behavior.

The extensive allocation of water rights to Endesa has had entry deterrence effects in other industries. In Aysen, a scarcely populated area in the south, Endesa holds 30 percent of available water rights, but does not have facilities in operation. The local state-owned generating plant supplies the entire demand for current with less than 1 percent of the area's water rights. This has inhibited the development of an aluminum plant that requires a large amount of electricity for its operation. Needing access to water rights, the Canadian company Noranda invited Endesa to be a (minor) partner in the $3 billion project. The project stalled when Endesa declined the offer.

Case 8. Regulatory Reaction to an External Shock (the 1998-99 Crisis)

This case illustrates how pitfalls in the regulatory framework and lack of technical know-how in regulatory institutions can impose high costs on consumers and create room for further litigation and disputes in the sector. In addition, it illustrates the damaging role politicians can play.

In 1998–99, Chile suffered its worst electricity crisis since the privatization of the industry. A severe drought caused a marked decline in hydroelectric generation, forcing the government to impose rationing. Despite the fact that water reserves were at very low levels, the government allowed Endesa's hydroelectric power plants to utilize a substantial amount of water from the country's main reservoir, Lake Laja. Díaz, Galetovic, and Soto (2000) estimate that, had this water been saved for the dry season, it would have been enough to avoid rationing. It seems that, at the time, CNE was confident that either it would rain or a power plant under construction would start producing in November. Unfortunately, it did not rain and the plant was still inoperative in July 1999.

This decision was a major mistake for two reasons. First, it signaled that the authorities were hesitant to impose rationing and face the political cost of doing so, leaving them vulnerable to lobbying. Second, it created space for opportunism because prices for the water transferred to Endesa were set at extremely low levels, well below the system's marginal cost and outage costs.[8] Furthermore, in October 1998, despite the fact that the country was suffering the worst drought since 1968, CNE announced that power was guaranteed until March 1999 and lowered regulated nodal prices (tariffs) by 10 percent.

---

[8] Outage costs (*costos de falla*, as it is called in the regulation) are transfer prices for energy in cases of system failure.

The 1982 electricity law stated that when conditions required rationing, consumers should be compensated at outage costs for unserved energy by firms unable to fulfill contracts. The need to compensate consumers should have prompted firms to install emergency equipment, purchase existing capacity from generators with surplus or self-producers with sufficient reserve equipment, or pay voluntary compensation to nonregulated consumers to be disconnected. However, the firms' legal responsibility was limited.

When implementing rationing and emergency measures, the authorities faced considerable opposition from hydroelectric generators. First, hydroelectric firms tried to convince the authorities that the drought was so severe that it represented a case of *force majeure* and they should be exempt from responsibility and compensations. Second, hydroelectric generators claimed that transfer prices from surplus generators should be valued at marginal costs, instead of outage prices. Third, hydroelectric generators disputed the amount of energy to be compensated and claimed that, according to the law, they were exempt from responsibility because, had the drought been as severe as that of 1968, they would have had a surplus of energy.

The response of the government was slow and irresolute. As a result, opportunistic incentives worsened the crisis. Without the guidance of the authorities, generators did not coordinate properly to reduce the extent of blackouts (for example, periodic maintenance was rescheduled very late) and, at some point, there was excess demand and unused capacity in the system. The authorities did not have the means to force firms to cooperate (for example, fines were too low to be effective). Finally, the reluctance of the government to set outage costs to value energy transfers encouraged firms to speculate that transfer prices were to be set at marginal costs. In turn, this led producers to continue supplying unregulated clients (worsening the shortage faced by households) in order to avoid paying disconnection fines that were above marginal costs but below outage costs.

In April 1999, six months after rationing was first imposed, the authorities finally declared that outage costs were to be used. The length and depth of the crisis led politicians to blame the private sector, question the performance of the authorities, and call for a revision of the regulation to tighten supervision and increase penalties. Congress passed a law determining that rationing should be implemented without distinction between regulated and unregulated consumers, thus destroying the incentives for an economically efficient response to the crisis. In addition, the new legislation significantly increased fines and required that compensation be paid in every case (no *force majeure*) for the entire amount of the deficit (no exemptions to compensations). These measures changed industry rules and will undoubtedly have long-run effects. Firms will have a more conservative approach to hedging contracts and, consequently, energy prices and unused capacity will increase. In a country subject to major earthquakes, the possibility of energy failures as a result of true *force majeure* events cannot be discounted, yet the law makes no exemptions. This creates the basis for future disputes.

In fact, firms disputed this law before the Supreme Court as unconstitutional (the case was dismissed). The structure of the law is so poorly designed that it is inconsistent with current regulation to the extent that the authorities cannot apply it without violating the law. In addition, according to some interpretations, the regulation may force firms with a surplus of energy during system failures to pay compensations.

The Role of Chilean Institutions in the Resolution of Conflicts

The five institutions in charge of regulating and monitoring the electricity sector (CNE, CDEC, SEC, the Antitrust Commission, and the Ministry of the Economy) convey a sense of acting in isolation of interest groups and political parties. However, the limitations of the institutions in terms of human capital and resources create inefficiencies in performance, resulting in high litigation costs and a certain randomness in their decisions. This section assesses the role of the Antitrust Commission, CDEC, and CNE in the resolution of conflicts.

The Antitrust Commission

Tables 3–2 and 3–3 present a summary of the trials and corresponding judgements for suits filed with the Antitrust Commission in 1988–97. In total, 16 suits with significant economic effects were filed at both the Prevention and Resolution Commissions. One episode led to a large number of disputes: 25 percent of all cases represent conflicts between Río Maipo (a small generating company near Santiago) and Puente Alto (a distributor serving areas close to Santiago). Several disputes are of no consequence to the electricity sector because they involve cases of commercial wrongdoing (for example, accusations of collusion to elect directors). In nine other cases (unreported here), individuals sued the electricity companies for minor issues, such as delays in connection or repair services.

Trials tend to be quite long; on average they last 12 months in the Prevention Commission and 20 months in the Resolution Commission. Since most disputes go through both commissions, a dispute may take around three years to be resolved. Once the Resolution Commission issues a judgement, appeals must go to the Supreme Court, an endeavor that could last a couple of years. The Antitrust Commission has filed two large lawsuits against Enersis on the grounds of abuse of monopoly power. These were extremely long trials (two to four years) and involved a large number of witnesses and technical reports. Since the National Economic Prosecutor is an officer appointed by the President of the

Table 3–2. Antitrust Commission: Proceedings of the Prevention Commission

(Selected cases from 1989 to 1997)

Date of proceeding	Date of judgement	Parties involved	Reason	Judgement
Nov. 10, 1989	Feb. 5, 1990	Sinel (d) against Chilectra (d)	Chilectra abuses its monopoly power delaying power supply increases required by Sinel. Overlap of geographic zone allows predatory practices.	Overlap of geographic zones is not allowed.
June 7, 1990	Jan. 29, 1992	CMET (telephones) against Enersis	Enersis abuses monopoly power because Chilectra uses posts installed in public access areas.	CMET withdraws accusations.
June 27, 1990	Jan. 27, 1992	Puente Alto (d) against Río Maipo (g)	Río Maipo abuses monopoly power in the devolution of payments for an eventual increment in the power supply.	Río Maipo is fined according to antitrust law.
Dec. 7, 1990	Nov. 25, 1991	Río Maipo (g) against Puente Alto (d)	Anti-competitive practices. Puente Alto does not publicly announce both tariffs and financial charges.	Vacated (the information was publicly announced).
June 12, 1991	Aug. 7, 1992	Puente Alto (d) against Río Maipo (g)	Rio Maipo abuses monopoly power when requiring excessive (illegal) guarantees.	Guarantees are monopoly practices. Río Maipo is fined.
Dec. 13, 1991	May 13, 1993	Pedro de Valdivia against Litoral (g)	Litoral abuses monopoly power on installation and power supply.	Dismissed.
July 29, 1993	Sep. 16, 1993	CORFO (asks advice)	CORFO asks whether procedures for auctioning Edelnor shares in stock markets are legal.	Auctioning adjusts to law.
Oct. 26, 1994	Oct. 5, 1995	Pullinque (d) against Endesa (g) and Gener (g)	Endesa and Gener abuse monopoly power by fixing tariffs.	Vacated.
July 4, 1996	Nov. 25, 1996	CNE (asks advice)	New water rights given to Endesa may affect competition in generation.	The court recommends that new water rights should not be granted until legal ambiguities are resolved.
	Dec. 23, 1996	Endesa	Endesa appeals previous sentence concerning water rights.	Vacated.

Note: (d) denotes a distribution company and (g) a generating company.

Table 3–3. Antitrust Commission: Proceedings of the Resolution Commission
(Selected cases from 1989 to 1997)

Date of proceeding	Date of judgement	Parties involved	Reason	Judgement
Nov. 4, 1988	March 13, 1990	VTR (telecom) against Endesa (g)	Endesa asked VTR to conduct a study but awarded it to a rival firm.	Vacated.
Feb. 14, 1990	March 27, 1990	Chilectra	Chilectra appealed the Prevention Commission's sentence.	Overlap of geographic zones is allowed but firms must charge the same tariffs.
June 5, 1990	June 2, 1992	Briones (particular) against Enersis and several AFP	Collusion to elect directors.	Vacated.
June 5, 1990	June 7, 1992	Pullinque (g) against Endesa (g)	Endesa abused market power. Excessive tariffs and tolls when using Endesa's transmission facilities.	Endesa won the case (3–2).
March 20, 1992	Sep. 15, 1992	Colbún (g) against Pehuenche (g), Endesa (g) and Chilectra (d)	Firms discriminated against Colbún.	Withdrawn by Colbún.
	Sep. 26, 1993	Briones	Appeal of the Resolution Commission's sentence.	Vacated.
	March 22, 1994	Río Maipo (g)	Río Maipo appealed sentence of Jan. 27, 1992.	Vacated. Río Maipo is fined for abuse of market power against Puente Alto.
Oct. 2, 1992	June 11, 1997	National Economic Prosecutor against Chilectra, Endesa, and Transelec	National Economic Prosecutor asked for divestiture to encourage competition and eliminate abuse of market power.	Rejected by both the Resolution Commission and the Supreme Court.
Oct. 10, 1995		Pullinque (g) against Endesa (g)	Appeal of previous Prevention Commission's judgement regarding abuse of monopoly power.	Vacated.
	Jan. 7, 1997	Endesa	Endesa appealed a previous sentence by the Prevention Commission.	Vacated.

Note: (d) denotes a distribution company and (g) a generating company.

Republic, the trial had some touches of political confrontation, but remained largely technical.

To a large extent, the inefficiency of the Antitrust Commission results from its lack of resources. Judges work ad-honorem, which may guarantee independence, but also implies they have little time for these matters, which, in turn, lengthens the processes. The Commission's technical staff is poorly paid and ill-suited for the job because most are lawyers with little training in economics.

The Resolution Commission is comprised of five members who are not necessarily trained to resolve technically complex and economically difficult disputes. The five members are a Supreme Court judge;[9] two public officers (usually lawyers) appointed ex-officio; and two university deans (one from a law school, one from an economics school), who are randomly selected from all universities.[10] As is apparent given its structure, the Commission must rely on expert witnesses to weigh arguments, facts, and opinions; however, given its limited financial resources, good advice is not guaranteed. In an effort to help resolve these problems, the government substantially increased the Commission's budget for 1998.

The legal system in Chile is antiquated, and operates largely on the basis of tangible proof of illegal activity. In fact, illegal practices must be fully specified as such in the law; judges cannot rule over nonspecified malpractice. Moreover, the Commission (a unit bound by public law) is only allowed to do things (instead of limited to do things, as is the case in the private sector). This limits the range of the Commission, in terms of both actions and the type of proof that is required to punish noncompetitive practices. To some extent, this legal structure reproduces the spirit of the Chilean legal system, which was designed in such a way so that discretion in the public sector is rare.

Paredes (1995) analyzes the decisions made by the Antitrust Commission since its inception in 1974. He finds that the behavior of the Commission regarding punishment for monopoly practices seems adequate. However, the relatively higher prosecution and punishment of vertical integration practices (which are largely justified in the literature as welfare improving in oligopolistic markets) seems inadequate. Paredes identifies two reasons for this behavior. First, there is a lack of clear definition of the purposes of antitrust regulation. Second, one of the monopoly practices that can most easily be specified corresponds to vertical integration.

---

[9] Judges in Chile have no formal training in economics.

[10] When the Antitrust Commission was formed in the mid 1970s, there were 7-10 high-quality schools of law and departments of economics in the country; most of them had highly trained staff and were independent of political or lobbying pressures. This makes the "academic" part of the Commission trustworthy. However, later the government deregulated higher education markets. To date, there are over 70 schools of law and economics of varied quality. The Commission has been fortunate in having highly trained appointees.

Furthermore, the fines are low compared with the potential benefits of wrongdoing. Fines levied by the Antitrust Commission between 1975 and 1987 averaged $29,000, and the maximum fine was $147,000. For example, on May 1, 1997, a system failure left 80 percent of the country without electric power for 55 minutes. The five largest generating companies and Transelec were fined after an investigation proved that their response to the emergency was excessively slow due to cost considerations (the expected delay should have been around three minutes). The investigation concluded that the main reason was that since support units have a higher operating cost than a failing unit, CDEC did not respond as fast as expected. Although the maximum fines were levied, they were minimal in comparison with the average sales or assets of the six companies: each company was fined less than $35,000.

Fines were increased substantially during the 1998-99 electricity crisis, reaching an estimated amount of $6 million. Certainly, this measure was in the right direction. However, the new law also extended the power of the authorities to impose such fines in a discretionary manner and located this new facility in the technically less apt regulatory body, SEC.

The Dispatch Center

A limited number of disputes have taken place in CDEC. An indirect way of assessing the number of disputes in determining the short-run marginal cost and allocating demand among different producers is through discrepancies. That is, we look at cases in which one or more members of CDEC have dissented from the majority decision. Since CDEC's inception, the number of dissensions has remained rather low.

Although the number is small, the trend is somewhat alarming and may reflect several aspects of the evolution of the industry. First, as more operators enter the market (for example, through changes in ownership) they are challenging the dominant role of Enersis.[11] Second, dissensions have been used as a negotiating tool in disputes in other areas not necessarily linked to the electricity sector. Third, the 1996–97 hydrological year was characterized by a severe drought and, for the first time in years, rationing was considered (it was not adopted, although voltage was reduced by 5 percent). In these conditions, CDEC was operating close to the point of "technical failure," a condition for which generators could be fined, thus exacerbating disputes.

---

[11] Pension funds have come to play an important role in the sector since they were allowed to invest in the stock market. Foreign investors also participate in the sector.

The case of Gener accusing Endesa of abuse of power in the dispatch of generating plants during the last months of 1997 exemplifies a conflict within CDEC that went beyond standard procedures. Instead of taking its complaint to the Minister of the Economy, Gener went directly to the Antitrust Commission. This may reflect the fact that Gener considered the issue to go beyond the boundaries of a standard CDEC conflict because the accusation dealt with intentional wrongdoing, not a simple technical discrepancy. Alternatively, it may reflect doubts regarding the ability or diligence of the Minister of the Economy to solve the issue. In any case, this lawsuit shows that conflict within CDEC has not only increased in frequency, but also in virulence.

Gener's allegation was that, invoking security reasons, Endesa had forced CDEC to allocate less energy than its capacity would allow to a crucial segment of the northern part of the Central Integrated System. In this segment, Endesa has no operations, so that Gener's ancillary, Guacolda, had to supply energy to cover the gap. Since Guacolda is a thermoelectric producer, at that particular time it would have been to its advantage to purchase energy in the spot market at marginal cost instead of producing it. Gener estimated the losses for the four months at $17 million.

The initial response of Endesa was to renounce its role as coordinator of energy dispatch in CDEC, in retaliation to the lawsuit. However, the parties reached an out-of-court settlement and the lawsuit was dropped. The terms of the agreement are not public, but it takes into consideration that Endesa may assume the economic cost incurred by Guacolda.

The National Energy Commission

CNE, the agency in charge of defining the sector's policies and calculating tariffs and prices, has played a crucial role in disputes in the electricity sector in Chile. CNE played an important role in promoting competition between energy markets in the design of the natural gas market, as discussed in case 6.

For over seven years, CNE was unable to issue the electricity sector statute despite the fact that an advanced draft was ready in 1992. The statute was necessary to provide detailed specifications to the general regulatory framework envisioned in the 1982 electricity law. Its absence was the source of several disputes. In particular, the statute should have specified the methodology for determining transmission tolls and investment charges. When it was finally enacted in December 1998, however, not only did it lack detailed specification on these issues, but also it actually introduced more ambiguities to the regulation by reinterpreting some of the original provisions of the law. Major generating companies have sued CNE before the Court of Appeals, as a result of which the statute has yet to become operative.

The magnitude of CNE's technical and political limitations was clearly evident during the 1998-99 drought. CNE was in charge of determining if it was necessary to impose rationing, ensuring that energy transactions were held at outage costs, and establishing the amount of compensation that producers had to pay to consumers for unserved energy. In retrospect, CNE failed in each of these areas. First, the authorities were vulnerable to lobbying and political interference and hesitated at the moment of imposing rationing. Second, CNE remained hesitant with regard to applying outage costs to value energy transactions for over six months during the crisis, thus encouraging opportunistic behavior by firms and deepening the crisis. Third, to date CNE has been unable to determine the magnitude of compensation, let alone force firms to pay consumers for unserved energy. Fourth, CNE was technically incapable of providing a solution to the crisis and, consequently, had to yield to political pressures and support the poorly designed law passed by Congress in June 1999 (allowing for generalized rationing and eliminating exemptions to compensations).

Applying the Regulatory Experience in the Electricity Sector to Highway Franchising

Highway franchising in Chile is a recent phenomenon. Contrary to the case of the electricity sector, highway franchising benefits from the rich regulatory experience the Chilean authorities have accumulated since the privatization program of the late 1980s. Highway franchising has relied on variations of the "build, operate, and transfer" scheme, in which the state transfers the legal right to invest in and operate highways, but retains ownership of the public works. This right lasts only a limited number of years, a period usually determined a priori by the government on the basis of the physical duration of the investment.[12] Upon expiration of this right, the government regains control of the operation and in principle can award it again to the private sector.

The allocation of the concession to the private sector is done through a transparent public auction that proceeds in two stages. In the first stage, firms interested in participating must qualify to bid on the basis of technical requirements and financial solvency. In the second stage, the prequalified bidders on the short list present their offers in a single-round, first-price, sealed-bid type of auction.

[12] Recently, the government proposed a new breed of franchise in which the total earnings of the concessionaire are fixed, but the length of the contract varies with demand. The private sector has been reluctant to accept this new mechanism on the basis of excessive risk.

A specific contract is designed for each concession based on the project's technical requirements and applicable legislation and regulations. The Ministry of Public Works performs the regulation and auctioning of highway franchises. Regulation comprises inspection of the construction and operation of concessions (including quality standards, safety provisions, compliance of the concessionaire with toll prices and user fees as stipulated in the contract, and technical specifications for different aspects of the highway), penalties for wrongdoing during construction and operation of the highways (to the point of stopping the work), and allowing minor changes in contract stipulations regarding changes in schedules, new investments, and extensions of the original contract.

Since the magnitude of investments in highways was deemed by the authorities to be too high for the capacity of the local financial sector, market design assigned an important role to foreign investment. However, in addition to the technical complexities of forecasting demand, costs, and exchange rate movements, highway franchising coincided with the transition to democracy, adding political uncertainty to the problem. To address these problems and the fear of having too few bidders in the initial auctions, the Chilean concession law gives the government the ability to offer guarantees to concessionaires. For instance, among other things, the government insures the concessionaires against low demand by guaranteeing a transfer of resources if flows fall below 75 percent of forecast demand. In addition, the government guarantees the expropriation of land to build the concession.

Table 3–4 presents a summary of highways and ongoing investment projects for which concessions have been awarded. As of November 1998, seven projects were in operation for a total investment of $620 million. The government had also auctioned nine other investment projects totaling $2.5 billion and six other projects were being studied.[13]

In general, the Ministry of Public Works has internalized several lessons learned from experience in other areas of the economy regarding concessions of public works to the private sector. In particular, the experience in the electricity sector, with which public works shares monopoly characteristics, has had a favorable impact on the institutional and regulatory design.[14] First, authorities

[13] According to the government, expected highway franchising amounted to nearly 80 percent of total expected concessions in public infrastructure in the 1990s. Nevertheless, it covers only around 50 percent of the estimated need for public roads. The remaining roads correspond to projects with low private profitability and, consequently, will be very likely undertaken directly by the government (for example, low-demand, inter-urban roads).

[14] Since the country is narrow, there are important economies of scale in having a single highway serving as the backbone of the highway network. In this regard, highway concessions share the same advantages and drawbacks of the electricity transmission system.

Table 3–4. Highway Concession Programs in Chile, 1993–99

Project	Total investment (millions of U.S. dollars)	Auction date	Status	Start of operations	Length of concession (years)	Payments to government	Subsidies and state guarantees
El Melón Tunnel	42	1993	In operation	3/1996	23	Yes	Minimum flows
Camino de la Madera	29	1994	In operation	5/1997	25	Yes	Subsidies and minimum flows
Access to Concepción	210	1994	In operation	4/1998	28	No	Minimum flows
Santiago-San Antonio	146	1995	In operation	1/1997	23	Yes	Minimum flows
Access to Santiago Airport	10	1995	In operation	2/1998	12	No	Minimum flows
Puchuncavi-Nogales	12	1995	In operation	11/1997	22	No	Minimum flows
Talca-Chillan	172	1995	In operation	9/1998	10	Yes	Minimum flows
Santiago-Los Vilos	255	1996	Construction	1999	23	No	
Santiago-Los Andes	137	1997	Construction	2000	28	Yes	Minimum flows
La Serena-Los Vilos	245	1996	Construction	2001	25	No	Subsidies and minimum flows
Chillan-Collipulli	210	1997	Construction	2001	22	No	Subsidies and minimum flows
Temuco-Río Bueno	190	1997	Construction	2002	28	No	Subsidies and minimum flows
Río Bueno-Puerto Montt	200	1997	Construction	2000	25	No	Subsidies
Collipulli-Temuco	226	1998	Construction	2002	25	No	Subsidies and minimum flows
Santiago-Talca	650	1998	Construction	2002	25		
Santiago-Valparaíso	383	1998	Construction	2002	Variable	No	
Quintay-Cartagena	100	1999e	To be auctioned				
Camino de la Fruta	100	2000e	Under study				
Chacao Channel Bridge	300	2001e	Under study				
Access Santiago North	150	1999e	Under study				
Valparaíso-Los Andes	200		Under study				
Interport Route	12	1999e	Under study				

[e] Expected.
Source: Authors' calculations based on information from the Ministry of Public Works.

have reacted quickly in response to perceived misconduct or regulatory weaknesses. Second, the government has been careful to avoid repeating the mistakes it made when privatizing the electricity sector, which led to the creation of a very large and politically powerful holding. Third, the government has incorporated mechanisms to reduce contract renegotiations and the cost of litigation.

Reaction to Possible Conflicts

The Ministry of Public Works has made an important effort to gain credibility regarding the cases with which it will engage in renegotiations and disputes. It sent a strong signal to the private sector in its tough stance with regard to claims by the concessionaire of El Melón Tunnel (the first concession awarded). According to the concessionaire, its initial demand estimates proved to be too optimistic, so that the annual transfer it has to make to the government makes the business unprofitable. The government has refused to change toll prices and transfers beyond the contract stipulations on the grounds that conditions have not changed, that a bidder in a concession must accept the demand risk, and that renegotiations are costly and hamper its reputation. In particular, it is difficult for the government to determine whether the firm was low-balling when it submitted its bid.

Limiting Concentration

The aggressive entry of a large foreign company with a bad record of renegotiating highway concessions led the government to promptly modify certain regulations. The modifications limited concessionaires to three of the 12 segments of Chile's main highway (the Pan American Highway). It should be recalled that, given Chile's geography, a single highway is likely to be the only profitable alternative.

Although there may have been an underlying political motivation for limiting the size of highway concessionaires, there are important economic reasons that support it. First, the government correctly gave priority to setting up a competitive market, rather than just attracting private investment. Considering the difficulties in regulating the electricity sector, it may be socially desirable to widen the entrepreneurial basis so as to promote the active participation of the private sector in a competitive environment. The existence of important sunk costs when bidding for highway concessions (estimated to be approximately $2 million for each bid) could lead firms to withdraw if one of the bidders already holds a large share of the market and the other firms think the probability of winning the auction is thus reduced.

Second, limiting the number of highway segments to be managed by a single firm provides the government more information to engage in regulation based on yardstick competition. In principle, operating costs should not differ markedly among concessionaires and could potentially serve as a benchmark for the government if renegotiations or contract adjustments are required. In addition, collusion among a larger number of concessionaires becomes increasingly costly, thus reducing a potential source of conflict.

Third, the government is concerned with the potential for political power of a large concessionaire of highways. Limiting the number of highway segments could reduce this power if firms can effectively be deterred from using third parties to disguise their participation. The Chilean Concessions Law includes several mechanisms to reduce this problem. These provisions arise largely from experience in the electricity sector, where concentration by Enersis has become a major political problem for the government.

Designing Conflict Resolution Mechanisms

The government has made an attempt to overcome the limitations of the judiciary system by designing and implementing entities that can, in principle, deal more efficiently with contract renegotiations. Due to design complexities and uncertainty, contracts in this area are likely to be incomplete and prone to disputes. Taking into account the limitations of the judiciary system when dealing with disputes in the electricity sector, the government created specific entities to deal with contract disputes between concessionaires and the Ministry of Public Works. For each concession, a conciliation commission is formed by three members (one for each party to the contract and an agreed-upon third member), which must resolve matters within 30 days of receiving a complaint. Complaints can be brought by either party, but the government is more limited than the concessionaire. If an agreement is not reached, the private party has two options: bring the case before either an Arbitration Commission (whose decisions are binding) or the Court of Appeals.

This is a novel approach to this problem, which inhibits incentives to renegotiate stemming from the weaknesses of courts to adjudicate complicated technical problems. However, to a certain extent, the current structure limits the impact of the conciliation commissions. Although conflict resolution mechanisms are an interesting component of the Chilean regulatory design, they present some shortcomings. First and foremost, the roles of the conciliation and arbitration commissions are distorted. In principle, their functioning should be diametrically different. The former should concentrate on easing disputes between the concessionaire and the government, but maintaining a neutral position with regard to both parties. The latter should focus only on providing solutions to the conflict in the form of legal judgements.

Consequently, the staff of both commissions should not overlap. A conciliation commission that, at the request of one party, transforms itself into an arbitration commission induces perverse behavior in both parties. In fact, each commission requires markedly different abilities of its members. In the conciliation commission, both parties ask mainly for neutrality, in exchange for which they are willing to reveal information to a third party regarding the extent to which they would yield to reach an agreement. By contrast, an arbitration commission is efficient if it gains a reputation for fairness. Since under arbitration one party will be penalized, any information divulged is of strategic value. Hence, parties will not release information to the conciliation commission if they believe that it can be used against them in the event of arbitration. In addition, a practical limitation of the scheme is that it is difficult to find candidates that are well suited for both commissions.

Finally, a number of minor issues show that conciliation and arbitration in this market could benefit from being redesigned. For example, conciliation and/or arbitration could be called for independently of the amount of resources involved in the dispute. Likewise, there are no criteria that justify calling third parties. A simple solution to this problem is to separate both commissions and redesign the rules by which they operate. In particular, the presence of representatives of the parties to the disputes in the arbitration commission does not play any useful role. Indeed, the representatives would probably hamper the efficiency of the independent member in assessing the situation and proposing solutions or penalties.

Conclusions

Chile's experience with private sector participation in the electricity sector provides ample evidence of the importance of adequately designing the structure of the post-privatization market, implementing the appropriate regulatory framework, and developing the institutional capabilities to enforce the regulation. In general terms, the Chilean case is characterized by a low level of conflict between the authorities and the regulated firms. However, Chile's experience shows that incomplete regulation and institutional weakness can become crucial limitations.

The lack of conflict in this case results from a fairly well-conceived design of the post-privatization market. It includes a clear separation of the different stages of production, sound regulatory principles in each stage, properly designed conflict resolution mechanisms, and no political interference. Notwithstanding some limitations, regulations ensure monitoring and control, guarantee access to the information necessary to regulate, and provide for appropriate interaction among private agents and between them and the regulators.

Disputes are concentrated in those areas in which regulation is incomplete, mostly where information asymmetry is high and regulatory institutions are less able to monitor private sector activities. The cases reviewed here suggest that conflict has stemmed from three main sources: (1) the existence of vertical integration; (2) the lack of definition of certain areas in regulation (for example, shortcomings in the procedures to set transmission tolls and investment cost sharing); and (3) the institutional weaknesses of regulatory bodies. One of the main problems resulting from Chile's privatization of the electricity sector is that it allowed the creation of a large vertically integrated conglomerate that could use its market power in the regulated segment of the market to reduce competition and raise its profits in the competitive segment. This dominant position would not be of capital importance if information problems were irrelevant and the authorities could properly regulate the market. Moreover, in such case vertical integration could be consistent with efficiency gains derived from scale economies and management. However, the analysis of the Chilean experience suggests that these efficiency gains are eclipsed when information asymmetry is important and the regulator cannot enforce regulation adequately.

The main source of conflict has been the perception that Enersis could engage in noncompetitive behavior in at least three areas. First, Enersis's distributor (Chilectra) could benefit its affiliated generators (Endesa, Pehuenche, and others) by issuing preferential contracts, in particular to reduce risk at a higher cost for other producers. Second, since two of the four directors of the dispatch center (CDEC) come from Endesa and its affiliate Transelec is a virtual monopoly in high-voltage transmission, the integrated firm could manipulate dispatch to its benefit. Third, since Transelec is a subsidiary of Endesa, the latter can obtain inside information from it and receive special treatment regarding transmission tolls and other contract specifications. It is apparent that in all cases the advantage of the integrated firm is based on the information asymmetry derived from the fact that the regulator has limited access to private contracts. To properly regulate the integrated firm, the authorities would require more information than is currently available. In this sense, requiring transmission contracts to be submitted to CNE (as is mandatory in several other countries) could be a useful reform to the regulatory mechanism.

The Chilean case also shows that once property rights have been allocated to firms in the privatization process, they become very difficult to modify. In addition, when regulation is not optimal, property rights can sometimes be used as legal entry barriers, as is the case of water rights. All these problems (which could have been anticipated at the moment of designing the privatization process) have caused much of the litigation that took place between 1990 and 1998.

A second group of disputes and conflicts are those arising from ambiguities in the regulatory framework. An ambiguous regulatory framework makes contracts incomplete and promotes opportunistic behavior in the market, which is exacerbated when institutions are weak or unable to enforce contracts. Chile's experience illustrates the perils of privatizing an industry characterized by natural monopoly segments and substantial information asymmetries without implementing a full regulatory body. The Chilean electricity sector was divested in the absence of the operational statute envisioned by the privatization law to determine key aspects of regulation, including transmission tolls and prorating of investment. Although the operational statute should have been enacted in the early 1990s, it was not issued until the end of 1998. The lack of definition and ambiguities in important aspects of regulation have led to a large number of renegotiations and disputes (some of which were legitimate business conflicts), but it has also allowed firms to behave opportunistically and extract rents from consumers and other firms.

The third source of conflicts is those arising from the limitations of regulatory agencies in terms of human capital, legal frameworks, and financial resources. An endemic problem is the lack of a trained staff to deal with their private sector counterparts. This problem affects the relative power of the government at the moment of renegotiating regulated tariffs. It has had a damaging effect in weakening the prosecutor's position in the vertical integration cases. The prosecutor lacked a consistent set of arguments to convince the judges that presumptions in cases of regulation can be as important as tangible evidence. In addition, lack of resources and low wages have created a fragile pool of human capital for Chile's public sector. Individuals obtain experience by working in the regulatory agency and then move on to better paid private sector employment in the regulated industry, leaving less qualified and dynamic personnel in the public sector.

Disputes in the electricity sector are often of an extremely technical nature, requiring not only an independent judiciary system, but also well-trained personnel to resolve disputes at reasonable cost. In addition, Chile's legal apparatus is quite inefficient in terms of the speed at which cases are processed, and has a tendency to rely on tangible proof of illegal activity. In cases of noncompetitive behavior, physical evidence is very difficult to obtain.

When the judiciary system is unable to provide quick and fair treatment in disputes, it is to the advantage of both parties to use the services of an independent arbitrator. The main drawback of arbitration is the lack of enforcement of decisions or penalties. Arbitrators have played an important role in Chile, but their inability to issue mandatory opinions limits their impact and has led the government to propose the creation of arbitration commissions with punitive power.

Several of the lessons stemming from the regulation of the electricity sector have been implemented in the highway-franchising program. In particular, the institutional and regulatory design has been positively influenced by the experience gathered in the electricity sector, which shares similar natural monopoly characteristics.

First, authorities have reacted quickly in response to perceived wrongdoing or regulatory weaknesses. The government has refused to change franchise conditions on the grounds that a bidder in a concession must accept the risks of the concession and that eventual renegotiations are costly and hamper its reputation. Second, the government has been careful to avoid the creation of a very large and politically powerful holding. By imposing restrictions on the number of franchises a firm can hold, the government signaled its commitment to setting up a competitive industry and to limiting the potential for political power of a large concessionaire. Third, the government has made an attempt to overcome the limitations of the judiciary by designing and implementing entities that can, in principle, deal more efficiently with contract renegotiations. Due to design complexities and uncertainty, contracts in this area are likely to be incomplete and prone to disputes. Taking into account the limitations of the judiciary system when dealing with disputes in the electricity sector, the government created specific entities to deal with contract disputes between highway concessionaires and the authorities.

References

Bitrán, E., and E. Saavedra. 1993. "Algunas reflexiones en torno al rol regulador y empresarial del estado." In O. Muñoz, ed., *Después de las privatizaciones: hacia un estado regulador.* Santiago, Chile: CIEPLAN.

Blanlot, V. 1993. "La regulación del sector eléctrico: la experiencia chilena." In O. Muñoz, ed., *Después de las privatizaciones: hacia un estado regulador.* Santiago, Chile: CIEPLAN.

Díaz, C. A., A. Galetovic, and R. Soto. 2000. "La crisis eléctrica de 1998-1999: causas, consecuencias y lecciones." *Estudios Públicos* 80(Primavera): 149-92.

Morandé, F., and J. M. Sánchez. 1992. "Incentivos y formas de discriminación en oferta de electricidad." ILADES/Georgetown University, Santiago, Chile. Unpublished.

Paredes, R. 1995. "Jurisprudencia de las Comisiones Antimonopolios en Chile." *Estudios Públicos* 58: 227–317.

Paredes, R., J. M. Sánchez, and A. Fernández. 1995. "Privatización y regulación en Latinoamérica." *Revista de Análisis Económico* 10(2).

Sáez, R. 1993. "Las privatizaciones de empresas en Chile." In O. Muñoz, ed., *Después de las privatizaciones: hacia un estado regulador.* Santiago, Chile: CIEPLAN.

CHAPTER 4

Private Participation in Infrastructure in Colombia: Renegotiations and Disputes

Juan Benavides and Israel Fainboim

Colombia began liberalizing and privatizing infrastructure and public utilities in 1991, following congressional approval of constitutional reform. Since then, private participation has been carried out mostly through concessions and joint ventures between public and private parties. Privatization has been less common so far, the important exceptions being the electric power sector and gas distribution. This institutional change took place in a country where rent seeking is deeply rooted and enforcement rules are not binding. The reforms have unfolded in a difficult environment in which the residual rights in public utilities and large civil works projects have often been placed in the hands of long-lived special interests. In addition, the constitutional reform created new rules and institutions that would function independently of the three state powers. These circumstances have encouraged affected parties to attempt to recover discretionary power, and explain in part the inefficiencies that arise in dispute resolution.

This chapter analyzes the renegotiations and disputes that occurred in specific infrastructure contracts and public utilities in Colombia between 1994 and 1999. It provides an overview of the institutional framework in which the disputes were conducted, and presents case studies in electricity, cellular telephone service, and road building. A background presentation by sector gives the reader information about the specific context that is important for understanding the rationale of the disputes. It sets forth the terms of each dispute, analyzes the efficiency and welfare features of each case, and outlines policy proposals. The cases of electricity and telecommunications pertain to institutional renegotiations taking place in a multiple-principals framework, where the issues at stake reflect concerns about the workings of new market and regulatory rules. The case studies of road and cellular concessions are accounts of ex post opportunistic behavior in a country where contract law is not binding and enforcement is weak.

Institutional Framework

The institutional framework in Colombia formally limits government discretion. The executive and legislature are chosen by public election and checks and balances are part of the political scheme. In turn, the judiciary has a long tradition of independent ruling. However, in terms of economic and legal practice, laws are often amended to satisfy special interests. Enforcement problems tend to be resolved by issuing additional laws.

Almost all Colombian public utilities and infrastructure companies are municipal enterprises. Few companies have national coverage. For decades, political interests captured many of the public utilities. Another form of capture was conducted by strong utility unions, which were able to extract part of the rents and even to establish some sector policies. This institutional landscape has changed since 1986, when the popular election of mayors was established, helping to limit the direct interference of political forces in public utilities.[1]

The 1991 constitutional reform was a key institutional event in infrastructure procurement. It achieved the following:

- Allowed private participation in all economic sectors.
- Created independent regulatory and control bodies.
- Transformed the judicial control systems over political power by creating the Constitutional Court.
- Created alternative mechanisms for the resolution of conflicts (conciliation and out-of-court proceedings).
- Introduced more control for the executive and the legislature over the judiciary while transferring almost total administrative autonomy to the judiciary.

These changes meant a significant reduction in legislative power over public utilities. The 1991 constitutional reform yielded the following laws governing infrastructure: Law 80 (administrative contracts, 1993); Law 142 (public utilities, 1994); and Law 143 (electricity, 1994).

Law 80 changed the public contracting system by expediting procedures, establishing public selection by contest as the basic procurement mechanism, limiting forfeiture cases of breach by the contractor, and providing for budget allocations to meet future obligations and contingencies. The legislation also requires feasibility

[1] However, some modernizing mayors willing to transform local utilities into stock companies or mixed-economy corporations have encountered strong opposition on the part of municipal councils. In addition, the very short (three years) term of office for mayors implies major risks for investors because an incoming mayor may renegotiate contracts.

and design studies before contracts are written in order to minimize construction risks. In addition, it establishes the principle of economic equilibrium in contracts, defining procedures for its restoration (either by direct agreement between parties or by arbitration). In essence, the state must preserve the financial conditions prevailing at the moment it signs a contract with a third party whenever events leading to distress are either provoked by the authorities or due to unforeseeable causes (changes in prices, for example) other than *force majeure*.

Law 142 created independent regulatory and consumer protection agencies to handle so-called domicile public services (fixed local and long-distance telephone service, electricity, gas, and water and sewerage). The regulation of other infrastructure activities (transport, ports, and mobile telephone service) was left in the hands of ministerial entities. The legislation's goal was to provide incentives for private participation in utilities under the principle of free entry. It defined parameters for sector regulation and state intervention mechanisms, and eliminated the need for permits, authorizations, and licenses for the provision of public services, except construction and environmental licenses.

In Colombia, regulation fits the dual role of being the principal of public utilities and the agent of multiple principals (Dixit 1996). It has been the subject of alternating and contradictory pressures from the Ministry of Finance and the National Planning Board. The struggle between regulation and special interests in state-owned utilities, which is the prevailing source of disputes, can be traced as follows: a measure affecting the revenues of a regulated company becomes a congressional issue and pressure is exerted directly (hearings before the Senate) or indirectly (threatening statements to the media). When the executive's administration needs support from the legislature, it increases pressure on the regulator.

Yet, a combination of facts explains the resilience of the regulatory institutions:

- Regulatory measures have had greater impact on those businesses with less effect on congressional reelections (generation and transmission of electricity, for example).
- The introduction of private capital, especially foreign capital, has given the process elements of irreversibility.
- Until 1997, the privatization of public assets responded to fiscal pressures. The need to raise revenues for massive public spending prevailed over any other competing goal.
- The utilities that were able to mobilize the legislature became totally discredited because of their financial and managerial problems.

The fact that the regulatory commissions have survived in a hostile atmosphere is positive. The most aggressive attempt to revoke the autonomy of the commissions altogether was the Council of State's decision in the middle of 1997, which argued that delegation of public service management to regulatory commissions was not legal (in Colombian legislation, the executive is responsible for public services). Nothing has come of the decision, but it indicates that the reforms could be rescinded if pressure mounts.[2]

The Electricity Sector

During the 1970s and 1980s, the expansion of electricity generating capacity was implemented using command and control procedures. The energy authorities calculated minimum-cost, supply-side schedules to meet demand forecasts and negotiated with multilateral agencies. In the process, all the incentives were aligned in the wrong direction, toward larger projects. As a result, Colombia has a large number of hydropower plants that require large money outlays per unit of capacity.

Hydroelectric projects involve high technical and input cost uncertainty.[3] The actual cost of capital in hydroelectric projects is usually higher than predicted. In a study commissioned by the World Bank, Merrow and Shangraw (1990) and Merrow and Schroeder (1991) find an ex post overrun bias in 76 percent of more than 80 hydroelectric projects funded by the World Bank. They also find that 53 percent of the projects exhibited overruns of more than 25 percent, and 30 percent had overruns of more than 50 percent. The bias was found to be nearly independent of the size of the facilities, the year of appraisal, and the region. The systematic nature of the overages suggests that project cost and schedule outcomes are predictable. Merrow and his colleagues successfully tested this hypothesis, showing that the total capital cost of the listed projects can be accurately and confidently predicted using a few variables.[4]

In Colombia, hydroelectric projects were shown as economic ex ante to facilitate approval; technical uncertainty was systematically overlooked. Once project construction started, cost renegotiations and contract extensions prevailed. The overrun bias is an indication of the informational rents captured by the procurement scheme.

---

[2] Attached to the French tradition, the judiciary considers the regulatory bodies as institutions foreign to Colombian tradition and appropriate to common-law countries.

[3] Technical uncertainty pertains to the unknown degree of physical difficulty of completing the project. Input cost uncertainty reflects fluctuations in factor prices during the construction phase.

[4] Merrow and Shangraw's (1990) and Merrow and Schroeder's (1991) results apply partially to Colombia. EPM (Empresas de Medellín) and ISA (Interconexión Eléctrica, S.A.) succeeded in building cheap (by international standards) hydroelectric plants in the Nare-Guatapé basin (Guatapé and San Carlos), while ISA and EEEB (Empresa de Energía Eléctrica de Bogotá) incurred enormous overruns in the process of building generating facilities like El Guavio and CHIVOR in the eastern branch of the Andes mountains due to geological problems.

Before laws 142 and 143 were issued, generation encompassed municipal and regional firms, which were often vertically integrated with distribution firms. Transmission was integrated with large generation assets and the system planning and operation functions. Local/regional governments owned distribution firms. Law 142 created the regulatory body for energy and gas (CREG). Law 143 split businesses in the electricity industry according to their potential competitiveness (allowing competition in generation), created a short-term market (pool), granted free entry into the grid, and set limits on vertical and horizontal integration. Prices in transmission and distribution were subject to regulation, although large consumers were allowed to directly purchase from the pool or through bilateral contracts with generators. The National Dispatch Center (CND, a division of the grid company) was given the responsibility of performing economic dispatch, controlling system security, settling contracts, and billing net financial positions by agent every month. Given that Law 143 provided only general guidelines needing further definition by CREG, pressure continues for redefining property rights and asset values by decree.

A privatization process was started more than a year after the reform was in place and has focused on generating assets. In 1999, 50 percent of generation capacity was in private hands. Private participation in distribution has taken more time, being completed first in firms that were in financial distress or had bad management. Privatization of more distribution firms is important, both for enhancing regulatory stability and for eliminating the debt of generation firms and distribution firms in the pool. The reform was weak in imposing penalties on distribution firms (traditionally in default regarding payments to generators). Therefore, default risk is still high.

The electricity market entered into operation in July 1995. The core of the market is a day-ahead, hourly pool, with predefined bidding rules for both fuel-fired and hydraulic generators. This is a *tight-pool* scheme: it is mandatory for generators to bid prices and quantities into the pool, and order-of-merit dispatch of all generating plants is then performed by CND. Within the pool, fuel-fired units must bid their avoidable cost. Hydroelectric plants (about 68 percent of total installed capacity) are supposed to bid the value of water, which is the present value of a probabilistically weighted average of the resources that today's stored water might substitute in the future. The demand side does not bid into the pool. Total consumption (assumed to be a totally inelastic demand schedule) is forecasted by ISA-Transmisión (ISA-T) for each of the forthcoming 24 hours.

The wholesale market is composed of the pool and a layer of bilateral contracts on top of it. Contracted energy met by own production is denominated at the contract strike price. This choice differs from the alternative used in the British pool, where all energy is denominated at the pool price, and then one-way (caps) and two-way (forward) contracts with payments for differences are settled bilaterally. Contracts are usually written for long periods (a year or more, henceforth called illiquid contracts). As shown in the first two case studies, the chosen format is problematic because participation rules are constrained to mimic centralized dispatch results and the supply side is composed of heterogeneous technologies, with a large share of hydroelectric plants.

Case 1. Reliability Payments in the Colombian Electricity Market

Terms of the Dispute

A coalition of congress members from a region endowed with abundant coal reserves has submitted a legislative proposal intended to establish an end-user mandatory payment (a reliability payment) to finance the building of 1,200 MW coal-fired plants. The coalition made two contentions. The first was that the electricity spot market, being a short-run mechanism, inherently yields low price signals that are unable to signal entry of private generators. The state must not abandon electricity supply. The second contention was that supply reliability cannot be preserved with gas-fired plants because gas will eventually be depleted.

This attempt to steer investment into precise technologies challenges the role of markets and prices, and calls for the return of centralized planning in electricity expansion. The introduction of a reliability payment on top of the capacity payment casts doubt over the dynamic efficiency of the pool price in yielding sufficient signals to potential investors. It amounts to a renegotiation of the existing institutional rules of energy supply, and was forced by special interests betting on the political liabilities of the executive's power during eventual shortages.

Analysis of the Case

The mechanisms chosen to handle competition in the spot market and the initial supply-side conditions yield difficulties that can be misrepresented as fundamental flaws of the market mechanism. According to calculations performed by the Ministry of Energy, the long-run energy cost must be around \$0.043/kWh to accommodate a normal return (10 percent for investment in power generation in Colombia) for efficient plants.[5] As of December 31, 1998, the spot price historical average was \$0.039/kWh, and the median was \$0.021/kWh. Discounting the capacity payment (expressed in energy units and designed to be a floor of about \$0.012/kWh in the spot price since 1997), the purely variable component of price has been no higher than \$0.009/kWh half of the

[5] Values are in U.S. dollars.

Figure 4–1. The Evolution of Electricity Pool Prices in Colombia, 1995-98

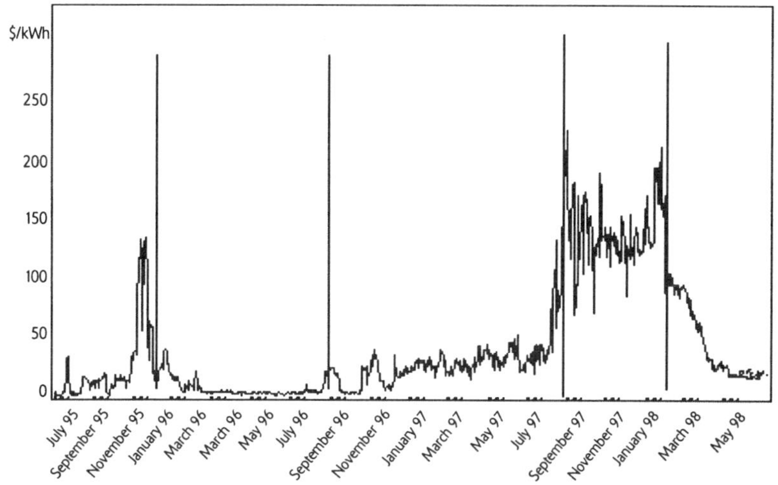

time. The spot price has unfolded as a flat, low-level signal most of the time, the pattern being interrupted by occasional spikes of short duration (as in period 4 in figure 4–1).

Every six or seven years, the surges coincide with the El Niño phenomenon (a quasi-periodic event), which reduces water inflow to reservoirs. Until now, just one El Niño event has taken place (1997–98) during the existence of the market. If (for the sake of simplicity) we assume a six-year period for El Niño and normal spot price behavior until completion of the current cycle, the hypothetical average price would shrink from $0.039/kWh to $0.031/kWh, and the median would shift downward from $0.021/kWh to $0.018/kWh.

Three factors have contributed to sustained low prices in the Colombian pool. First, because the system is energy constrained, excess peak capacity in conjunction with the large share of run-of-the-river plants and the weather cycle make it possible for hydroelectric plants to set the pool price most of the time, even during the dry season (December to April).[6] The daily load profile has two peaks, but they do not always translate into the corresponding shape of the price profile. Hydroelectric plants with large storage capacity tend to substitute fuel-fired generation during the peak period. The price signal does not "take off."

[6] The reader interested in price setting statistics is referred to case 2.

Second, the current rationing cost is too low to reward the reliability level implied by total existing capacity.[7] The threshold of the rationing curve is just $0.20/kWh, less than a tenth of the figure used in the England and Wales pool. Stored water is possibly undervalued. Only impending droughts raise the price level. It turns out that the system operator (CND) disseminates marginal cost forecasts on a weekly basis, with the help of a convoluted, minimum cost, medium-run optimization model. The routine is fed the rationing cost and the forecasts usually suggest low spot prices. In the absence of a futures market, such forecasts have a big impact on generators' expectations and the leeway for bids to move.

Third, the differentiated rules for denominating energy and the lack of payments for differences lead to competition between generators to enter into contracts for the maximum amount of energy deliveries. Whenever this strategy is chosen by the majority of generators, hydroelectric agents have an incentive to submit inframarginal bids into the pool during the wet season. Fuel-fired generators have an incentive to do the same thing during the dry season. By bidding low, generators seek to be fully dispatched, profit from the difference between high contract prices and the cost of procurement, and reduce the expected volume and purchase price (in case of having signed contracts in amounts higher than own generation). This arbitrage strategy occurred during the first three years of trading and was sustained by the lack of an open market for contracts, the long maturity of the first cohort of contracts (lasting in some cases three years and including high penalties for breach), the higher bargaining power of the supply side, and regulations that required distributors to contract most of their energy requirements for the regulated consumers.

With the benefit of hindsight, it is clear that a generator's pool cannot set marginal cost price signals and preserve the paradigm of order-of-merit dispatch at the same time (Bunn 1996). In the U.K. electricity market, the model that was adapted for Colombia, too much of the minimum-cost centralized dispatch ritual was preserved for two reasons. First, in 1989, experts doubted that decentralized spot pricing could support the operational security of a power system. Second, the alternative (a distributor's pool managed by the regional electricity companies based on a contracts market) could not meet the government's privatization time schedule. The combination of these two facts led to the well-known format in place in the United Kingdom and Colombia.

A capacity payment was designed to reduce the risk confronted by competitive plants of achieving zero income during wet multi-year periods

[7] Existing capacity is estimated by the Ministry of Energy. It is the leading indicator for calculating the value of water.

(Benavides 1997).[8] It converts a fraction of the expected income earned during future dry periods into a steady flow paid to those generators contributing the most to meet demand. Every year, by the end of the wet season, a model is run to determine the minimum-cost schedule to meet demand during periods of extremely low water inflow to hydroelectric plants. Each generating set required to meet demand in the routine is allocated a maximum capacity (MW) and paid $5.25/MW-month times this maximum capacity, adjusted by real availability. The monthly fee reflects the installment of the least-cost capital technology (an open-cycle gas turbine) and is ultimately charged to consumers. Payments are made regardless of states of nature and collected within the pool through each kWh generated. Incentives to keep and increase machine availability are explicit.

This solution evidences some distinctive features:

- Contrary to what has been observed in other electricity pools (like Argentina), the mechanism discourages the manipulation of availability declarations by generators.
- Newbery (1995) has illustrated how electric power generation contestability was transformed by the combination of modular technologies (gas turbines) and cheap fuel: long-term contracts make previously sunk investments ineffective to deter entry. The payment enhances the contestability of the generation market. Efficient plants might consider entering *without* contracts. In turn, debt is easier to obtain for potential investors.
- Payments are not differentiated by technology. They are kept at the minimum necessary to avoid rents for any fuel-fired technology.

Supporters of coal-fired generation found the introduction of the capacity payment to be insufficient to reduce the long-run risk of rationing during severe droughts, when the preferred expansion technology becomes the combined-cycle natural gas unit. The congressional coalition contends that the natural gas resource base will be depleted, while the domestic coal resource base may support "centuries" of continuous production. In the short-to-medium run, coal generation is likely to have the highest average cost: $40-48/MWh (utilization factor of 70 percent). Meanwhile, the combined-cycle gas unit, its closest competitor, costs $29-35/MWh with the same utilization factor. A coal plant has much larger capital costs ($1,100-1,400/kW) than a combined-cycle gas plant ($700-735/kW), and a more significant impact on the environment.

[8] The solution abstracted from conduct considerations, and focused on the implications of the supply-side structure inherited from the central planning period. The arbitrage strategy of dampening the spot price will disappear later rather than sooner.

Therefore, it is not cost-efficient to use coal plants to generate during peak periods or droughts (when hydroelectric production shrinks), since these are events of short duration that can be covered economically with technologies that have lower average cost. Other things equal, coal plants should not be turned on unless grid constraints force them to act as must-run units.

The valid claim of coal-fired generation supporters is that competition between natural gas and coal-based generation is distorted because natural gas faces price controls.[9] Were administrative controls eliminated, two things could happen: higher natural gas prices (increasing while the resource base is kept fixed and substitution remains uneconomic) could make coal generation competitive or induce further exploration and increase the resource base (Sundaresan 1984). Moreover, if natural gas trade agreements were reached with Venezuela, perceived scarcity would vanish.

Supporters of the reliability payment capitalized on the official distrust of the price mechanism in the spot electricity and natural resource markets. They said that the threat of natural gas depletion would be self-fulfilling if prices were not allowed to reflect scarcity. They used this excuse to draft legislation in congress establishing a reliability charge to prevent electricity rationing in the long run.[10] The reliability charge would compel every final user to pay the overrun of about 1,200 MW of mandatory-to-build, coal-fired plants. This would amount to an ironic introduction of future "stranded assets" to be reimbursed under a forced-cost recovery rule, which is incompatible with competition.

Regional interests would benefit by obtaining or controlling the royalties of the upstream (mining) business. Competitive generation firms and consumers would be harmed by the reliability payment. The implied threat for the regulatory body was that if it did not incorporate the requests into the regulation, the congressional coalition might reach its objectives anyway through the legislative process. The efficient solution includes additional liberalization of the market and elimination of price controls on natural gas. A revision of market rules and governance structure is being conducted with the help of a consultancy. It should align the bidding and contracting procedures to prevent systematic differences between spot and contract trading. Although the low-level price problem is central for preserving the market option, there is also a collection of equity and incentive problems in the wholesale market (see case 2).

The reliability payment has not succeeded in congress, but the dispute has not been settled. Legislative proposals are presented cyclically. Pressures to introduce the reliability payment in congress could reappear in periods of low

[9] Natural gas has been heavily subsidized and introduced in the residential sector on a massive scale.

[10] This happened after the coal lobby failed to convince the regulator to design a capacity payment with fees differentiated by technology.

pool prices, as seemed to happen during the first semester of 1999. The increasing share of the generation market owned by private investors (about 50 percent) is a counterbalancing force to acceptance of a rule of this sort.

Case 2. Requests for Light-Handed Regulation in the Electricity Market

Terms of the Dispute

By the middle of 1998, the Asociación Colombiana de Generadores (ACOLGEN, the syndicate of electricity generators who participate in the wholesale market) started debating the wisdom of spot price formation rules and the way of determining payments (especially capacity and transmission use charges). The number of ACOLGEN claims has increased since then. The generators are proposing a series of regulatory changes to deal with the following problems:

- Low level and high volatility of the spot price.
- Risk of changes in the value of generation assets as a result of discretionary changes in market rules.
- Inequity among generation technologies, including aspects such as bidding rules, constraints on the use of stored water, instability of regulated payments (calculated using large-scale optimization models), and the hourly bidding format.
- Inefficient rules for handling must-run generation, frequency control, and transmission charges.

The implications of low spot prices were discussed in case 1. The proposal to introduce a reliability payment is aimed at superseding private initiative in capacity investment. However, ACOLGEN's requests suggest that regulation should be more flexible and light-handed. The claims correctly identify market deficiencies. The issue under scrutiny is whether the initial regulatory scheme should be kept to signal commitment. Otherwise, CREG could be tempted to contend or must be adapted to allow welfare gains to be channeled through increased trading flexibility.

Analysis of the Case

The behavior of the price process responds to structural and strategic considerations. Some additional pieces of information help to explain the way prices move. Most of the generating plants in Colombia are hydroelectric (68 percent of total capacity, 12,000 MW in 1999). Five generators (EMGESA, EEPPM, ISAGEN, CORELCA, and CHIVOR) account for 75 percent of total capacity; the remaining 25 percent are spread among 18 other firms. Reservoirs

Table 4–1. The Percentage of Time that Different Types of Firms Set the Spot Price in the Electricity Market in Colombia, July 1995–February 1999

Firm	Type of firm	Time (percent)
CENS	Thermal, public	4.11
CHB	Hydroelectric, private	4.20
CHIVOR	Hydroelectric, private	3.21
CORELCA	Thermal, mixed ownership	3.61
EEPPM	Hydroelectric, public	24.39
EMGESA	Mostly hydroelectric, mixed ownership	8.79
ISAGEN	Hydroelectric, public	9.48
PROELECTRICA	Thermal, private	2.39
Others[a]		38.82

[a] Firms setting the price less than 2 percent of the time each; 50 percent of the time for other firms is hydroelectric.
Source: Authors' calculations.

store about 14.3 terawatt-hours (TWh), less than one-third of total annual consumption in 1998. Water inflows during the wet season are large enough to meet systemwide demand during the period and even to be spilled, due to storage limitations. However, water inflows during the dry season cannot meet average system demand. The firm owning the only multi-year storage facility (EEPPM, El Peñol reservoir, 4.4 TWh) generates the most in the spot market. The number of players is large (more than 25), but 79.3 percent of total water storage capacity is concentrated in EMGESA, EEPPM, and CHIVOR. Some large hydroelectric plants (more than 500 MW) are run-of-the-river, which increases price volatility.

Hydroelectric plants set the spot price most of the time (table 4–1). A single plant (Guatapé, from EEPPM) has set the spot price 14 percent of the time. During wet periods, hydroelectric plants set that price most of the time (table 4–2). In addition, fuel-fired firms do not reach a substantial percentage of spot price setting during dry periods (tables 4–3 and 4–4).

Spot price volatility is quite high. Annual volatility of crude oil prices in NYMEX is about 20 percent. Historical volatility in the Colombian electricity pool is around 238 percent, having reached 546 percent between September 1996 and September 1997. These high figures make hedging instruments costly. The premium of an ordinary call option may well be higher than the strike price.

The strategy of contracting most of the energy, where generators set low spot prices to produce the most and eventually purchase at very high pool prices to cover deliveries, is not sustainable. Distributors have gained experience and the mandatory contracting levels for the regulated sector have been progressively reduced. Almost four years after the market came into being, profits

Table 4–2. Spot Price Setting in the Electricity Market during a Sample Wet Period, September 1998

Firm	Time (percent)
CHB	9.4
EEPPM	50.6
EMGESA	7.8
ISAGEN	12.5
Others[a]	31.4

[a] Seventy percent of the time for other firms is hydroelectric.
Source: Authors' calculations.

Table 4–3. Spot Price Setting in the Electricity Market during a "Normal" Dry Period, January 1997

Firm	Time (percent)
CENS	7.12
CHIVOR	3.05
EEPPM	22.45
EMGESA	32.57
ISAGEN	13.58
Others[a]	21.23

[a] Fifty percent of the time for other firms is hydroelectric.
Source: Authors' calculations.

Table 4–4. Spot Price Setting in the Electricity Market during a "Severe" Dry Period, January 1998

Firm	Time (percent)
CENS	10.9
EEPPM	14.9
EMGESA	37.7
FLORES (T, PR)	11.9
ISAGEN	17.8
Others	6.9

Source: Authors' calculations.

from contracts were as low as profits from spot sales. This explains why generators' complaints about pool price behavior are fairly recent. The combination of a low mean and high volatility in the spot price, and low contract strikes is bad news for the supply side as a whole.

Other factors in addition to the energy component of sales influence the profitability of generation. The regulator computes a number of system charges using optimization models. The problems to be solved suffer from the multiple-solution syndrome because the corresponding objective functions are flat near the optimum solution. Different combinations of plants lead to roughly similar system costs. Slight parameter changes make allocation of capacity to be paid through capacity payments unstable, posing an equity problem for the regulator. This situation becomes critical because capacity payments could easily represent 50 percent of total income for some generators. Transmission (post-stamp) charges are affected by two problems:

- First, they are unstable because the national grid is divided into 10 areas (at least four of them representing no more than 1,000 MW) and the construction of a single medium-sized unit may easily change the predominant signs of load flows and use charges.
- Second, transmission charges are so high that they may become the factor determining profitability of generation in certain areas. In one area (labeled 4C), for example, the 1999 use charge for fuel-fired plants was $(-18)/kW-year. An investor could consider placing an open-cycle gas unit (receiving approximately $50/kW-year through capacity payments, assuming that 80 percent capacity is paid). In a very wet year, the unit may not be deployed at all, but it would collect $68/kW-year, more than the cost of capital ($48/kW-year). The remaining money ($20/kW-year) is close to the full-fledged fixed costs required to keep the machine in good operating condition ($26/kW-year). By choosing the proper nodes on the grid, entry of inefficiently cheap plants is facilitated and turned profitable by means other than direct competition.

Regarding the low figures characterizing the first moments of the spot price statistics, it must be emphasized that the mean heavily depends on the "power spectrum" of the price spikes occurring during extremely dry periods. A storage rule left over from the era of centralized operations prohibits a hydraulic plant from submitting price bids whenever its reservoir has hit a predefined upper limit.[11] The spot price is determined by administrative rules during

[11] The reservoir is said to be "intervened."

intervention episodes, which makes it vulnerable to unilateral regulatory modifications. This amounts to a discontinuity in the valuation of water because the implicit opportunity cost of mandatory storage is normally higher than the value of the water in the ongoing realization of the inflow process. This procedure also increases volatility: price bids become very high because hydroelectric plants do not want to get to the stage where intervention would affect their reservoir.

The constraints on free utilization of water resources act as forced insurance to hedge against supply shocks. The regulator does not ensure the payment of premia for generators that store water to increase supply reliability. It does not allow hydroelectric plants to capitalize on the entire potential of high spot prices because intervention also restricts generation. The operational minimum-level rules for reservoirs distort price formation in two ways. First, once the regulator has intervened in a sufficient number of reservoirs, thermal generators with just a fraction of their generation left to be sold within the pool have the incentive to increase the spot price (despite bidding rules that require the generator to explain costs). This strategy is feasible for fuel-fired firms because regulations prevent hydroelectric generators from competing. Stored water helps thermal generators to obtain temporary quasi-rents, which are unevenly distributed by technology. Second, if the water inflows are not low enough, but the operational limits are binding, additional inflows during the wet season will tend to lower the spot price. Given the limited storage capacity, some water will be spilled over.

Other equity problems disturb the workings of the market. Network constraints reduce the amount of energy traded through competition. Forced generation also replaces the output of efficient firms and harms their profits whenever they have to purchase at spot prices higher than self-procurement to fulfill contract deliveries. The unit commitment problem is poorly handled in a tight pool with hourly dispatch, which fills in the load-duration curve with vertical slices (Johnson, Oren, and Svoboda 1997). Fixed (starting) cost per period and heating/cooling time constants of fuel-fired units oblige thermal generators to submit bids with the hope of being continuously dispatched. Natural gas plants incur overruns in fuel purchases due to the take-or-pay clauses in gas contracts and the erratic nature of the dispatch process.

It is worth mentioning that the likelihood of unilateral action by the executive has influenced the perception of private investors. Law 143 stipulates that the government must expand the electricity grid if the private sector cannot do so. The government still owns generating firms (like ISAGEN) and controls Financiera Energética Nacional (FEN), the investment bank that finances energy projects. Therefore, government displacement of private investors remains a credible threat.[12]

---

[12] Fortunately, government decisions under implementation in the second semester of 1999 should have diminished the likelihood of intervention. Fiscal and financial efficiency considerations have led to the upcoming privatization of ISAGEN.

The organization of the wholesale electricity market and the energy regulatory body in Colombia are welfare enhancing measures in the public utility arena. But the chosen format is "only half a market" because the demand side does not submit bids into the pool. The paradigm of the tight pool has been superseded in other countries by more flexible institutional choices. A tight pool is an *artificial market* (Jacobs 1997) requiring ex post mechanisms (such as the capacity payment) to supplement administrative rules. The impact of mixed technologies in the pool was incompletely considered in the original design.

With hindsight, it is easy to see that too much of the old regime was preserved in the original design. In addition to the measures discussed in case 1, we propose a shift to a loose pool arrangement, allowing the demand side to play an active role, abolishing the mandatory bidding rules and reservoir limits, and focusing trading on a system of bilateral physical contracts. This proposal is closer in spirit to the Nord Pool approach. When the core of trading is a liquid market for standardized contracts, the risk of not being rewarded is diminished, even during the wet season. Financial constraints provide contract quotations a natural floor because capital costs can be recovered using either linear or nonlinear schedules. The discipline of competition and demand-side participation would keep the price within a narrow spread. Unit commitment and gas delivery could be better undertaken as well (Benavides 1998a).

The dynamic efficiency of this proposal is satisfactory if and only if a liquid market exists for contracts (Benavides 1998b). Trading through contracts can be viewed as an organizational procedure located between two extremes: a pure spot market and a spot market with a price ceiling. Incumbents' contracts act as a short-term entry barrier. New generators must wait for increased demand pressure and high dispatch factors to enter into the residual spot market. A large share of contracted energy, very long-term contract terms, and low pool prices are a bad combination for potential entrants.

In order to examine the possible evolution of ACOLGEN claims, it is necessary to identify how different interests coalesce and how they could influence the pool restructuring process that will take place in the short term.[13] ACOLGEN has four basic coalitions of generators: C1, hydraulic generators; C2, fuel-fired generators; C3, risk-averse generators; and C4, risk-taking generators.

These clusters are by no means mutually exclusive. Hydraulic generators have a 68-percent market share. Risk-averse generators (those contracting the most) include the majority of hydraulic generators and about half of the fuel-

[13] In the second half of 1999, CREG undertook a study aimed at establishing new institutions to handle the wholesale electricity market. The basic goals were to split the commercial and network operations that were in charge of the system operator, to set a self-regulatory scheme for transactions, and to improve the efficiency and equity of market rules.

fired generators. Risk-taking generators (those selling most of their generation within the pool) are mostly private foreign investors (both hydraulic and fuel-fired plants), representing a modest fraction of the total installed capacity. In the market restructuring process, it is likely that ACOLGEN will present itself as a unified front in all but contracting issues. The coalition of risk-averse generators is able to block any proposal in that regard because they are profiting from the strategy of depressing the spot price and selling through bilateral contracts. In addition, the San Carlos hydraulic plant (1,240 MW, ISAGEN) will be sold shortly. The major publicly owned hydraulic generator (whose largest plant is upstream San Carlos) is willing to purchase it. If this happens, the migration toward a loose pool, which is being considered, would be strongly opposed by the latter coalition.

Case 3. The Disputable Presumption of Undue Capital Reduction

Terms of the Dispute

Empresa de Energía de Bogotá (EEB), the public firm responsible for generation and distribution in the city of Bogotá, incorporated and became a holding company in 1997 in order to solve its serious debt problem. Once the process of capital injection was completed, regulatory limits on market participation meant that the new partners were prevented from investing in the electricity sector. A decision was therefore made to reduce the holding's capital. This measure faced strong opposition from some politicians and city council members, a former city mayor, and unions of other public utilities to be privatized. In the last week of February 1999, the Superintendencia de Sociedades (in charge of monitoring mergers and ownership structure) rejected a suit filed by the City Comptroller, who claimed that capital reduction was detrimental to the city. The claim disputed the scope of the sovereign rights of shareholders, presenting the issue of capital reduction as a transfer of public capital to private hands.

Analysis of the Case

Until 1997, EEB was one of the largest vertically integrated public electricity firms in Latin America. Its distribution network covered the metropolitan area of Santafé de Bogotá and about a hundred surrounding cities and townships (1.5 million billing accounts). Its generation plants accounted for 2,321 MW (21.5 percent of Colombia's supply). In 1997, total consumption was 10,000 GWh and the maximum peak load reached 1,850 MW (about 25 percent of total electricity demand).

EEB was organized as a municipal enterprise more than 60 years ago. Before 1986, the company's manager was named by the mayor who, in turn, was appointed by the president. Members of the city council sat on EEB's board of directors. The city council succeeded in establishing a pricing regime to cross-subsidize constituencies. In the end, tariff rebalancing was ineffective in covering operating costs.

A liquidity crisis in regional and municipal electricity firms began in 1990 and became an opportunity for centralizing ownership. Debt was swapped for increments of publicly owned shares and members of city councils were excluded from the boards of directors. These changes facilitated the search for a solution to EEB's debt, which was close to $1.5 billion in 1997, with payments concentrated between 1997 and 2000. The problem required measures beyond ordinary debt restructuring because between 1997 and 2000 estimated income was $5.3 billion and estimated spending was $6.5 billion, yielding an additional deficit of $1.2 billion.

An important percentage of EEB debt (59 percent) was financed by FEN. FEN's role was to pool capital resources from foreign banks for investment in public energy projects, and to provide the corresponding guarantees on behalf of the government. By August 1995, the City of Bogotá and the federal government restructured EEB's debt with FEN. The key condition for restructuring was a statement of purpose about incorporating private capital and splitting EEB into separate generation and distribution businesses. In turn, the city council authorized private participation for up to 48.5 percent of the capital, and the transformation of EEB into a holding company. The process itself was divided into two phases: restructuring and design of a competitive process to incorporate private capital.

Several alternatives were presented to foreign electricity companies (24 in total) in a poll designed to assess the interests and preferences of potential investors. It was clear that a vertically integrated structure would reduce the number of competitors (due to higher up-front payments) in a bidding process and would have higher regulatory risk (likelihood of future changes in vertical integration restraints). With that in mind, a reduced set of firm structures was evaluated. The final proposal was to structure a holding company that would be in charge of the transmission assets (EEBSA), encompassing a generation company (EMGESA) and a distribution/trading company (CODENSA). Debt would be transferred from EEB to the new companies at the moment of capitalization. The proposal included an agreement whereby EEB would regain 51.5 percent ownership in each firm, but only 36.5 percent in the form of common stock (with voting power). The remaining 15 percent of the shares would be issued as preferred stock (without voting power). A key decision was to pick a single private shareholder for the firms to be created in order to avoid the drawbacks of atomized ownership when efficiency-increasing measures are needed (Hart 1995). This restructuring choice attains the following welfare gains:

- Strategic decisions take place through stockholder initiative. Although 81.6 percent of EEBSA shares belong to the city, it no longer has full discretion over investment plans. Investors in CODENSA and EMGESA are also shareholders in EEBSA (11 percent), which serves to limit political interference.
- The investors own only 48.5 percent of the shares. However, given that only ordinary shares have voting rights, the investors have residual control of CODENSA and EMGESA's operational decisions (related to personnel and procurement). Before the incentive scheme was embedded in the voting structure (common versus preferred stock), capitalization never took off (Levy 1983).

EEB undertook a screening process, starting with 150 invitations to participate in the capitalization. Seventeen firms were considered eligible based on criteria such as financial strength and asset values in similar businesses. Finally, four pools of firms submitted offers to acquire 48.5 percent of CODENSA and EMGESA stock on September 15, 1997. The mechanism chosen for the allocation process was the sealed-bid, first-price auction with unknown reservation value to the bidders. The reservation value was set the day of the contest and made public knowledge just before disclosing the values of submitted bids. The reservation value was related to the amount of capital needed to turn CODENSA and EMGESA into financially feasible firms. Risk aversion prevailed in the auction design. The team in charge of the process probably felt that EEB history and the country context were more important than expectations in investors' calculations.

This was an unsatisfactory choice because it left too much room for uncertainty and misrepresentation of the capital reduction. It also cast doubt about the efficiency of allocation and indicated that further discussion about vertical integration, regulatory style, and capital scarcity was needed. Two factors explain the enormous gap between the reservation value ($500 million) and the sum of the two winning bids (about $2.2 million): uncertainty over the reservation value magnified bidders' risk aversion, with respect to the amount and to the rationale; and deep pockets.

By the time of the contest, the winning pools in both CODENSA (Endesa, Spain, and Chilectra and Enersis in Chile) and EMGESA (Endesa, Spain, and Enersis and Endesa in Chile) had strategic plans in the Latin American area. This meant higher bids due to the risk of losing presence in a new market. More important for the final outcome was the implication of acquiring a fixed fraction of the shares and the destination of fresh capital (short-term debt reduction). Once payments were made and the debt of the new firms became manageable through ordinary methods, excess capital made no sense. By design, this residual could not increase investors' shares.

Potential bidders probably anticipated this. Under the circumstances, the proposed auction form did not pursue efficiency objectives. It just performed the role of ensuring that stock purchase solved the debt problem. The auction winner was not necessarily the agent with the highest valuation, but the one with the deepest pockets, as residual capital eventually came back.

Once the capital injection ($2.1 million) was performed, about $1.2 million of the short-term debt of CODENSA and EMGESA was paid off. The remaining $300 million represented medium-term debt, a manageable level after the capitalization process. A decision had to be made with respect to the $1 billion of excess capital. In March 1998, the new companies agreed to reduce capital by about $1.4 billion. Under the regulatory measures in place, the alternatives for the new stockholders were to allocate the residual capital in portfolio investment or to expand operations in the Colombian electricity market. The former possibility was inefficient, as the opportunities of EEBSA were more constrained than the possibilities of private shareholders. The latter was not feasible in the short and medium run because the regulatory body had set limits to vertical and horizontal integration, and CODENSA and EMGESA were already close to the size limits.[14]

Claims against the reduction of capital started in April 1998. Detractors argued that the investors were receiving a generous discount of about 30 percent of the initial outlay, while keeping the original shareholding (48.5 percent of CODENSA and EMGESA, and 11 percent of EEBSA).[15] However, from the standpoint of property rights, shareholders were free to dispose of capital in their best interest. There was nothing irregular about it. Once the debt problems were solved, reduction of capital was the only feasible solution. Moreover, the city government as well as the investors would get back a corresponding percentage of the reduction. The city would receive about $700 million. If these resources are properly invested and managed, the well-being of city residents can be improved.

The issue of foreign capital investment in public utilities is an easy target for old-guard politicians and unions (Spiller 1996). For example, the privatization of Empresa de Teléfonos de Bogotá has been repeatedly blocked by the city council and its labor union. This case was intended to challenge the adequacy of capital reduction after EEB became a share corporation. Interested parties argued that the decision was harmful to the city. If the capital reduction had not been approved, some politicians and municipal unions would have gained momentum

---

[14] A single generation firm may own no more than 25 percent of the generation market; a single distribution firm may own up to 25 percent of the regulated market; and a generation/distribution firm may hold no more than 25 percent of the distribution/generation market.

[15] Castro (1998).

in their argument and Colombia's reputation as a country where property rights are enforced would have suffered. The solution is efficient and it was confirmed by a decision from the Superintendencia de Sociedades, which was issued in February 1999 after the City Comptroller filed a claim against the capital reduction.

Two final caveats about the capitalization procedure arise in this ex post assessment. First, auction theory indicates that reduced uncertainty increases efficiency and reduces the emergence of a winner's curse situation. Reduced uncertainty can be attained in mechanisms other than the first-price, sealed-bid auction. An open auction in which the reservation value per share is common knowledge would have minimized the occurrence of overcapitalization. Second, harsh limits on horizontal property may not be necessary to deter the exercise of market power. This issue is relevant in times of credibility crisis for investment in emerging economies. Unless pure yardstick competition is the regulatory choice for distribution, $RPI - X$ schemes could approximate competitive results without recourse to hard limits in horizontal property.

The Mobile Telephone Sector

At the end of the 1980s, the Colombian telecommunications sector was a technologically backward industry that provided low-quality service, exhibited reduced national coverage, and faced excess demand in the largest cities.[16] These inefficiencies were the outcome of provision through public monopolies in long distance (TELECOM) and local telephone service.

Law 72 (1989) initiated the beginning of private participation in telecommunications, through concessions to private operators. The first four years of the liberalization process were plagued with obstacles as well as opposition from municipal councils and the unions of incumbent firms.[17] To minimize organized resistance to private participation, the government adopted a new strategy for the sector: "new" services (such as value-added services and cellular telephone service (*telefonía móvil celular*, TMC) were readily granted as concessions. The rendering of TMC was approved by Congress (Law 37, 1993) and regulated by Decree 741 (1993). These measures assigned the Ministry of Telecommunications the duty of granting the service by means of auctions.

The demonstration effect of the concession of cellular telephone service as a means to foster the privatization of other services explains why the government was interested in the successful outcome of the process. Its concerns were reflected in the allocation design and in the resolution of subsequent disputes.

[16] The density was approximately eight telephones/100 inhabitants.

[17] A landmark in this process was the 1992 attempt to privatize TELECOM. TELECOM's union organized a national strike that forced the government to abandon its target of immediate privatization.

Cellular concessions were designed to maximize government revenue. Competition for the market was open to firms possessing sufficient technical and financial capacity. Competition within the market was designed to allow for the consolidation of regional duopolies. The national territory was split into three regions: eastern, western, and the Atlantic coast. The service would be provided through two networks for each of the regions (A and B), with two operators competing in each region. The concessions (granted in 1994) gave the operators exclusive rights for five years; from 1999 onward, the Ministry of Communications could grant additional licenses in each of the regions. Three hundred channels were allocated in 800 MHz and 900 MHz bands.[18] There was no spectrum left in these bands available for new operators. Firms willing to enter the market in 1999 would use other bands of the spectrum, which are less convenient for the TMC service.

The concession was not designed to maximize welfare in the Chadwick-Demsetz style, where it is granted to the firm bidding the lowest rates. The government had to use revenue as the bidding variable. The government included coverage objectives in the concession contracts. Bids had to include the cost of a plan to serve the poorest municipalities within the franchise region. These plans should be implemented within five years. The operators should also provide road coverage, although the scope for this was left open.

Each bidding firm was ranked according to organizational and technical capacity, experience in cellular telephone service, and planning and financial capacity. The scores of this preliminary ranking represented 5 percent of the total. The definitive evaluation (95 percent of the total) selected the bid with the maximum total value (the concession and the expansion plan sums offered). The concession term was set for 10 years, which could be automatically extended for 10 more years. However, the contracts did not set forth the mechanism for the license extension price.

Since cellular telephone service would compete with fixed telephone service operators, both public and mixed-economy firms were allowed to participate in the concession of network A. Private firms that were incorporated in Colombia could participate in both networks. Private concessionaires were required to transform themselves into open corporations within five years from the date of the contract allocation.[19] The scheme left open the possibility of establishing two

[18] The following frequency subranges belonging to bands of 800 MHz and 900 MHz were reserved: (1) 824 Mhz to 849 Mhz for transmission and 869 Mhz to 894 Mhz for reception; and (2) 890 Mhz to 915 Mhz for transmission and 935 Mhz to 960 Mhz for reception.

[19] Colombian law defines an open corporation as a firm inscribed in the stock exchange to which no natural or juridical person may be entitled, by himself or by an intermediary, to more than 30 percent of the stock.

national networks, each operating in three regions. Cellular operators were forbidden to provide direct national and international long-distance services, except with prior legal authorization. However, the concession allowed companies to offer intraregional call delivery, a close substitute for fixed long-distance service. Cellular concessionaires may also provide value-added services, under previous authorization of the Ministry of Communications. The concession contract could not be transferred totally or partially within three years of the subscription date. In addition, shareholders could not sell or transfer their shares during this period, and could not sell shares in a way that would change the nature of the business. Prices were left unregulated; however, each operator had to report price changes to the Ministry.

Eleven firms registered to submit bids (eight proposals for the private network and three for the mixed network). The opening date of the tender was October 28, 1993. The first-price, sealed-bid auction form was used in the process. Concessions for network B were granted first (January 1994). Bids for network A (granted in February 1994) should reach at least 95 percent of the figures offered by network B auction winners.

The winners of network B were Celumóvil in the eastern region, Celumóvil de la Costa in the Atlantic coast region (together they comprise the Celumóvil Temporary Union), and Cocelco in the western region. Three of the most important economic groups in the country (the Santodomingo Group, the Ardila Lulle Group, and the Luis Carlos Sarmiento Organization) and their foreign partners (ATT and Telefónica de España, among others) make up these firms.

The concessions for network A were granted to Comcel in the eastern region, Celcaribe in the Atlantic coast region, and Occel in the western region. Comcel is made up of two of the largest public telecommunications firms in the country (TELECOM and Empresa de Teléfonos de Bogotá) and Bell Canada International, among others. Celcaribe is made up of Millicom International and a few local telephone companies. Occel is made up of Cable and Wireless and the Empresas Públicas de Medellín (EEPPM), among others. The tender yielded $1.2 million to the government (1.2 percent of 1994 GDP).

Consolidation has been an anticipated response to personal communication system (PCS) entry, accompanied by concentration of the voting majority. Consolidation had the following consequences:

- Roaming charges were eliminated.
- Interconnection charges were reduced because the local operator could be bypassed as well as domestic long distance (LDN) for calls between cellular telephones.
- Sales costs were reduced when advertising costs were distributed among a larger base of subscribers.

Celumóvil absorbed Celumóvil de la Costa in October 1997. Bell Canada, the largest shareholder of Comcel (the operator in the eastern region) bought 69 percent of Occel (the operator in the western region) on March 26, 1998. Comcel is also interested in buying Celcaribe, which would allow completion of a national cellular network. Grupo Sarmiento is now the largest shareholder of COCELCO, after buying an additional 39.8 percent of its shares from Telefónica de España. These changes in ownership have been possible because the period ended in which the sale of shares was banned. Companies have realized operational profits since 1996, but high up-front payments mean that total profits are still negative.

Case 4. Industry Consolidation with Government Support

Terms of the Dispute

In 1994, the Colombian government granted six cellular telephone service franchises through auction, receiving $1.2 billion in entry fees. This large up-front payment makes profitability fragile for the concessionaires. However, the legal vacuum in the licensing of contracts has been favorable for them. Key disputes over the license extension price, the level of coverage, the transfer of assets, and the future structure of the mobile telephone market have been solved in a manner that reduces the impact of the large up-front payment. The direct regulation of cellular telephone service by the Ministry of Communications has facilitated the benevolent treatment of disputes. The Telecommunications Regulatory Commission (CRT) regulates local and long-distance telephone services.

The combination of a high license price and steep investment requirements forced operators to rely on debt denominated in U.S. dollars. High financial leverage placed operators in a vulnerable position with regard to devaluation and demand fluctuations. Both of these risks became apparent in 1999, when operators faced strong declines in demand as well as accelerated devaluation. It was expected that the national economy would not grow in real terms in 1999-2000. In this context, the government seemed to be inclined to protect the industry against new competitors and the impact of contingencies. The government's delay in submitting legislation defining the rules to grant PCS concessions confirms this attitude. As of July 1999, the project had not been examined by congress, which probably would delay the entry of PCS until the year 2000. The benevolent regulatory treatment that characterized the entry and consolidation periods of the cellular market could persist. The long-term effect of this could be the establishment of a duopoly in the mobile telephone service business.

Analysis of the Case

Law 142 defines cellular telephone service as a "nondomicile" public service. This implies that it is regulated by the Ministry of Telecommunications and not by CRT. It also implies that it is not monitored by the Superintendency of Domicile Public Services (SSPD). The Ministry of Telecommunications monitors the coverage and quality of cellular services. It also collects 5 percent of total cellular revenue to fund universal service provision, allocates the spectrum, and resolves consumer complaints.

In addition, Law 80 (which regulates public contracts) applies to concession contracts. Cellular concession contracts have failed to consider many issues. They hardly specify what must be done once the term of the concession expires. If the concession is renewable, the renewal mechanism is not specified ex ante; neither are the methods to determine the renewal price. If the concession is not renewable, rights of asset ownership are poorly defined.[20] These contracts do not state future awarding procedures (auction or administrative mechanism) and do not specify whether current concession holders may participate. Although they include a long list of triggering events that can be invoked in case of breach of contract, contractors do not use them to terminate contracts; they prefer to renegotiate.

In December 1998, nearly four and a half years after operations were initiated, service penetration was around 3 percent, equivalent to 1.2 million subscribers. This fast penetration happened in spite of the fact that the tariffs are among the highest in Latin America because of the high up-front (license) payments, coverage requirements, and a series of additional charges and taxes. Cellular firms have differentiated the market, offering a menu of service packages and rates. The plans offered by the firms operating in the same region are almost identical. Their current strategy includes penetration to low-income subscribers, extension of consumer contracts, continuous introduction of additional services, and the consolidation of two national networks. Firms currently offer almost the entire variety of services that PCS offers, as well as those offered by the value-added and trunking and paging firms. Cellular firms also compete with local and long-distance operators.[21]

Most of the conflicts and disputes that emerged after the concessions were granted have been resolved in favor of the firms. This might be because a key government aim is to open the telecommunications market and the most

---

[20] Disputes have arisen about the nature of assets that must revert to the government.

[21] National and international automatic roaming permits competition with LDN and international long-distance (LDI) firms. Some cellular firms offer continental roaming as well. Contracts with subscribers were extended from one to two years from 1998, with high fines for breach of contract.

important economic groups are found among the concessionaires. Some of the solutions to the dispute have been welfare enhancing, but the decision-making process has lacked transparency. The conflicts in cellular telephone service fall into two categories:

- Disputes pertaining to key issues that were left undefined in the contract, such as the license extension price, coverage level, transfer of assets to the government, and entry of services that are close substitutes.
- Disputes regarding quality of service, consumer price discrimination, and uneven tax regimes across competing firms.

The analysis and evaluation of each controversy and the welfare issues of the corresponding solutions are addressed individually.

Early Extension of Contracts

In January 1997, the Ministry of Communications decided to move up the due date for license extension from 10 to 13 years. The Ministry accepted the concessionaires' argument about the difficulty of obtaining long-term credit due to uncertainty regarding the extension of the contract. The concessionaires agreed to pay $130 million for up to 10 additional years. The present value of this figure is $560 million charged in year 2003.[22]

Elimination of the uncertainty regarding license duration and price facilitates investment and enhances welfare. However, the ex post license price definition was discretionary. An ex ante competitive mechanism would have revealed the correct extension value. In spite of all the drawbacks, the firms and subscribers gain with the measure because coverage will increase.

Change in Service Coverage Obligations

In 1995, the government eliminated from the concession contracts the obligation to serve the poorest municipalities. The firms raised the contention that cellular telephone service is not suited to deliver this service. Neither the law nor the contract specified the scope of the obligation. Instead, they left undefined the level of coverage and the obligation to operate the service. The concessionaires capitalized on contract incompleteness and convinced the government to exempt them from the obligation to operate. The technological argument is valid. But

[22] It may be argued that such a low figure was charged because during the second 10-year period the current cellular firms would face competition from PCS. An alternative explanation is that firms could have gained the concession by "low-balling," with the expectation of a favorable extension price.

the concessionaires, by giving back to the government the amount originally intended to serve those municipalities, benefit because they end up with a more focused and homogeneous business.

Transfer of Assets to the Government

Law 80 establishes that concessionaires' assets must be transferred to the government once the concession term expires. The concessionaires argued that the transfer of assets should be understood as the devolution of assigned bandwidth, but not of equipment. There are valid reasons for converting a BOT (which denies ultimate ownership) into a BOO contract. If the risk of opportunistic behavior by the government is large and the assets are extremely specific, a BOO deal is superior to a BOT deal because the BOO deal yields increased investment and facilitates incorporating new technologies. The dispute has not been settled yet.

Competition with Close Substitutes

In 1996, the government announced that PCS licenses would be granted in 1997 or 1998; pressure from cellular operators successfully postponed this event until 1999 or 2000. Cellular operators are requesting to participate in the PCS auction. The licensing of PCS raises two issues. The first is that increased competition in mobile telephone service could lead to sharp price cuts. The second is that cellular firms could face financial losses if the PCS licenses are auctioned by minimum tariff instead of maximum price offers, and if current cellular operators are forbidden to enter the PCS contest.

The government used an inefficient mechanism to grant cellular concessions that might force its replication in the PCS licensing process. The efficient solution is easy to state, but difficult to carry out: the cellular firms should be reimbursed for the license payments.

Dispute over Consumer Rights

A 1998 auditing report commissioned by the Ministry of Communications pointed out problems with consumer rights, among them:

- Users are required to give up their right to file legal suits against the firm.
- The Ministry does not adequately handle consumer complaints and claims.
- Each concessionaire has defined its own regime to deal with unilateral termination of contracts.

- If the telephone of the receiver rings three times, a minute of use will be charged even if the call is not completed.

The decision of the Ministry was to form a consumer complaint committee including CRT and SSPD, institutions lacking legal rights over mobile telephone service. This is a clear instance of conflict between technological convergence and regulation by service. The easiest way to channel consumer claims would be to extend the jurisdiction of SSPD over close substitutes of domicile public services.

Prohibition of Promotional Packages

In April 1995, Comcel and Celumóvil were sued before the Industry and Commerce Superintendency (the agency in charge of anti-monopoly control) for offering promotions. The Superintendency stated that promotions could discriminate among users of the same plan. Seven months later, responding to the Superintendency's request, Comcel and Celumóvil made a commitment to eliminate this discrimination by raising the rates of users that benefited from the promotion. Comcel requested to be allowed to phase in the increase over 18 months, but the Superintendency forced the measure to be completed in 30 days. This gave way to suits against the operators, filed by consumers claiming changes in contract conditions. Unless limit-pricing strategies are being used, promotional packages must not be prohibited.

Conflicts on Tax Discrimination

Article 16 of the Colombian Tax Statute (Decree 624, 1989) exempted mixed-capital firms from paying income taxes. In 1995, a suit contended that the article violated the right to equal treatment and freedom of enterprise. The exemption was finally eliminated. The Constitutional Court did not take an explicit position in this case, arguing that the statute makes no reference to cellular telephone service. The response to the suit reflects the difficulties of the courts in facing the requirements of a new model for the provision of public services. The conflict was motivated by discrimination in favor of public or mixed firms, which is customary in many public agencies. The solution is efficient, as it levels the playing field for utilities, regardless of property structure.

Highway Concessions

Colombia has a national road network of approximately 12,400 km, which makes it one of the least-covered countries in Latin America.[23] Only 10 percent of the roads are paved. The country has 310 km of paved roads per million inhabitants, as compared with 1,059 km in Costa Rica, 858 km in Argentina, and 820 km in Mexico. Despite the deficiencies in coverage and quality, road transportation prevails in Colombia. In 1997, 95 percent of passenger transport and 92 percent of cargo transport were carried by roads.

Until 1993, roads were built through public works contracts. In this scheme, the government assumed the overruns and delays. Therefore, all aspects of the contracts were subject to renegotiations—design, technical specifications, deadlines, unit costs, and additional works. Road-building firms took advantage of their bargaining power during the construction period because the political and economic cost for the government of breaching a badly performing ongoing project was higher than continuing the work with the same contractor. The scheme gave way to delays and overruns as well as to corruption. Delays were up to four times the programmed schedule and overages were twice the amount budgeted (Sarmiento et al. 1996).

Since 1992, the Instituto Nacional de Vías (INVIAS) has been in charge of the contracting process for construction and maintenance of the national road network. INVIAS is funded with national budget resources, taxes on gasoline and the increased value of properties, and toll collection. INVIAS is often late in its payment schedule to road contractors. This has become a permanent source of conflict, leading to periodic requests for cost readjustment and interest for delayed payment. Most of the delays occur because the Ministry of Finance is the institution with the residual control over national budget funds. The government cuts investment budgets when it faces fiscal restrictions, directly affecting the execution of civil works. Under these circumstances, concession contracts may become a better procurement alternative because they improve the structure of incentives associated with public works contracts and also attract additional funds.

However, the scope for concessions is limited because the majority of roads in the country have reduced traffic levels and the government must provide direct budget contributions. Public outlays are recovered in part through taxes on the increased value of property. The government's ability to enforce contracts will determine whether concessions represent an improvement over public works contracts.

---

[23] Road coverage in Colombia is about 100 meters/km^2, occupying the second-to-last place in Latin America (the average for Latin America is 118 meters/km^2).

A "first generation" of road concession contracts started in 1994. Guarantees on construction and commercial and regulatory risks were conferred to the concessionaires. Land acquisition and license procurement were left in the hands of the concessionaires. Initially, INVIAS subscribed 13 concession contracts. The program included the rehabilitation of 1,220 km and new construction of 306 km, at a cost of about $830 million. During the operational phase, the concessionaires will be in charge of maintaining 1,375 km (approximately 10 percent of the road network).

First-generation contracts conferred too many government guarantees to concessionaires. The corresponding financial burden led the government to devise a new design for the concession contracts (the "second generation").[24] In order to reduce delays and uncertainty in construction costs, it was agreed that project designs should be completed before licenses are granted.[25]

INVIAS is now allowed to purchase land and obtain environmental licenses before the design is finished. A new scheme of guarantees was established to reflect the complexity of the works. Construction risks assumed by the government were limited to 20 percent in new projects, to 10 percent in roadside construction, and totally eliminated in rehabilitation projects. INVIAS requested to ensure "future disbursements" with the Ministry of Finance. This is a mechanism by means of which the government makes a commitment to include line items for the necessary amounts to cover the guarantees during the term of the concession.[26]

Second-generation contracts limited the time period for minimum revenue guarantees and introduced the concept of expected present value of revenues. The concessionaire has 25 years to realize this amount, at which point the road is transferred to the state. The World Bank provided a liquidity guarantee (a contingent credit granted to INVIAS), which acts as a bridge credit from the moment when the guarantee is made effective until it is possible for INVIAS to cash the scheduled outlays. The World Bank also offered a partial risk guarantee that protects project lenders from eventual breach of contract by INVIAS.

Concession contracts show fewer delays and overruns than in the public works contract scheme (Hidalgo 1997b). The average delay of the projects under concession has been 17 months, compared with 3.5 years for public works contracts. Concession projects had average overruns of 40 percent, compared with 300 percent in public works contracts. Nevertheless, the figures for

---

[24] The second-generation concessions include 27 projects (1,819 km) at a cost of $4.3 million.

[25] This means that the engineering design must be performed along with studies on traffic, revenues, environmental impact, value appraisals, and financial feasibility.

[26] The mechanism, however, does not imply the liquidity of such guarantees.

concessions are still high by international standards. Increased costs in concessions come from civil works (58 percent) and land acquisition (40 percent). Increases in the costs of civil works are due to changes from preliminary to definitive design, and to additional works requested by the contractor. Changes in design explain 57 percent of the increments, while additional works explain the remaining 43 percent (Hidalgo 1997b).

Case 5. First-Generation Road Concessions

Terms of the Dispute

The construction of the Bogotá-Villavicencio road was contracted with private firms using public works contracts for two stretches, a concession scheme for the third stretch, and the operation and maintenance of the entire road. Although each type of contract shared risks between parties ex ante, in practice the government bore most of the risks ex post. Each and every project contingency ended up in claims. Pass-through of increased costs was easily accomplished by the contractors, who found almost no resistance from the government. The disputes in this project arose from the following:

- Failure of the government to comply on time with land acquisition, environmental licenses, and other permits.
- Deficiencies in technical information and engineering studies, leading to changes in design and the periodic imposition of additional works.
- Inadequate methodologies for estimating cost, expenses, traffic, and rates.

Analysis of the Case

The original road linking the country's capital with Villavicencio has a sinuous design. Frequent landslides make maintenance costs high ($30 to $35 million a year). These factors led to the decision to construct a new road, considered as the pilot project for the first-generation road concessions. In 1993, the government declared the project viable and stated that the 92 km of road would be completed by 1996.

The project included construction, operation, and maintenance. Construction was divided into three stretches. Stretch I, between km 8+000 and km 39+200, would be developed under concession. The concessionaire would also take responsibility for operation and maintenance of the entire road. From km 39+200 to Villavicencio (stretches II and III), construction would be undertaken through a tender system with INVIAS resources. The concession contract included guarantees on maximum overruns, minimum traffic, and adjustment of toll rates. The concessionaire, by means of a fiduciary contract, was required to establish an autonomous fund to collect and manage the resources for financing, constructing, and operating the project.

For stretch I (km 8+00 to km 39+200), two consortia submitted bids for the original contest, which was declared void. The consortiums were ICA (Mexico)-CORFIGAN-ODINSA and Concesionaria Vial de los Andes (made up of Dragados y Construcciones, from Spain, and Corporación Financiera de los Andes, part of Coviandes). In the summoning for direct contracting, the same two firms participated again. The stretch was granted to the second consortium and the contract was signed in August 1994. The delivery of works was set for September 1999. The works included construction and rehabilitation of the existing road, construction of a 2.3 km tunnel (El Boquerón), and construction of the bypass of Cáqueza (9.6 km) with resources from INVIAS. Operations would last 178 months, including the transfer of assets to the government.

Time spent obtaining environmental licenses and in acquisitions and road design delayed the start of construction by 15 months. This forced the signing of an amendment to the contract on May 28, 1996, which extended the delivery date by 17 additional months. The length of the stretch was reduced, as it initially included km 0+00 to km 55+00. It was later modified to run from km 8+00 to km 38+200. In spite of the reduction, operation and maintenance costs were not reduced in proportion. The term for operation and maintenance was extended from 178 months to 196 months. The concession now expires in 2013, three years after the original date.

Before filing the May 1996 amendment, Coviandes filed a $15 million claim of pecuniary loss from nonfulfillment on the part of INVIAS, equivalent to 30 percent of the value of the contract. The claim originated in a delay in the initiation of the works when the alternative of building the tunnel of El Boquerón was still being studied. The claim was not justified because the concessionaire was committed to submitting a complete design. Moreover, the 1994 contract foresaw the construction of this tunnel. In addition, the 1996 amendment modified the costs and terms of the work in order to adjust it to the new design. The Cáqueza backup road (km 39+100 to km 55+100) was introduced as a modification of stretch I. The work was assigned to Murillo Lobo Guerrero-Gayco S.A. in May 1997, to be completed by August 1998. The work has been completed, although with widespread flaws in pavement quality (Contraloría General de la República 1997).

Stretch II (km 55+300 to km 87+500), which entailed road rehabilitation, was initially assigned to the Brazilian firm Andrade Gutierrez Constructora S.A. in 1994, and scheduled for delivery in April 1997 (contract 290/94) and December 1997 (contract 291/94). The contract was declared void by mutual agreement before completion on April 18, 1997, just 12 days before the deadline.[27] INVIAS called three construction firms to submit quotations for completion of the work. On April 22, 1997 INVIAS invoked the state of "manifest emergency," which allows it to sign contracts bypassing normal procedures. INVIAS hastily used this power to write a contract with Inconstruc Ltd. to deliver the remaining works within nine months. INVIAS subsequently granted an extension of two additional months. The works were finally completed in April 1998. Poor quality led to further negotiations to permit the contractor to improve the quality of the work. Delivery in inadequate conditions reveals auditing problems related to the lack of adequate incentives and penalties to undertake this task in an efficient way.

The work for stretch III (km 87+512 to the Intersection Villavicencio-Acacias) included construction and rehabilitation of the existing road and the construction of two tunnels (Bijagual and Buenavista, 185 and 4,519 meters long, respectively). The project was assigned to Recchi Grandi Livori Fincosit in August 1994, for delivery by October 1997. The firm did not meet scheduled dates and costs; however, no penalties were imposed. The deadline was extended by one month and finally the contract was declared void in January 1998, at which time close to 50 percent of the construction had been completed. Recchi Grandi Livori Fincosit has requested compensation of $55 million from INVIAS for breach of contract.

The delay originated mainly in the Buenavista tunnel (which was only 47 percent complete). In February 1998, INVIAS again invoked the state of manifest emergency and made a direct contract with Conconcreto in March 1998 for the completion of the tunnel. Works are to be finished in 2001.[28] The bypass of Pipiral, which should take at least two years to complete, has not been contracted yet. Costs increased 38 percent over the face value of the original contract.

The delays in the delivery of the third stretch forced the government to make disbursements to maintain the financial equilibrium of the contract. INVIAS tried to transfer those cost overruns to the consumers by raising toll rates before the works were completed. User and community opposition to the measure has prevented changing the rates, forcing INVIAS to provide additional funding. By delivery time, toll rates will be adjusted by about 62 percent. Renegotiations on quality have delayed the application of the new rates.

---

[27] The Brazilian firm withdrew for safety reasons, since some of its engineers were kidnapped by the guerrillas. Andrade Gutierrez is currently requesting $6 million in compensation from INVIAS.

[28] The Buenavista tunnel is five km long and it is situated at the entrance of Villavicencio. Its final costs are still uncertain, since serious geological problems were encountered during construction. Moreover, solving tunnel ventilation problems may cost INVIAS around $25 million.

According to calculations performed in November 1998, the road will eventually cost twice the original contracted value.[29] Four firms had to be hired to complete the works. By 1998, the execution level reached only 60 percent.

In practice, the seemingly superior contracting scheme of concessions has not worked. INVIAS has not levied fines. Consumers have borne delays and cost overruns. The weak bargaining power of INVIAS led to substantial changes in the road's design, as well as delays and renegotiations in the construction schedule and the cost of the works. In addition, the government has shown a willingness to increase its contributions to the project. The financial equilibrium of the concessionaire has prevailed to the detriment of consumers and the government. Contract design has improved, but enforcement remains ineffective. Efficiency gains depend on strengthening the institutions responsible for enforcement.

Case 6. Second-Generation Concessions

Terms of the Dispute

In October 1997, the El Vino-Puerto Salgar concession was granted in a multi-attribute contest in which the bidding variable with the highest weight was "requested government contributions." The bidding variable "expected present value of revenues" was given a very low weight, in spite of being more competitive. The firm Concesionario del Magdalena Medio won the bidding process by submitting the highest requested present value of revenues and the lowest requested government contributions, and foregoing requests for guarantees. After the concession was awarded, the concessionaire requested a change in design to reduce project costs and risk. This strategy aimed to capitalize on the high chance of contract modification ex post. It attained perfect hedging because high present value of revenues is ensured. The variable with the highest impact in the bidding process is loosely related to performance.

Analysis of the Case

The El Vino-Puerto Salgar project comprises the following:

- Operation and maintenance of the stretch El Vino-Tobia Grande-Villeta Intersection (51 km).
- Rehabilitation, operation, and maintenance of the stretch Villeta-Honda (72 km).

---

[29] The road was contracted for $160 million in 1994 and will end up costing $320 million as of 1998.

- Construction, operation, and maintenance of the stretch Intersection Tobia Grande-Intersection Puerto Salgar (68.5 km).
- Operation and maintenance of the stretch Honda-La Dorada-San Alberto (380 km).[30]

The concession contest was organized in two stages: a preliminary qualification (May 1997) followed by the bidding process itself (October 1997). The bidding variables and weighting factors were: requested government contributions (69 percent); minimum requested revenue (10 percent); expected present value of requested revenue (3 percent); requested liquidity guarantees (6 percent); and items subject to geological risk (12 percent). In practice, this arrangement could be labeled as "minimum value of requested government contributions," where the winner is granted the right of collecting the proposed expected revenues. This differs from the Engel et al. (1997) approach (least present value of expected revenues). The winner here was precisely the firm that proposed (and ensured) the highest expected revenue, winning by requesting the lowest amount of government contributions. Colombia committed itself to funding the project with $285 million at most. Minimum revenue guarantees were limited to the period 1998–2006 and overrun guarantees in tunnel construction were limited.

Four international consortia participated in the contest. The winning consortium was Concesionario del Magdalena Medio (made up of the Colombian and Spanish firms Sacyr-OCP CONSTRUCCIONES–IFI), which asked for $137.1 million in government contributions and gave up the option of government guarantees.[31] Moreover, the consortium did not request a guarantee for cost overruns in the construction of the tunnels, or for the minimum income and liquidity guarantees. Instead, it asked for the highest expected value of revenue. Accordingly, one-third of the project cost would be financed with government contributions,[32] the remaining two-thirds being funded by the concessionaire. The work was scheduled to start in July 1998.

INVIAS was in charge of purchasing 95 percent of the land needed to start the project. It hedged inflation risk by hedging with toll indexation to RPI. It hedged revenue risk by allowing extensions of up to five additional years. If expected revenues are not realized during the extension, INVIAS will not hand out additional money. The concessionaire bears *force majeure* risks, except for

[30] The total length is 571.5 km, of which 68 km correspond to new works, 442 km to maintenance, and 60 km to rehabilitation. The estimated cost is $411 million. This is a complex project, including 20 km of tunnels with an estimated cost of $244 million. The road will have six tolls.

[31] Some national civil engineering firms believed that undertaking this project would be impossible under the conditions offered by the winner (Poder y Dinero 1997). They determined that project profitability required government contributions ranging between $240 and $260 million.

[32] The government was authorized to finance contributions through foreign credit (DNP 1998).

terrorist attacks and coups d'état, which INVIAS bears. INVIAS bears risks stemming from changes in the law related to environmental issues and tariff policies.

As soon as the concession was granted, Concesionario del Magdalena Medio proposed a new design eliminating all the original bridges, reducing the number of viaducts from 35 to 26, and reducing the number and total length of tunnels (from 15 to 9, and from 19.6 to 6.2 km, respectively). This proposal challenged the contract clauses, as presentation of alternative designs was forbidden.

A decision about the acceptance of the new design had not been made as of March 1999. The new design avoids the geological risk and cost of tunnels, but adds seven kilometers to the road. Were the proposal accepted, concessionaire profits would increase (seven kilometers of open road are cheaper than 13.4 km of tunnels), but the cost reduction would not be passed on to the users.

This case illustrates two government weaknesses in the design of procurement mechanisms and the credibility of enforcement. Contests granted through multivariate ranking are easier to manipulate and the winner may not be the bidder with the highest valuation. In this case, the bidding variable with the highest weight (requested government contributions) bears no relationship to effort. With respect to the credibility of enforcement, poor understanding of incentive compatibility is less harmful than the perception of bidders that breaching the major contract dispositions ex post will have few, if any, consequences on their finances or reputation. In this case, not only were rents ensured (due to the almost irrelevant role of expected present value of requested revenues in the ranking), there was also an attempt to change the whole object of the contract ex post.

INVIAS must undertake a serious process of reviewing and redesigning contest rules. It should grant concessions with a single bidding variable linked to the contractor's effort, and improve the process of choosing the route (involving road users and the community) to reduce the temptation of proposing unilateral modifications.

General Lessons and Remarks

In Colombia, regulation is a new institutional choice, created as a delegation of authority that can revert to the executive's administration at any moment. This change has redistributed the control of public utilities, which had been held by politicians (both at the legislative and city levels) before 1994. Private participation in power generation and cellular telephone service has increased the number of parties interested in public utilities. This creates an implicit system of checks and balances that could keep economic rents under control in the long term. Further private investment will occur if politicians are blocked in their attempt to maintain control over firms through public control or regulatory capture (Shleifer and Vishny 1994).

Regulation of public utilities faces two major difficulties: the interference of politicians (to recoup managerial rights or increase residual control) and the lack of economic guidelines in the courts for settling disputes. These are characteristics of a country whose legal tradition follows the principles of French civil law principles.

The technical skills and strength of individual regulatory commissions are limited. By merging the existing regulatory bodies into a single one, the likelihood of capture would diminish and the technical skills could be shared. Regulatory coherence in common issues (open access policies, for example) could also be attained. The benefits of this rearrangement are larger in the telecommunications sector. Technological convergence makes business regulations obsolete.

With regard to contract law, it has been observed that legal rules and contracts are not binding. Both the concessionaires and government agencies rely on extrajudicial agreements because they are cheaper and easier to renegotiate than resorting to the prevailing enforcement system. Enforcement is weak and does not replace or compensate for the quality of contract law. This situation is also found in other French law countries (La Porta et al. 1998).

The combination of weak enforcement and nonbinding contracts keeps the cost of provision through concessions high. Extrajudicial agreements amount to bilateral bargaining between a firm and a monopolistic government agency. In this legal and enforcement context, renegotiations (additional works; majority of risks borne by the government; and changes in design, quality standards, coverage, and unit costs) tend to be settled in favor of the concessionaire. Following the line of reasoning of Shleifer and Vishny (1993) regarding the equivalence of corruption and taxation, these case studies show that as long as the end consumer is charged the social cost and not the social value of a concession, renegotiations become equivalent to revenue-maximizing taxation. Renegotiations have possibly worse welfare consequences because the rents (except for bribes to public officers, if any) go to the concessionaire.

Better contract design, a correct auction objective function and contest format to grant concessions, and stronger reliance on incentive-compatible regulations are needed to increase the efficiency gains of private participation in public utilities and infrastructure. However, any effort in this direction will be irrelevant if enforcement remains weak.

Addendum 2001. Enforcement of Infrastructure Regulation

This addendum is about enforcement, the critical theme raised after examining the characteristics of renegotiation in infrastructure in Colombia. First, we discuss a model (Laffont 2001) that represents enforcement as an imperfect technology of endogenous efficacy.[33] Then we give an alternative explanation for the Colombian case and identify measures to improve the quality of infrastructure regulation.

Laffont's basic model describes an environment where:

- Either the regulator succeeds in forcing the regulated firm to fulfill the contract or renegotiation takes place.
- There are two types of firms (cost-efficient and inefficient). Renegotiation is driven by the fact that an inefficient firm has an ex post negative utility.
- Institutions are weak and ensure only an imperfect enforcement of regulatory contracts. When a firm obtains an ex post negative utility, it attempts to renegotiate its regulatory contract.
- With probability p (a function of the expenses incurred to set up an efficient enforcement mechanism), the regulator is able to impose the implementation of the contract, and with probability $1 - p$, the regulator is forced to accept a renegotiation.
- Renegotiation is modeled using the Nash bargaining solution and it is costly. Efficient firms never renegotiate.

Laffont extends his model to the case of a nonbenevolent regulator that must be rewarded to avoid collusion with the agent. The reservation value of the regulator is set proportional to an exogenous parameter measuring the level of corruption of the country.

This framework provides a fresh view on problems incompletely treated when reforms were set in place in the mid 1990s. We agree with the description that enforcement makes firms comply with a predefined set of allocations, but does not solve asymmetric information problems. This fits well the workings of enforcement and regulation in Colombia. The treatment of enforcement as endogenous and the nonbenevolence of the regulator are also important contributions to understanding these types of regulatory processes.

Institutional and new political economy ideas—including how cultural beliefs sustain renegotiation—can shed more light on enforcement. Cultural beliefs are expectations about how other individuals act in various contingencies (Greif 1994), determining whether the stakeholders of the regulatory game are willing to allocate resources to defend its rules. They are determined in a larger context, but a few actions to alter them will be pointed out in this addendum.

Our story of renegotiation incorporates an explicit role of institutions and a different typology of firms (not related to cost). The standard version of regulation

---

[33] The paper can be found at *www.idei.asso.fr/English/EPresent/index.html.*

begins with a set of norms issued by a commission. If conflicts about norms arise, they can be submitted to the judiciary or to a body dealing with monopoly and antitrust affairs. This version illustrates the issue of complementarity: regulation requires backing by a system of institutions for its norms to be followed. Aoki (2000) states that, "if the institutional structure of a particular economy reflects equilibrium strategies in its underlying economic game, complementarity is likely to exist between the elements of that structure. That is, the operations of one institution will be reinforced by the existence of other institutions."

Institutions in Infrastructure

Institutions are comprised of organizations and beliefs. We examine here the legal system (including the antitrust tradition) and beliefs related to regulatory reform. At the beginning of the regulatory game, the performance of former institutions triggered the shaping of the latter. Paraphrasing Greif, cultural beliefs that were crystallized with respect to a specific context affect future strategic decisions.

In Colombia, regulation of public services appeared as a delegation of power from the executive to specialized organizations that would not suffer from the same opportunistic temptations. Although delegation has been accepted by the courts for monetary and fiscal matters, its application in infrastructure is viewed as a threat to the legal mindset (based on the French Code). Influential lawyers look at regulation with antipathy on the following grounds: (1) Delegation is permissible if it does not dilute the responsibility of the executive branch; more precisely, if it *maximizes* the possibility of intervention of the executive in strategic economic sectors; and (2) more ideologically, economic regulation is viewed as an Anglo-Saxon instrument that is alien to the country practice. It is no surprise that the courts have studied the possibility of giving the regulatory functions back to the executive, with the explicit endorsement of many politicians.

The country tradition in antitrust and antimonopoly issues is poor because the state used to favor concentration of industry and vertical relations in both private and public firms. The four major economic clusters produce about half of the country's industrial output, and maintain strong relationships with the political power. Two regulatory experiences that do not rely on the existence of an antitrust body are worth being mentioned here:

- The hard limits on horizontal and vertical integration set by the electricity regulator have been respected so far. With hindsight, they may well have been the only way to deter market power, given the inexperience of the entity in charge of monitoring mergers and acquisitions. The limits are self-enforcing because violations would be contested in the wholesale electricity market by other firms.

- Open access provisions via direct agreements between telecommunications firms have yielded exceedingly few disputes, suggesting the presence of collusion. This illustrates the other well-known side of the coin: excess rents may sustain an inefficient world without renegotiation.

We constrain the discussion of beliefs to the expectations about the consequences of deviant behavior in regulatory contracts and about the gains from privatization. Beliefs like those presented below help coordinate expectations on the reform of public utilities, thereby influencing enforcement.

The sketchy relation of the rule of law is a judiciary perceived as either incompetent or malleable in settling disputes between the state and powerful firms. This perception is more pronounced in the case of highway concessions. International civil works firms that were granted concessions usually enjoy political leverage (lobby at the highest political levels). Legal disputes lost by the state were common in the first group of highway concessions granted after Law 80. Renegotiation cases have reduced with improvements in the technical capacity of the regulator and the quality of design, which have made information harder. But in projects where design uncertainty is high (due to the presence of tunnels, for example), renegotiation has been persistent.

With reference to privatization, it is worth reviewing the *Latinobarómetro* surveys.[34] Trust in privatization has never been dominant in Colombia and it is fading at a quick pace. In 1998, about 50 percent of the population either strongly disagreed or disagreed with the following statement: "The privatization of state companies has been beneficial." In 2001, this percentage reached 78 percent. Worryingly, the increase is totally explained by an increment in those who strongly disagree. The percentage of those who strongly disagree with privatization in 2001 (44 percent) is the highest in Latin America, and the total percentage of those who distrust privatization in 2001 is the highest in the region, along with Argentina. Although concessioning to private firms is logically different from ownership, there is no evidence that trust in private participation in general enjoys a significantly better consideration than direct privatization.

The conclusion of this section is terse: low organizational complementarity + dismal beliefs = weak institutions in infrastructure.

Enforcement and Equilibrium

To complete the picture, it remains to describe types of firms and the driver of renegotiation. Firms are classified according to their willingness to force a

[34] Complete data are available for purchase at *www.latinobarometro.org*.

renegotiation process. Type combines size, corporate culture, networking, long-term goals in the country, and access to scarce resources (elite lawyers). "High" types can be called *sharks* for expositional purposes. Renegotiation is not driven in this description by negative utilities due to cost inefficiencies, but by the smell of positive net profits after renegotiating the regulatory contract. Uncertainty in project design and weak institutions intensify the smell. The strength of outside options available for international sharks (for example, the threat of deterioration of international relationships if they are able to get their government's endorsement) leads to asymmetric bargaining.

Because of the reinforcing nature of working institutions, types, enforcement, and beliefs are self-fulfilling: if expectations are of state impotence whenever sharks have a legal claim, renegotiation will occur whenever sharks sign regulatory contracts. Neither the legal institutions nor the public will tend to support regulation or privatization.

What to Do

Institutions are inertia-driven. Complementarity implies that a change independent of other elements will have only a limited impact. Aoki (2000) believes that "effective institutional change requires that the expectations of a significant portion of the population regarding future change be coordinated." Programs confined to strengthening the regulatory capacity are, of course, the first action to undertake. In particular, regulators must be able to sustain a system of incentive contracts, provision of hard information, and contract design and surveillance. But a switch to a different equilibrium in institutions is needed to attain improved enforcement. This is costly, and many things have to re-accommodate in a certain sequence. Moreover, no single actor has control over the implementation of any reform proposal.

If we owned the option to decide where to start a program to enhance the quality of regulation, the choice would be the judiciary. Either a record of consecutive disputes settled properly or the application of punishment to a major breach would help start a change in beliefs. This requires increased regulatory efforts to provide information that can be verified by the courts. Regulatory complexities do not help in that regard.

Laffont (2001) starts his paper this way:

> "Regulatory contracts, as any other contractual relationships, suffer in less developed countries (LDCs) from a severe lack of enforcement. Good laws and rules are rather straightforward to import from the developed world. A good set of lawyers can transfer this institutional knowledge quite easily (if not cheaply)."

In light of institutional complementarity, this proposal is of little help because it is not evolutionary stable. Pistor (2000) states that:

> "(...) to be effective, law needs to have local constituencies with a strong interest in and understanding of the laws. This is a prerequisite for the new laws to become part of the continuous process of legal change, without which the formal legal system will remain largely irrelevant."

Once beliefs have started to move in the desired direction, based on exemplary results, channels to promote effective participation of stakeholders are needed to consolidate the persistence of the initial move. Again, exemplary results are required to stimulate stakeholder mobilization. A buildup of achievements in the two fronts needs to be formed.

The seeds of reputation effects are also required in this context to attain an efficient level of self-enforcement. Litigious firms must suffer in future concession contests.

We understand the extraordinary costs (and luck) required for this sequence of events to unfold. A reformer has the humble duty of leading feasible changes that maintain open the possibility of future welfare improvements.

References

Aoki, M. 2000. *Information, Corporate Governance, and Institutional Diversity*. Oxford, UK: Oxford University Press.

Benavides, J. 1997. "Capacity Payments in Predominantly Hydroelectric Electricity Markets: The Case of Colombia." Proceedings of the 18th Annual North American Conference of the USAEE/IAEE, September 7–10, San Francisco, CA.

_____. 1998a. "Pushing the Reform Ahead in the Colombian Wholesale Electricity Market." Proceedings of the 21st Annual International Conference of the IAEE, May 13–16, Quebec City, Quebec, Canada.

_____. 1998b. "Irreversible Investment and the Role of Contracts in Imperfectly Competitive Electricity Markets." INFORMS 98, June 28–July 1, Tel Aviv, Israel.

Bunn, D. W. 1996. "Review of the Electricity Pool of England and Wales from a Demand-Side Perspective." In G. MacKerron and P. Pearson, eds., *The UK Energy Experience - A Model or a Warning*. London, U.K.: Imperial College Press.

Castro, Jaime. 1998. "Las generosidades del gobierno distrital."*El Tiempo,* 3/E, September 26.

Contraloría General de la República. 1997. "Informe de seguimiento al proyecto vial. Santafé de Bogotá-Villavicencio, Colombia.

Dixit, A. K. 1996. *The Making of Economic Policy. A Transaction-Cost Politics Perspective.* Cambridge, MA: MIT Press.

DNP. 1998. *Documento Conpes* No. 2997. Departamento Nacional de Planeación.

Engel, E., et al. 1997. "Infrastructure Franchising and Government Liabilities." Presented at the seminar, Managing Government Exposure to Private Infrastructure Projects, May 29–30, The World Bank, Cartagena, Colombia.

Greif, A. 1994. "Cultural Beliefs and the Organization of Society: A Historical and Theoretical Reflection on Collectivist and Individualist Societies" *Journal of Political Economy* 102: 912-50.

Hart, O. 1995. *Firms, Contracts, and Financial Structure.* Clarendon, UK: Oxford University Press.

Hidalgo, D. 1997a. "20 años de infraestructura de transporte. Grandes planes, algunas realizaciones." *Estrategia económica y financiera* 264 (September).

_____. 1997b. "Los impactos de las concesiones viales en Colombia : ¿Vamos por buen camino?" *Estrategia económica y financiera* 258 (June).

ISA-T. 1999. *Análisis del mercado mayorista de la electricidad en Colombia.* ISA-T, Medellín, Colombia.

Jacobs, J. M. 1997. "Artificial Power Markets and Unintended Consequences." *IEEE Transactions on Power Systems* 12: 968–972.

Johnson, R. B., S. S. Oren, and A. J. Svoboda. 1997. "Equity and Efficiency of Unit Commitment in Competitive Electricity Markets." *Utilities Policy* 6: 9–20.

Laffont, J. J. 2001. *Enforcement, Regulation and Development.* IDEI Working Paper, Toulouse, June 12, 2001.

La Porta, R., et al. 1998. "Law and Finance." *Journal of Political Economy* 106: 1113–1155.

Levy, H. 1983. "Economic Evaluation of Voting Power of Common Stock." *Journal of Finance* 38: 79–94.

Merrow, E. W., and B. R. Schroeder. 1991. "Understanding the Costs and Schedules of Hydroelectric Projects." Paper presented at AACE Transactions, 35th Annual Meeting.

Merrow, E. W., and R. F. Shangraw, Jr. 1990. *Understanding the Costs and Schedules of World Bank Supported Hydroelectric Projects.* Energy Series Paper no. 31, Industry and Energy Department, The World Bank, Washington, D.C.

Newbery, D. M. 1995. "Power Markets and Market Power." *The Energy Journal* 16: 39–66.

Pistor, K. 2000. "The Standardization of Law and Its Effect on Developing Economies." *G-24 Discussion Paper Series* 4. Cambridge, MA: Center for International Development. Harvard University and United Nations.

Sarmiento, E., et al. 1996. *La crisis de la infraestructura vial.* Escuela Colombiana de Ingeniería, Bogotá, Colombia.

Shleifer, A., and R. W. Vishny. 1994. "Politicians and Firms." *Quarterly Journal of Economics* 109: 995–1025.

———. 1993. "Corruption." *Quarterly Journal of Economics* 108: 599–617.

Spiller, P. 1996. "Institutions and Commitment." *Industrial and Corporate Change* 5: 1–32.

Sundaresan, S. M. 1984. "Equilibrium Valuation of Natural Resources." *Journal of Business* 57: 493–518.

CHAPTER 5

Settlement of Disputes in the Power Sector in Argentina

Juan A. Legisa

Transformation of the electricity sector in Argentina started a decade ago as a consequence of necessity and as an outcome of a general consensus arising from theoretical discussion prevailing at the end of the 1980s and the beginning of the 1990s. The accelerating factor was the serious crisis that the sector suffered in 1988/89 as a result of many years of problems in government administration.

In 1989, the government approved and enacted State Reform Law No. 23,696 and Economic Emergency Law No. 23,697, representing a landmark in the role of the state in the country. These laws institutionalized the government's decision to give up its entrepreneurial role. The government assumed the role of a designer of policies and regulator of essential activities, while exercising control over the development thereof.

Law No. 24,065 and Law No. 15,336 created the Electricity Regulatory Framework, which marked a turning point in the sector. The Framework replaced former reorganization projects with a comprehensive transformation project. As a consequence, the government has refocused its attention on the role of regulating the activity and controlling the private concession-holding companies.

The reform process attracted private investment, which reversed the trend of lack of electric power and low quality of service. The investment helped in paving the way for reliable service at lower prices.

A national law created a regulatory entity as a self-governing body enjoying full legal capacity to act in the fields of public and private law. Ente Nacional Regulador de la Electricidad (ENRE) is responsible for following the principles and rules contained in the Regulatory Framework; ensuring that services are rendered under conditions of reliability, competitiveness, equality, free access,

The author would like to acknowledge the contributions of Víctor Agüero, Ciro Bohorquez, Mariano García Cuerva, Ernesto Kerszberg, Silvia Merzi, and Alejandra Robles.

and fair and reasonable rates adapted to the expected service quality; protecting the rights of users; and guaranteeing long-term supply.

Congress enacted and approved the Regulatory Framework. Therefore, it properly fits the criterion subsequently upheld by the 1994 Constitutional Reform, which states that legislative action is an essential requirement for the formulation of the regulatory framework for privatized utilities. This chapter describes two of the most significant disputes that have taken place in the power sector in Argentina: the cases of EDESUR (one of the two private distribution companies in Buenos Aires) and TRANSENER (the private transmission company).

The Disputes

According to Law 24,065, ENRE has primary jurisdiction over any and all disputes arising between wholesale market agents and electricity users or other interested third parties. The term "jurisdiction" is understood to mean the power to determine the fair solution to conflicting positions between the above-mentioned subjects.

The law made a distinction between disputes involving market agents and those involving market agents and users or interested third parties because, in the first case, the conflict has to be solved through ENRE's jurisdictional action. This means that conflicts between agents cannot be filed with the courts if ENRE has not previously issued a decision in the matter. Conflicts between public service users and providers or between other interested parties and market agents require that a claim be filed with ENRE so that it can exercise its jurisdiction, but they may also resort directly to the courts.

ENRE's jurisdiction is restricted to issues falling under its vested powers. Law 24,065 specifies that the origin of such disputes must be the supply of electric power transmission and the distribution of public services. The interested parties are entitled to file two kinds of administrative procedures against resolutions issued by ENRE in the exercise of this function: reconsideration, to be filed with ENRE itself, or an appeal, with the Energy Secretariat. Other than filing any of these administrative procedures, an interested party may also file a direct judicial appeal with the National Administrative Disputes Court of Appeals. Therefore, the parties are not required to resort to the lower courts.

The main problem arising from these rules refers to controlling compliance with quality standards and with the duties of electricity carriers and, particularly, distribution concessionaires, toward their users. The provisions clash with the ability of users to resort to the courts instead of filing a claim with the regulatory entity. This is because it is likely that alterations in distribution quality levels affect large numbers of users simultaneously. In addition, concession contracts provide an administrative procedure for applying penalties according to the frequency and duration or the departure from established voltage levels.

In exceptional situations, there may be several court actions overlapping an identical activity concurrently carried out by the regulatory authority. The National Constitution, as amended in 1994, includes article 42, which protects the rights of electricity consumers. Article 42 states that: "Legislation shall establish efficient procedures for the solution of conflicts." The types of disputes discussed here fall under this constitutional provision, although the congress has yet to enact a law to regulate the resolution of these types of disputes.

EDESUR

On February 15, 1999, an electricity failure and a subsequent fire occurred at the Azopardo substation, which is owned by EDESUR S.A. The fire left almost 160,000 users without electricity in the City of Buenos Aires, affecting the neighborhoods of Almagro, Balvanera, San Cristóbal, Boedo, and Montserrat. The distributor fully restored service 10 days later. The event took place in the course of recently commissioned works intended to connect the existing 132 kV grid to the new 220/132 kV Azopardo substation.

The failure of one of the cable joints, due to a single-phase short circuit, ignited a fire that ultimately destroyed all the cables in the affected area of the tunnel. It also did away with the reserve represented by redundant three-wire line number 136, which was not fire-protected. Three-wire lines 135 and 136 supplied the 132/13.2 kV Azopardo, Pozos, Once, and Independencia substations. At the time of the event, there were no technical personnel present in the Azopardo substation; only one watchman was there. The joints had been made inside the tunnel under the station, where all the 132 kV cables entered and left the station, without any measures to protect the other wires. Moreover, the site did not have a fire detection system.

After several failed attempts to reconnect the cables at Azopardo, EDESUR S.A. decided to bypass the cable outside the station. This would restore the previous setup for the Pozos, Once, and Independencia substations. ENRE carried out an expert examination according to technical standards and the state of the art. The examination showed the following:

- The tests performed at the Azopardo substation to transfer the load were carried out at insufficient test voltage levels and, purportedly, without previously treating the cables and accessories with oil.
- Negligence turned the splicing failure, which from the electrical point of view was a simple contingency, into a double contingency, canceling out the possibility of load recovery from the high-voltage grid.
- The absence of specialized personnel during load delivery, given the significance of this task—initial transfer of the public electricity service

to the substation's 160,000 customers—caused the fire to go undetected for 30 minutes, and the firefighters began fighting the fire by gushing water into the tunnel.

- Of the 16 oil samples taken from the tunnel cables, 10 exceeded the moisture limit for installed cables (25 parts per million, ppm) and all 16 of the new cables exceeded the limit (10 ppm). In the samples taken from the bypass, the moisture content was 11 ppm or less.

The power cut largely exceeded the downtime limits established in the concession contract. The outage caused serious damage and affected a large number of users, jeopardizing the safety and health of the citizens. The power cut was not the result of a *force majeure* event, but of faulty facilities in EDESUR's own distribution system, located in an area under its sole jurisdiction. Accordingly, there are no reasons that could possibly exempt EDESUR from its liability.

In view of the extent of the aforesaid failure, ENRE proceeded to immediate identification of the affected users, as well as to determine the contractual penalties to be acknowledged to each under the concession contract. Consequently, on February 17, 1999, ENRE issued Resolution No. 222/99. It disallowed *force majeure,* instructing EDESUR to credit to the affected users the amount of contractual penalties in their next bill, and to extend the due date of bills until March 3rd in order to allow time to include said credits.

Because the power cut lasted more than 10 days, ENRE understood that the concession contract's normal contingency provisions referred to determining the amount to be discounted for energy not supplied. That would fix maximum admissible periods for interruption of the power distribution service for systems similar to the grid transferred to EDESUR S.A. at the time the concession contract was executed. The penalties provided for in the contract were intended to compensate only marginal interruptions exceeding the reference standard.

In the present case, many of the users affected by the event had been left without effective, normal service for several days. In addition to the contractual penalties, ENRE issued Resolution No. 292/99. It provides that, in view of the exceptional characteristics of the event (supply cut off for an extraordinarily long time), the provisions of the preestablished penalties had been exceeded and that, according to the general principles of law, the affected users were entitled to compensation for all damages suffered. The legal grounds for this resolution arose from the contractual relationship between the distributor and the service users, and from the jurisdictional powers granted to ENRE by Law 24,065 to solve conflicts in the distributor-user relationship.

The resolution led to the problem of seeking a way to resolve approximately 160,000 claims, a number that was impossible to treat following the normal dispute resolution procedures. To this end, ENRE decided to determine uniform, minimum estimated damages to which all residential users were entitled without any claim or evidence of damage. It established compensation levels of Arg$90 for those who had no electricity for less than 24 hours and of Arg$100 plus Arg$3.75/hour for those who had no electricity for a longer period.[1] This compensation did not limit claims for other, larger damages, if duly proved. The compensation was based on ENRE's jurisdictional powers and on the fact that the distributor acknowledged having caused damage to users. Insofar as shops and industries were concerned, they were required to prove the damages suffered to be entitled to collect the pertinent compensation.

EDESUR S.A. filed an appeal against the resolution based on purported formal flaws in the contested act, which would originate in the failure to comply with specific administrative provisions. The appeal also referred to other purported flaws of content that would affect the rules regulating electricity distribution and prejudice the constitutional right to defense and to ownership of property. Therefore, EDESUR S.A. claimed annulment of the appealed resolution. According to Resolution No. 471/99, ENRE disallowed the distributor's appeal to reconsider, setting forth the legal arguments supporting its action and decisions, which were then expressly accepted and consented to by the distributor.

TRANSENER

Within the framework of the transformation of the electricity sector, which began in 1991, a concession for high-voltage electric power transmission service was granted to the firm TRANSENER S.A. Because it is characterized as "public service" (section 1, Law 24,065) and in view of its monopolistic nature, the electric power transmission activity is subject to regulation, both with respect to rates and service quality. Upon expiration of the first five-year pricing period, ENRE proceeded to revise—in light of applicable rules (Law 24,064 and the concession contract)—the remuneration payable to TRANSENER S.A. and the issues relating to service quality.

The concession contract provided that, in principle, it was necessary to approve a new value for the remuneration for transmitted power (RVT), to fix an efficiency encouragement factor, to establish a premium system for quality, and to reclassify transmission line categories for the application of penalties.[2] For this purpose, CAMMESA (Compañia Administradora del Mercado Eléctrico Mayorista) was asked to estimate the average annual income forecast for RVT for the second pricing period. CAMMESA adopted three demand hypotheses,

[1] Values are in Argentine pesos.

[2] The High-Voltage Power Transmission Remuneration System establishes that the carrier's remuneration is comprised of the following items: connection, transmission capacity, and transmitted power.

which yielded a maximum of Arg$33.17 million and a minimum of Arg$23.45 million. For the first pricing period, the RVT was Arg$55 million.[3] The decrease in income was mainly due to improved energy supply, both in volume and efficiency terms, and a consequent decline in prices.

As set forth in the prevailing rules, ENRE convened a public hearing to discuss four issues related to the transmission remuneration payable to carriers. The issues were the variable remuneration for transmitted electric power, the efficiency encouragement coefficient, the premium system, and the reclassification of line categories.

The First Public Hearing

ENRE convened a public hearing, which was held on May 29 and June 2, 1998. At the hearing, the various interested parties had the opportunity to express their respective positions regarding the four issues that would be subject to ENRE's decision.

At the hearing, TRANSENER S.A. stated that, if the decision to be adopted by ENRE were limited to the four issues under review, the resulting remuneration for the second pricing period would not meet the principles applicable to rates provided for in Law 24,065. In the carrier's view, even if the highest RVT value were approved, the remuneration to be collected during the second five-year period would not provide enough income to meet service operating costs, taxes, repayment, and a reasonable rate of profit, as provided for in sections 40 and 41 of the law.

In view of this situation, ENRE requested the concessionaire to supply more detailed and complete information with respect to operating expenses, investments, capital base, and expected rate of profit. Once the requested information was obtained, ENRE decided to revise the calculation of the remuneration to be fixed for the second pricing period and to determine whether the amount to be approved would comply with the provisions of Law 24,065. Without prejudice thereto, ENRE passed resolutions on the four issues for which the public hearing had been convened.

Remuneration for Transmitted Electric Power

Through Resolution No. 1319/98, ENRE approved an RVT value equal to Arg$33.17 million/year for the second pricing period, according to the highest hypothesis taken into account in CAMMESA's calculation.

---

[3] At the end of the first rate period, the RVT value, adjusted according to the terms of the concession contract, was Arg$59.21 million.

Efficiency Encouragement Factor

ENRE fixed the efficiency encouragement factor, the annual reduction percentage with respect to remuneration for connection and transmission capacity, as follows:

Year	Reduction to be applied (percent)
1999	0.0
2000	0.2
2001	0.2
2002	0.4
2003	0.4
2004	0.6
2005	0.6
2006	0.8
2007	0.8
2008	1.0

Premium System

ENRE established a premium system using a formula that takes into account the quality level observed in the first pricing period, and that is proportional to the amount of penalties applied during the period. The formula is:

$$\text{Premium}_{Ii} = \max[\text{PMMH}_I * \text{ut}_I]* \max[(\text{DAM}_{Ii} - \text{DMH}_I)/(1 - \text{DMH}_I); 0]$$

$$+ [(\text{Tfamp}_I - \text{Tfam}_{Ii})/(\text{Tfamp}_I); 0],$$

where Premium_{Ii} is the premium in the first period for equipment i. For each type of equipment, PMMH_I is monthly average penalties in the first pricing period, ut is the total number of units, DAM_{Ii} is variable annual average availability each month, DMH_I is average availability in the first pricing period, Tfamp_I is the variable annual average failure rate for the first pricing period, and Tfam_{Ii} is the variable annual failure rate each month.

ENRE also approved the values for PMMH, DMH, and Tfam for each type of equipment, and the procedure according to which CAMMESA must collect payments among the agents of the wholesale electricity market. The premium formula applies, on a monthly basis, to the different types of transmission system equipment, lines (categories A, B, and C), transformers, connection equipment (connections), and reactive power compensation equipment.

Reclassification of Line Categories

With regard to line categories, ENRE decided that they should be reclassified on a yearly basis, starting on November 1, 1998. The classification takes into account the cost overruns determined by CAMMESA with the seasonal schedule, and the significant changes foreseen in the system for the following year.

The Second Public Hearing

At the same time, ENRE convened a new public hearing, intended to discuss TRANSENER S.A.'s report on operating expenses and investments, expected capital base determination and rate of profit, and the remuneration implicitly expected by the concessionaire. A further purpose of the hearing was to assign the payment, by the different transmission service users, of an eventual difference between the remuneration to be finally adopted and the remuneration that arose from strict application of the four issues resolved.

After the second public hearing, and taking into account the information gathered—particularly regarding disbursements already made and those estimated for the next five-year period—ENRE evaluated operating costs and investments in order to determine expenditures on terms compatible with reasonableness criteria established by Law 24,065.

Operating Costs

ENRE obtained a reasonable estimate of operating costs for the second five-year period, as follows (in millions of Argentine pesos):

1999	34.75
2000	34.65
2001	34.65
2002	34.65
2003	34.65

The estimate of a reasonable amount of total operating costs should be understood, in the context of a "price cap" price revision, as an amount consistent with efficient and effective management of the utility concessionaire. A more efficient performance would allow the concessionaire to provide the service according to this level of expenses as well as to increase its profitability. However, a lower efficiency level, in which actual expenses exceed those estimated by the regulator—either itemized or in the aggregate—would not entitle the concessionaire to request any adjustment whatsoever.

Investments

ENRE analyzed the investments to be made during the next pricing period according to TRANSENER S.A.'s report, and determined which of the proposed investments should be considered for inclusion in the carrier's regulated remuneration. ENRE purged the investment list to avoid inclusion of those investments that, according to the rules in force, should be treated as enlargements and, therefore, should not be taken into account for the purpose of fixing TRANSENER S.A.'s rate. As a result, ENRE determined the following investment amounts for the next five-year period (in millions of Argentine pesos):

1999	5,845.2
2000	10,469.1
2001	11,438.0
2002	15,780.3
2003	15,045.3

Capital Base

In order to determine the reasonable profitability level to be computed as a component of the carrier's remuneration, ENRE analyzed the question of capital base and the rate of profit. Since the concessionaire carries out nonregulated activities, from which it obtains part of its total income, ENRE determined that the reasonable rate of profit should be calculated on a portion, not the whole, of the capital base. Therefore, ENRE took into account that, in compliance with the provisions of section 19 of Law 23,696, the enforcement authority had appraised the concessionaire's assets, and that this appraisal had been taken into account in valuing the capital applied to regulated activities in the amount of Arg$310.9 million.

Profitability Rate

To determine the reasonable rate of profit provided for by Law 24,062, ENRE used the calculation method known as the capital assets pricing model (CAPM), assuming that it was acceptable for the case in question. The CAPM was used because it builds the rate of profit on the basis of a risk-free rate to which an allowance is added that represents an average of profits earned by private investments over and above a risk-free investment. In order to fully adapt the rate to the case under examination, the CAPM applies a multiplier—the beta factor—to the market premium to obtain the margin to be added to the risk-free rate to make the specific activity in question profitable.[4] Lastly, the method includes a "country risk" rate.

TRANSENER S.A. considered that the applicable rate of return should be between 12.44 and 15 percent (similar to the rate of return of a company operating with its own capital). ENRE analyzed the situation and concluded that the concessionaire's rate of profit should be 10.54 percent. ENRE arrived at this value using a 5.178 percent risk-free rate, a 0.58 beta factor applied to a 3.03 percent market premium, and the 3.6 percent estimated country risk.

By comparison, regulations in the United Kingdom indicate that a range of 6.5 to 7.5 percent was considered for the cost of capital when that country revised carrier prices (OFFER 1996). Therefore, considering a country risk rate of 3.6 percent, ENRE's value of 10.54 percent for the rate of profit falls within a comparable range of 10.1 to 11.1 percent.

Calculation of Reasonable Remuneration

Based on the foregoing definitions, ENRE calculated the remuneration for TRANSENER S.A. for the pricing period starting on July 17, 1998. ENRE decided that Arg$94.6 million would be allocated to TRANSENER for the second pricing period.[5] This new income level implied an 8-percent reduction with respect to the high-voltage carrier's income during the first five years of operation.

ENRE's study to decide on this matter showed that, indeed, establishing TRANSENER S.A.'s remuneration for the second pricing period only on the basis of the four items dealt with in the first public hearing would not comply with the pricing principles established by Law No. 24,065. In other words, the remuneration of approximately Arg$77.5 million that would have applied in the first case would have been clearly insufficient to meet said principles. Examination of the nature of the RVT showed that the method provided for in the concession contract for calculating remuneration in each pricing period had become unreasonable, because it may lead to establishing remuneration at levels contrary to the reasonableness criteria upheld by Law 24,065. Therefore, ENRE concluded that it was empowered to make a broad revision, including both the carrier's remuneration and the questions related to service quality. At the same time, it was required to act to ensure compliance with the provisions of the law.

[4] For calculation, the beta factor includes the (higher) risk difference between operating in a price-cap pricing system and a price calculated according to a rate-of-return system.

[5] The carrier's regulated income at the end of the first pricing period was equal to about Arg$103 million, before penalties.

Assigning Payment among Users

Lastly, ENRE clarified the issue of assigning payment of the difference between the remuneration fixed for TRANSENER S.A. and the remuneration that would have resulted from taking only the new RVT approved by ENRE Resolution No. 1319/98. Although the remuneration was determined in accordance with the provisions of Law 24,065, the RVT would still be part of the fund collection mechanism under which the payment obligations undertaken with the concessionaire would be met. Therefore, the remuneration for connection and capacity was determined taking into account that users of the transmission system share in the payment of the costs thereof, to the extent of their respective utilization.

To that end, and in order to ensure a total annual remuneration of Arg$94.6 million, through its Resolution No. 1650/98, ENRE changed the connection remuneration values established in paragraph 1.1, Sub-Annex II-C, of the TRANSENER S.A. concession contract. The values were changed as follows (in Argentine pesos):

Type of connection	First period	Second period
500 kV	10.766/hour	28.186/hour
220 kV	9.689/hour	25.366/hour
132 kV	8.613/hour	22.549/hour
For each dedicated transformer	0.054/hour/MVA	0.141/hour/MVA

Legislative Issues for Further Reflection

The regulator's reactions to EDESUR's outage and TRANSENER's remuneration revision have received wide approval. However, we should not adopt a complacent attitude. A sufficient amount of time has to elapse so that the advantage of hindsight, together with events unfolding at home and abroad, will permit a fair historical judgement of these decisions. In the meantime, a host of issues remain open and call for further debate.

Making private profit compatible with public service is no easy task, as the two examined cases show. Private companies face the conundrum of deciding on investments aimed at fulfilling quality requirements, incurring the minimum cost, and avoiding the cost of penalties. Penalties and remuneration systems should be designed in a way that encourages efficiency, safety, and consumer welfare.

As for punishment of breach, the regulator's duty is to carefully weigh the amount of the penalties to impose. Besides assessing the seriousness of the failure, this requires taking into account the merits of the distributor, based on its prior performance. The regulator has the obligation of protecting the interests of consumers. However, imposing high penalties on companies may not be consumer friendly beyond the short term. Enduring heavy penalties might lead utilities to strengthen investment in skills and equipment, thus facing the complicated tradeoff between costs incurred in preventing system failures and costs derived from increased investment and its implications in terms of rate increases.

There is not yet enough evidence to ascertain the extent to which the regulator's intervention in the two cases examined contributed to minimizing service costs and rates, or to helping to increase system reliability and resilience. However, evidence so far seems to point to a drastic reduction in failures, consistent with the fact of private agents taking over management responsibilities.

Even if the risk of outages cannot be eliminated, the prevailing compensation system considerably mitigates the vulnerability of consumers. However, further regulatory attention should be devoted to estimating penalties and apportionment. Likewise, regulation of transmission tariffs should be revised on a regular basis in order to avoid drastic corrections of the sort implemented in the case studied here.

Reference

OFFER. 1996. *The Transmission Price Control Review of the National Grid Company* (August).

Part II. Promoting Competition in the Provision of Public Services: Access Arrangements to Network Industries

CHAPTER 6

Practical Rules for Pricing Access in Telecommunications

J. A. Ordover and R. D. Willig

During the past several years, many countries have embarked on a process of liberalizing their telecommunications. The key element in this process entails opening up the sector to market competition. In some cases, telecommunications services are already fully competitive, although a monopoly provider continues to control other services. Often, access to the local network—to the loops and wires—that connects subscribers is fully controlled by the incumbent telecommunications services provider. This stranglehold on access creates public policy challenges for those responsible for regulating the sector and for ensuring its continued development as well as progress toward full-fledged competition.

Two main policy problems stem from monopoly control over access. In the first place, it creates the ability and incentives to overprice access to those who need it. This problem is not unique to telecommunications. In fact, in many network industries, some elements of the network are likely to be monopolized, either for cost or regulatory reasons, or both. Many countries have developed regulatory mechanisms for constricting the monopoly power of incumbents.

The second policy challenge stems from the fact that the incumbent provider of network access is likely also to compete with the new entrants who require access as a necessary input into the provision of final telecommunications services. In this case, the incumbent may have insufficient incentives to offer new entrants access to the network on nondiscriminatory terms, both in terms of the price that it charges for access as well as the level of quality of access. Consequently, by abusing access to the input, the incumbent may stymie or even derail the development of competition in the provision of end-user services. At the same time, if the incumbent is allowed to charge a full monopoly price for access, its incentive to discriminate against new entrants is likely to be less as compared with a regime in which the access price is tightly regulated. This confronts the regulator with a difficult trade-off: on one hand, tight regulation of access enhances incentives to discriminate, especially if the new entrants are likely to divert lucrative end-user customers from the incumbent; on the other hand, relaxed regulation of access creates the danger that access—hence end-user prices—will be set significantly above the competitive level.

Regulation of access must reflect all these concerns plus several others. First, access regulation should create incentives for efficient entry into the provision of end-user telecommunications services. That is, access rates should not be so low as to encourage entry from potential vendors that are less efficient than the incumbent. Second, access rates should not be so high as to discourage efficient entry or create incentives for inefficient bypass of the incumbent's access network. Third, access rates should be sufficient to ensure that the incumbent has correct incentives to invest in the network both by installing new access lines (loops) as well as by deploying economically efficient technologies in the network.

It is also important to emphasize here that access prices cannot correct all the inefficiencies that are present in the sector. For example, in many countries, end-user prices are significantly distorted from the underlying true economic costs. In particular, local rates are frequently set below cost and long-distance (inter-urban) rates are set above cost. This being the case, it is critical that regulators should engage in rate rebalancing, possibly even prior to full liberalization of telecommunications services. Economically sound end-user and access prices are required to ensure that competition takes root and generates the desirable outcomes.

Basic Methodological Approaches to Access Prices

The economic literature has proposed a variety of different methods for setting access prices. The methods can be roughly divided along two key dimensions. The first dimension pertains to the institutional setting in which access rates are determined. In particular, the regulator can set access rates directly (that is, an independent body determines the rates according to some well-defined and transparent set of rules), or the parties can voluntarily negotiate the prices (subject to some general legal principles, such as competition laws that guard against abuse of dominance). We know of no country in which there are no regulatory or antitrust constraints on the terms on which access can be obtained. This makes perfect sense in view of the fact that there is little or no competition in the provision of access. Until such competition develops at a workable level so that market forces can keep access rates at competitive levels, there have to be some other means for ensuring that access is not denied or priced excessively.

However, it also follows that once a workably competitive market in the provision of access develops, regulatory strictures on the pricing of access will not be required.

The second dimension pertains to whether access rates are *built up* from costs (the bottom-up approach) or *derived from* end-user prices (the top-down approach) of services that have access as an input. Both methods have been used in practice. Neither one is unambiguously superior to the other as a practical tool for setting access rates. It is commonly agreed, however, that the top-down approach provides a tool for gauging whether the seller of the access deals with itself on a preferential basis. It is also important to note that neither regulation nor negotiation is unambiguously superior to the other. Regulation may be desirable in those countries in which antitrust laws are poorly developed or nonexistent and in which the agency (and the courts) enforcing the competition policy may lack the required expertise to resolve disputes regarding access. Alternatively, the incumbent (or potential entrants) may gain control of the regulatory agency and pursue access policies that are not necessarily in the public interest. In sum, from the policy perspective, there is no single correct method for setting access rates in all circumstances.

Some Relevant Cost Concepts for Setting Access Rates

Access prices should be based on true economic costs. In most countries, it is difficult to estimate the economic costs of providing telecommunications services—including access services.[1] This is so for many reasons. First, there is no reason to believe that the costs as reported by the government-owned incumbent telecommunications monopolist in any way approach an efficient level. It is more likely than not that the incumbent has not been operating efficiently. And there is no reason to believe that its embedded technology is the proper measure of forward-looking costs (that is, costs that will be incurred as the network is built using the currently available technology). Second, in previously planned economies in transition to the market, accounting costs are often fictional inasmuch as they reflect nonmarket-determined valuations of inputs.

These difficulties in estimating the pertinent levels of cost obviously constrain the degree of precision with which access prices can reflect underlying costs. However, these difficulties should not cause the regulator to set the rates in a haphazard manner or in a manner that pays only lip service to the requirement that rates be efficient. Given that much of the technology used in providing

[1] In fact, such costs are generally difficult to estimate, as is evidenced by the ongoing debate in the United States following the passage of the Telecommunications Act of 1996.

access is available on world telecommunications equipment markets, some cost elements of providing access should not differ greatly from country to country. Consequently, regulators should rely on international benchmarks for determining the (forward-looking) costs of providing access services (principle 6–1). The pertinent costs should be forward-looking in the sense that they ought not reflect the distorted current accounting measures, but, instead, should reflect the costs as they likely will be incurred in the future as telecommunications networks are built in a cost-efficient manner.

Principle 6-1. *Regulators should utilize world cost benchmarks (appropriately modified to reflect specific domestic conditions) that reflect forward-looking costs rather than historic costs as reported by the incumbent telecommunications service provider.*

What types of costs does the regulator have to know in order to implement a rational, pro-competitive access regime? It is important to remember that whether access prices are calculated using a bottom-up or top-down methodology, much of the same cost information is necessary.

In a competitive market, prices tend toward (long-run) marginal costs. Since regulation should mimic the workings of a competitive market, the policy prescription is that access should be priced at the level of long-run marginal cost. Assume that it costs 0.05 cents to provide one incremental unit of access (say, one minute). If access were priced at less than marginal cost (that is, less than 0.05 cents per minute), its usage would be over-stimulated (other things equal) relative to the efficient level. Note that the marginal benefit from this additional minute of access would (approximately) equal the price of access, but the social cost of additional access would be less than that. Conversely, the provision of access would be repressed below the socially efficient level if access were priced at more than 0.05 cents. Ideally, long-run marginal cost is the (first-best) efficient level of the access price (principle 6-2).

Principle 6-2. *Access should be priced based on long-run incremental costs of provision.*

However, even if we set aside the fact that the regulator may lack precise knowledge of the long-run marginal costs of access, there are other reasons why pricing access at marginal cost may not be feasible (or even desirable). Provision of access might entail significant fixed costs. Fixed costs are those types of costs that do not vary with the amount of access provided. For example, the cost of the switch is not sensitive to the volume of switching that it actually performs. The cost of the switch depends on the number of loops that are attached to it. Costs of local transport—that is, transport between local wire centers—or transport between the point-of-presence of the long-distance carrier and a local switch are also likely to be insensitive to usage (at least on the margin). Principle 6-3 addresses these issues.

> ***Principle 6-3.*** *The regulator needs to be familiar with the underlying technologies and the pertinent costs as a precondition for setting economically rational access rates.*

In referring to the fixed costs of providing access, we do not mean the costs associated with installing and maintaining a loop (a pair of copper wires) that connects the end user to the switch (or to some point between the customer's premises and the switch). These costs should in principle be recovered from the customers by means of installation fees and monthly line charges. In many countries, revenue from these charges together with (local) usage fees generated by customers do not recover the full costs of the loop. This situation has policy relevance for pricing access.

When there are significant fixed costs, marginal cost pricing of access need not generate enough revenue to recover the full costs of providing access.[2] The presence of fixed costs can create scale economies in the provision of access. In this case, marginal cost pricing is not feasible because it generates revenue that does not cover the associated total costs (principle 6-4).[3]

> ***Principle 6-4.*** *When there are scale economies in the provision of access (or any other service), marginal cost pricing is not feasible. In such a case, the prices of some services sold by the access provider must deviate from the pertinent marginal costs.[4] That is, if access is priced at marginal cost, the prices of some other services must be set above marginal cost.*

The total amount of costs that can be directly attributed to any service, in particular, the provision of access, is termed the total long-run incremental cost (LRIC).[5] It seems a reasonable requirement that revenue from the provision of access (or any other service) should at least cover the LRIC of access or any

---

[2] This revenue includes implicit revenue that the vertically integrated telecommunications service vendor charges itself for access. Of course, a vertically integrated vendor does not charge itself for access. However, these implicit charges (and the concomitant revenue) can be calculated using observable data.

[3] See Baumol and Sidak (1994).

[4] We do not advocate that the revenue shortfalls be covered by general subsidies from the budget. In any case, such subsidies will not be politically sustainable once the incumbent monopoly telecommunications service provider is privatized.

[5] For example, the monthly flow of costs directly attributable to usage could be LRIC = \$1 million + (\$0.0005) x (#access minutes).

other service (principle 6-5). The rationale for this requirement is that if access revenue did not cover the LRIC of access, then the vendor would run a deficit that would have to be made up from the other services it sells. Those services would have to be priced above levels that would be required if access covered its own direct costs. Such a situation would not be tenable in the long run if the vendor faced effective competition in the provision of the overpriced services. Rivals who were not burdened with the need to subsidize access could charge lower prices and steal the vendor's business. It also follows that if the regulator desired to subsidize access, it would have to either find some other source of subsidy or prevent competition from undercutting the access provider.

> ***Principle 6-5.*** *The revenue from access (including the implicit revenue that the access provider charges itself) should at least cover the total long-run incremental cost.*

However, revenue from access should not be excessive relative to the cost of providing access (principle 6-6). The stand-alone cost of access provides a correct revenue ceiling.[6] Stand-alone cost is defined as the cost that would be incurred by a vendor that provides only access service. By definition, it includes both the direct costs as measured by the LRIC and all the other costs that cannot be directly attributed to any other services offered by the vendor. Hence, by definition, stand-alone cost cannot be lower than the LRIC as long as there are *scope economies* in the provision of access and other telecommunications services.[7] By the same reasoning as before, if the vendor were to earn in revenue more than the stand-alone cost of providing access in a liberalized telecommunications market, another vendor could come in and under-price the incumbent.

> ***Principle 6-6.*** *The revenue from access (including the implicit revenue that the access provider imputes to itself) should not exceed the stand-alone cost of providing access.*

We have now presented the various cost concepts that are pertinent to the process of setting access rates. To sum up our discussion so far, access rates should be set in such a manner that revenue from access should not fall below the LRIC floor or exceed the stand-alone cost ceiling. If rates (hence revenue) are outside of these bounds, it means that full competition in the provision of access and other telecommunications services is impeded either by government regulation or by some other entry barriers.

---

[6] Of course, the stand-alone cost can be calculated for any service, not only access.

[7] It is not likely that there should be diseconomies of scope because provision of access does not impinge negatively on the technological ability of the firm to provide other telecommunications services.

Pricing Principles in the Presence of Scale Economies

We now proceed to a more detailed analysis of pricing principles when there are significant scale economies (that is, declining average costs) in the provision of access. When there are scale economies, setting prices equal to marginal (or incremental) cost does not generate enough revenue to cover the vendor's full costs of its operations. Consequently, prices have to diverge from marginal (incremental) costs. The extent of such divergence is determined by the extent of the revenue shortfall. In any case, since prices in excess of marginal costs distort usage levels away from efficient levels, the regulator ought to keep the aggregate economic cost of these distortions to the minimum.

The regulator can employ several strategies. It can allow the vendor to implement more sophisticated pricing schemes, such as two-part tariffs.[8] A two-part tariff is a pricing scheme whereby the purchaser of access pays a (monthly or quarterly) fixed fee that does not depend on the volume of access (as measured in minutes of switched access, for example) and a variable fee that depends on volume. This pricing scheme reduces the inefficiencies from nonmarginal cost pricing by bringing the usage price closer to the pertinent marginal cost. This stimulates usage and thereby improves allocative efficiency. However, if the fixed fee is the same for all potential buyers of access, some potential purchasers—especially the smaller ones—might be unable to afford the fee. This would foreclose them from the market(s) in which they intended to participate. Thus, the fixed fee would diminish competition and reduce allocative efficiency. Hence, we have principle 6-7.

> ***Principle 6-7.*** *Sophisticated pricing schemes (such as two-part tariffs) can alleviate the inefficiencies caused by the need to price access above the marginal cost, but generally cannot solve all the inefficiencies engendered by such departures from marginal cost pricing.*

Besides two-part tariffs, the regulator could also approve (or recommend) volume discounts, whereby the usage charge varies with the amount of access purchased. Again, this pricing scheme reduces the unavoidable distortions, but, of course, cannot eliminate all of them. The discussion thus far leads to an important point, principle 6-8.

> ***Principle 6-8.*** *In the event that marginal cost pricing of access is not feasible, the regulator should consider more complex pricing schemes in order to ameliorate the inefficiencies caused by deviations from marginal costs.*

---

[8] See Laffont and Tirole (2000).

We consider this an important point for two reasons. First, some countries might lack familiarity with more sophisticated pricing mechanisms. Lack of familiarity could create suspicions as to the motives behind such pricing, especially when proposed by a concessionaire whose goal is to maximize profits. Second, in some countries, sophisticated pricing schemes could be viewed as evidence of dominance and its abuse. While it is true that only firms with some market power can deploy complex pricing schemes, it does not follow that such pricing is tantamount to abuse of dominance.[9] This is especially true if the regulator constrains the overall earnings of the provider (either through price caps or some other regulatory mechanism).

So far, we have implicitly assumed that "access" is required by all users to produce the same final service, such as long-distance calling or data transport. This is not the case in reality. Access is required by vendors selling rather distinct products, such as long-distance, international, or local calls; data transmission; mobile services; and a host of other end-user telecommunications services. However, to the provider of access, "access" is a homogeneous product whose marginal cost is the same irrespective of the identity of the buyer. It costs the same amount to provide one minute of switched access to an international carrier as it does to a long-distance carrier or to a switched data vendor. This raises the question of whether access should be priced equally for all buyers. The answer would be "yes" if marginal cost pricing were feasible. If marginal cost pricing were not possible, then economic theory suggests that the answer would be negative. Economic theory suggests that different users may pay different rates for access depending on the service they provide (principle 6-9).

> ***Principle 6-9.*** *When there are significant fixed costs in the provision of access, differential pricing of access to different user groups could be in the public interest.*

The extent to which different users may be required to pay different rates is determined by the differences in their (derived) demand elasticities for access (principle 6-10).[10] Those buyers of access who have low derived demand elasticity may end up paying more for access compared with those buyers whose demand for access is more elastic.

---

[9] By definition, any firm that faces less than perfectly elastic demand for its service has some market power.

[10] Two forces determine the extent of derived elasticity of demand for access by any particular user. First is the ability to substitute away from buying access from the incumbent access provider to some other sources (such as bypass). Second is the elasticity of demand for the end-user service itself. For the (derived) demand elasticity to be low, both of these forces have to be weak. That is, both the demand elasticity must be low and the substitution elasticity must be small.

Principle 6-10. *Roughly speaking, prices for access charged to different classes of buyers should be inversely proportional to the buyers' elasticity of demand for access.*

Several comments on principle 6-10 are in order. First, in many countries, there is already discrimination in the pricing of access. In particular, operators of local networks charge each other different rates for completing local calls on their networks compared with what they charge third parties for completing a long-distance call. That is, one-way access rates are different from two-way access rates. Second, although in many countries price discrimination could be challenged as abuse of dominance, regulators should be sensitive to the fact that price discrimination may be a necessary evil.

Third, having said that, we note that there are sound public policy reasons to insist on uniform rates for access for all classes of users (principle 6-11). It is quite plausible that—for one reason or another—inelastic users may be especially valuable to the society. Then the application of the inverse elasticity rule stated in principle 6-10 does not lead to the socially most desirable outcome. In addition, price discrimination creates incentives for its avoidance. There are social costs associated with such avoidance that need to be reflected in the assessment of feasible price discrimination.[11] The regulator (and the provider) will likely not know the requisite elasticities precisely. As a result, there will arise errors in the calculations of optimal rates for access. The more severe these errors, the less desirable the price discrimination.

Principle 6-11. *Although discriminatory pricing of access is in theory socially optimal (in the sense that it reduces the social cost of nonmarginal cost pricing), in practice there are sound public policy reasons why uniform pricing of access to all users is likely to be the most prudent public policy.*

The Implications of Scope Economies for Pricing: The Ramsey Pricing Rule

Here we focus on general implications for pricing that arise in the presence of joint and common (network) costs. When there are scope economies, the prices charged by the vendor must recover not only the fixed costs that can be directly attributed to any particular service, but also fixed costs that are joint and common

[11] A great deal of evidence from telecommunications markets indicates that service providers are quite skilled in getting around market price distortions. Services such as call-back, hubbing, and others aim to reduce the costs of international calls, which are significantly above marginal cost. In the future, voice and data calls will be most likely indistinguishable. The growing presence of Internet and cellular telephone service also puts severe limits on the extent of sustainable market distortions.

to several services (we call them network costs). Among experts on the costing of telecommunications networks, there is no agreement yet about whether these joint and common costs are significant or whether most of the costs can in fact be attributed to individual services.

We assume that joint and common costs exist and consider the implications for the pricing of services (including access). Building on our discussion in the preceding section, we observe that the presence of such fixed costs requires that all prices be marked up above marginal costs. And, in principle, revenue from each and every service offered by the firm should exceed the LRIC of that service.[12] The rule for marking up services (including access) above marginal costs is summarized in principle 6-12.

> ***Principle 6-12*** *(Ramsey optimal pricing rule). Prices should be marked up above the corresponding marginal cost in an inverse relationship to the corresponding elasticities of demand. That is, services that have inelastic demand should be marked up by more in percentage terms than services that have elastic demand.*

Some general conclusions follow from principle 6-12. First, this rule applies to all the services offered by the incumbent, including access that the incumbent sells to third parties. Second, the access price derived from the application of the Ramsey (or "inverse elasticity") rule is generally sufficiently high to contribute to the recovery of the fixed (network) costs incurred by the incumbent provider of access. From this, it follows that a buyer of access cannot justifiably complain to the regulator (or to the court) that the incumbent is exercising market power (or abusing its dominant position) in the provision of access merely because the incumbent sets the access charge above the long-run marginal cost (or even the LRIC) of providing access (principle 6-13).[13]

> ***Principle 6-13.*** *When there are (significant) network joint and common costs, pricing access above LRIC does not constitute abuse of market power and should not be prohibited either by the regulator or by the courts.*

The third implication from the Ramsey pricing principles is that when new entry occurs, the entrant will be required to contribute to the recovery of network

---

[12] The more precise statement is that each price should exceed the corresponding product's marginal cost. However, if there are no impediments to entry, then each price should exceed the product's average direct cost.

[13] In some countries, access rates are determined through arms' length negotiations between the parties, subject only to scrutiny under the antitrust rules. The mere fact that the incumbent refuses to sell access "at cost" should not be the basis for a valid antitrust complaint.

costs. This is for two reasons. First, the entrant is likely to divert sales from the incumbent. To the extent that those sales contributed to the recovery of the network costs, the incumbent would suffer a revenue shortfall and might be forced to raise prices on which there is no competitive pressure. Second, even if the new entrant does not divert sales from the incumbent (because it offers a brand-new service), the ability to sell access to the entrant relieves some of the pressures on the incumbent to cover all of the network costs from the mark-ups on preexisting services.

These observations still leave open the question of the magnitude of the markup on access that the incumbent can justifiably levy. Economists have advanced two distinct approaches to this issue, the bottom-up approach, which invokes the Ramsey pricing principles, and the top-down approach, which utilizes the efficient component pricing rule (ECPR).

Ramsey (Efficient) Access Pricing Rule

The Ramsey pricing rule directs the decisionmaker to set prices by taking into account the pertinent marginal costs, the pertinent demand elasticities, and the tightness of the budget constraint facing the incumbent. With respect to the pertinent marginal costs, we reemphasize the fact that the current costs of the incumbent operator need not be efficient. Thus, care must be exercised in using them for setting efficient prices for access or for any other services.

Consideration of the tightness of the budget constraint basically reflects the fact that the extent to which prices must deviate from the underlying marginal costs depends on the magnitude of the fixed costs. The fixed costs can be divided into two categories: those that can be attributed to a particular service (or a group of services) and those costs that are joint and common to all the services. The magnitudes of the costs in the various cost categories are not known with exact precision. Moreover, the current levels of fixed costs incurred by the operator may be excessive, as compared with efficient, forward-looking levels (principle 6-14).

> ***Principle 6-14.*** *Current rates incurred by the operator are likely to be a poor guide for setting Ramsey prices and determining the tightness of the budget constraint.*

The standard feature of Ramsey pricing has to do with the pertinent demand elasticities (principle 6-15). The novel element that enters into the calculation of efficient access rates is the effect of access fees on the demand for end-user services offered by the incumbent operator. To illustrate, assume that the services offered by the incumbent and by the competitor are substitutes in the eyes of the consumers. For example, assume that both carriers offer long-distance (interurban) service. In this case, an increase in the access fee above marginal cost has three effects. First, it reduces demand for access. Second, it increases revenue from access above the initial point. Third, the novel effect is that the increase stimulates demand for the long-distance service offered by the incumbent, which contributes to the recovery of the fixed costs.

> ***Principle 6-15.*** *When setting efficient access rates, the regulator must account for the effect of the level of the access rate on the demand for the incumbent operator's end-user service(s). In particular, the markup should reflect the fact that the entrant's service can compete with the incumbent's offerings, which reduces the contribution that the incumbent operator earns on the sale of its services.*

Another case arises when the entrant adds a service that does not compete with that of the incumbent operator. In this case, access is just another source of revenue that potentially contributes to the recovery of the fixed costs. It is reasonable that access revenue should be required to make such a contribution and thereby lessen the burden carried by other services (principle 6-16).

> ***Principle 6-16.*** *Even if the entrant's offering does not compete with those of the incumbent, there are sound public policy reasons to burden access rates with some contribution toward the recovery of the fixed costs.*

In general, the optimal access price, *a*, can be expressed by means of a simple formula:[14]

> a = [marginal cost of providing access] + [revenue impact on the incumbent's sales of end-user services from end-user offerings of the competitor] + [contribution from access to the recovery of the network costs].

Although the elements of the formula seem simple enough, the calculation of the terms in the square brackets is far from simple. It is also clear that the incumbent operator and the purchaser of access will have incentives to misrepresent the magnitudes of the effects. For example, the incumbent will overstate the amount of diversion of sales to the rival (hence, the magnitude of lost contribution), and the rival will try to convince the regulator that its product does not compete with that of the incumbent and will only stimulate the use of the network. Similarly, the new entrant will try to argue that its product should

[14] See Armstrong, Doyle, and Vickers (1996).

not contribute significantly to the recovery of fixed costs, either because these are small in any case or because, as a new entrant, it is already at a competitive disadvantage vis-à-vis the incumbent.

Global Price Caps

The application of the Ramsey principles developed in the preceding sections leads to the so-called *global price cap* rule for pricing access. Under that rule, the regulator sets all the rates including access at the (Ramsey) efficient level and then determines the appropriate permissible price increases for every basket of services, including access, as well as for the total basket of services offered by the operator.[15]

An important point to bear in mind here is that it is necessary to "start" the price caps using proper exogenous weights in the formula for calculating the average price (principle 6-17).[16] In particular, these weights must be proportional to the level of output that would be realized if Ramsey prices were set initially. Otherwise, the operator will not be given the right incentive to set the efficient level of prices, including the access price. In this respect, global price caps are no different from other price caps. If the regulator does not start the price cap regime with appropriate weights, there is no assurance that the actual price path will ultimately converge to efficient prices.

> ***Principle 6-17.*** *For the global price cap regulation to implement efficient prices (including the price of access), it must assign proper weights to the services included in the cap.*

In some countries, the problem of choosing the proper weights is made rather complicated by the fact that the level of penetration of telecommunications services is low. Consequently, the assessment of the correct weights in the formula may require a good deal of guessing. Moreover, current prices are totally distorted so that current consumption levels of telecommunications services are very poor indicators of future levels.

The problem of selecting the correct weights in the formula is also exacerbated in the case of global price caps because the calculation of the global price cap requires that the regulator estimate the likely future sales of the new

---

[15] That is, the regulator develops the appropriate CPI (consumer price index) for each basket of services and for the total basket of services.

[16] If there are two services plus access, the global price cap formula is $(w_1)(p_1) + (w_2)(p_2) + (w_3)(a) \leq p^*$, where the w's are weights for the services, including access, sold by the incumbent, and a is the price of access.

entrants. (This is because access revenue enters into the price cap formula.) This is not a trivial undertaking, especially because the level of sales could be affected by the strategic behavior of the incumbent operator. Indeed, the incumbent operator may have an incentive to manipulate the access price during the transition to disadvantage its rivals. However, principle 6-18 indicates that the opposite effect may result.

> ***Principle 6-18.*** *The application of the global price cap regime lessens the incentives for the incumbent to discriminate against its rivals because the global price cap enables the incumbent to earn some portion of the monopoly profit from selling access.*[17]

In general, the more constrained is the access price toward cost, the stronger is the incentive for the incumbent to exclude rivals (or disadvantage them in competitive downstream markets).

In sum, the global price cap rule offers an attractive policy mechanism for setting access prices. However, it may be informationally too demanding in countries with poorly developed telecommunications. It is also a rather sophisticated regulatory rule that requires careful revisions in the event that the initial weights are not chosen optimally at the start. The value of the rule is especially obvious when it comes to pricing access for services that do not compete with the services of the incumbent. Although we have argued that "access is access" so that uniform access fees may be an appropriate policy to follow, it is also plausible that an exception can be made for services that do not compete (or compete only very weakly) with those of the incumbent (principle 6-19).

> ***Principle 6-19.*** *For services that do not compete with the services of the incumbent operator, the incumbent should be free to select any access fee it wishes, subject only to the global price cap constraint. That is, the revenue that the incumbent earns from selling access to noncompeting users will be debited against the revenue earned elsewhere. The result will be that the operator will be forced to lower prices on these other services in order not to violate the global cap.*

The bottom-up approach to setting access fees starts with the LRIC for access and builds on additives that reflect the need to cover the operator's revenue deficit. The deficit would be realized by the operator if it were to charge

---

[17] In fact, if the incumbent operator earns the same profit by selling access as by selling its final product that competes with the product of the rival, the incumbent's incentive to increase the costs of its rival disappears. See Ordover and Willig (1981).

marginal cost prices for all of its services. This approach leads to markups over pertinent incremental costs that reflect both the demand-side considerations (through various elasticities) as well as the size of the deficit that needs to be recovered. It is essential to recognize that whatever surpluses or (more likely) deficits the operator is running (or was running) before privatization and liberalization are largely irrelevant to these considerations. These surpluses (or deficits) likely do not reflect the types of considerations that enter into the construction of efficient prices. Of course, the big problem facing the regulator is that the current prices are frequently vastly distorted, which makes it especially important that prices be rebalanced as much as possible prior to liberalization.

The Efficient Component Pricing Rule

An alternative approach to setting access rates starts with the vector of rates charged by the incumbent operator and recovers from these end-user prices the implicit rates that the operator charges itself for access. This is the top-down approach that some countries have used, most notably New Zealand. The United States uses this approach for setting wholesale rates.[18]

Principle 6-20 states the efficient component pricing rule (ECPR).

> ***Principle 6-20.*** *The access price charged by the incumbent to a rival on a competitive segment should not exceed the opportunity cost to the operator from forgoing the sale of the competitive service.*

The only novel concept in this principle is the notion of the opportunity cost. This can be defined as the amount of net revenue that the incumbent loses as a result of selling one unit of access to the rival operator. To illustrate, assume that one minute of a long-distance call sells for 10 cents. Assume that the incumbent incurs a cost of three cents in producing one unit of long distance, excluding the cost of providing access (that is, originating and completing the long-distance call). Then, if the incumbent loses one minute of long-distance sales to the rival, it loses seven cents in contribution (or gross revenue). To the incumbent operator, seven cents is the opportunity cost of providing access to the rival. It is important to note that the cost of providing access does not enter into this calculation. This is because the operator has to incur that cost regardless of whether it sells the final product (one minute of long distance) or whether it sells access to the rival who then sells the final product. This leads to principle 6-21.

---

[18] Following the passage of the U.S. Telecommunications Act of 1996, incumbent local exchange carriers are required to sell at wholesale local exchange service to new entrants who can resell these services to final consumers.

> ***Principle 6-21.*** *Under the ECPR, the access price should not exceed the direct cost of providing access plus the opportunity cost of providing access.*

This access pricing rule ensures nondiscriminatory treatment of the rival by the incumbent operator. Indeed, since the operator recovers the full opportunity cost of providing access to the rival, in principle it should be indifferent between selling one unit of a final service itself or selling the necessary input to the rival. The ECPR provides a meaningful test of whether the incumbent is engaging in rate discrimination against the rival.

The regulator first *derives* the level of the opportunity cost from the price and cost information that pertains to the incumbent's operations. This is calculated as the margin that the operator earns on the end-user service in question. In the second step, the test considers whether the incumbent *imputes* to itself the same access charge as it charges the rival. If the access charge is set higher than the imputed charge that the operator sets for itself, then we have *prima facie* evidence of discrimination (principle 6-22).

> ***Principle 6-22.*** *If the operator charges itself less for the provision of access than it does another operator, there is a presumption of price discrimination. The operator now has the burden of proving why it should charge itself a lower access charge than it charges the other operator.*

To rebut this presumption, the incumbent must offer a convincing demonstration that the cost of providing access to the rival is significantly higher than the cost of serving itself. Although there may be reasons why this is so, the regulator (or the court) should not accept such cost evidence without thorough examination. For example, one reason why such a cost differential could arise may be because the incumbent's network and operation support systems are not equipped to serve a rival. This creates a serious public policy issue regarding whether entrants should be burdened with the costs of equipping the incumbent for a liberalized marketplace. Whatever the outcome of the public policy debate, it should clarify the incumbent operator's cost burden. Ideally, this type of information should be provided at the time of the concession bid.

Although there are legitimate reasons why the incumbent may be required to charge the other firm more for the provision of access, there are also reasons why a lower charge may be appropriate. For example, if the new entrant offers a service that does not compete with the current offerings of the incumbent, the opportunity cost to the incumbent is zero. In such a case, the ECPR would set the access fee just at the level of the direct cost of providing access (principle 6-23).[19]

[19] Recall that the bottom-up Ramsey pricing approach would set the fee at a higher level to reflect the fact that the access fee should be used to relieve some of the budget constraint facing the incumbent operator.

Principle 6-23. *When the entrant's service is an imperfect substitute for the service(s) of the incumbent, the opportunity cost component of the access fee should be reduced to less than the net revenue that the incumbent earns on the service that is the closest substitute for that of the rival.*[20]

The application of principle 6-23 offers a realistic upper bound on the opportunity cost additive that can be charged by the incumbent to the new entrant. Of course, as we noted before, the extent to which the entrant's new service competes (or will likely compete) with that of the incumbent is not easy to determine. Perhaps some pertinent information can be gained by analyzing competitive interactions in other countries. The relevant information can also be revealed through the burden-shifting procedure of setting the level of the access fee in the top-down procedure.

In particular, we suggest that such a procedure can be implemented in a situation where the level of the access fee is fixed by means of arms' length negotiations between two parties, subject to some sort of judicial oversight. During the negotiations, each party would have a shifting burden to demonstrate the appropriate level of the opportunity cost additive. The default rate could be set at the dollar-for-dollar amount, which would be appropriate if the new entrant were proposing to offer a service that (in broad terms) looks like the current offering of the incumbent. For example, if the entrant proposes to compete with the incumbent in the provision of long-distance service, the starting point for the negotiations could be a dollar-for-dollar additive. Then the entrant could offer evidence why a lower additive should be appropriate (for example, because of imperfect substitutability or demand stimulation). In turn, the burden would shift to the incumbent to explain why the reduction would be inappropriate. There is no reason why such a process could not be readily implemented in most countries.

We should comment also on the fact that some economic models of access indicate that the opportunity cost component of the access fee should be further adjusted for the ability of the entrant to substitute away (to another input).[21] In

---

[20] To illustrate, assume that the incumbent offers five different end-user services. Assume that the entrant's service is most competitive with service #2. By this we mean that the cross elasticity of demand between the service of the incumbent and the price charged by the entrant is the highest for service #2. Cross elasticity is defined as the percentage change in demand for a particular service of the incumbent when the entrant changes its price by 1 percent. Often, the evidence on cross elasticities will not be precisely available. However, the fact-finder may be able to determine which of the products is the closest substitute for what the entrant proposes to offer.

Continuing with the example, the opportunity cost additive should be bound by the difference ($P_2 - C_2$), which is the margin that the incumbent earns on service #2. In this expression, C_2 is the cost that the incumbent would save if it were to reduce by one unit its supply of service #2.

[21] Note that if the price that the incumbent charges to end users makes a contribution to the recovery of joint and common costs, the access fee calculated using this price as a starting point will also make such a contribution. The point is that under the ECPR, wholesale services (such as access) do not make a different level of contribution than does the incumbent's own service.

addition, these models indicate that the fee could be adjusted to reflect the degree of post-entry competition between the incumbent and the entrant. With respect to the first adjustment, we suggest that the parties themselves should in principle have the correct incentives to ensure that the entrant does not substitute away to the less efficient input. Since both parties gain from using the most efficient access mode, there are strong private reasons to ensure that the efficient arrangement will be implemented.

The second adjustment is more difficult to implement. Clearly, the intensity of ex-post competition cannot be determined before entry occurs. Moreover, since the intensity of competition will likely change over time, there is no obvious benchmark for making the appropriate choice when the level of the additive is determined for the first time. Principle 6-24 addresses this issue.

> ***Principle 6-24.*** *As under the global price cap regime, the regulator should be required to review the level of the opportunity cost additive after some pre-specified period of time. Alternatively, if the fee is negotiated between the parties, the provisions for renegotiations should be explicitly built into the contract. Moreover, the parties should have access to the courts to reopen the contract.*

In sum, the top-down approach using the principles of the ECPR is well suited to the private negotiations for access. The bottom-up approach, with its concomitant adjustments to overhead recovery, is better implemented in a full-blown regulatory setting. Indeed, there is no obvious way to implement the various adjustments required by the Ramsey pricing mechanism in the private negotiations. We note also that the ECPR provides a useful test for ensuring that the incumbent does not abuse the global price cap mechanism during the transition phase.

Efficiency of Entry

We did not consider in the analysis of rules for access fees the desirability of entry (principle 6-25). We assumed that entry was in the social interest and that the public policy concern was to ensure that the entrant could compete on a fair footing with the incumbent. Indeed, the ECPR ensures that the entrant who is at least as efficient as the incumbent in the provision of the retail (end-user) service can compete with the incumbent. This is true provided, of course, that the entrant has already expanded the costs necessary to enter the provision of the retail service. In a sense, then, the ECPR ensures that on the margin the (more) efficient firm will provide the service. That is, if the entrant can pay a compensatory access fee (direct cost plus opportunity cost) and still take the business away from the incumbent, then the efficiency criterion is satisfied. The same problem plagues the Ramsey pricing approach: the standard models seem to assume that the entrant has no fixed costs. If there are fixed costs, welfare optimization needs to account for them.

> ***Principle 6-25.*** *Entry may not be socially desirable, counting the fixed costs of entry and the fact that the incumbent already invested in the sunk costs. Duplication of facilities has its social costs.*

Entry and the threat of entry are the most potent economic mechanisms for inducing efficient behavior by the incumbent and for lessening the grip that the incumbent may have over the political-regulatory regime. Consequently, even if entry may result in some duplication of facilities and even if it may result in stranding some of the incumbent's assets, public policy should be biased–if only mildly–toward favoring entry rather than discouraging it.

The danger here is that the incumbent could be a recently privatized, former state-owned monopolist with significant foreign participation. The presence of foreign capital could encourage the policy of (partial) expropriation through entry. Such temptations ought to be discouraged because they lead to strong disincentives for future participation of foreign capital in the process of economic transformation. Such participation is especially important in network industries (see Ordover and Uribe 1999).

This analysis does not fully address the question of the level at which entry should be allowed or promoted, or which types of technologies should be encouraged. It may sound circular and obvious, but as a rule public policy should promote competition in those segments of the network where competition is, in fact, viable. The temptation to create parallel networks early in the development process should be avoided. Instead, entry should be directed toward those parts of the network where scale and scope economies are small (relative to demand), where the incumbent's presence is not well established, and where new technologies can trump the entrenched position of the incumbent. In all instances, it is important to ensure that at least the rudiments of an access regime are in place.

For example, if entry is allowed into local telecommunications markets, such entry would waste social resources in the absence of an interconnection agreement. Still, we often see in countries in transition that entry into local telecommunications is promoted because penetration rates are low and the government seeks sources of capital other than the incumbent to finance development. As we mentioned, this should not be a source of concern as long as interconnection rules are in place. However, regard must be paid to the fact that such entry could frustrate the reasonable business plans of the incumbent. For example, its investment in switches and local transport facilities could have been based on expectations of exclusivity. This creates the problem of stranded investments. ECPR rules can be deployed to compensate the incumbent not only for the sales actually diverted (as in the standard setting), but also for sales that it would have made but for entry.

Additional Considerations in Designing Access Pricing Rules

Our discussion thus far has focused on rather streamlined models of access pricing. Even in these simple situations, there are many considerations that impinge on the design and choice of the rule for pricing access. In reality, the regulator/ policymaker must deal with many additional considerations that further complicate the assessment and selection of access pricing rules.

Nonlinear Pricing of End-User Services

In network industries characterized by significant fixed costs and diversity of consumers, linear pricing is in general not optimal.[22] That is, the service provider can do better (in terms of profits and overall social welfare) if it deploys sophisticated pricing schemes. For example, the service provider can offer volume discounts whereby the marginal (or average) price falls with the volume of purchases. The service provider can also offer a variety (menu) of purchase plans for the service in question. For example, Plan 1 might offer the consumer a low fee for the right to access the network and a high price for usage and Plan 2 might offer a high fee for accessing the network and a very low fee for usage. Offering such a menu of choices—with many intermediate versions—will be optimal when consumers have variegated tastes for the service in question (public policy prescription 6-1).[23]

> ***Public policy prescription 6-1.*** *Differentiated access fees are necessary if the regulator wants to implement differential pricing for the final service to consumers. Differentiated pricing is welfare-desirable when consumers have variegated tastes and marginal cost pricing is not feasible.*

To make matters concrete, assume that the vendor offers two plans $[P_1{:}\{F_1, r_1\}, P_2{:}\{F_2, r_2\}]$, where plan P_1 entails a higher entry fee, F_1, than plan P_2, and $r_1 < r_2$ is per unit price.[24] Under the simple interpretation of the ECPR, the access fee paid by the entrant could be either $a_1 = r_1 - m$ or $a_2 = r_2 - m$, where m is the

---

[22] Linear pricing entails charging a consumer the same price irrespective of the volume of purchases.

[23] We can write $v(q,t)$ to denote the willingness to pay by consumer of type t for q units of service. The type reflects the consumer's taste for service or income.

[24] Where the unit of service could be a telephone call or an impulse.

marginal cost of the (potentially) competitive service. It is easy to see that if the entrant's access fee is set at a_1, the entrant cannot compete for consumers choosing P_2. On the other hand, if the fee is set at a_2, it is now the incumbent that cannot compete against the entrant for customers who choose P_2.

Thus, either ECPR-based fee causes the sophisticated pricing scheme to unravel. In fact, the scheme will also unravel if the fee is cost-based (that is, based on the LRIC). The problem stems not from the basis for the fee, but, rather, from the fact that entrants are offered a single access fee while the opportunity cost to the incumbent depends on which customer switches to the entrant—whether it is a customer selecting P_1 or P_2. Indeed, this is an issue that is familiar in the U.S. long-distance telecommunications market. In the United States, facilities-based carriers (such as AT&T or Sprint) sell wholesale long-distance minutes to resellers. Basically, the facilities-based long-distance carriers sell access to their networks at rates that are below retail rates. Resellers are then in a position to arbitrage against the sophisticated tariff schemes deployed by the underlying carriers, thereby making these schemes less feasible.

Getting back to our problem, we note that a sophisticated version of the ECPR would reflect the fact that the incumbent's opportunity cost that is pertinent to the derivation of the access price is the cost of losing a particular customer. The opportunity cost of losing a marginal unit of demand for a competitive service (such as a minute of long-distance calling or a kWh of energy) varies with the customer. The entrant should be presented with a different fee depending on which customer it diverts from the incumbent. Note also that a cost-based access fee cannot be made to vary with the customer unless it is augmented by additives such as those described above (which, in essence, transform the LRIC access fee into an ECPR-based access fee). In addition, in principle, the Ramsey access fee scheme can also be made to depend on the customer served.[25]

In sum, the problem facing the policymaker stems from downstream price discrimination. If the policymaker wants to replicate such price discrimination in a competitive regime, it cannot do so with a single access price for offer to the entrant. However, if the policymaker is not convinced (as much as we are) of the social benefits deriving from complex pricing schemes, the concern discussed here may not be that relevant. In addition, in many countries, the information available to the incumbent monopolist that is necessary to implement such pricing schemes may not be available in the first place, in which case the issue will be moot.

---

[25] If there is a continuum of customers with different tastes, then the incumbent should offer a continuum of two-part tariffs. Each customer would self-select the optimal tariff. This means that the entrant would in effect end up paying a different access fee depending on which customer it captures.

Peak and Off-Peak Pricing

Demand for a service may differ also by the time of day (morning/evening) and by season (summer/winter). In this case, like in the case discussed above, it may be necessary to vary the access fee to the network to reflect these demand shifters. There are additional considerations that affect the setting of rates in these types of situations.

We start with a very stripped-down, peak/off-peak model of the electricity industry. We assume the relevant network is the transmission grid for the provision of electric power. We assume that the cost of building a unit of transmission capacity is r. Once capacity is built, it costs nothing to transmit power over the grid up to capacity. Generation has a constant short-run and long-run marginal cost of g, whether it is used for base load or peaking usage. We also assume that demands are independent so that there is no shifting peak as a function of electricity prices.

With these assumptions, we obtain efficient unit prices for electricity as $p^L = g$ and $p^H = r + g$, where p^L is off-peak and p^H is a peak price, in the event that all the demand is satisfied by the incumbent. Clearly, if the access fee were set at zero (consistent with off-peak margin), then the entrant would divert all the business from the incumbent during the peak period (by charging a price lower than p^H). This, in turn, would impose a strain on the network with a capacity chosen to serve the efficient level of demand. Moreover, the entrant would be able to gain sales even if its unit generation costs were higher than those of the incumbent. Alternatively, if the fee were set at $(p^H - g_I)$, then an efficient entrant would not be able to serve off-peak demand. This leads to our public policy prescription 6-2.

> ***Public policy prescription 6-2.*** *Different access fees should be set for peak and off-peak periods in order to induce efficient use of the network. All other things equal, the peak access fee should be higher than the off-peak access fee.*

In this example, we assumed that peak and off-peak periods are independent of each other. Often consumers can (imperfectly) substitute consumption between periods. In such a case, the level of the access fee can affect the distribution of demand between the periods. Using the same example, if the entrant has low generation costs, it can reduce the off-peak price, stimulate demand during the off-peak period, and divert some demand from the peak period. The result might be that the incumbent would be stranded with excess capacity at the peak period although it has been charging efficiently for peak usage.

Alternatively, if the entrant lowers the peak price because its operating costs are lower, then it will impose additional demand on transmission both from stimulated peak demand and diverted off-peak demand. Stimulated demand lowers quality (brownouts, more blocked calls) and creates consumer dissatisfaction, which undermines support for opening markets to competition (public policy prescription 6-3).[26] Note, however, that if the incumbent receives access price $a^H = r$ during the peak period (as calculated before), it should have the correct incentive to expand the size of the network to accommodate the stimulated demand. Over the long term, this should alleviate the capacity constraint. The obvious problem occurs during the transition period from monopoly to competition. The extent of the problem depends on the level of congestion in the network before competition opens up.[27] It also depends on how immune the incumbent is to incentives to expand the network.

> ***Public policy prescription 6-3.*** *The regulator should set the peak access fee at a level high enough to induce appropriate investment in the network to accommodate stimulated demand at the peak due to competitive entry. Otherwise, quality will fall and public support for competition will erode. This would be an adverse outcome for transition to a market-based regime. Hence, the access fee should cover (at least) the incremental cost of expanding capacity. However, such a fee is inefficient in the off-peak period.*

Technological Choices for Serving Peak and Off-Peak Demand

We have assumed that serving peak and off-peak demand can be accomplished with identical technology (which can be deployed more efficiently either by the incumbent or by the entrant(s)). In some industries, such as electricity, the reality can be quite different. Hence, the access fee must also drive the correct choice of the technology for serving the two periods (public policy prescription 6-4).

> ***Public policy prescription 6-4.*** *The peak access prices should reflect efficient use of technology (as is the case in all other circumstances).*

To illustrate, assume that base-load demand is 300 MWh and peak demand is 350 MWh with a load duration of four hours a day. Given the data, the generator can choose between a generator of 300 MW capacity and a 50 MW peaker, or a 350 MW generator that will be underutilized for 20 hours a day.[28]

---

[26] In the United States, one still hears the sentiment that the telephone system worked better when AT&T was the monopoly. There have also been concerns with the performance of electricity markets after even limited deregulation. Some commentators have expressed the view that deregulated markets will experience more brownouts and higher prices during peak demand periods.

[27] We are concerned that in many countries moving from (state) monopoly to competition, transmission may be tight (and also inefficient).

[28] This could be power purchased elsewhere.

With these data, it is likely that the incumbent will install a 300 MW generator and the entrant will try to compete for the incremental peak demand. In order to be able to compete, the entrant should be charged an access fee that reflects the net revenue foregone by the incumbent on the incremental peak demand. Obviously, if the calculation reflects only the saved variable cost on the energy that will be replaced by the entrant, the (hourly) access fee is likely to be high (since the peak price also covers the cost of the peaking generating capacity). If the fee reflects the total cost that would be saved if the peaking capacity were removed and sold elsewhere, the fee would be low.

A high fee might discourage entry of an efficient entrant whose technology may be different from that of the incumbent; a low fee might induce entry and strand investment (peaking generating capacity).

Another complication arises when the incumbent and the entrant can select from the menu of technologies with different fixed (base) and variable costs. The total cost is given by

$$\phi(Q;K) = rK + v(K;\, w)Q,\ Q \geq K \text{ and } v' < 0,$$

where r is per unit cost of capacity, K is installed capacity, Q is output, w is a vector of input prices, and $v(.)$ is a function defining variable cost. By moving first and installing the technology, the incumbent may have an incentive to use a very capital-intensive technology with low variable cost. The markup forgone on sales lost to the entrant would be $p - v'$, which may be artificially high and may preclude a less capital-intensive entrant with somewhat higher variable cost. The incumbent could strategically over-invest in order to foreclose entry. In this case, the best guidance for the regulator is to rely on the LRIC as the base for assessing the proper level of the fee. This issue has been debated in the United States following the passage of the Telecommunications Act of 1996, regarding the proper basis for access fees.

Avoided or Avoidable Cost in Setting Access Fees

The discussion above hints at a possible problem when the incumbent cannot immediately shed all the costs. In the example, the incumbent will likely not be able to divest itself of the generating capacity the moment the entrant comes in. In other circumstances, there may even be long-run fixed costs that may be incurred in the provision of the competitive service (that is, service that can be contested in the marketplace). For example, local exchange carriers have argued that they will continue to incur significant costs of providing local calling. Thus, in contrast to the standard model, the competitive service cost is:

$$TC = f + cQ,$$

where f is fixed cost, c is marginal cost, and Q is output. The average cost is $f/Q + c$.[29] Now the issue is how access should be priced when an entrant diverts only a portion of the incumbent's sales. A possible approach is to use the avoided cost standard as advocated by the local exchange carriers in the United States. Under this standard, access would be priced at $(p-c)$, which in principle yields enough in margin for the incumbent to recover the fixed cost (possibly more, but also possibly less). At this price, an entrant who has yet to invest in the provision of the competitive service will likely not be able to earn an adequate return. Note that the entrant's total cost is

$$TC^E = f_E + (c_E + a)Q^E,$$

where E denotes the entrant and a is the access charge. Hence, on the assumption that the entrant captures all of the incumbent's sales, the profit of the entrant is

$$pQ - (f_E + [(c_E - c) + p]Q) < 0$$

if the entrant's variable cost is not significantly lower than that of the incumbent. Thus, even if the entrant's long-run, forward-looking costs are lower for the same volume of output than those of the incumbent, the entrant will not be able to participate in the market.

Alternatively, the access fee could be based on the avoided cost standard in which the entrant pays the fee that reflects long-run savings in cost that would be realized by the incumbent if it were to exit the competitive function and only provided the network function. Thus, under this standard, the access fee would be set at

$$a = p - (f/Q + c).$$

Note that here the fee is sensitive to the pre-entry level of output produced by the incumbent. This is the case because the average cost depends on the scale of output. Constant returns to scale would obviate this problem. This access fee induces the efficient choice of the supplier (that is, the one with the lowest long-run cost), but potentially leaves the incumbent stranded with the amount equal to the fixed cost.

---

[29] We are not implying that this is necessarily a realistic cost function in actual applications. In fact, it is perhaps more plausible to assume that the cost function exhibits constant returns to scale (in the long run).

Conclusions

This chapter has reviewed some important issues in the analysis of access pricing. Although we have provided some answers to the problems facing regulators in countries that have embarked on deregulation of telecommunications (and other network industries), many thorny policy questions remain. Indeed, economic analysis of access issues is one of the most important research topics in regulatory and antitrust economics. From the work thus far, several important regulatory prescriptions emerge.

First, access arrangements should be designed to promote efficiency, including entry of new firms into the segments of the network industry where competition should and can flourish.

Second, access arrangements should not be used to maintain the incumbent's market power.

Third, access arrangements must reflect economic costs to the maximum extent possible. Insofar as there are inefficiencies in the manner that the network is arranged and costed out, the regulator should deal with these inefficiencies separately.

Fourth, if the retail prices charged by the incumbent are distorted for public policy or other reasons, then an efficient access pricing rule must account for these distortions. In particular, if the incumbent is required to cross subsidize some customer groups, then the entrant should also be required to bear the same burden; otherwise, efficiency will not be realized.

Fifth, access prices cannot be expected and should not be relied upon to solve all the industry problems during the process of transition from monopoly to competition. The regulator must deploy a full range of regulatory instruments to guide the transition process toward effectively competitive market arrangements, including rebalancing of retail rates.

Sixth, the access regime should create incentives for the incumbent firm to innovate and to lower its costs.

Seventh, as far as possible, the access regime should rely on voluntary contractual arrangements between the affected parties. The regulator should step in when private negotiations are not likely to be successful or conducive to efficient allocation of scarce economic resources.

These desiderata for an efficient access regime are far from simple or easily satisfied. However, given the importance of the access regime in fostering competition, access rules should be at the center of public policy concerns.

Bibliography

Armstrong, M. Forthcoming. "The Theory of Access Pricing and Interconnection." In M. Cave, S. Majumdar, and I. Vogelsang, eds., *Handbook of Telecommunications Economics*. Amsterdam, Holland: North-Holland.

———. 2001. "Access Pricing, Bypass and Universal Service." *American Economic Review, Paper and Proceedings* (May).

Armstrong, M., C. Doyle, and J. Vickers. 1996. "The Access Pricing Problem: A Synthesis." *Journal of Industrial Economics* 44(2): 131–50.

Baumol, W. J., J. A. Ordover, and R. D. Willig. 1997. "Parity Pricing and Its Critics." *Yale Journal on Regulation* 16(1): 145–164.

Baumol, W. J., and J. G. Sidak. 1994. *Toward Competition in Local Telephony*. Cambridge, MA: MIT Press.

Laffont, J. J., and J. Tirole. 2000. *Competition in Telecommunications*. Cambridge, MA: MIT Press.

Ordover, J. A., and R. D. Willig. 1981. "An Economic Definition of Predation: Pricing and Product Innovation." *Yale Law Journal* 91(1): 8–53.

Sidak, J. G., and D. F. Spulber. 1997. *Deregulatory Takings and the Regulatory Contract*. Cambridge, U.K.: Cambridge University Press.

CHAPTER 7

Efficient Network Access Pricing Rules for Developing and Transition Economies

Jean-Jacques Laffont

The movement for privatization, liberalization, and deregulation extends to developing and transition economies that have reconsidered the former natural monopolies for public services in telecommunications, electricity, gas, and transportation. Parts of these public firms are now viewed as potentially competitive, such as long-distance service in telecommunications and generation in electricity or gas. Other elements—for example, the transmission grid in electricity and the tracks in railways—are still considered natural monopolies and remain regulated.

Management of the interface between the competitive and regulated sectors is crucial for the success of liberalization. The conditions under which competitors can access the regulated sector, which is an essential input for their activities, determine the profitability of entry. These conditions therefore affect the level of competition in the sectors opened to competition as well as the efficient utilization of the natural monopoly elements.

Despite their vital role for the success of liberalization, there are no specific proposals for desirable access-pricing rules for developing economies. This chapter aims to start filling this gap. Some main features of developing countries might call for specific rules. Many developing countries are characterized by the high cost of public funds, poor auditing and monitoring facilities, low transaction costs of corruption, weak counterpowers, weak ability to commit, and inefficient tax systems.[1]

The author thanks Robert Willig for his comments on a first draft.

[1] See Laffont (1996, 1998) for more details on characteristics of developing countries.

The Optimality of the Market Structure

The pricing of interconnection is highly dependent on the market structure. We distinguish three different situations. In case 1, there is vertical disintegration. The firm controlling the bottleneck (the natural monopoly) is not allowed to compete in the provision of services using the bottleneck as an input. In case 2, the firm controlling the bottleneck is one competitor among many providing services that use the bottleneck as an input. In case 3, competition takes place between vertically integrated firms and each firm controls a bottleneck and provides services.

Do the characteristics of developing countries favor a particular market structure? The comparison of cases 1 and 2 rests essentially on a comparison of the economies of scope that vertical integration makes possible and the problems of favoritism it raises. Since the economies of scope are likely to be independent of the characteristics of developing countries (at least for given technologies) and developing countries find it difficult to fight favoritism, there should be a bias toward vertical disintegration in these countries. However, the comparison of cases 2 and 3 rests on a comparison of the fixed costs associated with competition in the provision of the bottleneck and the gains that competition would yield.[2] This comparison is difficult in developing countries, where the high cost of public funds increases the costs of the duplication of fixed costs as well as the information rents of monopolistic provision of the bottleneck.

These comparisons are further complicated by the dynamics of the industry, which may be moving toward case 3, as in the telecommunications industry. Vertical disintegration might in fact slow down the emergence of competition among vertically integrated firms that provide both local and long-distance telephone services. Thus, vertical disintegration might be particularly inappropriate. By contrast, vertical disintegration might be strongly advised if competition in services is introduced for railway tracks, gas pipelines, or the electricity grid. Each case presents a choice between single ownership of the tracks, the pipelines, or the grid, and shared ownership of the bottleneck by the users who agree on rules for using it. The comparison is between the inefficiency of regulation and the free-rider problems of joint ownership. In a country where regulation is easily captured, joint ownership would be the more favorable scenario.

Currently, the main difference between telecommunications and the other industries is that the local network that is a bottleneck for long distance is providing a service of its own for which consumers can compete. For gas, electricity, and railways, consumers are not interested in purchasing separately the service provided by the bottleneck. And, in general, different firms will not provide the

[2] See Auriol and Laffont (1992).

piece of the pipeline, electricity grid, or track that is of interest to the consumer. An exception might occur in railways, where several firms might provide roughly equivalent itineraries. It might be more likely that a different company than the incumbent local telephone company would provide the copper fiber optic line to the consumer, and that this bottleneck would be rented to different users, including local telephone service companies.

Structural Separation and Pricing of Access to Independently Owned Infrastructure

The utility that owns the infrastructure sells wholesale services to other firms, which market final services to the consumers. Here we consider competitive and noncompetitive uses of independently owned infrastructure.

Competitive Usage

The simplest case arises when the *n* final services are produced by competitive industries at some constant marginal cost. It is as if the utility produced the final services itself at a unit cost equal to its own cost of providing access to the competitive downstream firms plus the latters' unit cost of producing the final services.

The Ramsey formula can be applied to the prices charged for access to the utility's infrastructure and the prices can be decentralized through a price cap on access charges. Ramsey pricing entails the following:

$$\frac{P_k - C_{Ok} - C_k}{P_k} = \frac{\lambda}{1+\lambda}\frac{1}{\hat{\eta}_k} \quad k = 1,\dots,n,$$

where P_k is the price of service *k*; C_k is the producer's long-run marginal cost of producing the final service, *k*; C_{Ok} is the long-run marginal cost of access to supply service *k*; $\hat{\eta}_k$ is the price superelasticity of service *k* and λ is the shadow price of the utility's budget constraint.

Under competition, $P_k = a_k + C_k$, where a_k is the access price. Therefore, the induced access-pricing rule is:

$$\frac{a_k - C_{Ok}}{P_k} = \frac{\lambda}{1+\lambda}\frac{1}{\hat{\eta}_k} \quad k = 1,\dots,n.$$

Alternatively, we can define the demand for access, D_k, for service k (access k) as:

$$\tilde{D}_k(a_1, \ldots, a_n) = D_k(P_1, \ldots P_n).$$

The price superelasticity of the demand for access k is

$$\tilde{\eta}_k = \frac{a_k}{P_k} \cdot \hat{\eta}_k.$$

We obtain a classic Ramsey type of pricing (see principle 1):

$$\frac{a_k - C_{0k}}{a_k} = \frac{\lambda}{1+\lambda} \cdot \frac{1}{\tilde{\eta}_k} \quad k = 1, \ldots, n.$$

Principle 1. *The excess of the access price over the marginal cost of access for service k relative to the access price for k should be inversely proportional to its demand price superelasticity.*

The decentralization of Ramsey pricing by price caps enables the regulator to rely on the demand information of the regulated firm (see warning 1). This is true even if we still have the difficult choice of weights in the price cap.

Warning 1. *In developing countries, for a very competitive usage of the infrastructure, Ramsey pricing of the infrastructure should be based on broad categories of usage that do not raise complex inspection issues and should be decentralized by price caps.*

Figure 7–1 illustrates the typical market structure and raises several informational issues. The demand information is naturally located with the users of the infrastructure. The utility can infer this demand information from the demand for access as long as the users report truthfully the type of final good for which they use the infrastructure. The following examples illustrate the importance of reporting truthful information.

- For railways, each shipper must specify truthfully the content of its cargoes. This additional agency problem may be a serious issue in countries where corruption impacts the inspection system, especially if there is a large number of users, as we implicitly assume in this section.
- For the Internet, pricing independent of usage is still necessary because of the technical difficulties in identifying the type of usage.
- In telecommunications, long-distance carriers that face higher access prices than local carriers may bypass their interconnection by sending traffic directly to a local carrier that benefits from lower access prices.

Figure 7-1. The Typical Utility Market Structure

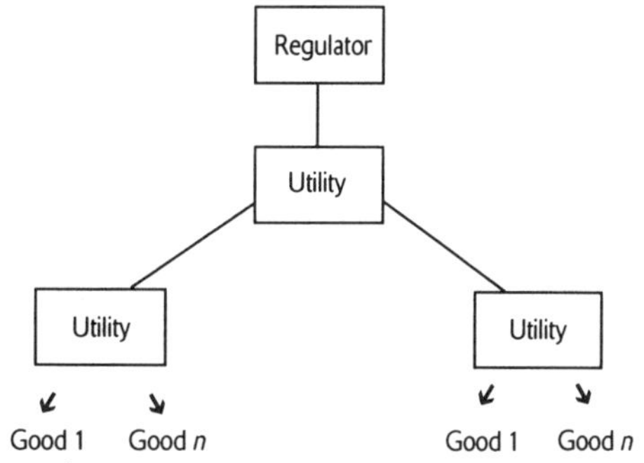

- In electricity, the pricing of transmission should depend on the demand or supply elasticity at each node of the network. This creates a lot of discretion for the system operator. Therefore, pricing should be based on a single injection price and a single extraction price, that is, prices that reflect easily observable characteristics. Congestion brings the further difficulty of having to rely on nodal pricing that accounts for the externalities due to Kirchoff laws. Again, there should be a uniform price that reflects the local treatment of congestion.

There are technical limits for the best possible use of Ramsey pricing, as well as institutional limits that are needed to curb corruption activities. Laffont and Tirole (1993) show that optimal regulation may require no price discrimination and therefore may entail "political" cross subsidization. Note that decentralization is only partial in the sense that the regulator will still have to make sure that the firms use the correct classification of services into the different categories. Ramsey pricing is often criticized for its informational requirements. Note that price cap regulation does not require the regulator to know the price elasticities. It uses firms' knowledge of these elasticities. Of course, the calculation of the optimal weights in the price cap formula requires the same type of information.

The Market Power of Users

Consider the simple case in which each user is a monopoly in one independent market. The monopoly will charge a monopoly price computed according to the usual formula:

$$\frac{P_k - (a_k + C_{Ok})}{P_k} = \frac{1}{\eta_k}$$

where η_k is the price elasticity of good k. Since Ramsey pricing requires

$$\frac{p_k - C_{Ok} - C_k}{P_k} = -\frac{\lambda}{1+\lambda}\frac{1}{\eta_k},$$

the monopolistic mark-up of the user should be undone by a discount on the access price defined by:

$$\frac{a_k - C_{Ok} - C_k}{P_k} = -\frac{\lambda}{1+\lambda}\frac{1}{\eta_k}.$$

These marginal access charges can be supplemented by a fixed payment to form a two-part tariff, $a_k q_k + A_k$, where q_k is quantity and A_k is a fixed fee, and which ideally can extract the monopolist's profit (see remark 1). More generally, nonlinear pricing can be used.

> ***Remark 1.*** *For competitive usage of the infrastructure, two-part tariffs cannot be used because competition would drive prices to marginal cost and bankrupt users.*

> ***Principle 2.*** *With market power of users, the marginal access charges should subsidize access; users' excess profits should be recovered by fixed charges and more generally by nonlinear pricing.*

Principle 2 requires a lot of knowledge from the regulator and raises issues of favoritism in price discrimination. In the absence of long-term contracts, there is potential for expropriation of some large users' investments. Warning 2 addresses the complexity and potential discretion involved in countries with little technical expertise and low transaction costs of collusion. For example, the control of a user's monopoly power could be undertaken by the regulatory agency or by an appropriate policy of marginal subsidization cum profit tax. The regulator could use a simple price cap regulation. The regulator really needs more instruments, but in general is not given tax instruments and can only very imperfectly achieve multiple objectives with the single instrument of access prices.

> ***Warning 2.*** *In developing countries, the regulator should not attempt to undo the monopoly power of the infrastructure users. Alternative policies should be used to foster competitive use of the infrastructure.*

Additional Problems with Ramsey Pricing

One problem with Ramsey pricing is regulatory capture. That is, when the regulator designs the tariffs, the discretion surrounding the determination of elasticities raises the problem of capture (when a price cap is used the problem is transferred to the choice of weights). Warning 3 addresses this problem. In practice, the choice of a good starting point is difficult and is generally based on past prices. Expert benchmarking is crucial for the success of developing countries in this task.

> ***Warning 3.*** *A nondiscretionary method for choosing weights in the price cap should be selected (for example, last year's quantities and an exogenous change in the level).*

Another problem with Ramsey pricing is the risk of expropriation. The best and simplest way to strike a balance between rent extraction and incentives for cost minimization is to use price cap regulation with reviews. However, in countries with little credibility, regulation of the rate of return might offer a more reassuring environment. First, in addition to the traditional problems of rate-of-return regulation, the specificities of developing countries (for example, lack of reliable accounting and lack of regulatory expertise) favor price cap regulation. The drawback of giving up too much rent is weakened by the urgent need to attract capital. Second, rate-of-return regulation does not necessarily represent a more effective commitment to fair treatment when the government has little credibility to fulfill its promises.

One-Way Access with Vertical Integration

We consider the case of a vertically integrated utility (the incumbent) that provides access to the infrastructure and that also sells a service using the infrastructure. The problem is to price access for other providers of services using the infrastructure. A situation of noncompetitive entry would require regulation of prices of services. Here we consider the pricing situation when competitive users with constant marginal cost provide a service that is not provided by the incumbent (case a) and when they provide a service that is a close substitute for the service provided by the incumbent (case b).

Let good 1 refer to the service offered by the incumbent with the long-run marginal cost of access for good 1 denoted by C_{01} and the long-run marginal cost of producing good 1 denoted by C_1. Let good 2 refer to the service offered by the competitors with the long-run marginal cost of access for good 2 denoted by C_{02} and the long-run marginal cost of production denoted by C_2. There is no fixed cost in the production of services.

Let a be the access price to be charged to competitors. Ramsey pricing of access leads to:

$$a = C_{O2} + \frac{\lambda}{1+\lambda}\,\frac{P_2}{\hat{\eta}_2}$$

with $P_2 = a + C_2$ from perfect competition. Alternatively we can write:

$$a = C_{O2} + \delta[p_1 - C_{O1} - C_1] + \frac{\lambda}{1+\lambda}\frac{P_2}{\eta_2}. \tag{1}$$

$\delta = (\partial q_1 / \partial P_2)/(\partial q_2 / \partial P_2)$, where q_1 and q_2 are the retail sales of goods 1 and 2, respectively, δ is the displacement ratio (the change in the incumbent's retail sales divided by the change in its sales to rivals as the access price varies).

In case a, competitors provide new products that the incumbent does not (or cannot) provide. That is, $\delta \approx 0$. For example, the mobile phone industry illustrates this case when the incumbent provides local and long-distance services by fixed link (δ is small). In this case, a global price cap appears particularly promising (principle 3). The cap would take the following form: $\bar{q}_1 p_1 + \bar{q}_2 a \leq \Pi$, where $\bar{q}_1$ and $\bar{q}_2$ are the equilibrium quantities of goods 1 and 2. The global price cap Π would provide good incentives for the owner of the infrastructure to favor interconnection that would increase its business.

> ***Principle 3.*** *If the services provided by users of access to the incumbent do not compete seriously with the services sold by the incumbent, a global price cap should be favored; more generally, regulation of such access should be treated just like regulation of an end-user service.*

However, congestion and inflexible pricing might cause problems in allocating the infrastructure with prices. If rationing occurs, favoritism could be a problem, particularly in developing countries. An example of this problem is an incumbent railway that serves only freight and passenger cars (see the appendix example of Argentina). The problem of favoritism brings up two issues. First, it is important to allow peak-load pricing of access and end-user service symmetrically to avoid favoritism. Second, an increase in the number of users decreases the shadow price of the budget constraint and therefore leads the incumbent to lower the access price.

In case b, competitive users offer services that are very close substitutes for the services provided by the incumbent. Equation 1 shows that the access price should be higher than in case a in order to avoid inefficiency and balance the budget of the incumbent (principle 4). A regulation that does not allow this "competitive" response of the incumbent will create incentives for exclusionary behavior. Examples include telecommunications in Ghana and Colombia (see the appendix).

> ***Principle 4.*** *When entry leads to business stealing, the access price should be higher than the marginal cost corrected by the Ramsey own-elasticity term.*

A good policy would allow an access-pricing rule that is generous for the incumbent and that focuses regulatory resources on implementing quick and high-quality interconnection. The policy could be based on the efficient component-pricing rule: $a = P_1 - C_1$. If data were not available for calculating the incumbent's cost, C_1, in the competitive context considered here, pricing could be based on the marginal cost of the entrants, unless the incumbent can demonstrate that its cost is lower (warning 4).

> ***Warning 4.*** *When competitive entrants offer services that are highly substitutable with the incumbent's services, pricing can be based on the efficient component-pricing rule supplemented by active regulatory oversight to favor nondiscriminatory interconnection. Alternatively, pricing could use a global price cap supplemented by maximum access prices defined by the efficient component-pricing rule.*

Two-Way Access

When network competition develops, reciprocal access charges between networks must be determined. This situation of network duplication is not common in the developing countries considered here, but it may arise in telecommunications and railways.

If final prices are regulated, the networks can negotiate interconnection charges. The regulatory resources can facilitate interconnections and agreements, especially when the networks are asymmetric in size. When the final prices are unregulated, reciprocal access prices should be regulated, but two dangers must be avoided. First, networks might collude on high reciprocal access charges that induce monopolistic final prices (see principle 5). Given that we can expect weak competition among networks, we favor the "bill and keep" doctrine of zero access charges because of its simplicity (warning 5). Indeed, for such situations the access payments wash out whatever the access price, and a low access price encourages competition in the final prices.

> ***Principle 5.*** *When symmetric networks compete in linear prices, the optimal access charges should be below the marginal cost of access to undo the monopolistic competition of networks on final prices.*[3]

[3] This principle assumes that the fixed costs of the network are recovered. Otherwise, principle 5 must be combined with recovery of such costs.

Warning 5. *For symmetric networks competing in linear prices, we favor the "bill and keep" doctrine of zero access charges.*

The second danger is that networks might choose not to be interconnected. Again, regulatory resources should focus on ensuring good interconnection. Theory shows that if networks compete under nonlinear tariffs, the collusion effect disappears and access should be priced at marginal cost. The bill and keep doctrine leads to marginal prices that are too low and to fixed charges that are too high, with high levels of exclusion for consumers.[4] However, such a situation is unlikely in developing countries.

A more difficult situation occurs when networks (fixed and mobile networks) are asymmetric in their marginal costs of access and in size. When networks are of mature size, regulatory resources are likely to be on the high side. In this scenario, a reasonable option would be negotiated access tariffs under the threat of competition policy.

The most difficult case corresponding to the second danger (lack of interconnection of networks) is when a small network tries to enter. The incumbent network is likely to use access charges to block entry. Therefore, it is important to make sure that network competition does not interfere with network development in areas of interest. If network competition, say, in an urban area, is still desired, it must be because large unsatisfied demand exists and the networks may develop without interconnection (for example, the telecom sector in Colombia). At some point the regulator will be able to mandate negotiated access prices with a fallback option of using international benchmarking (see warning 6).

Warning 6. *In the cases where network competition is desirable, mandated negotiation under the threat of arbitration by an international body is an interesting option.*

Conclusion

Recommendations about access pricing—including the optimal use of the network when cost recovery is a constraint—depend on many factors. In practice, further considerations must be kept in mind. First, the type of available accounting information is crucial to assess the workability of cost-based access-pricing rules. In the absence of such data, price cap regulation and international benchmarking are the only possible options.

---

[4] A menu of tariffs including linear prices might then emerge.

Second, the rules should depend on the other types of instruments available. Often access-pricing rules are also used for accommodating entry. With fixed costs of entry, there is no simple solution to this problem and one should not use access prices for this purpose. Instead, other instruments should be used to encourage entry.

Third, the main entry problem in developing countries is in infrastructure. Access rules should make sure that investors in infrastructure can recover their costs; generous access rules may be needed for this purpose. From this point of view, the obsession with long-run incremental cost goes in the wrong direction.

Finally, nonprice conditions for interconnection are as important as pricing for efficient liberalization. Regulatory attention to these issues by independent technical staff is essential.

Appendix. Pricing Rules in Telecommunications in Selected Countries

Argentina

Argentina was divided into two territories of approximately equal size and each one was assigned to a monopoly regulated by price caps. The northern part of the country (north of Buenos Aires) was awarded to France Télécom and the southern part to Telefónica. As tariffs between the two regions were balanced, interconnection charges washed out and the pricing of interconnection did not matter.

Since fall 1999, competition has been open to many operators. The two incumbents will be regulated with price caps on their initial territory until "competition is a fact." Interconnection charges are negotiated, but the regulator can intervene if deviations from forward-looking incremental costs are important. In addition, if operators do not agree, the regulator will impose a price with reference to the forward-looking incremental cost. Given the uncertainty surrounding this cost, it is possible that the two incumbents will set high interconnection charges to blockade further entry.

China

China first introduced competition in the mobile telephone sector without having any problem of interconnection. Now Unicom, which was initially owned by various ministries and the army, is facing problems in trying to enter the fixed-link market, which is controlled by the incumbent China Telecom. After four years, interconnection agreements have been reached in only three cities; for example, Chongching is not interconnected.

Colombia

A constitutional amendment prohibits monopolies, even public ones. There are several regional public companies offering local telephone service: Bogotá Telecom Company, with 25 percent of the market; Medellín, 10 percent; Cali, 7 percent; and four mobile phone companies.

There appears to be no problem in setting interconnection charges for mobile phones or for long-distance service. The services are sufficiently complementary, so that both operators gain from quick interconnection. However, the access charges might be too high.

When the Telecom and Medellín companies entered Bogotá's local market, access was refused by Bogotá Telecom. Now there are three fixed-linked companies in Bogotá that are not fully interconnected. Indeed, access charges are not included in the price cap on final prices. Access prices are determined by historical costs according to the fully distributed method. Bogotá Telecom makes no money on access and has all the incentives for exclusionary behavior.

Côte d'Ivoire

Competition has been introduced only in the mobile phone market where prices are unregulated. The operator of the fixed link (Citelcom) has been a monopoly for years and its final prices are regulated.

Here we consider the interconnection agreement between Citelcom and the mobile phone operator, Comstar Cellular, which was accepted by the regulator. Citelcom has committed to the following tariffs (where p_l is the local tariff and p_L is the long-distance tariff):[5]

For a call from Citelcom to Comstar:

Local $p_l = 25 + a_l$, where a_l is the access price of Comstar
Long distance $p_L = 130 + a_2$, where a_2 is the access price of Comstar.

For a call from Comstar to Citelcom, the access prices are (in CFA francs per minute):

Local $a_1^l = 25$
Long distance $a_1^L = 130$

Citelcom uses an "efficient component pricing rule" if we interpret (a_1, a_2) as the avoided costs of Citelcom. Citelcom's access price equals its opportunity cost of losing a customer:

Local $p_l - a_l - 25$
Long distance $p_L - a_2 - 130$

Comstar's access and final prices are unregulated. The idea is that the mobile phone market is competitive and the avoided costs of Citelcom are approached by the costs of the mobile phone competitors.

These prices must be contrasted with Citelcom's tariffs (in CFA francs per minute):

Local calls	10
Long-distance calls	180.

[5] We neglect some taxes and some factors taking account of unpaid invoices.

However, given that tariffs are unbalanced, it is not possible to relate the prices of access to Citelcom's costs.

A danger of the efficient component pricing rule for Citelcom is that mobile phone operators collude in choosing high access prices, reducing Citelcom's revenues from the outgoing calls of its own subscribers. However, Citelcom's subsidiary in the mobile telephone sector could maintain a downward pressure on prices. But this is not really the case because competition to attract consumers has no effect on the high charges that consumers of the fixed-linked network have to pay to access the mobile network.

Note that we have focussed on marginal prices. There are fixed parts both in consumer tariffs and in interconnection pricing. Finally, the mobile companies have a zero reciprocal access price, but must pay Citelcom's local access price.

Ghana

Competition was introduced in the telecommunications sector starting in 1992. Three mobile operators entered and developed interconnection agreements with the incumbent, Ghana Telecom, through largely bilateral negotiations. However, as theory would predict, access charges are very high. Ghana Telecom charges cellular companies for interconnection more than its local tariff (note, however, that tariffs are unbalanced). Ongoing disputes surround the issue of sharing revenues from access.

A second license for fixed-linked telephone service was sold to Westel, which has not started its activities. Due to the weakness of the regulator, the future of competition is not assured.

References

Auriol, E., and J. J. Laffont. 1992. "Regulation by Duopoly." *Journal of Economics and Management Strategy* 1: 503-33.

Laffont, J. J. 1996. "Regulation, Privatization and Incentives in Developing Countries." In M. G. Quibria and J. Malcolm Dowling, eds., *Current Issues in Economic Development.* Oxford, U.K.: Oxford University Press.

———. 1998. "Competition, Information and Development." *Annual World Bank Conference on Development Economics.* Washington, D.C.: The World Bank.

Laffont, J. J., and J. Tirole. 1993. *A Theory of Incentives for Procurement and Regulation.* Cambridge, MA: MIT Press.

CHAPTER 8

Open-Access Issues in the Chilean Telecommunications and Electricity Sectors

Carlos Díaz and Raimundo Soto

The recent wave of infrastructure restructuring and privatization in Latin American countries has been characterized by the introduction of competition in areas that in the past had been considered natural monopolies. Regulation efforts have successfully expanded the scope of competition in various sectors with network and natural monopoly characteristics. Industries like electricity, natural gas, telecommunications, and even transport are restructuring. The degree of competition introduced depends on particular market conditions. In most of these industries, the competing activities still need to use the existing networks, heightening the policy relevance of access conditions and pricing. Development of effective competition and of the advantages of network externalities will require open access to some still-regulated facilities of these industries.

Policymakers must create proper conditions for entry into the competitive sector, but not induce excessive entry, not expropriate previous investments or discourage future investment in the monopolized part of the industry, and not generate inefficient bypass. In this respect, Chile has had a pioneering role. Its two decades of experience provide valuable insights with regard to the effects of different institutional arrangements on access, access pricing, and tariff-setting mechanisms, as well as the role of the authorities in fostering competition and reducing the adverse effects of ambiguous or incomplete regulation. This chapter describes the Chilean experience up to 1999 in regulating access to networks in two sectors: electricity and telecommunications.

Regulatory reform to facilitate the transition to competition began almost two decades ago in Chile. The government has engaged in an active policy of

The authors would like to thank Jorge Fritis, Leonardo Mena, Felipe Morandé, and Ricardo Paredes for valuable information, and Federico Basañes for detailed comments.

restructuring and transferring services and publicly owned firms to the private sector. The policy has removed the limitations to market entry and allowed private sector participation even when transfer of property was deemed inefficient or politically unacceptable (for example, franchising public infrastructure). The process has involved both privatization and liberalization, with the latter aimed explicitly at promoting market entry. In general, the sectors involved were characterized by the existence of barriers to entry, the degree of market power by incumbents, and sufficient economies of scale and scope so that the most efficient industrial organization was a regulated (private) monopoly.

The objective of the Chilean government was to implement the necessary conditions for market competition in all areas in which monopoly power could not be exerted by incumbents or imposed by technology. In areas in which monopoly power could be exercised, strict regulation was designed to provide incentives to incumbents to behave as if they were in a competitive market and to avoid noncompetitive practices upstream or downstream. Consequently, provisions were made to facilitate the introduction of competition in different segments of the markets. Such was the case for generation and commercialization in the electricity sector and, more recently, for mobile, long-distance, and local telephone service.

Despite the government's efforts, deregulation and privatization have not been as coordinated and smooth as would be desirable. The privatization process in some cases we study in this chapter was implemented before the regulatory framework was in place, allowing incumbents or newcomers to exert market power and obtain rents. In particular, the privatization of electricity led to a degree of vertical integration, which, in the context of incomplete regulation regarding transmission tolls, has hampered access and competition in retail markets. By contrast, in telecommunications the government has had a significant role in fostering competition by modifying the regulation to induce increasing degrees of competition in the different segments of the market. In particular, the introduction of a multi-carrier system in long-distance service is perhaps the most significant accomplishment of the regulator.

Analytical Issues in Network Economics

The recent economic literature provides ample evidence of the benefits a society can reap from privatizing and deregulating public services such as the electricity and telecommunications sectors. In particular, the literature describes the benefits of expanding coverage, reducing costs, enhancing productivity, and improving quality and product/service diversity. However, those benefits depend to a large extent on the particular form in which the private sector is allowed to participate in markets characterized by monopoly power. Chile was one of the first Latin

American countries to engage in full-scale market deregulation and public sector divestiture and, consequently, presents a number of interesting case studies.

Traditional reasons for regulating telecommunications and electricity services are the presence of scale economies leading to natural monopoly, the presence of network externalities, a dominant position by incumbents, and the existence of bottlenecks in essential facilities. In the last two decades, fundamental changes have reshaped the structure of telecommunications and electricity markets. Technological and regulatory developments have lowered entry barriers and increased the ability of new firms to enter these industries at different productive stages. In turn, this has substantially altered the way in which both industries operate and mitigated the importance of monopoly power to justify economic regulation. Nevertheless, the changes also raise new challenges to regulation derived from network competition.

In several countries, technological and regulatory changes in the telecommunications industry have led to a significant degree of competition, to the point that many observers argue that traditional justifications for regulating network industries no longer apply.[1] In fact, Laffont, Rey, and Tirole (1998) predict that decades of regulatory scrutiny will give way in the near future to a competitive marketplace from which detailed regulation will withdraw. Sidak and Spulber (1997) describe the following characteristics in the United States: (1) local telephone networks have lost or are losing their monopoly nature, and the existence of a natural monopoly in a market is not necessarily a barrier to entry; (2) there is a problem of duplicate facilities, and the sunk-cost argument no longer applies; (3) entry barriers are not an issue because costs have already been sunk for multiple networks; (4) erosion of the local exchange monopoly eliminates the possibility of leverage and self-dealing; and (5) local networks are no longer essential facilities.

It is no longer correct to argue that the entire electricity sector presents natural monopoly properties. The decline of scale economies in generation and the fact that energy as a product can be separated from transmission as a service have opened the market to competition (Hunt and Shuttleworth 1996). Technological improvements have created more opportunities for competition and increased the contestability of these markets. However, in some segments of these industries, bottlenecks remain and need to be regulated to accelerate the transition toward competition and to avoid the social cost of duplicating essential facilities that would otherwise arise. For example, by controlling access to an essential facility or input necessary for

[1] The many alternatives to monopoly products and services make competition possible. Potential facility-based competitors include access providers, long-distance telecommunications companies, cable TV operators, gas networks, cellular and digital phone (PCS) carriers, and electricity utilities.

competition, the incumbent could raise entry barriers in a market that would otherwise be competitive.

In the telecommunications sector, local exchange companies still hold a dominant position and control access to some essential inputs. Therefore, for competition to succeed requires open access to some components and services of the local network. Regulations, usually in the form of network interconnection and the unbundling of services, are key in creating conditions for effective competition.

In the electricity sector, regulators must harmonize the introduction of competition in production and marketing with maintaining natural monopolies in transmission and distribution services. To achieve wholesale and retail competition, regulators ought to require each electricity utility to transmit energy for others on equal terms and to wheel power generated by its competitors over its transmission and distribution network. Open access to transmission and distribution wires would allow all customers to choose between trading directly with producers or through the intermediaries of their choice.

Another reason that justifies implementing regulatory schemes in the form of open access or common carriage is the presence of externalities in networks. These externalities drive a wedge between private and social prices, so that efficient resource allocation would require regulation. Network externalities make a fully interconnected network the most efficient supply structure and, consequently, allow an incumbent provider to preserve its dominant position by refusing or overpricing interconnections.[2] When new subscribers join the telephone service network, existing subscribers benefit because they can receive calls from new subscribers and make calls to them without paying an additional charge. Likewise, in the electricity sector, a producer benefits from interconnection not only by being able to sell energy to a larger market, but also because it can rely on the capacity of other producers as backup instead of having to build its own reserve units.

The existence and enforcement of open access to multiple networks are crucial for bringing the benefits of competition and network externalities to the telecommunications and electricity industries. To implement this policy, regulators have to specify clearly the technical and economic conditions under which the incumbents shall grant competitors access to their network services. The incumbents must follow those specifications and allow competitors, customers, and suppliers to have access to their facilities with a level of ease that is comparable to that of the company's own access. Pro-competitive reforms will not achieve their objectives and might even prove counterproductive, unless prices and terms of access become economically efficient signals to guide investment and production.

---

[2] Occasionally an incumbent would like to subsidize rivals entering the market in order to appropriate those externalities (market and network creation), for example when new technologies are introduced (Economides 1996).

To be effective, open-access policies under the presence of incumbent monopolies need to be supported by detailed regulations including technical procedures, efficient pricing formulas, and explicit time frames for interconnection. These clear rules together with an adequate regulatory structure are needed to enforce interconnection rights without incurring long, costly disputes.

The methodologies for setting access tariffs must be technically sound and firms must know about them in advance. If the regulation is not well designed, the setting of incorrect interconnection and access charges could jeopardize the introduction of competition into network industries. However, this is a difficult matter and there is an active discussion among scholars regarding how to set these prices, ranging from the efficient component pricing rule—the Baumol-Willig rule (Baumol and Willig 1982)—to Ramsey and accounting prices (Armstrong and Doyle 1995; Economides and White 1995).

From an institutional point of view, lack of access to information by regulators and the need for strengthening of regulatory agencies are also important limitations to the effective regulation of these sectors. Access and interconnection charges require detailed information about an incumbent's cost structure, so it is important to ensure that regulators can collect the necessary information from market participants. In the regulatory process there also exist some areas in which it is not possible to eliminate all ambiguities, so regulators need to have the autonomy and the resources to shield technical decisions from lobbying and political interference by interest groups.

Expanding the number of potential suppliers and customers is likely to make the electricity and telecommunications industries more efficient and more competitive. However, even under open-access conditions and an adequate regulatory framework, there may be circumstances in which dominant firms, occasionally vertically integrated, are able to exercise market power. Therefore, the authorities must continue to address competition problems in concentrated and vertically integrated markets. Developing a competitive market when there is an important dominant operator is a costly and long-term process. These costs might justify engaging in schemes to reduce market power through industry restructuring and divestiture.

Open-Access Issues in the Telecommunications Sector

Prior to the restructuring of Chile's telecommunications sector in the early 1980s, state-owned firms dominated the sector. Compañía de Telecomunicaciones de Chile (CTC), a network the government acquired from International Telephone and Telegraph Corporation (ITT) in 1974, provided local telephone service. Empresa Nacional de Telecomunicaciones (ENTEL), a firm the government created in 1964, provided long-distance telephone service. Only telex service was to some extent competitive, as Telex-Chile, ITT, and Transradio Chilena Compañía de Telecomunicaciones (VTR, a joint venture by RCA and local investors) split the market. The Chilean authorities made it a standard practice to set tariffs at very low values for political reasons. As a result, the return on investment was negligible, the quality of service was minimal, cross subsidies were widespread, and customers had to wait for prolonged periods in order to obtain a telephone line.

Deregulation started in the mid 1970s with the elimination of anti-private sector regulation and with modernization of the management of state firms. In 1977 the government created the Undersecretary of Telecommunications (Subtel), an agency of the Ministry of Transport and Telecommunications, and put it in charge of enforcing the law. The main functions and attributions of Subtel are (1) to draft sector policies; (2) to develop, issue, and enforce technical standards for the operation of the industry; (3) to overview compliance with local regulations and international agreements; (4) to grant licenses and franchises; and (5) to enforce sanctions on illegal practices.

In 1978 Subtel allowed the entry of private firms into the local telephone service market. Two small, privately owned telephone companies were established and granted concessions overlapping parts of CTC's service areas in Santiago (Complejo Manufacturero de Equipos Telefónicos, CMET, and Compañía Telefónica Manquehue). These companies took advantage of the severe shortage in the supply of telephone lines, especially in affluent residential and commercial districts. CTC was required to interconnect with the new networks, which partly duplicated CTC's own network.

The entry of private firms in local telephone service and the desire to privatize the sector led the government to issue the 1982 telecommunications law, which reshaped the structure of the sector along the lines of tariff deregulation, open access to the market, and private sector management. The government's announcement of the privatization of CTC and ENTEL and the sale of its participation in Telex-Chile gave momentum to the reform movement. Between 1985 and 1987, the authorities sold 25 percent of CTC and 33 percent of ENTEL, and transferred control of the firms to private investors. By 1990 the two firms had been completely privatized.

Table 8–1 shows the evolution of the telecommunications sector since 1987. It has been dynamic in all five segments of the telecommunications market: local telephone service, long-distance telephone service, mobile phones, cable TV, and Internet service.

As of 1998, CTC continued to dominate local telephone service, with 87 percent of the market (table 8–2). Other firms—such as CMET, Manquehue, Entelphone, and VTR Telesat—also operate in local telephone service (table 8–2). They tend to concentrate on particular segments of the market, such as high-income families, commercial users, or closed systems. Investment in network

Table 8–1. The Telecommunications Sector in Chile, 1987–98

	Local telephone service			Long-distance telephone service		
Year	Lines (thousands)	Density (lines per 100 inhabitants)	Waiting list (thousands)[a]	Domestic (millions of minutes)	International (millions of minutes)	Mobile phone subscribers (thousands)
1987	581	4.65	232			
1989	689	5.40	284			
1991	1,056	8.02	241	597	57	36
1993	1,516	11.10	198	984	72	85
1995	1,894	13.42	117	1,847	137	197
1997	2,693	18.20	N/A	2,704	242	410
1998	3,046	20.40	N/A	2,975	259	964

[a] CTC only.
Source: Subtel's database and Melo and Serra (1998).

expansion has been substantial: line density increased from less than five lines per 100 inhabitants in 1987 to over 20 lines in 1998. The entire network is digital.

Before the multi-carrier system was implemented in 1994, CTC monopolized domestic long-distance telephone service, although the majority of its lines were leased from ENTEL. The latter dominated the international segment, despite some competition by Chilesat, which entered the market in 1992. The entry of a large number of carriers dramatically altered the functioning of the market and tariffs were reduced by 60 percent for international calls and by 40 percent for domestic long-distance calls. Currently, 10 firms operate at the national level. ENTEL and CTC continue to have an important share of the market, but they do not enjoy monopoly status. In 1998 ENTEL's participation reached 39 percent in domestic long-distance service and 35 percent in international long-distance service. CTC's share was 34 percent in domestic and 20 percent in international long-distance service. Chilesat and Bellsouth held 18 and 10 percent, respectively, of the international long-distance service segment.

In 1989 Subtel decided to split the country into three areas and franchised two concessions for mobile telephone service in each area. Startel, a company formed by the fusion of CTC's and VTR's cellular phone branches, holds one concession in each area. ENTEL holds one concession in two of the areas and Bellsouth holds the third one. Startel has a participation of 57 percent of the market, while ENTEL has 23 percent and Bellsouth has 20 percent. Digital telephone service, PCS, was introduced in 1996 when Subtel auctioned three concession areas with national coverage. The mobile telephone branch of ENTEL obtained two of these concessions and its rival, Chilesat PCS, won the third one.

Cable TV is offered nationwide by two companies: Metrópolis Intercom, a CTC subsidiary that rents its parent company network, and VTR, which operates

Table 8–2. Market Shares in the Telecommunications Sector, 1998
(Percent)

Company	Local exchange	Long distance: Domestic	Long distance: International	Mobile	Cable TV	Internet
ENTEL and affiliates	1.5	39.0	35.0	23.0		60.0
CTC and affiliates	87.0	34.0	20.0	57.0	40.0	35.0
Telex and affiliates	1.2	18.0	15.0			
VTR and affiliates	0.7	2.8	9.7		58.0	
Bellsouth			10.0	20.0		
Manquehue	2.2					
CMET	2.6					
Other companies	4.7	6.2	7.3		2.0	5.0

Source: Duff & Phelps (1998).

with its own network. As of 1998, 23 percent of households (680,000) were connected, of which VTR's participation reached 56 percent and Metrópolis Intercom held 42 percent. Internet service is a relatively new segment of the market, serving around 75,000 households. Nevertheless, it is a dynamic segment with monthly growth rates of over 12 percent (DCR 1998). There are more than 30 Internet providers, but two firms dominate the market: ENTEL (60 percent) and a CTC affiliate (CTC-Reuna, 35 percent). Until May 1999, the expansion of the market was severely limited by the high tariffs charged by CTC to customers for local calls to connect to the Internet provider. A reduction of 50 percent in the regulated tariff eliminated this distortion.

After 15 years of deregulation, the most striking characteristic of the structure of this sector is undoubtedly the dominant role of the two former state monopolies in local and long-distance telephone service. As shown in table 8–2, CTC maintains its dominant position in local telephone service and has been able to move into other complementary markets, such as Internet service and cable TV. By contrast, ENTEL has reduced its share of the long-distance market, but has gained access in mobile phones and Internet service, thus diversifying its portfolio.

Evolution of Regulations in Telecommunications

Until 1982, the telecommunications sector did not have a regulatory framework of its own; the electricity law regulated it. The sector was organized in state monopolies and the authorities did not need to implement specific regulatory procedures. The 1982 telecommunications law substantially changed the concept of how telecommunications markets should operate. It granted open access on a nondiscriminatory basis, allowed market determination of tariffs, and made interconnection mandatory for all firms operating in the market. Table 8–3 presents a summary of the main innovations introduced by the telecommunications laws to the previous regulatory framework in terms of entry, tariffs, interconnections, and regulatory authorities.

Although the 1982 telecommunications law introduced important changes in the regulation allowing for private sector entry to the market, it presented several limitations for efficient operation of the industry after its complete privatization. Therefore, in 1987 the law was modified in several areas. The local and long-distance telephone service segments were differentiated for regulatory purposes. This allowed the authorities to set different quality standards, technical requirements, and, eventually, tariffs in these two segments of the market.

The modified law sanctioned that in cases where the Antitrust Commission determined that competition in a market was unlikely, the methodology for setting tariffs should be based on the incremental (marginal) cost of an "efficient-firm" model. Tariffs were to be set so that the net present value of expansion projects was zero, discounting at a rate reflecting the sector's capital cost. The capital cost was estimated using the capital asset-pricing model. If no investment was to be undertaken, tariffs were to be based on marginal costs. Rather than using actual costs, those of ideally efficient companies were used, reflecting the situation that would result from using the most appropriate technologies available. In case the incremental costs were not enough to cover total costs, they were to be increased in order to obtain a set of tariffs that would ensure near-maximum economic efficiency as well as self-financing for every service, region, and company. An indexation formula was included in the model for each company.

The sector operated under this framework until 1994, when a new telecommunications law was passed. In the interim, there were numerous disputes concerning interconnections, tariff-setting procedures, and vertical integration. The 1994 telecommunications law introduced a major modification in the regulatory framework by opening the long-distance segment to competition through a multi-carrier system. In order to foster competition, it established the necessary technical requirements to guarantee open access to network facilities and services, provided for equal access to different carriers, and allowed for vertical integration.

Open-Access Issues

In 1978 and 1980, Subtel granted concessions to CMET and Telefónica Manquehue in areas of Santiago where line shortages were acute. Telefónica Manquehue had been founded to increase the value of property in a large real estate development project in an affluent neighborhood of Santiago. The incumbent in the surrounding areas, CTC, had expected to serve the areas but did not have the capacity to provide timely service.

Table 8–3. Changes in Regulations of the Telecommunications Sector, 1959–94

Regulation	Law of 1959 (DFL 4)	Law of 1982 (no. 18.168)	Changes in 1985/87	Law of 1994
Entry	Only a government license was required to operate local telephone service. In practice, licenses were not granted in areas covered by existing concessions. Monopoly operation was the norm. Telegraphs and long-distance telephone service were public monopolies by law.	Any person can apply for concessions and licenses. Concessions have no limitations in terms of the nature of services (for example, local telephone service or long distance) and locations (geographical overlaps allowed).		The law implemented a multi-carrier system in long-distance service, allowing vertical integration. It required local companies to provide consumers equal access to carriers.
Service tariffs	In principle, tariffs were fixed in order to guarantee a fixed rate of return on assets of 10 percent. In practice, tariffs were usually set in nominal terms and eroded by inflation.	Tariffs are determined by private negotiation, unless the National Economic Prosecutor determines that market structures inhibit competition. In such case, the Ministry of the Economy and the Ministry of Transport and Telecommunications set tariffs. However, the law did not establish specific procedures.	The Antitrust Commission determines which service tariffs should be regulated. The Ministry of the Economy and the Ministry of Transport and Telecommunications set the tariffs. Service tariffs are to be determined according to an efficient-firm model.	
Network intercon-nection	No specific regulations.	Firms are required to inter-connect (easement) under the technical standards determined by Subtel.	The law set technical standards and connection points for network interconnections. It established time limits for interconnection in long-distance service.	

Table 8–3. (Continued)

Regulation	Law of 1959 (DFL 4)	Law of 1982 (no. 18.168)	Changes in 1985/87	Law of 1994
Intercon-nection tariffs	No specific regulations.	Tariffs are determined by private negotiation, unless the National Economic Prosecutor determines that market structures inhibit competition. In such case, the Ministry of the Economy and the Ministry of Transport and Telecommunications set tariffs. However, the law did not establish specific procedures.	The Antitrust Commission was in charge of determining whether interconnection tariffs should be regulated. In such case, the Ministry of the Economy and the Ministry of Transport and Telecommunications set the tariffs. Tariffs are set according to an efficient-firm model.	The Ministry of the Economy and the Ministry of Transport and Telecommunications have to set tariffs in any case according to an efficient-firm model.
Regulatory institutions	Bureau of Electrical Services and Interministry Tariff Commission.	Undersecretary of Telecommunications (Subtel). Antitrust Commission. Ministry of Transport and Telecommunications Ministry of the Economy.	Allowed referees to resolve disputes within a six-month period. Judgments can be appealed to the Supreme Court.	

CTC began to delay and sometimes obstruct interconnections with its network because the company visualized that entrants would become important rivals in the market. CTC's practices led to substantial litigation in the Antitrust Commission, as reflected in table 8–4. Litigation costs and the slowness of the Chilean judiciary system effectively delayed the entry of these companies and retarded competition. To a large extent, CTC was able to succeed with its strategy because the regulatory framework was ambiguous and incomplete with regard to the conditions in which interconnections should be achieved.

The 1982 telecommunications law established mandatory interconnections for concessionaires of public services under the technical standards of Subtel. In case of disagreement between the parties regarding connection fees, interconnection could be initiated before the courts reached a final judgment. The main drawback of the law was that it did not specify procedures and deadlines for interconnections and compensatory fees for the use of the incumbent's network.

It is noteworthy that telex companies did not engage in disputes with CTC during this period, despite the fact that telephone service is a substantial part of their costs. According to Coloma and Herrera (1990), there are two nonexclusive explanations. First, CTC did not provide telex service, so those telex operators did not represent a threat; in fact, service was usually complementary. Second, since the telex market is somewhat modest, the returns to monopolizing would be small. CTC feared that its dominant position could be challenged if it pursued an aggressive strategy in this additional area.[3]

In fact, disputes over telex service actually involved the other state monopoly, ENTEL. In 1980 ENTEL applied for a license to operate telex service. The existing companies complained to the Antitrust Commission that ENTEL had a legal monopoly over international long-distance service that explicitly precluded it from pursuing other commercial interests. After the claim was accepted and ENTEL was restricted from participating, it formed a joint venture with TEXCOM (currently its subsidiary) to offer telex services. Again, existing firms complained to the Antitrust Commission, which ruled that ENTEL must offer TEXCOM the same prices and quality standards it supplied to the existing telex firms.

By the end of 1985, the authorities implemented a legal mechanism to reduce litigation costs and delays. It allowed interconnection tariff disputes among parties to be reviewed and sanctioned by a referee chosen by the firms in advance (or, if necessary, nominated by Subtel). The disputes would be reviewed within a maximum period of six months. Appeals of the referee's decision could be reviewed only by the Supreme Court. In addition, Subtel was granted additional powers to obtain information and data from concessionaires to speed up decisions.

---

[3] Economides (1996) discusses the incentives of the incumbent to block or foster entry based on the complementarity or substitutability of the services provided.

Table 8–4. Proceedings of the Antitrust Commission Regarding Interconnections in Telecommunications, 1981–99

Case	Accusation	Judgment
CMET against CTC (1981)	CTC fetters interconnections with CMET.	CMET and CTC reached an out-of-court compensatory agreement in 1982.
CMET and National Economic Prosecutor against CTC (1982)	CTC engages in anti-competitive practices Unauthorized sale of lines in CMET's concession areas and continues to make interconnection difficult.	In 1983 the Antitrust Commission sanctioned that CTC engaged in anti-competitive practices, abusing its monopoly power to create entry barriers. The Commission set a deadline of 15 days to interconnect CMET and CTC in two cities.
Telefónica Manquehue against CTC (1982)	CTC engages in anti-competitive practices Unauthorized sale of lines in Telefónica Manquehue's concession areas and continues to make interconnection difficult. Unjustified delays in interconnections. Abuse of monopoly power by charging an access fee.	In 1983 the Antitrust Commission sanctioned that CTC engaged in anti-competitive practices, abusing its monopoly power to create entry barriers. The judgment includes a procedure for the interconnection of networks.
Post Office, ITT, and Transradio against ENTEL (1981)	In 1980 ENTEL applied for a concession to operate telex services. In January 1981, the three companies sued on the basis that ENTEL's status as a legal monopoly in international communications precluded its participation in telex services.	In 1983 the Antitrust Commission accepted the claim and ruled that ENTEL was not allowed to operate telex services.
Transradio, ITT, and National Economic Prosecutor against ENTEL and TEXCOM (1982)	A contract between ENTEL and TEXCOM allowed the former to operate in the telex market, thus defying the judgment of the Antitrust Commission. Terms and access conditions of this operation were discriminatory with regard to Transradio and ITT.	In 1983 the claim was accepted by the Antitrust Commission, which ruled that ENTEL should give TEXCOM the same conditions given to other private firms.
CMET against CTC (1986 and 1989)	CTC makes interconnections with CMET forward: willfully contrary, not easily managed.	The Antitrust Commission ruled that, according to the 1985 law, arbitration or Subtel should resolve disputes.
CMET against CTC (1988)	CTC does not allow CMET to install components (trunk lines) in a facility leased to a third party.	The Antitrust Commission ruled that CTC could not impede such practice if it was technically feasible (1990).
Subtel against Startel (CTC) (1999)	Startel engages in anti-competitive practices when introducing the Calling Party Pay system.	Startel was fined US$500,000.

These measures reduced time delays and might have helped improve the quality of judgments, but did not solve the ambiguities and limitations of the regulation.

Furthermore, the authorities did not show interest in attacking one of the main impediments to competition in the sector—interconnection procedures and fees—as reflected in the reforms of the 1987 law and in the 1988 tariff-setting process. The former related mostly to setting the institutional framework for competition; it did not address the manner in which such competition was to be carried out. The latter focused on reducing cross subsidies, but maintained access fees that were substantially above marginal costs (Tabja 1997).

During this period, CTC continued to enjoy substantial monopoly power and was able to keep entrants under control by means of inducing continuous interconnection problems. As is apparent from table 8–4, entrants had recourse to arbitration, the Antitrust Commission, and the judiciary system to solve disputes. However, fines were too low to deter CTC from anti-competitive practices. The largest fine applied to CTC in this period barely reached US$500,000.

High long-distance tariffs for both domestic and international calls generated high profitability in this segment of the market. Consequently, several local telephone service firms applied for concessions in long-distance service and firms operating in the long-distance sector applied for local telephone service concessions. For Subtel this action posed the problem of allowing vertical integration in the market. It also confronted the authorities with the fear of regulating a powerful integrated firm. This was a reflection of the lessons learned in the electricity sector, where integration made regulation very demanding.

In 1988 and before granting any franchise, Subtel required the Antitrust Commission to state its opinion as a "legally binding statement" regarding the costs and benefits of vertical integration in telecommunications and the advantages of segmenting markets, forbidding firms in one segment to participate in the other. The Antitrust Commission sanctioned the enforcement of competition in long-distance telephone service; local telephone service companies could not participate directly or indirectly in long-distance services (decision 718/763 of 1989). This judgment was based on the notion that local telephone service had monopoly power and could use it to monopolize the long-distance market. According to the Commission, efficient participation of local telephone companies would require an agency overseeing a large number of conditions. However, the authorities lacked the necessary technical and operative capabilities to monitor vertically integrated firms in a context of asymmetric information.

Later in 1988, an appeal by local telephone companies to the appeals court of the Antitrust Commission successfully revoked the aforementioned judgment (decision 332 of 1989). It sanctioned that local telephone service firms could participate in the long-distance market if such market was organized as a multi-carrier system. In addition, it sanctioned that long-distance firms could participate in the local telephone service market if certain conditions were satisfied.

For example, the judgment ruled that firms should guarantee egalitarian treatment of access to network interconnection service, including interfaces, network intelligent functions, switching services, maintenance, customer information, and billing and ordering systems.

The incumbent monopoly in long-distance telephone service, ENTEL, appealed to the Supreme Court. In 1990 the Supreme Court ruled that the Antitrust Commission had technically failed to prove its case and that the previous judgment was not valid. The Court determined that the Antitrust Commission "omitted the necessary technical and expert reports to support the ruling, although it was required to do so." In September 1990, the Antitrust Commission ruled to maintain the legal monopoly status of ENTEL. This situation remained unchanged until ENTEL's long-distance monopoly was abolished in 1992. However, real competition did not begin in this market until the 1994 telecommunications law was passed.

Meanwhile, in April 1990 the Antitrust Commission studied a complaint against Telefónica of Spain. The complaint claimed that, according to the Chilean competition law, it was forbidden to participate in CTC and ENTEL simultaneously. The Antitrust Commission ruled (decision 735/240) that Telefónica could hold interest in only one of these companies or should seek special consent from the government to be allowed to own shares in both companies simultaneously. Several telecommunications companies, against and in favor of the ruling, appealed to the appeals court of the Antitrust Commission. In 1992 the latter resolved (decision number 368) that Telefónica should sell its participation in either CTC or ENTEL within an 18-month period. In the end, Telefónica sold its share in ENTEL and kept CTC.

Despite some limitations, the 1994 telecommunications law established a regulatory framework that enforces open access and stimulates competition, particularly in the long-distance market. Among the conditions that it requires from local exchange companies in order to foster long-distance competition are: (1) to provide consumers equal access to carriers so they can select the carrier dialing the same number of digits; (2) to provide nondiscriminatory and equal access to interconnection and network services in terms of quality and time frames; (3) to operate with regulated interconnection fees; and (4) to allow market participants to have access to the necessary information about subscribers, including the volume of traffic generated.

In addition, the new law established more detailed procedures and norms related to interconnection of networks in general. Some important aspects of the new law were: (1) that it applies to all telephone operators; (2) that it defines the location of points of interconnection; and (3) that the prices of all network services should be in any case subject to regulation according to procedures described by the law. These changes were important in order to improve the negotiation capabilities of entrants and small competitors to enforce their interconnection rights, reducing disputes and lawsuits related to the technical and economic conditions of the interconnection of multiple networks.

In spite of this significant reform, the authorities did not introduce detailed norms with regard to the procedures and timing in which local interconnections should be implemented. As a consequence, interconnection problems among local telephone companies persisted. During 1995 CMET and CTC had a dispute derived from interconnection problems that ended with the application of a fine to the latter. In September 1995, in an attempt to solve these problems, Subtel established a detailed procedure and a three-month deadline for setting and accepting telephone interconnections. From this date on, local interconnection regulations specified timing and procedures. These detailed interconnection rules and procedures make it difficult for incumbent monopolies to deny, delay, or overprice the interconnection of multiple networks in an attempt to preserve their dominant position. However, problems continue in setting tariffs on services.

Interconnection and Access Tariffs

The 1982 telecommunications law established that service prices should be unregulated unless the National Economic Prosecutor determines that market structures inhibit competition. In such case, the Ministry of Economy and the Ministry of Transport and Telecommunications would be in charge of setting tariffs according to direct costs and a profit margin. In 1982 and 1985, the National Economic Prosecutor found that some local telephone services were not offered under competitive terms, so they should be subject to tariffs. However, given that the law did not establish specific procedures, the tariffs were not recalculated, but rather only adjusted by a price index.

The law was modified in 1987, introducing the procedure of setting tariffs according to an efficient-firm model, and assigning to the Antitrust Commission the responsibility of specifying which service tariffs should be regulated. This tariff-setting methodology was first applied in 1988.

In 1993 and 1998, the Antitrust Commission listed the telecommunications services that should be regulated and in 1994 the law established that certain services have to be in any case subject to tariff setting. The Antitrust Commission identified the services for each firm and for regional markets as shown in table 8–5.

To set service and interconnection tariffs, companies are required to present their own studies along the technical and economic lines developed in advance by the government. After the study is submitted to the authorities, the Ministry of the Economy and the Ministry of Transport and Telecommunications—operating together through Subtel—have 120 days to make objections and propose alternative tariffs. In case of conflict, the parties can consult a panel of three experts (one selected by each party involved and the third chosen by mutual consent) for a recommended solution. However, the Ministries retain

Table 8–5. Main Services Subject to Tariff Regulations, 1994 and 1998

By law of 1994	By resolution in 1998[a]
Network interconnections and services. Switching services, maintenance, customer information, and billing and ordering systems.	CTC and some other local exchange companies in specific areas: • phone lines • telephone connections • local calls within a company • access for long-distance and wireless providers • switching and transmission services provided as private circuits • local segments of calls originated in a local exchange company, transmitted to the network of another local company, sent to a long-distance network or to a wireless firm. Long-distance switching and transmission services provided by ENTEL, CTC, and Chilesat. Services provided to suppliers of complementary services.

[a] Resolution number 515, April 22, 1998.

the right to set definitive tariffs and their decisions can be appealed only to the Supreme Court.

The procedure for setting tariffs contains several pitfalls. In turn, these shortcomings facilitate disputes among incumbent firms and regulators.

- First, when using an ideally efficient company as a benchmark, it is very difficult to reach an agreement with regard to costs and efficiency parameters. In particular, the privatization of CTC as a single provider of local telephone service impeded the government's ability to use the yardstick of competition to measure CTC's performance.
- Second, tariff models are still unable to solve the problem of allocating common carriage costs among different services and regions. In turn, this hampers network expansion by introducing incentives to free ride.
- Third, the current regulation does not provide a procedure for determining unambiguously the ideal, efficient network design. Hence, ex ante definitions of the network used to evaluate investment projects at the firm level might not match ex post evaluations by the authorities, and price wedges between both parties might lead to sub-optimal investment plans.

Tariffs tend to be quite sensitive to the cost of capital used in simulation models. But, in general, the authorities do not have enough information to calculate the cost of capital and a proxy has to be adopted. Moreover, the tariff-setting process assigns to the regulated company an important role in providing information regarding its operating and capital costs. This leads to substantial problems of providing asymmetric information to the disadvantage of the regulators.

Throughout the years, the authorities have shown a tendency to overcome a number of institutional limitations that weakened the regulatory framework beyond the above-mentioned shortcomings. In particular, Subtel has developed the capabilities to enforce regulation, monitor compliance with technical and economic norms, and provide guidance for the tariff-setting procedures. This has been an important counterbalance to the large power, both economic and political, of incumbents. Technical proficiency also tends to shield the authorities from political pressures.

Unbundling Services

The most recent impulse toward transparency and competition in the telecommunications sector is the extensive unbundling of the services provided by local exchange companies, which was implemented in 1999. Unbundling refers to the separate sale of lines, switching, and transmission services.

The 1994 telecommunications law does not contain any provision in this regard. However, it allows the authorities to set tariffs—on an individual basis—for those services identified by the Antitrust Commission as being offered noncompetitively (see table 8–5). In 1998, the Commission issued the corresponding list of services with the proviso that Subtel ought to develop the most disaggregated tariff scheme possible to value the services provided by local exchange companies. Although the definition of individual services and network components is necessarily arbitrary (since any service is a bundle of features), the spirit of this mandate was to further the unbundling of facilities to induce more competition at the local telephone service level. Since by law the tariffs were to be revised in 1999, Subtel produced a detailed technical report to serve as the basis for tariff setting.

In May 1999, the authorities issued a new tariff schedule for CTC that was immediately disputed by the firm. However, the Court of Appeals and then the Supreme Court rejected the claim. In addition to legal matters, several aspects of the process have been controversial and deserve particular attention: (1) the absence of detailed procedures for using CTC's facilities; (2) the extent to which unbundling requirements are excessive or economically justifiable; and (3) the efficient firm cost standard used for setting prices for unbundled elements. Table 8–6 shows that for most services there was a substantial cut in tariffs, reflecting the unbundling requirements, cost reductions due to technological changes, and the fact that in some cases previous tariffs were set too high.

Open-Access Issues in the Electricity Sector

Open-access issues in the electricity sector arise in two areas where monopoly power is customary: high-voltage transmission and electricity distribution. Access

Table 8–6. Tariff Revisions for Some Services Offered by CTC, 1999
(Chilean pesos)

Service	Previous tariff	New tariff
Fixed cost	6.304	5.213
Local calls within CTC's network		
Normal hours (per minute)	15.4	13.3
Discount hours (per minute)	2.6	2.2
Local segments of calls originated in CTC's network and transmitted to the network of another company		
Normal hours (per minute)	15.4	5.7
Discount hours (per minute)	2.6	1.0
Domestic long-distance access charge		
Normal hours (per minute)	9.7	3.5
Discount hours (per minute)	1.6	0.6
International long-distance exit access charge		
Normal hours (per minute)	9.7	3.5
Discount hours (per minute)	1.6	0.6
International long-distance entry access charge		
Normal hours (per minute)	135.8	3.5
Discount hours (per minute)	135.8	0.6

Source: Subtel and CTC's tariff setting decree (August 1999).

problems in the Chilean case are exacerbated by the rugged, mountainous topography of the country and by the property structure of the sector that emerged from the privatization process. Despite its careful design, the regulation of the sector remains incomplete, fostering inefficient resource allocation and allowing rent-seeking activities.

Structure of the Electricity Sector

This section describes the main characteristics of the Chilean electricity sector in terms of its structure, the privatization process, and the regulatory framework in which it operates.[4] Chile is a long, narrow country (4,400 km long with an average width of 200 km) located alongside the Andes mountain range. The northern half of the country comprises one of the driest deserts in the world and is largely uninhabited. Power generation relies mostly on thermoelectric facilities (gas and coal-based) and demand concentrated in mining activities. By contrast, in the southern half of the country, rain and snow accumulation is abundant (rendering hydroelectric generation efficient) and consumption is concentrated in industrial and residential uses. There

[4] For a more detailed analysis of the regulatory framework, see Basañes, Saavedra, and Soto (this volume).

are two main and independent electricity systems (the Greater Northern Integrated System and the Central Integrated System).[5] Each system comprises its own generation plants, transmission lines, and distribution networks (see map 8–1).

Currently, four institutions rule the activities in the electricity industry (excluding the Antitrust Commission and the judiciary system):

- The *National Energy Commission (CNE)* advises the government on all matters related to energy (including electricity, fuel, and nuclear power). Its duties include defining the sector's policies and development strategies, studying and proposing economic and technical norms, and calculating tariffs and prices.
- The *Ministry of the Economy* sets tariffs (as proposed by CNE) and promotes the efficient development of the generation, transmission, and distribution of electricity.
- The *Superintendent of Electricity and Fuels (SEC)*, an independent supervisory agency related to the Ministry of the Economy, monitors compliance with the law and regulations, controls the quality of service and safety of facilities, processes applications for concessions, and prepares the information required to set tariff rates.
- The *Economic Load Dispatching Center (CDEC)* is a coordination entity designed to optimize the operation of the generation system and energy dispatch. In the short run, CDEC acts as a clearinghouse in the energy market; in the long run, it is in charge of planning the operation of the combined generation-transmission system.

The geographical situation configures a peculiar situation for the electricity industry and suggests the importance of open-access issues. Since the country is narrow, the generally accepted opinion is that a unique, high-voltage transmission line is the only economically viable structure. Important scale economies in transmission reinforce this view. After privatization, regulation of the electricity sector was based on the notion that this configures a natural monopoly for transmission. The law explicitly considers the access problem that arises in this context. However, the regulation is plagued with inconsistencies and ambiguities that have rendered this area a major source of conflicts and legal disputes.

The structure of consumption also raises access issues. In the Greater Northern Integrated System, consumption corresponds mostly to large, isolated mining operations that directly negotiate supply contracts with generators. By

[5] There are two other isolated, state-owned systems in the extreme south of Chile, which we exclude from the analysis in view of their small size (23MW and 88MW).

Map 8–1. Electricity Systems in Chile

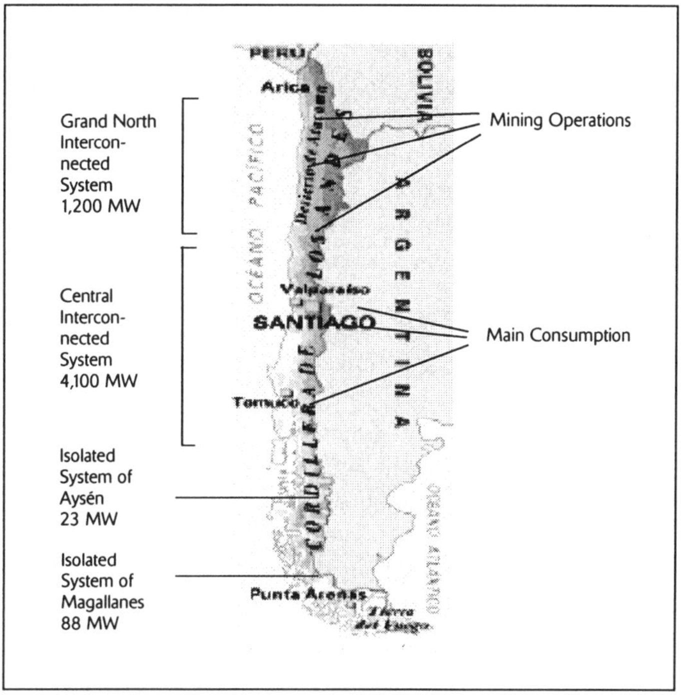

contrast, in the Central Integrated System, electricity consumption is largely concentrated in Santiago (50 percent of industrial and residential consumption), where more than 45 percent of the population lives. This concentration of demand makes the Santiago distribution company (Compañía Chilena de Electricidad, Chilectra) a large local monopoly and an important player in the industry. Although strict regulation has been implemented concerning tariffs, service quality, and required investments, access to unregulated clients within the concession area remains controversial as discussed below.

Access problems are exacerbated by vertical integration structures resulting from the privatization process. The electricity sector in Chile was traditionally dominated by state-owned enterprises at the generation, transmission, and distribution levels. Vertical and horizontal integration was widespread. The privatization process initiated in the late 1980s was carried out under the presumption that generation was a potentially competitive market, while distribution and transmission were local and natural monopolies, respectively.[6] For the latter two, the plan envisioned a scheme combining private property and management under strict government regulation.

[6] For a detailed description of the institutional evolution of the electricity sector, see Soto (1998).

However, the privatization process produced a market structure inconsistent with the design envisioned in the regulatory framework in two important areas. First, high-voltage transmission lines were sold as part of the main generating firm, Empresa Nacional de Electricidad (Endesa), thus conforming de facto to a vertically integrated firm. Although Endesa was required to separate transmission lines from generation plants, it retains 100 percent of the property of the transmitter Transelec. Second, the government did not enact the necessary restrictions on ownership across segments of the industry. As a result, a large conglomerate (Enersis) was able to control the main distribution company (Chilectra), the main producer (Endesa), and the monopoly in high-voltage transmission lines (Transelec, a subsidiary of Endesa).[7] Table 8–7 shows the market structure in the electricity sector.

The authorities have repeatedly claimed that Endesa's dominant role in generation and transmission does not allow fair competition in the sector. This vertically integrated structure has been the source of many legal disputes and conflicts. The first major attempt to separate the integrated firm started in 1990 when the National Economic Prosecutor filed a complaint with the Antitrust Commission against Chilectra, Endesa, and Transelec for noncompetitive behavior. The complaint was rejected, as was an appeal to the Supreme Court. The prosecutor initiated a second procedure immediately after the first trial ended. The second trial lasted until June 1997 and was again rejected.

The government could have imposed tighter ownership controls after privatization to prevent Enersis from holding simultaneous interests in distribution, transmission, and generation. Ownership is not the main issue when regulation is correctly enacted and informational asymmetries are not significant, however, this was not the case in Chile (Shapiro and Willig 1990).

Open-Access Issues in Transmission

Both scale economies and Chile's particular geographical conditions support the notion that high-voltage transmission is a natural monopoly. Consequently, to ensure competition, the law guarantees open access to transmission lines in the form of an easement. That is, as long as lines have excess capacity, a transmission company cannot refuse to serve any producer interested in dispatching energy to a consumer, or in selling in the spot market, even if the tariff has not been agreed on in advance. However, the regulation is incomplete in two important areas: transmission tolls and new investments required to expand the network when necessary.

---

[7] In addition, Endesa benefits from privileged information on new commercial areas, water rights, and reserve management, and would have been able to discriminate or block entry of potential competitors (see Basañes, Saavedra, and Soto, this volume).

Table 8–7. Market Structure in the Electricity Sector, 1997
(Percent)

Market	Central Integrated System	Greater North Integrated System
Generation		
Endesa and affiliates	59.2	8.0
Gener and affiliates	22.1	11.0
Colbún	12.0	n.a.
Tocopilla	n.a.	50.0
Edelnor	n.a.	21.0
Others	6.7	10.0
High-voltage transmission, 500KV		
Endesa-Transelec	100.0	0.0
High-voltage transmission, 220KV		
Endesa/Chilectra	80.4	0.0
Gener	5.0	0.0
Edelnor	0.0	100.0
Distribution		
Chilectra (Santiago)	40.0	n.a.
Chilquinta (Valparaíso)	20.0	n.a.

n.a. Not applicable.
Source: Energy Commission.

The 1982 electricity law did not establish clear procedures for setting transmission charges. The legal framework was modified in 1990 to establish a price system for the transmission sector based on influence areas (for valuing operation costs) and incremental-cost estimates (for network expansions). Although the 1990 law did not detail the manner in which such tariffs were to be calculated, it mandated that within one year CNE must issue the corresponding technical and economic details of the procedures to be used in calculating transmission tolls and other regulated features of the sector. This electricity sector statute was not issued until early 1998. Regulated firms have gone to the Supreme Court, disputing the statute as inconsistent with the electricity law. The eight-year period before the statute was issued induced uncertainty, inefficiency, monopoly, and rent-seeking activities.[8] When it was finally released, the statute did not contain a useful methodology for determining transmission tolls.

The law specifies only that tolls are prorated between users and that tolls should cover facilities within the area of influence of a generating unit, that is, the network of transmission lines and other installations necessarily affected by

[8] In a number of cases, loopholes in the regulation induce grave anti-competitive practices (see Soto 1998).

injections of power by a user.[9] The definition of the area of influence is ambiguous because any action by a user must necessarily affect the entire system. As discussed extensively in Díaz (1998) and Soto (1998), however, the ability to affect the network does not necessarily imply that tolls should be paid.

The problem of the lack of definition of transmission tolls has become increasingly important because of recent, substantial investment in gas-based thermoelectric plants installed around Santiago. A number of disputes and lawsuits have been initiated, but to date the authorities have not advanced a solution and court settlements have not produced a useful methodology for valuing these services. In some cases, the parties have used private arbitrage to settle disputes.

The absence of a clear mechanism for setting transmission tolls is aggravated by vertical integration. Although open access to lines curtails the monopoly power of the high-voltage transmission company (Transelec), it still retains important informational advantages that could benefit its parent company, Endesa. For example, when bidding for a supply contract, an important component of the offer of all generators is the transmission toll. Being a subsidiary of Endesa, Transelec cannot guarantee fair treatment to other generators and, as a result, competition is not always achieved.

When capacity is limited or new transmission lines are necessary, the law presumes that interested firms and the transmission company can negotiate an agreement to undertake the required investments. The potential user can choose to connect with the transmission company's network (thereby avoiding undertaking the investments) or to build the lines to satisfy its own requirements and connect with the network at the points the user deems most suitable. The law does not consider the possible asymmetric bargaining power of firms, in particular when the additional demand is not substantial. In the Greater Northern Integrated System, large mining operations are able to deal efficiently with this problem through public auctions of their demand for energy. In these cases, the negotiation usually involves generation and transmission companies. As is usually the case, when a satisfactory offer is not possible, the generating company offers to build its own (dedicated) transmission line. However, this option is limited in the Central Integrated System, where a substantial number of customers have small demands for which a dedicated line is not economically viable. In this latter case, the transmission company can exert its market power.

The authorities have been lenient toward the problems of vertical integration. In 1994 the Supreme Court judges issued a number of recommendations to achieve more transparency in the transmission sector (recommendations are considered mandatory in spirit):

[9] The law also establishes that the transmission company should calculate the value of the toll, the areas of influence, the capital replacement value, and the prorated toll. A user who does not agree with the toll calculated by the company has recourse to arbitration, but faces litigation costs.

- The pertinent authorities must issue a statute for the sector as soon as possible. To resolve existing ambiguities regarding the use of transmission lines and the setting of toll charges, the authorities must make all necessary changes to existing legislation.
- Because of the existence of information asymmetries, Transelec must become the owner of the assets it now manages. This should be undertaken in a manner determined by Transelec shareholders but within a relatively near time horizon.
- Given the lack of adequate procedures for ensuring the expansion of the transmission network when that becomes necessary, Transelec should open itself up to participation by other interested firms, regardless of whether they are involved in generation.
- In order to increase transparency, distribution companies should purchase energy and power by means of a public auction. The rules and regulations governing the auctions should be established freely by the distribution companies. These should apply generally to all and be nondiscriminatory, and public information should be readily available (contrary to current practice). The latter is necessary in order to eliminate any possibility of arbitrary or illicit discrimination and to transfer any potential cost reduction to users.

Of these provisions, only the second one was implemented, but it was done in a way that made Transelec behave as an Endesa subsidiary and not as an independent company. The government has not demanded compliance with the other three recommendations.

The statute is technically complex, in particular with respect to network expansions. Calculating prorated tolls under asymmetric (and largely unobservable) information is very difficult. In addition, the provisions will affect large players in the market in different ways, leading to political difficulties. The two main holdings in the electricity sector (Enersis and Gener) have commercial interests in several other areas of the economy and in other countries in Latin America, and are thus important players in the political arena. In addition, executives in the private sector consider CNE to be politically and technically weak; the recent mismanagement of the severe 1998–99 drought supports this notion (see Díaz, Galetovic, and Soto 2001 and 2000).

Open-Access Issues in the Distribution Segment

The law separates retail sales of energy in Chile into two markets: consumers with a power demand above 2MW are allowed to directly negotiate with generators (unregulated clients), while consumers below that benchmark pay regulated prices to distribution companies. Since electricity distribution presents large-scale economies at a local level, regulated prices are required to inhibit distributors from using their monopoly power.

These tariffs are determined based on two charges: the basic cost of energy and the value added in distribution. These charges are determined according to two independent methodologies. First, every six months the authorities calculate the *nodal price of energy*, which corresponds to the production costs at each point in the network, including transmission losses. Nodal prices consider a forecast of the short-to-medium-run cost of energy production optimized with regard to the availability of water. Second, every four years the distribution value added is revised according to an efficient-firm model. Since such an efficient firm does not exist, a simulation model is used as a benchmark. Under symmetric information, the mechanism should provide adequate incentives to firms to reduce costs by forcing them to compete against the simulated optimal firm. Under asymmetric information, however, this mechanism has the obvious drawback that the regulator does not have enough information to determine the cost structure of the efficient firm because actual market data costs are strongly influenced by those of the existing monopoly. Hence, the mechanism tends to converge to the standard rate-of-return model.

To avoid discrimination, the law requires that distribution companies serve all customers within their concession areas at equal tariffs and equivalent quality conditions. Nevertheless, there are two areas in which the original regulation was incomplete: concession overlaps and the access to unregulated clients within a concession area.

Regarding the overlapping of concessions, distributors were granted concession areas that are usually exclusive and based on historical (preprivatization) precedents. The regulators can grant concessions without limitations, but have traditionally expressed doubts about allowing overlapping distribution networks given the economic cost of duplicating facilities. CNE supports the notion that concession areas are largely determined by technical rather than economic factors. Concession areas can be urban or suburban, facing different legal and regulatory treatment (for example, different regulated prices). However, the regulation does not address the issue of which prices should be applied when urban and rural concessions overlap.

In 1990 conflict arose when a rival firm (Sinel) accused a large distribution firm (Chilectra) of predatory practices in an area where concessions overlapped. When Chilectra began to sell in Sinel's concession area, the latter feared that it would be eliminated from the market if cross subsidies from urban to semi-urban consumers were allowed (semi-urban distribution costs are 15 percent higher than in the urban case). The Antitrust Commission interpreted the electricity law as setting tariffs for customers, not for geographical areas, and, hence, sanctioned that concession areas were not exclusive (thus allowing overlaps) but that prices could not differ.

The main access problem, however, relates to the effective capacity of generators to compete with distribution companies for those clients located within the concession area. In the Greater Northern Integrated System, this is hardly a problem because large mining operations—which comprise a substantial portion of the unregulated clients—are invariably located outside the limits of concession areas. However, in the Central Integrated System, a significant fraction of unregulated clients—mainly industrial and commercial firms—are located within distribution areas.

In this regard, the regulation is incomplete in two areas. First, electricity transformation from high voltage to industrial or commercial standards is a largely nonregulated service and an important component of end-user costs. Determining an appropriate return to transformation is crucial for efficient operation of the market, in particular when contracts are auctioned. When bidding for an energy contract involving large consumers, generators also find it efficient to provide the transformation service by installing the necessary equipment. However, for medium-size clients (a significant part of the market), this option is economically inefficient and generators are usually forced to hire services from distributors. In this case, distributors have monopoly power and can extract rents from the market. This problem is aggravated when there is an ownership relation between distributors and generators (for example, Chilectra and Endesa) and contracts made by distributors are not public knowledge.

Second, when servicing an unregulated client within a concession area, the generator must negotiate sub-transmission tolls with the local distributor or build a sub-transmission line and install the necessary equipment. These tolls are not regulated but left to negotiation among the interested parties. The law implicitly presumes that their negotiating power is equivalent. In general this is hardly the case and it is certainly not true when there is vertical integration between generators and the distribution company. It is easy for a distributor to benefit its affiliate generator in energy auctions by simply charging rival generators a higher sub-transmission fee. In the largest Chilean market (Santiago), the situation is even worse because the distributor is allowed to compete against generators for unregulated clients within its concession area. Obviously, competition under these circumstances cannot be fair since the distributor will not undercut itself.

Final Remarks

Chile was one of the first Latin American countries to engage in full-scale market deregulation and divestiture of state-owned enterprises. The electricity and telecommunications sectors are among the most interesting cases of network privatization. The benefits of divestiture in both sectors have undoubtedly been significant in terms of increasing the efficiency of production, improving the quality of services, and extending coverage. However, the evolution of these sectors presents an interesting contrast from a regulatory point of view. While regulation in the electricity sector was once considered pioneering, it has not properly adapted to market evolution and is now to a large extent outdated. On the contrary, in the telecommunications sector, the initial regulation was weak and incomplete, but it has steadily progressed and adapted to changes in the industry. Open-access issues are at the center of deregulation processes, but they are hardly sufficient to guarantee a successful outcome from market restructuring. In both sectors, open-access provisions were a key component of the design of regulation.

Ambiguities and limitations in the regulatory framework regarding the practical application of the open-access principle led to substantial distortions in the functioning of the electricity sector. Vertical integration has deepened the adverse effects of poor regulation. In the telecommunications sector, implementing open-access provisions has demanded a substantial effort by regulators to overcome both the limitations of regulation and the economic and political power of telephone service incumbents.

The evolution of regulation in the telecommunications and electricity sectors offers an interesting contrast regarding the role of the authorities in overcoming the limitations imposed by regulatory ambiguities and inefficient privatization outcomes. In the telecommunications industry, the authorities have pursued an active stance of attacking the sources of monopoly power and introducing competition policies in local and long-distance telephone service markets. By contrast, in the electricity sector, lack of regulation has led to substantial litigation over monopoly power, over-investment in transmission facilities, and friction among competitors in the generation market.

Several lessons emerge from the Chilean experience that can be useful to other countries. First, the existence and enforcement of provisions guaranteeing open access to networks are crucial to reaping the benefits of privatizing the telecommunications and electricity industries.

Second, while it is true that without open-access clauses incumbents can easily use their monopoly power, it does not follow that open-access provisions are sufficient to guarantee adequate and efficient operation of the industry. Open-access policies need to be supported by detailed regulations including technical procedures, efficient pricing formulas, and explicit conditions for interconnection. These rules are essential for enforcing interconnection rights without incurring long, costly disputes.

Third, the methodologies for setting tariffs must be technically sound and known in advance by firms. Setting incorrect interconnection and access charges could jeopardize the introduction of competition in network industries. Setting correct charges requires detailed information about the incumbent's cost structure, so it is important to guarantee that regulators have access to the necessary information from incumbents. Insufficient access to information by regulators is an important limitation in achieving effective regulation in the sector.

Fourth, incumbents can exercise market power even if open access is guaranteed and other firms participate in the market. Consequently, the authorities must still address competition problems in concentrated markets such as cream skimming, segmentation, and blockading. Developing a competitive market when there is a dominant operator is a costly and long-term process. These costs may justify the implementation of market power reduction schemes before the divestiture of the industry, and the introduction of vertical integration restrictions during the privatization process.

Fifth, the strength of regulatory institutions and agencies from an institutional point of view is crucial for promoting competition and shielding technical decisions from lobbying and political interference. Even if privatization leads to quasi-competitive market structures, the operators of public utilities tend to have important political and economic power. In the presence of ambiguities in regulation, lobbying and disputes are likely to appear and, although some may be legitimate, they would mostly reflect rent-seeking behavior. In addition, since conflict is not unusual, it is important to design the regulatory structure so as to minimize litigation costs.

References

Armstrong, M., and C. Doyle. 1995. *The Economics of Access Pricing.* OECD Report. Organisation for Economic Co-operation and Development, Paris, France.

Baumol, W., J. Panzar, and R. Willig. 1982. *Contestable Markets and the Theory of Industry Structure.* Harcourt Brace Jovanovich.

Coloma, F., and L. Herrera. 1990. "Análisis institucional y económico del sector telecomunicaciones en Chile." *Cuadernos de Economía* 27(82).

Díaz, C. A. 1998. "Análisis del sistema tarifario de transmisión eléctrica." Universidad de los Andes, Santiago, Chile. Unpublished.

Díaz, C. A., A. Galetovic, and R. Soto. 2001. "Anatomía de una crisis eléctrica." *Revista de Análisis Económico* 16(9): 1–71.

———. 2000. "La crisis eléctrica de 1998–1999." *Estudios Públicos* 80(Spring): 149–92.

Duff & Phelps Chile Clasificadora de Riesgo. 1998. "Informe sector de telecomunicaciones." Sectoral Report published by Duff and Phelps (December).

Economides, N. 1996. "The Economics of Networks." *International Journal of Industrial Organization* 14(2).

Economides, N., and L. White. 1995. "Access and Interconnection Pricing: How Efficient is the 'Efficient Component Pricing Rule?'" *Antitrust Bulletin* XL(3): 557–579.

Hunt, S., and G. Shuttleworth. 1996. *Competition and Choice in Electricity.* London, UK: John Wiley & Sons.

Laffont, J. J., P. Rey, and J. Tirole. 1998. "Network Competition: I. Overview and Nondiscriminatory Pricing." *Rand Journal of Economics* 29(1): 1–37.

Melo, J., and P. Serra. 1998. "Competencia y regulación en telecomunicaciones: la experiencia chilena." *Perspectivas* 1(2): 215–47.

Shapiro, C., and R. Willig. 1990. "Economic Rationales for the Scope of Privatization." In E. N. Suleiman and J. Waterbury, eds., *The Political Economy of Public Sector Reform and Privatization.* Boulder, CO: Westview Press.

Sidak, G., and D. Spulber. 1997. *Deregulatory Takings and the Regulatory Contract. The Competitive Transformation of Network Industries in the United States.* Boston, MA: Cambridge University Press.

Soto, R. 1998. "Ambigüedades en la tarificación de la transmisión eléctrica en Chile." Universidad Alberto Hurtado, Santiago, Chile. Unpublished.

Tabja, R. 1997. "Análisis de la tarificación en telecomunicaciones." Universidad de Chile, Santiago, Chile. Unpublished.

CHAPTER 9

Access Arrangements in Argentina's Public Utilities: Electricity, Natural Gas, and Telecommunications

Santiago Urbiztondo, Sebastián Auguste, and Federico Basañes

The current wave of infrastructure privatization in Latin American countries is characterized not only by an ownership change, but also by the introduction of competition in areas that in the past were considered natural monopolies. Deregulation efforts have successfully expanded the scope of competition in various sectors with network characteristics. Countries have restructured (or are restructuring) electricity, natural gas, telecommunications, and transport industries. They are introducing competition, depending on the particular characteristics of the markets, in the generation of electricity, production of natural gas, retail of electricity, nonlocal telephone service, and among different train operators using the rail system. In most of these cases, the competing activities still need to use the existing network to provide the service.

The benefits of promoting competition in the competitive segments of these industries cannot materialize unless rival firms gain access to the networks that are essential inputs for the provision of final services. In the electricity industry, rival generators must have access to transmission facilities. Similarly, for retail competition, access to the distribution network by intermediaries (retail suppliers) and large users needs to be fair in order to have some competitive pressure and improve the alternatives open to final

The authors thank María del Carmen Tettamanti, Gabriela Larrauri, Alicia Federico, Inés Valdez, and Juan Manuel Magliano for discussions. A previous version of this chapter was presented at the Workshop on Second-Generation Issues in the Reform of Public Services at the Inter-American Development Bank, Washington, D.C., October 1999.

users.[1] In the gas sector, producers require access to transmission pipelines and retailers and large users need access to the distribution network in order to have competition in both ends of the market. In the telecommunications industry, access to the local loop—by suppliers of long-distance services and cellular operators—creates a bottleneck. Such access is needed because strong network externalities can be attained only through interconnection, and because it is neither economically efficient nor generally feasible for new competitors to duplicate the existing facilities.

Regulating access to the network is crucial for the efficient functioning of these industries. Indeed, with the progressive introduction of competition, a greater number of rival firms will seek to interconnect to the networks. Therefore, an access price has to be determined at each interconnection point. Prices should be sufficiently high to be compensatory (at least cover the long-run incremental cost of the use of the network by the entrant), yet not so high as to preclude efficient operation by the entrant. Regulation should ensure that there is sufficient pressure on the owner of the infrastructure to operate in an efficient manner, but that no unnecessary duplication of network construction takes place while preserving incentives for maintenance and expansion of the existing net.

A major consideration for the introduction or deepening of competition is to examine the legal room for doing so and also the fairness of recovering admissible stranded costs. The determination of access charges, as well as the rest of the regulated prices, is related to this problem. The economic literature offers two major approaches to the efficient pricing of access to networks: the efficient component pricing rule and the global price cap rule.[2]

The efficient component pricing rule maintains that the holder of the bottleneck facility should offer its services at a price that yields it the same contribution that it would earn by performing the end-user service itself. When the holder of the network sells the final product, it makes a certain profit; for it to be indifferent between selling the input to a competitor or using the input (network) to produce and sell the service itself, both options should yield the same profit. Consequently, there would be entry only when the potential competitor could compensate the network holder, pay its own costs, and still make a profit, that is, when the competitor is more efficient than the network holder. The efficient component pricing rule is consistent with efficient competition—it ensures that the responsibility for supplying the service is

[1] Naturally, the definition of "fair" is in itself arguable. Conceptually at least, it should resemble the outcome in the absence of any barriers to entry, but then again, the definition of a barrier (and its dynamic effect on competition) is not unequivocal. See Costello (1998) for a discussion of this issue regarding the regulation of a public utility and its affiliated market retailer.

[2] See Willig (1979); Baumol and Sidak (1994); Laffont and Tirole (1996); Armstrong, Doyle, and Vickers (1996); and Armstrong and Vickers (1998).

distributed in such a way as to minimize total costs. However, the rule is not sufficient by itself to allow competition to fulfill its other important functions of eliminating allocative inefficiency and eroding monopoly profits. The ultimate determination of the economically efficient retail price (and therefore the level of contribution that should correspondingly be incorporated in access charges) must be determined by regulation.

The global price cap rule recognizes the fact that the profit of the integrated network holder is an increasing function of both the access charge and the final retail price (under a break-even constraint, a higher access charge would permit the regulated firm to lower its final price). A regulator concerned with consumer welfare would take this tradeoff explicitly into account and regulate the owner of the essential facility according to a global price cap that includes both access charges and final goods prices. If the firm is constrained by perfect global price caps, then it has incentives to set appropriate prices both to end users and to rivals. The optimal level of the access charge will depend on the benefits of reducing the retail price (which will depend on the elasticity of demand) and the effects of raising the access charge on productive inefficiency (which will depend on the competitors' elasticity of supply).

However, despite their powerful theoretical results, the information requirements for both schemes are considerable. The translation of either approach into practical rules for guiding regulators and their accountants and engineers has proven to be a difficult task so far. Even the efficient component pricing rule, distinguished by its low information requirements, needs an estimate of the opportunity cost of access, which is subject to strong disagreement. Looking ahead, the implementation of the global price cap rule could be feasible through delegation of price authority to the regulated firm. However, there would be an interval in which potential predatory behavior or political unsustainability would require some sort of cross subsidies. Implementing the rule would mean that prices would be weighted corresponding to the quantities to be supplied, which is not an easy task but is much easier and "doable" than complete calculation of prices. Weights would be needed because private incentives over the structure of tariffs coincide in this case with social interests as represented by Ramsey prices, which minimize distortions in the allocation of resources (Laffont and Tirole 1996).

In Argentina, the introduction of competition has been explicitly planned. The country experienced an unprecedented transfer of services and publicly owned firms to the private sector, both by transferring property and by contractual agreements (concessions) with or without exclusivity. In general, but not always, the sectors involved have been characterized to some degree by sufficient economies of scale and scope that the resulting natural monopoly required the direct regulation of the acting private firms. However, some provisions were made regarding the introduction of competition in different segments of the markets. Such was the case for generation and commercialization in the energy sector (both electricity and natural gas); the use of infrastructure in the railway concessions; and progressively mobile, long-distance, and basic telephone service.

However, the "open access" policy has had different degrees of progress in these sectors. Competition in electricity generation has been strong. Instead of creating problems in symmetry of access, vertical separation of production, transmission, and distribution led to conflicts concerning externalities and financing of further capacity. In natural gas, the underdevelopment of an integrated transportation net, the rigidity of supply contracts, and potential problems with insufficient competition upstream have meant that the production market is not sufficiently integrated and therefore problems with access to the network come from the demand side. Access in telecommunications is now of particular importance in light of the opening to competition of long distance in 1999 and basic telephone service in 2000.[3]

The particularities of access arrangements in the electricity, gas, and telecommunications utilities allow us to identify common and individual issues of interest for international comparison and future public policy. Considering each sector in turn, we describe the industry, summarize the initial legislation and regulatory adaptations applying to access up to 1999, and describe the kind and degree of competition in place. We interpret the conflicts of interest involved among the different participants and the effects of the rules and legislation.

Electricity

Argentina's power sector has undergone important restructuring since 1992. This process has included the vertical disintegration of generation, transmission, and distribution of electricity; the privatization of all the activities at the federal level; and the introduction of a new set of pricing and regulatory schemes.

The legal basis of these reforms was established in 1989. The federal government began by franchising the distribution and commercialization of SEGBA, the utility supplying electricity to Greater Buenos Aires. In 1992, SEGBA's electricity generation and transmission activities were privatized through international bids. Since then, major assets in all segments of the power sector have been privatized or concessioned, with the exception of some distribution utilities that are still in the hands of provincial governments.

[3] Interconnection with cellular companies and some local operators has provided some observations regarding access to a basic facility by noncompetitors, as the services provided by those entrants have been complementary to those provided by the owners of the essential facility.

The Wholesale Electricity Spot Market (MEM) was also created in 1992 to allow all generators, distributors, transport utilities, and large users to trade electricity.[4] A gradual deregulation of distribution systems has permitted large users to enter the market and negotiate contracts directly with generators. As a consequence of deregulation and privatization, more than 2,000 agents participate in MEM. Of these, 44 are generators, eight are high-voltage transport and transmission utilities, 31 are federal and provincial distribution utilities, and the rest are large users.

A highly competitive electricity market has emerged as a consequence of this restructuring of the wholesale segment. MEM permits the spot price of electricity to be set hourly with due consideration to fluctuations in demand. MEM defines the spot price but also employs a special mechanism known as "seasonal prices" to moderate short-run fluctuations through special provisions of averaging and compensation. Under the new regulatory scheme, the seasonal price is the only rate that can be passed through to end-users by distributors. The scheme also permits a transitional pass-through of prices for electricity included in contracts sold together with the assets of national companies, although these contracts expired in the year 2000.

Any firm wishing to produce electricity can enter the market if it meets technical and safety standards. The main actors in the generation end of the market are independent power producers, national government generators, bi-national utilities, and foreign producers. In order to prevent vertical reintegration of the power sector, firms already operating a distribution network are not allowed to generate. To protect generators and distributors, transmission carriers are not allowed to buy or sell power. This prohibition results from the assumption that transmission is a natural monopoly (and monopsony), and thus those carriers could end up enjoying excessive market power.

Although competition in the operation of the given transmission network was deemed impossible or inefficient, the government has introduced market auctions for the right to deliver the transmission services, and sometimes threatens to replace the concessionaire. The concession for transmission is exclusive for 95 years.[5] Insufficient investment in the transmission grid has been one of the main problems associated with the reform, as lack of adequate property rights has required the introduction of voting mechanisms with certain inefficiencies.

Both distribution and transmission companies are regulated as to tariffs and quality standards. The three largest distribution companies in Argentina buy

[4] Argentina has two independent systems, MEM and MEMSP—the latter operates the Patagonian System.

[5] There are five regional transmission companies and new firms are allowed to build and operate new transmission lines under the technical supervision of Transener, which operates the main transmission network.

almost 60 percent of the country's electricity generation. All the other distribution companies are or will be regulated by the provincial governments according to some variation of the national model, which gives an exclusive concession to distribute electricity in a specific geographical area. The exclusive concession is subject to three main legal obligations: (1) to meet present demand and any increase in it; (2) to be responsible for an investment program that can satisfy predetermined technical and commercial quality standards; and (3) to grant any generator or large user open access to its network.

A detailed regulatory framework governs the operation of the three segments of the power sector. In particular, this framework has encouraged strong investment in generation, provided stable rules that have resulted in strong declines in the spot and contract prices of electricity, decentralized power decisions, and enhanced reliability and quality of supply. Further, average electricity prices are lower in Argentina than in many developed countries, and they are in line with previous medium-term historic trends. Naturally, some difficult issues remain unresolved, but these are generally attributed to the insufficient market orientation of the regulatory system introduced in 1992.

The Secretary of Energy, under the Ministry of Economy, formulates nationwide energy policies, sets guidelines for economic dispatch in MEM, and oversees the functioning of CAMMESA. CAMMESA is the nonprofit agency acting as system and market operator of MEM, and is jointly owned by the Argentine government and associations representing generators, transmission companies, distribution companies, and large users.

The National Electricity Regulation Agency (ENRE) is the federal regulatory entity. An autonomous agency, it supervises the nationwide transmission and distribution of electricity in the concessions following the privatization of SEGBA in Greater Buenos Aires. ENRE authorizes tariff updates, controls the quality of service, applies penalties, approves expansion projects, and mediates conflicts. The municipal and provincial governments regulate the privatized municipal and cooperative distribution companies, respectively, through analogous regulatory bodies. Although ENRE has no authority over provincial or municipal companies, it consults with the provincial regulatory bodies and influences the entire power sector through rulings that govern the interconnected system.

Access

Open access to the transmission and distribution networks can be defined from two sides: generators have to be treated without discrimination, and large users need to be able to pay for and use available capacity also without specific constraints. Considering the upstream generators, the common pool within which supply is constructed in Argentina guarantees this open access and therefore the issue is easily accomplished. Thus, it is more relevant to consider open access to final users and intermediaries who commercialize energy and apply competitive pressure to the distribution companies.

According to Law 24.065, transporters and distributors may not grant or offer advantages or preferences with regard to access to their facilities other than those based on specific classes of users or particular differences established by ENRE. They may not engage in acts that imply unfair competition or abuses of a dominant position, with ENRE representing the authority of first instance in charge of establishing such violations. The regulator may be asked to intervene in cases where an agreement cannot be reached in regard to required service conditions. In these cases, the regulator has to settle the dispute with the basic goal of ensuring supply of the service.

Commercial and physical bypass of the distribution company is allowed for large users, creating two types of competition: (1) among generators, to sell in blocks to the distribution companies (who now receive stronger competitive pressure to procure energy efficiently); and (2) between generators and distribution companies to sell electricity to the large users.

The legislation recognizes three types of large users: major large users (grandes usuarios mayores, GUMAs), medium-size large users (grandes usuarios menores, GUMEs), and individual large users (grandes usuarios particulares, GUPAs). The legislation classifies the large users according to their consumption; all of them are allowed direct access to MEM in order to make their energy purchases.[6] These categories of large users were created gradually over time: GUMAs started to operate in MEM in February 1993, GUMEs in February 1995, and GUPAs in February 1999. The number of large users participating directly in MEM has been growing since the reform of the sector in late 1992, especially the GUMEs. In June 1999, there were 1,983 large users operating in MEM (figure 9–1).

The original law contained no provisions in regard to retail suppliers or marketers. This concept was introduced later, in Resolution SE 186/95. This resolution defined MEM operators as companies licensed by the Secretary of Energy to market electricity supplied by international interconnections, binational enterprises, and companies other than MEM agents making block sales of electricity.

Access to the Distribution Network by Third Parties

Large users that require more than 50 kW of power have free access to MEM. Figure 9–1 shows that the use of access to MEM increased from 1993 to 1998. This occurred for different reasons. Naturally, bypass might allow large users to

[6] The different categories of large users have various technical requirements, including provisions for minimum proportion and length of energy contracted in the futures market.

Figure 9–1. The Number of Large Users (MEM and MESP)

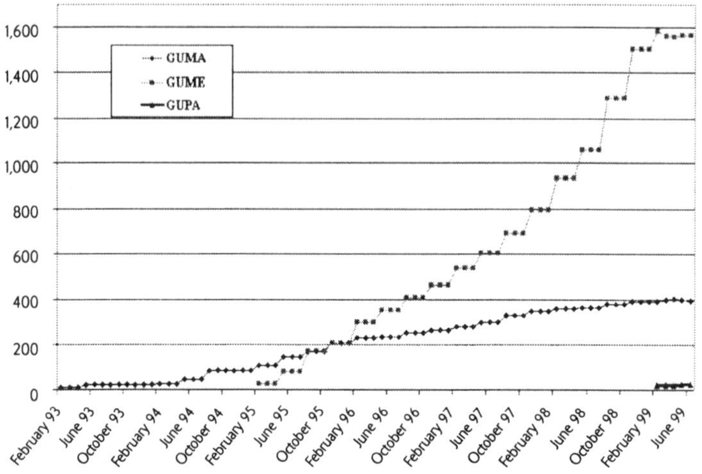

Source: CAMMESA.

procure cheaper energy by paying the spot price instead of the seasonal price that the distribution companies are allowed to translate to final users. But there are other possible sources of differences in prices. For example, due to tax asymmetries, bypass allows users to avoid some provincial and municipal taxes and charges applied to transactions in general (that is, the tax on gross income, which is lower when the energy component is brought directly to the exporting jurisdiction) and to energy directly. In addition, other types of constraints imposed on distribution companies make them less competitive in buying energy.

One of the problems engendered by commercial bypassing and the subsequent enlargement of the definition of a large user has to do with so-called assigned contracts. These contracts for purchasing electricity were assigned to the distribution companies (Edenor, Edesur, and Edelap) as part of the process of privatizing the former government enterprise SEGBA S.A. The contracts covered up to 50 percent of electric power needs. However, the slump in power prices on MEM in the wake of privatization efforts left prices under the contracts unduly high, constituting a kind of stranded cost. Thus, large users that engage in bypassing create increased costs for other captive users, since a larger percentage of the energy purchased under these contracts is allocated to them.

To correct this problem, the Secretary of Energy issued Resolution SE 425 (August 1998). The goal was to neutralize (at least temporally) the effect of the expanded definition of a large user (as established under Resolution SE 423, which created the concept of GUPAs), and the increased trend of GUMAs and GUMEs becoming agents of MEM and bypassing the distribution companies.

This resolution introduced a variable transition charge (CTV) on those large users that choose to commercially bypass the distribution company at any time after February 1999.[7] The intention of the CTV is to protect captive residential users, who would have to pay increasingly high energy prices because of the stepped-up use of commercial bypassing.[8]

Figure 9–1 indicates that the number of large users becoming new agents of MEM stopped growing in 1999, which reflects the effectiveness of the CTV. Indeed, it is tempting to conclude that avoiding these assigned contracts has been the only motive for commercial bypass. However, it could also be true that a number of larger users who became agents of MEM had reached an equilibrium by the end of 1998, independent of the CTV.

A related issue is the generalization of the right to choose an electric power supplier. In June of 1998, the Secretary of Energy publicly announced plans for a project designed to extend to all power users the right to choose an electric power supplier. The project was to begin with those users with a consumption level of more than 50 kW (this phase was successfully implemented with the inclusion of GUPAs as MEM agents). As part of this project, billing procedures would be modified as of 1999 to differentiate between wholesale energy and power costs and the costs of services provided by the distributor (network expansion costs, operating and maintenance costs, retail-level marketing costs, and costs of technical losses).[9] It was planned to later extend this right of choice to users that require more than 30 kW (Intermediate Phase II), and to all users by the year 2000.

This project, which has been informally abandoned since the new Secretary of Energy took over in late 1998, spawned debates over the feasibility of its implementation within the envisaged time frame. However, the experience in Great Britain and Norway suggests that granting universal open access to all end users of electric power service is technologically feasible. In addition, the assigned contracts were scheduled to lapse in 2000, making it likely that competition would be introduced in the retail electric power market in the not-so-distant future. Taking full advantage of this new kind of competition will require updating certain regulatory provisions with respect

[7] According to the preamble to this order, the CTV was established to prevent possible over-procurements under the assigned contracts by establishing that, if such a situation did occur, its full effects could not be passed on in corresponding charges to final users.

[8] The CTV added to the technical transportation function usage charge is figured according to the time period and distribution area. ENRE is the agency responsible for setting this charge at quarterly intervals until the assigned contracts lapse in 2000, ensuring that it is equitably divided among users continuing to deal with distribution companies and large users in proportion to their energy consumption.

[9] Energy and power costs include the costs of the various phases of transportation plus energy, power, reserve, and service costs, which ought to be passed on to users according to their corresponding consumption patterns.

to setting wholesale energy prices and exclusive transportation rights. In particular, full competition downstream will require deregulation of final tariffs charged by the distribution companies, development of a true contract market, declared contracts with final users, and deregulation of the construction of new transmission lines.

Access to Transport by Large Users

Access to the distribution net leads to commercial bypass and puts competitive pressure on the distribution companies, reducing the use of cross subsidies among different types of users. The possibility of physical bypass—for example, direct connection of the user with the transmission line without using the distribution network—also helps to induce efficient operation and pricing of the distribution network by placing additional competitive pressure on the distribution companies. Users can credibly threaten physical bypass to gain strategic positions for negotiating better prices for use of the distribution network. In general, except for particular types of users (located next to the transmission line or new users who demand extension of the network), physical bypass is unusual. It should be used only in cases of inefficient bargaining between distribution companies and bypassing users (perhaps due to regulatory rigidities preventing price differentiation).[10]

The competitive threat of physical bypass rests on the clarity of the rules for accessing the transmission lines. There are clear rules for setting transmission charges. Clear ground rules with regard to the expansion, financing, and usage of private transportation lines connecting the user to the transportation system are also needed to ensure that physical bypass is a real possibility.[11]

Argentina's initial regulations in this area were criticized for their failure to adequately spell out the corresponding property rights.[12] The expansion of private lines was to be determined by negotiations between the interested parties. Charges for third-party use of resulting excess transportation capacity were to be calculated in all cases as if they were existing facilities, ruling out any possibility of passing on the amortization costs of corresponding expansion projects to these third parties.

[10] Instead of referring to "price discrimination" we speak of "price differentiation." The reason is to avoid the common mistake of confusing differences in prices related to differences in costs with those that are unrelated to costs (only the latter being discrimination). Indeed, the confusion often leads to thinking that price averaging is the prohibition of price discrimination, when in fact it might be the opposite.

[11] Current regulations contemplate three types of transportation system expansion: (1) under contracts between interested parties; (2) through competitive bidding; and (3) small-scale expansion.

[12] Prior to Resolution SE 179/98, regulations in this regard were provided by Article 31 of the regulatory framework (Law 24.065) and by Resolution SE 2743/92 establishing regulations for access to existing capacity and expansion of the transportation system.

In the face of repeated complaints by MEM agents demanding priority of use to those bearing the full amortization cost of the corresponding investments, the Secretary of Energy issued Resolution SE 179/98. It allows priority in accessing new transportation capacity to the agent engaged in expanding a line supplying power to high-demand users (particularly industrial users). Nevertheless, this priority status is regulated and limited to a specific time frame to allow for the possibility of third parties accessing this transportation capacity at some future point.[13]

The resolution establishes the following requirements for authorizing construction of a transportation line or other transportation facility designed for private use:

- The line must be radial and extremely short in length.
- The line must be connected to the point technically closest to the electric power network.
- There should be no foreseeable public convenience or necessity for sharing the line or facility use with third parties, even in the long term.
- The party applying for authorization must have the written consent of all third parties with ownership rights to public or private property impacted by the layout of the line or the site of the facility in question.

In sum, compensation for expansions of transportation capacity made under contracts between interested parties is the same as for existing facilities. Corresponding amortization costs may not be passed on to the user population, which operates as a major deterrent to physical bypassing. However, effective as of 1998, parties making expansions designed to meet energy demand from the interconnected system through a radial line have priority over other third parties as far as access is concerned, which affords at least a partial solution to this problem.[14]

Determination of Charges

The regulatory framework establishes that transportation and distribution tariffs cannot differ among clients except due to location or type of service as approved

[13] From a technical standpoint, expansions of the electric power transportation network tend to be modular in nature, making it that much more difficult to bring the expansion project completely in line with demand and generally requiring that excess capacity be built. Thus, third parties are legally entitled to access any excess expansion capacity even during the period in which the construction agent is given priority over the new line.

[14] Priority status with respect to access to a radial line lapses immediately upon the granting of authorization to access such line that makes the radial line an integral part of a network. In no event may such access be denied on the grounds of engendering the lapse of this priority status.

by ENRE (Article 44, Law 24.065). That is, the general principle applicable is nondiscriminatory pricing, although this is not fully the case regarding access charges.

ENRE regulates the transmission tariff, which is the same for all types of users, based on technical parameters. Thus, the transmission cost per kWh between a given node and given zone is the same for all consumers using that part of the network at that particular time, regardless of their level of consumption or of whether they are customers of a distribution company. This charge is made up of two basic components: fixed charges (connection and transportation capacity charges) and variable charges (based on losses and the probability of power line failures). The total charge paid to the transporter is calculated based on these fixed and variable charges as a fixed sum for each rate period.[15]

The technical transportation function is the connection service provided by the electrical facilities making up Argentina's interconnection system or those directly or indirectly connected to this system (physically linking buyers and sellers of electricity and also linking them to MEM). In other words, any MEM agent can perform the technical transportation function; when this function is served by an agent whose main business is not transportation, such an agent is called a "nontransporting agent."[16] This service is provided under the principle of open and equal access, regardless of the agent performing it.

The determination of the access charge to be paid to the nontransporting agents (that is, the distribution and subdistribution companies) falls under Resolution SE 159/94 by the Secretary of Energy. This resolution amends Resolution SE 61/92, and provides that charges for access are to be freely negotiated by the parties concerned.[17] The agreed terms must be offered under the same conditions to every large user. These contracts have been rare because they must be made public. Instead, discount agreements have generally been informal and covert. In the absence of an agreement, the Secretary of Energy sets the charge and other contractual conditions. According to Resolution SE 406, which was passed in June of 1996, ENRE sets default maximum charges (and discounts for low-quality transportation) for the technical transportation function. ENRE calculates the value added by distribution, which varies slightly among provinces (and is often lower than that calculated by the provincial governments).

---

[15] Nevertheless, variable charges continue to be used as an indicator in setting node prices. Therefore, total income received by the transportation company is fixed, but users face positive marginal costs.

[16] There are two types of electrical facilities: high-voltage (with voltage of 132 kV or higher) and low-voltage (with voltage under 132 kV). Nontransporting agents typically operate low-voltage facilities, and the transmission companies operate high-voltage ones.

[17] There are two exceptions. The first is the case of the transportation of high-voltage power and trunk distribution transportation systems, which continue to be governed by the procedures established under Resolutions SE 61/92 and 137/92. The second is the case of concession holders operating distribution utilities with respect to the service provided to the large users in their respective areas, which continue to be governed by the provisions of their respective concession agreements.

Negotiations about the access charges for the technical transportation function are free within a regulated interval that varies from province to province but is set by the national regulator. In this sense, differentiation of access charges is possible, but extreme inefficiencies or exploitation of monopoly power in provincial concessions or distribution companies is federally constrained. One example of this is a conflict in the province of Córdoba, where ENRE resolved that the access charges should be those under Resolution SE 406 instead of the higher ones that the provincial distribution company EPEC demanded (see ENRE Resolution 1726, December 1998).

According to the regulations, all large users requesting the services of the technical transportation function must enclose a copy of a supply contract with a generator. The toll is made up of three components:[18] a monthly charge for transportation capacity usage, a charge for transported energy, and a surcharge for the use of transportation systems owned by other agents. The first two elements are calculated by the Organismo Encargado del Despacho (OED, Dispatch Administration Office) according to pre-established formulas. The provider of the technical transportation function is liable for the payment of charges due to all other transportation service providers, such as fixed-trunk distribution and high-voltage transportation charges (variable charges are not included in the usage charge).[19]

Evolution of Third-Party Access

According to CAMMESA, there are 380 GUMAs, 1,556 GUMEs, and 22 GUPAs operating in MEM, and 18 GUMAs and seven GUMEs in the wholesale electricity market in Patagonia (MEMSP). Total demand contracted by large users reached 852,645 kWh in March 1999, and purchases in the spot market added up to 322,377 kWh (table 9–1).

In 1998, large users originated 10.7 percent of total transactions in the futures market and 4.3 percent in the spot market. Large users bought 69 TWh in MEM (about $2,000 million) and 3,435 GWh in MEMSP ($95 million, table 9–2).[20]

Considering the evolution of commercial bypass since the privatization of SEGBA and the reform of the industry, figure 9–2 shows the percentage of total commercial energy in MEM by large users and self-generating plants. The figure indicates that commercial bypass by large users increased continuously, reaching 20 percent including self-generation.

---

[18] The usage charge includes the cost of expanding necessary networks to preserve service quality.

[19] Variable charges for usage of the high-voltage and trunk distribution transportation system are not included in the usage charge; they are collected directly by OED on behalf of and in the name of the transporters, and are calculated based on the MEM node corresponding to the provider of the technical transportation function.

[20] Values are in U.S. dollars.

Table 9–1. Energy Traded by Large Users in the Wholesale Electricity Markets, Argentina, March 1998

Energy transaction	MEM[a]	MEMSP[b]
Contracted demand	840,853	11,792
Purchases in the spot market	226,390	95,987
Sales in the spot market	83,179	

[a] Argentina's Wholesale Electricity Spot Market.
[b] The market that operates the Patagonian System.
Source: CAMMESA.

Table 9–2. Energy Traded in the Wholesale Electricity Markets, 1998
(Millions of dollars)

	MEM[a]			MEMSP[b]		
Agents	Spot market	Futures market	Total	Spot market	Futures market	Total
Generation	620	1,151	1,771	43	37	80
Distribution	764	905	1,669	6	1	7
Large users	62	246	308	53	36	88
Transportation			248			15

[a] Argentina's Wholesale Electricity Spot Market.
[b] The market that operates the Patagonian System.
Source: CAMMESA.

Related Observations

According to estimates by the Secretary of Energy (1998) based on a survey of 23 distribution companies in Argentina, tariffs for industrial users are reasonable and comparable across the country, whereas residential tariffs are also reasonable for low levels of consumption. Nevertheless, as consumption increases, 45 percent of the distribution companies have very high residential tariffs, and 30 percent have high tariffs for commercial users. That is, the tariff disparity in the provinces is more pronounced for commercial and residential users, which in turn means that the potential advantages from the generalization of bypass and the right to choose the energy supplier in the future vary regionally.

The implementation of bypass, both commercial and physical, has often required intervention by ENRE and the Secretary of Energy. In general, ENRE has granted permission for bypass as requested by the distribution companies. However, in 1996 ENRE denied MEM access to New Shopping S.A. as a GUMA, following protest by Edenor S.A. because New Shopping redistributed electricity to a shopping center on its property. After the appeal, the Secretary of Energy

Figure 9–2. Commercial Bypass in Electric Power (Percentage of commercialized energy in MEM)

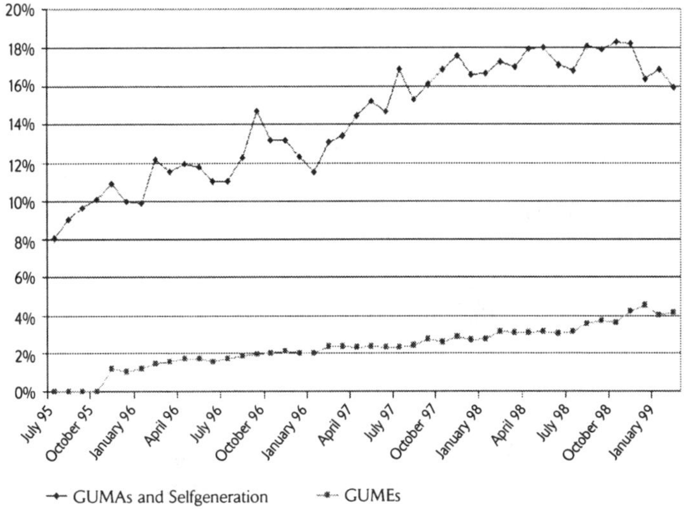

Source: CAMMESA.

granted in 1998 (Resolution SE 394) the requested permission (which enables New Shopping S.A. to bypass Edenor). The ruling considered that New Shopping S.A. was always treated as a sole client by Edenor, and therefore commercial units within the shopping center were not third parties. The Secretary of Energy noted in the resolution that previous resolutions by ENRE in comparable cases granted the permission for commercial bypass in the first place.

Natural Gas

Since the privatization of Gas del Estado S.A. in late 1992, natural gas in Argentina has been provided through nine private distribution companies (eight until 1998), all of which are supplied from the three main production areas in the country (Norte, Neuquina, and Austral) by two different pipeline operators (north and south). As in the case of electricity, the gas industry was vertically separated to favor the development of competition wherever it was technologically and economically feasible. To avoid vertical integration, restrictions were imposed on ownership of production, transportation, and distribution (no more than 20 percent of the existing stock in these areas can be held by the same owner). In particular, large industrial users may buy gas directly (through brokers) from producers, bypassing the distribution companies either commercially or physically.

Considering the structure of tariffs and final services provided, residential and commercial users receive a firm (noninterruptible) service, but industrial users and power generators can choose (and pay accordingly) the order of preference in case of a shortage. Shortages commonly occur during the winter (peak shaving is very limited) despite the important growth—28 percent—in the maximum volume of gas injected and a 30 percent growth in transportation capacity since 1993. Distribution companies need to contract firm transportation capacity. Due to seasonal fluctuations, this has meant important under-utilization in the summer months, resulting in an average utilization of approximately 75 percent over the entire year.

Despite this regional separation at the distribution level, regulation of transportation and distribution is centralized at the federal level, and is carried out by the Ente Nacional Regulador del Gas (ENARGAS), an autarkic entity created at the time of privatization. The regulatory framework and operation licenses constrain and guide ENARGAS's decisions. Upstream, at the production fields, various producers competitively set prices. The most important producer—YPF, recently acquired by Repsol from Spain—sells more than 60 percent of the gas produced, raising some concerns about the degree of actual competition. In particular, prices at the wellhead have increased since 1993 (by approximately 17 percent in real terms), introducing pressure on the regulatory adjustment to accommodate this development in tariffs for final users according to the passthrough formulas.[21]

In accordance with Law 24.076 and Presidential Decree 1732/92, ENARGAS is responsible for approving tariffs (margins) for transportation, tariffs for final users, and the passthrough of gas costs. It also verifies safety and quality requirements and environmental conditions. Other federal and provincial agencies regulate upstream activities, but prices and entry are freely determined. The federal government granted transportation and distribution licenses for 35 years, renewable for 10 additional years, at the end of which a new auction will have to be carried out to determine which private entities will continue to provide transportation and distribution services.

The development of this market has been quite satisfactory in different dimensions. Overall tariffs have become normal as compared with the structure in other countries. Both tariffs and margins of joint transportation and distribution are somewhat higher than in Canada, but much lower than in Great Britain, Germany, and France. Other indicators of coverage, productivity, and quality have improved significantly compared with previous trends.

---

[21] Some arguments might explain this increase in prices at the wellhead as a natural competitive development. See Urbiztondo (1999).

Access

The regulatory framework created by Law 24.076 establishes the principle of open access, prohibiting transporters and distributors from engaging in acts involving unfair competition or abuses of a controlling market position. The law also requires them to allow third parties equal access to their transportation and distribution capacity (commercial bypassing) so long as it does not jeopardize their ability to meet demand by providing contracted services. The transporters and distributors may not grant or offer any advantages or preferences with respect to access to their facilities other than those based on specific differences as established by ENARGAS.

Distributors are assigned clearly demarcated geographic areas, purchasing gas under agreements entered into directly with the gas producer or marketer. According to the provisions of Article 13 of Law 24.076, in principle any consumer may purchase natural gas directly from the producer or marketer, freely negotiating the conditions for such transactions. However, the consumer must give ENARGAS and the distributor six months' advance notice of its intention and must also finance the corresponding metering equipment.[22] Moreover, the licenses limit the definition of consumers eligible for bypassing the distribution company to large users (users with consumption over 10,000 cubic meters per day in the case of firm distribution or firm transportation service or over 3,000,000 cubic meters per year in the case of interruptible distribution and interruptible transportation service) and subdistributors.

Determination of Charges

The regulatory framework does not allow transportation and distribution companies from engaging in price discrimination. However, this is enforced only regarding transportation. The prohibition holds for distribution through the regulated tariffs for the different categories of users defined by ENARGAS, but it does not apply to access charges to large users engaged in commercial bypass.[23] Indeed, the transportation charge is the same for all users (depending on the type of service) and is not discounted. Thus, in principle, there are no gains to be made in this area for parties engaging in bypassing.[24]

[22] As an alternative, the consumer may choose to pay a surcharge on top of the charges set by ENARGAS. With the exception of parties with direct connections to a producer or transporter (physical bypassing), such consumers must meet all obligations incurred under the provisions of the distributor's service regulations. Compressed natural gas (CNG) stations cannot bypass the regional distributor under Article 13 of Law 24.076.

[23] Assuming the equal prices do not constitute a discrimination of prices, when in fact some cost differences for users of the same categories would imply the opposite.

[24] There are certain discounts made for firm transportation service that are prohibited in the case of interruptible transportation service. Discounts on firm transportation are minor because contracts between transporters and distributors allow the latter to reduce their contracted capacity in the event of the loss of any of their customers.

By contrast, the interested parties freely negotiate the terms of access to the distribution network, although they have to be lower than the regulated value added by distribution. Since the resulting discounts are confidential, the differentiation (and perhaps discrimination) of prices exists even when theoretically it is not allowed. ENARGAS may be asked to intervene in cases where an agreement cannot be reached. It would hold a public hearing within two weeks from the filing of the request for intervention and settle the matter within a period of 60 days from the commencement of the proceeding.

In other words, the regulations do not specifically require the access charge to the distribution facilities to be necessarily lower than the price of combined distribution and marketing services, and parties engaging in commercial bypass could be paying for a service that, in principle, they are not using (marketing).[25] The distributor will negotiate different charges according not only to the different cost of servicing each user, but also considering its alternatives (that is, their price elasticity of demand).

Resale Market for Transportation Capacity

The development of competition requires clearly defined (and transparent) access and transportation rules and a pricing system that can (among other things) efficiently allocate transportation capacity. In this regard, the regulatory authority has tried to streamline the resale market for transportation capacity.[26] ENARGAS Resolution 419/97 superseded Resolution 267/95, which caused numerous complaints from distributors and transporters, including claims that it would disclose confidential information. Resolution 419/97 established regulations for the resale of transportation capacity. Its stated objective is to expand the resale system, grounding it in the principles of open access, equity, efficiency, transparency, immunity, and confidentiality. This resolution creates a capacity resale market for the resale of all or part of transporters' transportation rights with a minimum daily volume of 10,000 cubic meters.[27]

The administrator records all offers, requests, and transactions made on the capacity resale market. Awards are made by means of open bidding according

---

[25] Distribution companies offer discounts and still face commercialization costs after commercial bypass (for instance, they still bill final users).

[26] Alger and Toman (1990) first proposed the creation of a resale market of transportation rights in the natural gas industry in the United States, pointing out the positive effects on the allocation of resources (signals for investment), the immediate expansion of transportation capacity, and the flexibility over the length of purchase contracts chosen.

[27] These regulations do not apply to the resale of capacity where the transference is through an "open bid," or the buyer of capacity is a distribution service provider during days in which the system is in a state of emergency.

to the best request (capacity demanded) under prevailing supply conditions (capacity supplied), thereby concentrating the information coming from both sides and speeding up the award process. Moreover, in order to ensure that competition in retailing is feasible, distribution companies may not refuse to provide transportation service as long as there is available capacity. And they may not discriminate against users that have purchased capacity on the capacity resale market and therefore do not use the transportation capacity contracted by the distribution company.

Tariffs involved in the resale of transportation capacity are determined in the following way. First, the outgoing loader, who sells its contracted capacity in the resale market, must pay the transporter the established price under the original transportation contract. Second, the incoming loader, who buys capacity, must pay the outgoing loader the capacity reserve charge established under the resale contract. That charge may not exceed the ceiling charge approved by ENARGAS for the receiving and delivery points established in the original contract. The incoming loader also pays the ED or TI charge to the owner of the transportation net, depending on whether it is in the same subzone as the outgoing loader. The incoming loader pays this charge regardless of whether it has the same delivery point as in the original contract and whether it is located upstream or downstream from the original receiving point.[28]

Thus, one advantage of the capacity resale market is that it makes some contractual conditions more flexible (such as changes in the receiving point or deadlines), which would otherwise–under an award mechanism based strictly on open bidding–be more rigid. The ceiling over prices paid by the incoming loader might prevent speculative buying of capacity for future resale, but more generally could avoid a transaction that is economical (assuming that seller and buyer do not find some hidden compensation mechanism).

The capacity resale market began to function only recently. Only eight transactions were recorded on this market in 1999. In general, sales are made by large users that, for a variety of reasons such as delays in investment schedules and bankruptcy, are not using their contractual capacity. In lieu of this market, firm capacity sales have been made through open bidding (generally for the remaining term of the original contract).

The explanation for the small volume of transactions on this market and the indifference on the part of larger users lies in its very structure. Distribution companies must contend with seasonal demand (peaking in the winter season) and, as a result, have an excess capacity in the summer that could be temporarily sold. However, larger users have consumption patterns that are not subject to

[28] The resolution specifies that, in the event of the payment of an ED charge, such charge must be exactly equal to the charge approved by ENARGAS and may not be discounted.

seasonal fluctuations (which explains why they enter into medium and long-term contracts for fixed volumes). Thus, large users engaged in bypassing have capacity contracts allowing very little margin for seasonal transactions, while large users supplied by distribution companies are required to give six months' advance notice of their decision to terminate service, which imposes constraints making it difficult to get out of these contracts.[29] No distribution company has brought to the market any of its contracted capacity, which means that contracted capacity is at the desired level either according to the distributors' own supply responsibilities or for avoiding firm transportation space that facilitates full commercial or physical bypass by large users. Furthermore, a natural rejection of this mechanism, coincident with the official interpretation, comes from transporters, as its general use would mean a decreased direct market for them. Consistent with this, the volume of resales of interruptible capacity is somewhat larger than that of resales of firm transportation capacity.

From a global perspective, the successful promotion of competition through open access of large users and retailers to both the distribution and transportation networks (resulting in commercial and physical bypass) requires three conditions. First, it requires a clearly defined, transparent access and transportation (transportation per se plus distribution) pricing system. Second, it needs a benchmark spot market to expand the supply and demand for gas and to provide guidance for long-term contracts.[30] Third, it needs a network code system allowing for individual access and the identification of transactions under a balanced system. This would avoid giving third parties information about private transactions and at the same time assure that choice of supplier is not instrumentally problematic (regarding the British experience, see Waddams Price, 1997). Even if these conditions are not fully met in Argentina (due to rigidities in the capacity resale market), competition through direct access to the distribution and transportation networks (in the form of commercial and physical bypass) has been strong. However, this does not prove that distribution companies were operating inefficiently. It could be due to the attempt by large users to avoid paying for implicit cross subsidies in the regulated tariff structure and in the computation of transportation costs for the determination of final tariffs, on the one hand, and to obtain certain tax benefits on the other hand.

---

[29] An additional factor might be the values of the regulated ED, which, if too high, might discourage purchase of the unused transportation capacity of an outgoing loader. Some flexibility over the determination of this charge would certainly be positive (or at least it would not provoke visible costs).

[30] Without such a market, distribution companies and large users must ensure their own gas supplies and tend to enter into medium and long-term contracts with producers, thereby limiting their flexibility and opportunities for engaging in different courses of action, making commercial bypassing an attractive option. The degree of upstream competition is also an important factor.

Forms, Determinants, and Effects of Bypassing

The final gas tariff is the sum of the price of gas, the transportation charge, and the distribution charge. Direct access by large users (bypassing the distribution company either commercially or physically) may be prompted by differences in the alternative prices to be paid in these segments or by differences in tax liabilities.

The prices paid by distribution companies in each basin are no higher than those paid by large users purchasing their gas supplies directly, with the exception of certain electric power generating plants holding extremely long-term contracts. However, there are advantages in purchasing gas directly because the user is free to choose the supply basins. Therefore, the user can select a combination that differs from that offered by the distribution companies, which are subject to price-setting regulations. That is, the price of gas passed on to final users is an average of the prices the distribution companies pay in the different supply basins. Users adversely affected by this averaging process are prompted to engage in commercial bypassing.

There are no significant discounts on the (firm) transportation charges, which means that, in principle, there are no gains to be made in this area for parties engaging in bypassing. Nevertheless, in those cases where distribution companies are supplied by two different basins, a full commercial bypass (the users contract their transportation directly) might result in lower transportation costs. This is due to the fact that the direct purchase avoids the averaging of transportation charges from the two different basins included in the price charged by the distribution company, which perhaps is not arbitrated at the point of delivery to the large user.

There is a regulated ceiling over the price for the transportation service provided by the distribution companies. The ceiling is equal to the value added by distribution, but free negotiations of discounts to lower it are allowed. It stands to reason that certain discounts would be made in the face of a plausible threat of bypassing, depending on the potential losses to the distributor engendered by this practice.

Both commercial and physical bypassing generally produce tax benefits, which vary from one province to another. These benefits stem from the avoidance of provincial taxes, such as the "stamp tax." A large user might enter into tacit, informal agreements with producers or under-declare the value of the contract. At the same time, the distribution companies must have formal contracts with the actual values involved in order to recover the cost of the gas in controlled distribution charges. Bypassing might also help users avoid the "tax on gross income." The tax paid to the distribution company is figured on the full invoice value, while engaging in bypassing can reduce the amount payable for the gas component as a result of the lower tax rate applicable to the hydrocarbons sector. Depending on the circumstances, this benefit could amount to as much as 3 percent of the gas price. Moreover, certain provinces levy taxes on the marketing of gas (the tax rate in Santa Fe, for example, is 7 percent), which can be circumvented through direct commercial bypassing (or, in other words, bypassing the gas retail marketer).[31]

From the standpoint of the distribution companies, the damage caused by the loss of large users choosing to engage in commercial bypassing depends on the extent of bypassing. However, foregone savings from large-volume gas purchases cannot explain the extent of bypassing. In the case of commercial bypassing that is limited strictly to the purchase of gas, the company continues to collect the distribution charge, although it may be forced to grant discounts to head off larger losses. These larger losses are sustained in two cases. In the first case, commercial bypass also includes the transportation service (called hereafter "full commercial bypassing").[32] The distribution company is unable to make use of its year-round firm contractual transportation capacity, which goes unused during the summer months when consumption by residential customers falls off. Second, in the case of complete (physical) bypassing, the user cuts all ties with the distribution company and therefore the company loses the full value added by distribution allocable to such customer and, where applicable, any possibility of reselling its excess transportation capacity during the summer season.

Thus, the mere possibility of sustaining a loss affects the distributor's bargaining power with respect to distribution charges (discounts) and, in this sense, the threat of bypassing, in and of itself, is damaging to the distribution company. The plausibility of the threat of full commercial or physical bypassing depends on whether it is really to the large user's advantage to build its own access to the transportation network or to purchase capacity other than from the distribution company at controlled prices.

Large users currently exhibit a pattern of behavior that the distribution companies consider opportunistic. In principle, if a large user engaging in full commercial bypassing has continuous service and wishes to keep such service, it should enter into a contract with the transporter for continuous service and should also pay the distribution company for continuous service. However, the expansion project carried out by the distribution companies to originally offer continuous service to the large user might have no alternative use. Or it might have excess capacity, so

[31] Gas retail marketers have the advantage of flexibility over distribution companies in the sense that they are able to grant large discounts compared with controlled charges, while distribution companies are also required to have contracts in place meeting 50 percent of their demand before the beginning of the season and are subject to certain requirements with respect to their firm transportation capacity that are not imposed on marketers.

[32] Full commercial bypassing occurs when the distribution company performs only the technical transportation function (in return for which it collects the distribution charge, less a possible discount in the face of a plausible threat of physical bypassing), while the large user makes its own contractual arrangements for the purchase of gas and transportation service, either directly or through a marketer.

that the large user has an incentive to contract with the distribution company for interruptible service at a lower rate while maintaining its contract with the transporter for continuous service to ensure supply of the desired volume of gas. That is, once the distribution company has carried out the irreversible investment to provide continuous service, full commercial bypass allows the user to pay for continuous service only to the transport company and not necessarily to the distributor.

Obviously, this type of behavior creates financing problems for distribution companies, which are forced to meet demand (in this case for continuous service). The distribution companies can bill only for what is theoretically a lower quality service (at a lower price), but which is the same service as initially demanded. The problem lies in the fact that, as a consequence of the imperfect design of the tariff structure, the large user would (to a certain extent) pay twice for transportation capacity by continuing to receive firm distribution service while engaging in full commercial bypassing. This is so because the value added by distribution (which determines the ceiling for the distribution tariff) includes a charge for firm transportation that needs to be paid for again in contracting with the transporter for continuous service. Thus, this so-called "opportunism" on the part of large users represents their escape from the double payment of transportation capacity for continuous service after full commercial bypass.[33]

The key problem is that the rate structure for financing the distribution service does not ensure that investments will be recouped in the expansion of the distribution network to meet new demand. At the same time, the cost of transportation capacity is included in the charge for firm distribution when it should not be included.

In sum, the main functions of direct access by users in Argentina's natural gas market are to reduce price distortions produced by the implicit cross subsidies created by regulation, and to procure tax benefits. Large users engaged in bypassing get tax breaks by avoiding or lowering provincial and municipal taxes on wellhead gas. They also circumvent higher gas prices in certain basins or the higher transportation costs associated with regulatory efforts to keep prices down for residential users (through a better choice of basins and/or a smaller load factor in the transportation charge).[34] The close ties between gas marketers and certain distribution companies are a clear indication that the reasons for engaging in bypassing are much more general in nature than a mere desire for greater

[33] Arguing that the problem disappears if the price for interruptible distribution covers the unbundled cost of this service is unsatisfactory. First, if such were the case, there would be a serious problem with the level of tariffs overall. Second, it should not be acceptable that investments are made under one condition (firm demand), for which a given price is regulated, and later payment is revised according to its computed cost.

[34] The load factor for residential users is 0.35, which, in the opinion of sources consulted at ENARGAS, makes adequate provision for differences in transportation costs for users with different seasonal patterns of consumption, thereby making this less of an incentive for resorting to bypassing.

efficiency through better business management. In particular, regulatory rigidities are key determinants. The degree of regulatory rigidities and distortions aimed at cross subsidizing from industrial users to residential ones would be higher if open access provisions did not exist or were less applicable.

Moreover, the resulting cost to distribution companies depends on the type of bypassing practiced. Partial commercial bypassing (in which distribution companies continue to provide transportation service) will not cause the distribution companies to sustain sizeable losses. However, physical bypassing causes distribution companies heavy losses in terms of the value added by distribution and the cost of their firm contractual transportation capacity for residential users, which they are unable to sell off to large users during the summer months. Lastly, full commercial bypassing by a user with interruptible service produces an intermediate cost for the distribution company. It is limited to the cost of the excess firm transportation capacity going unused during the summer season that it is unable to resell. A user that switches from continuous service to interruptible service as a result of its decision to engage in full commercial bypassing will cause the distribution company to suffer considerably heavier losses (requiring an appropriate adjustment in the rate structure, at the very least including a minimum commitment term for future service). It is noteworthy that a (plausible) threat of full commercial or physical bypassing constitutes a potential loss capable of triggering discounts and losses for distribution companies, even if the event never actually materializes.

Evolution of Competition

Growth in Bypassing

The number of customers taking advantage of commercial bypass possibilities has grown steadily since 1993 to as many as 99 users as of late 1998, or 23.7 percent of all eligible large users (figure 9–3). Naturally, the first customers to exercise this option were those with the highest consumption figures. They were later joined by large users with smaller average consumption figures that, over time, have reduced the average size of users engaged in bypassing. A breakdown of the volume of gas supplied by all distribution companies in 1998 shows third-party demand (commercial bypassing) accounting for 31 percent, a larger share than that supplied to residential users (25.6 percent) and to large users not engaged in bypassing (24.7 percent).

Table 9–3 shows trends in commercial and physical bypassing in 1993–97, broken down by distribution area. The slow but steady growth in physical bypassing (mainly concentrated in the south and northeast) contrasts with the

Figure 9–3. Percentage of Large Users Commercially Bypassing the Distribution Companies

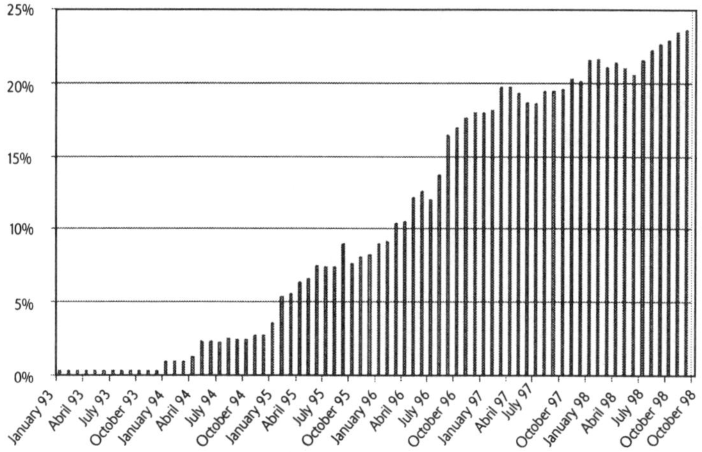

Note: The number of large users is the sum of users within service categories provided directly (ID, IT, FT, FD) and users demanding transportation service to the distribution company.
Source: ENARGAS.

consistently strong growth in commercial bypassing. The different license areas report different growth rates, averaging 31 percent of all gas supplied.[35]

So far, there have been no discernible attempts to broaden the definition of large users eligible to engage in bypassing, as was the case in the electric power sector. However, ENARGAS is considering this possibility. More specifically, it is considering extending bypassing to include users with a daily consumption of over 5,000 cubic meters (down from the requirement of 10,000 cubic meters/day). For the more distant future, ENARGAS is considering the possibility of including residential users, subject to the amendment of corresponding distribution licenses.

In contrast to the electric power industry, it is more difficult to promote bypassing in this sector and to generalize the right of natural gas users to choose their own supplier because the corresponding licenses do not provide for the eventual lapse of exclusive rights. These provisions were made in the concession contracts granted after the privatization of SEGBA in the electric power sector, which anticipated that the revision to be carried out in 2007 could be terminated if technology allowed competition in the distribution segment. The legal room for furthering competition is also present in the telecommunications industry due to the limitation of the term of exclusive licenses to a maximum of 10 years

[35] Note that the heavy impact of bypassing on the Litoral gas company is tied to the 7 percent provincial tax on the marketing of gas in the province of Santa Fe, as well as to the large share of industrial users in this province.

Table 9-3. Natural Gas Delivered, by License Area and Marketing Arrangement, 1993–97
(Percent)

License area and type of bypass	1993	1994	1995	1996	1997
Metrogas					
Commercial	0	0	3	28	40
Physical	0	0	0	0	0
Ban					
Commercial	13	13	14	15	19
Physical	0	0	0	0	0
Litoral					
Commercial	0	14	29	41	57
Physical	0	0	0	0	0
Pampeana					
Commercial	0	5	12	11	13
Physical	0	0	0	0	0
Sur					
Commercial	0	1	18	15	21
Physical	5	7	5	9	7
Centro					
Commercial	0	0	0	8	24
Physical	0	0	0	0	0
Cuyana					
Commercial	0	22	23	25	31
Physical	0	2	1	2	1
Noreste					
Commercial	0	18	30	43	34
Physical	13	23	21	20	36
Total country					
Commercial	2	7	14	24	31
Physical	2	3	2	3	5

Note: Figures do not include wellhead gas consumption in the Sur area and supplies for the Cerri plant in the Pampeana area.
Source: ENARGAS.

in the case of the privatization of Entel. It is important to keep in mind that the government has limited ability to reinterpret contracts compared with governments in other more politically and economically stable countries. In Argentina, the government has a negative reputation in terms of arbitrary policies adopted in the past, which would lead to an increase in the country risk that might produce more damage overall than the benefits from furthering competition in these regulated industries.

Discounts

In the past few years, ENARGAS has published information on discounts offered by distribution companies. The type of information furnished has changed over the years, from a general benchmark figure in 1995, to a breakdown of discounts by type of service in 1996, to a breakdown of discounts to different industries and to power plants in 1997. In its annual report for 1995, ENARGAS furnishes piecemeal data on discounts offered by distribution companies on ceiling prices charged to customers, including a 33.4 percent average discount in December 1995 for all types of services. This figure is not broken down by type of user or service and provides only a rough idea of the discounts offered at that time. In its annual report for 1996, ENARGAS breaks down discounts granted by the distribution companies according to the type of service; the average discount was 28.8 percent.[36] Discounts for the subset of services subject to commercial bypassing were quite a bit higher, at an average of 35.2 percent. Finally, in its annual report for 1997, ENARGAS breaks down these discounts by industrial origin, providing separate figures for discounts going to thermal power plants. The average discount for all types of users was 26.8 percent, compared with 33.1 percent for power plants and 19.5 percent for industrial users.

In other words, distribution companies offer large discounts to industrial users and electric power plants and, while the type of data published by ENARGAS do not show secular trends, a survey conducted by FIEL in 1997 showed larger discounts offered in 1996 compared with 1995 (FIEL 1999). Commercial bypassing was prohibited under the government monopoly until the early 1990s and, in general, there was less of an incentive to optimize pricing. Thus, it seems that there has been a strong surge in discounts since 1993, thereby magnifying the real effects of the competition engendered by open access reflected in the equally high level of bypassing.

Telecommunications

The telecommunications sector was one of the first and most important privatizations in Argentina. The formerly public firm ENTEL was privatized in 1990, when the country had not yet recovered from the severe macroeconomic conditions of the 1980s. The sector was made up of two firms (Telefónica de Argentina and Telecom Argentina), called Licenciatarias del Servicio Básico (LSBs), which provided local and long-distance domestic services. One firm provided service to the northern part of Argentina, and the other to the southern part. The firms shared the Buenos Aires metropolitan area in equal parts. They shared the provision of international services in a joint enterprise, and owned one of the three main mobile telephone companies. They also owned one of the three leading data transmission companies and entered the cable-TV business only recently.

[36] Discounts granted to large users vary according to the type of service provided, ranging from 24.5 percent for IT service to 25.2 percent for ID service, to 33 percent for FD service, to as high as 53.4 percent for FT service. This shows that the cost of full commercial bypassing is higher in the case of a user with continuous service (FD and FT service) that "opportunistically" switches to interruptible service in resorting to bypassing, thereby causing the distribution company to sustain heavy losses.

Perhaps because it was an early privatization, this experiment was affected by many design imperfections. One of the major problems was that the previous tariff structure (based on pervasive cross subsidization with a clear distribution purpose) was transferred to the new setting, bringing with it all the tensions associated with a heavy cross-subsidized price structure regarding its sustainability in the face of competitive pressures. The sustainability problem and the need to prepare the industry for a future competitive environment across its different segments resulted in a very conflictive and profound tariff rebalancing in 1997, reducing drastically the size of many cross subsidies, but retaining the important ones.

Another important weakness had to do with institutional design. The institutional regulatory framework was defined immediately after the bidding process with the creation of the Comisión Nacional de Telecomunicaciones (CNT). During its first year, CNT was an autonomous body, although its members were appointed by the executive without open contest. In 1991, the executive created the position of Undersecretary of Telecommunications within the scope of the Ministry of the Economy and Public Works and Services. Since then, CNT (which was renamed CNC in 1996, when the postal service came under its supervision) has remained under the control of the executive.[37] In 1996, the Undersecretary of Telecommunications was moved from the Ministry of the Economy and upgraded to Secretary of State in the Office of the President. CNC was the most unstable and politically dependent regulatory agency in Argentina following privatization. For all practical purposes, the regulator of the telecommunications industry has been the Secretary of Telecommunications.[38]

In any case, the situation at the time of privatization was one of a monopoly in local, short-to-long distance, and international services, along with limited competition in the other segments, where both firms have important interests. Competitive pressures were therefore supposed to be negligible during the licensing period. The licensing period was a seven-year concession of exclusivity rights in all voice transmission services (except for the mobile segment) under CPI-X price regulation (with X set at 2 percent per year), along with quantitative targets dealing with the expansion of lines and quality of service. The exclusivity of the license could be extended in 1997 for three years, with an increase in X to 4 percent per year, only if some additional coverage and quality targets were met.

When the time came to decide whether to extend these exclusive licenses, it was considered that the general targets set by Presidential Decree 62/90 had been met (the provisions of the decree may have been somewhat vague with respect to certain minor points). However, the government decided to extend

[37] Late in 1993, the positions on the Board of Directors were filled by contest, but in 1995 a new intervention changed the Board.

[38] In the following, we call the regulator the Secretary of Communications although this is the name by which it has operated only since 1996.

these exclusive license rights for only two additional years, formulating a policy of controlled deregulation to ensure real competition by strengthening new operators as well as existing independent operators. More specifically, Presidential Decree 264/98 provided for what was referred to as "controlled" deregulation of the telecommunications industry. Four companies—Telefónica, Telecom, and two consortia led by cellular operators—were competing in the long-distance market as of November 1999, and in the local market as of November 2000. Three additional companies were competing in the long-distance market in 2000.[39]

However, Law 25000 approved Argentina's commitment to the World Trade Organization to eliminate restrictions on access to the local market and to grant licenses in line with the provisions of domestic regulations, effective as of the year 2001. Regulations in this area had been implemented under the provisions of Resolution SC 16200 in June 1999 by the Secretary of Communications. The resolution approved the "General Licensing Regulations and National Licensing Plan." In line with previous legislation, Resolution SC 16200 sets stringent requirements for the obvious purpose of keeping out small operators targeting a small number of local areas or concentrated in small geographic zones within these areas. Thus, in essence, there is still a negative attitude toward competition for telephone service in official circles: the only welcome and acceptable type of competition preserves or limits changes in the existing pattern of cross subsidies.[40]

Stranded costs in the telecommunications sector are particularly low. Indeed, the licenses granted in 1990 provided temporal exclusivity for seven years and three-year extensions that contained payments compensating otherwise uneconomical provision of service in rural areas. Only mandatory, uneconomical investments set for the extension period between 1998 and 2000 should be considered as stranded costs to be recovered in the following years. In that sense, the scope for introducing competition in the telecommunications sector is very high from the technological, legal, and reputation points of view.

Interconnection during the Term of Exclusive Licenses

Prior to 1998, the following articles and decrees governed the legal framework regulating interconnection in telecommunications: Articles 23 and 24 of the Telecommunications Act (Law 19798); section 10.4 of the Terms and Conditions approved under the provisions of Presidential Decree 62/90, as amended; Articles 27 and 28 of Decree 1185/90; and relevant provisions of Decrees 506/92,

[39] There are several problems with the government's decision to limit the number of licenses. These problems cannot be resolved by restricting market access for new service providers as part of the deregulation process in Argentina (Urbiztondo, Aguste, and Basañes 1999; Spiller and Cardilli 1997).

[40] For more on the main provisions of Resolution SC 16200, see Urbiztondo, Aguste, and Basañes (1999).

663/92, 1461/93, and 1587/93. The Telecommunications Act allowed service operators to enter into agreements for the sharing of services, networks, equipment, and buildings. The terms and conditions provided for the two LSBs, the international service operators, and the competing service operator to interconnect their networks to ensure the continuity, expansion, and quality of telephone service.

All operators were required to furnish adequate numbers of connection centers and facilities with the necessary capacity to meet demand in a transparent, equitable manner. This interconnection requirement included all networks providing local calling service within the Buenos Aires Metropolitan Area, service between the north and the south, and international service. The license holders were free to negotiate the conditions for these interconnections, without this affecting the provisions of the terms and conditions in any way. In cases where an agreement could not be reached, the Secretary of Communications had the authority to set these terms and conditions. Interconnections involving license holders and independent local network operators were governed by these same principles.

In general, interconnection charges were to be set at a level that covered the cost of service delivery, including a reasonable return on fixed operating assets used in providing service, although there were no details or agreements with respect to the cost criteria to be used for this purpose. Moreover, rival service providers were to be given equal access to the existing network based on availability at regular, nondiscriminatory prices reflecting the use of network facilities and services. Once their exclusive rights lapsed, former license holders were required to allow their users to access the networks of rival service providers under conditions equivalent to those under which such service was furnished to their own users on their own respective networks, subject to technical constraints.

There were four main types of interconnections, namely: (1) between LSBs; (2) between an LSB and an independent operator (IO), a small telecom in the interior of the country, mostly local cooperatives; (3) between an LSB and cellular telephone service operators; and (4) between an LSB and value-added service providers (for example, an Internet service provider). Interconnection arrangements between LSBs were of the "bill and keep" variety (with each party keeping the value of its own billings), assuming a balanced two-way flow of traffic. The Secretary of Communications was concerned about obtaining the necessary information to enable it to enforce interconnection requirements vis-à-vis other operators. Therefore, the Secretary required that LSBs provide information on their interconnection agreements. However, this requirement did not meet with success and, in turn, led to the imposition of sanctions on LSBs in 1997 for failing to include in their interconnection agreements guidelines that were consistent with those established in Presidential Decree 62/90.

Independent operators (primarily cooperatives) providing basic service in small population centers under exclusive licenses were initially treated like end users under arrangements for their interconnection with LSBs. The independent operators entered into agreements with a number of such cooperatives (including Copelco in Cuatralcó). Based on background information in those agreements, the Secretary of Communications made Resolution SC 61/97, which established terms and conditions for the interconnection of IOs and LSBs, pending the lapse of the exclusive rights conferred under licenses for the operation of basic telephone service. The resolution included the following: (1) the IO would receive 78 percent and the LSB 22 percent of revenues from long-distance calls initiated by a customer of the IO (using the LSB-owned network); (2) the LSB would keep all revenues from calls initiated by one of its own customers; and (3) each company would keep 100 percent of the value of billings for local telephone traffic (included in the long-distance charge for toll calls).

It turned out that 78 percent of outgoing long-distance traffic is more than adequate compensation for use of the IO-owned local network for outgoing and incoming traffic. This means that basic service in areas serviced by IOs has been subsidized by the long-distance service provided by LSBs (in addition to a 10-cent-per-minute subsidy for international calls initiated by their LSB customers).[41] Moreover, Resolution SC 18971 by the Secretary of Communications (establishing general universal service regulations) provided that Resolution SC 61/97 was effective until November 2000 (at which time only eligible IOs could obtain a universal service subsidy).

Cellular telephone service operators are required to pay the final price of calls carried by LSBs as if the cellular operators were the end users. In other words, there are no discounts for savings on nonallocatable network costs, while LSBs pay 35 cents per minute of airtime when one of their customers makes a call to a cellular phone.[42] This is a ceiling value on which cellular telephone service operators could offer discounts, particularly during off-peak periods. It is obviously a way for cellular operators to subsidize their own customers, thereby effectively discriminating against incoming traffic. The lowest marginal charge for an outgoing call from a cellular phone is approximately 20 cents, well below the 35 cents paid by LSB customers.

The problem with connection charges for value-added services does not lie in the pricing of the use of corresponding lines. Rather, it lies in the pricing of the outgoing connection to Telintar, the operator that held exclusive license rights for long-distance service until October 1999. Connection prices have plummeted over the course of the past few years (from $50,000 to $5,000).

---

[41] See Urbiztondo, Aguste, and Basañes (1999).

[42] Apparently, this value was set by the regulator in response to requests from cellular telephone service operators for a rate of 45 cents per minute during peak periods and 20 cents per minute for off-peak periods. Further study of costs seems to be warranted in order to regulate the terms of interconnection with cellular operators.

Interconnection and Competition

Despite legislation in effect at the time establishing basic principles and guidelines for interconnection arrangements, the Secretary of Communications issued Resolution SC 49 in January 1997 (ratified by Presidential Decree 92/97). The resolution established the regulations on interconnection, which would define the scope of these guidelines and address unforeseen problems expected with future growing competition. Thus, the new order established more precise basic principles and guidelines for interconnection arrangements effective as of 1998, including the following general principles:

- Free negotiation of interconnection agreements by interested parties, with the freedom to agree on corresponding prices, terms, and conditions, subject to intervention by the regulatory authority either at the request of the parties concerned, in the face of the refusal of a service provider to make the requested interconnection, or at its own initiative in the public interest.
- Equitable treatment with respect to corresponding technical or economic conditions.[43]
- Mutual compensation by service providers for transportation and for completing calls.
- Use of open architecture networks by the primary service provider, with the obligation, where requested, to furnish billing service, customer assistance service, information service, directory assistance service, emergency service, collect or operator-assisted calling service, and calling card service under equitable conditions and at least one switched-access interconnection point to all users in each local service area with more than 2,000 customers.
- Prices based on long-term incremental costs, with cross subsidies prohibited.
- Resale of services under equitable conditions.
- An obligation on the part of the primary service provider to keep accounting records as required by established regulations.

In other words, interconnection charges were to be freely negotiated by the parties concerned. However, in the event the interested parties were unable to reach an agreement in this respect, the Secretary of Communications would

[43] Interconnection agreements must be filed with the regulator and published in the Official Gazette, setting aside a 30-day period for the presentation of any comments or objections. The concept of equitable treatment also refers to the fact that the interconnection must be of the same or better quality than that provided by the primary operator to itself, with the same access as offered to its own customers.

set these charges based on long-term incremental costs. Moreover, in cases where long-term incremental costs cannot be established, corresponding price controls would be based on a comparative schedule of prices and conditions for similar services, functions, or components in Australia, Chile, France, Germany, Italy, Mexico, New Zealand, Peru, Spain, the United Kingdom, and the United States.

The requirement to use long-term incremental costs as the basis for setting interconnection charges meant that such costs were defined as including the direct costs of only those functions, components, facilities, and assets strictly necessary for interconnection purposes. These costs include planning, operating, and maintenance costs associated with necessary infrastructure, without taking into account their historical or replacement costs, with capital costs established based on market indicators. This was an innovative measure for Argentina, similar to the benchmark or model-enterprise-based price controls used in Chile.

As revealed by different international experiences, access pricing poses a major problem in the sense that the companies owning corresponding networks have made certain investments that they may have trouble recouping (historical costs for which long-term computations are impossible). These investments are often required to maintain implicit cross subsidies, making it difficult to base price computations on long-term incremental costs. In the absence of complete free-market pricing, it is unreasonable to require that only a single price (namely the access price) be set equal to the long-term marginal cost when, even with this flexibility, conditions associated with a natural monopoly justify using Ramsey prices rather than the aforesaid costs.

There is also the problem of overhead, which is exacerbated by the absence of a cost breakdown for different service components, particularly because established operators are not required to unbundle service components. These problems are further compounded by the danger of so-called stranded costs engendered by previous decisions taken by the regulator, that is, historical costs making their way into the estimates of incremental costs.

Possibly as a result of these problems, a number of provisions of Presidential Decree 92/97 were amended under Decree 266/98 approving new interconnection regulations. (Decree 92/97 was judicially challenged and was never enforced as far as interconnection is concerned.) The superseding order provides a clearer definition of the concept of long-term incremental costs (with corresponding computations including indirect costs or overhead) and of a number of previously ambiguous concepts associated with the issue of interconnection (such as physical interconnection, transit, and costing). It establishes a number of mandatory services, such as billing and collection services, access blocking for system customers with unpaid bills, and pre-subscription requirements in all locations with more than 5,000 customers. And it gives primary service providers certain obligations, including the obligations to provide dedicated long-distance links under equitable conditions and to refrain from making changes in their local service areas without prior authorization.[44]

However, there is a major qualitative difference between Decree 92/97 and Decree 266/98 in terms of the level of detail in establishing the individual service components that the primary operator must offer to its competitors. Decree 92/97 required an extensive unbundling of these components, in that any service components requested by a new operator entering the market not initially identified were to be considered by the Secretary of Communications for inclusion as essential components, to be offered separately under corresponding interconnection agreements. Decree 266/98 limited the identification and unbundling of essential components. This difference demonstrates how efforts to promote competition are focused on network duplication. This puts new competing basic telephone service operators at a strategic disadvantage compared with LSBs in the negotiation of interconnection agreements, and exposes the new operators to a greater financial risk from the larger investments required by network duplication. In general, network duplication is still just a future possibility, although several operators have indicated that they have definite plans in this respect, at least in certain high-profit areas.

The new legislation contains specific provisions regarding access pricing and various deterrents to changing service providers. It points to the government's intention of promoting competition strictly through network duplication, while preserving a rate structure that implicitly subsidizes certain users in the absence of a clear definition of the concept of universal service and of its form and sources of financing and recipients.[45]

Decree 266/98 set the following interconnection charges pending implementation of the above-mentioned pricing systems based on incremental costs or pegged to the so-called basket of benchmark countries: (1) local transit charges were set at $0.015 per minute for the duration of existing exclusive licenses (until November 8, 1999) and at $0.010 per minute thereafter; (2) access charges or fees for completing local calls were set at $0.035 per minute until November 8, 1998, $0.0315 for the period from November 8, 1998 to November 8, 1999, $0.0235 until November 8, 2000, and $0.0215 thereafter; and (3) the average network access charge for international calls was

[44] Decree SC 266/98 also modifies the basket of benchmark countries, eliminating France, Germany, Italy, Peru, and Spain. At the same time, it adds greater flexibility with a reference to the possible inclusion of other countries with similar regulatory frameworks.

[45] Resolution SC 18971/99 of June 1999 approved the General Universal Service Regulations and called for the establishment of a fund fed by contributions from telecommunications service operators based on the value of their billings. However, it also reflected the government's continued desire to refrain from making significant changes in the current rate structure and, in particular, its desire to keep residential rates at their present level, even at the cost of implicit cross subsidies.

set at $0.15 per minute, plus an additional $0.10 per minute under the concept of "network development" until November 1999 (which is an implicit reference to the financing of investments earmarked for the provision of universal service or the fulfillment of other types of contractual obligations).

According to the data presented in table 9–4, a cross-country comparison shows high access charges for completing calls. That is, such charges seem to be out of line with the medium-term guidelines established under Decree 266 based on a sample of countries with comparable regulations. At the same time, the network transportation charge appears to be comparatively low.[46] Moreover, it is noteworthy that, in absolute terms, the local access charge is higher than the transit charge, unlike the case in the other countries (where local access is less costly than network use for transit purposes). With a final price of $0.025 per minute for a local call in Argentina, the spread for local service competitors requiring access service does not become positive until 2000 (when they are actually allowed to enter the market).

The competition model behind the new regulations regarding access charges in telecommunications provides incentives for investment to duplicate the network (in order to avoid paying those charges). This might be reasonable for a country in which the telephone network is still underdeveloped (with a penetration rate of about 20 lines per 100 people). However, these incentives might reduce retail competition, particularly in less-populated areas where regulated final prices are cross subsidized from higher-than-cost tariffs in more densely populated areas.

Furthermore, the pre-subscription regulations (Resolution SC 2724/98 of December 1998) stipulate that, at least initially, competition in domestic and international long-distance telephone service will be grounded in the pre-subscription of customers to different telephone companies. According to the resolution, beginning in 2000, callers would be able to select a carrier on a call-by-call basis by dialing a three-digit prefix identifying the selected service provider (if other than the primary carrier to which the caller was pre-subscribed). In other words, each customer would be required to select a long-distance company to carry all its calls. Moreover, there is a minimum subscription period of two months, and customers would be charged for switching service providers (although the charge itself is not specified). Thus, together with other regulatory measures, it is conceivable that this mechanism was designed to curtail competition by making it more difficult and more costly for callers to choose their service providers. This would soften the kind of adjustment in tariffs that would follow from a more deregulated and

---

[46] For more on transit access charges in Argentina, see Urbiztondo, Aguste, and Basañes (1999).

Table 9–4. Interconnection Charges for Phone Calls in Selected Countries, Late 1990s
(U.S. cents/minute)

Country (year)	Local access	Transit
Austria (1998)	1.96	1.96
Chile (1998)	2.60	2.60
Denmark (1998)	1.07	1.98
France (1998)	0.76	1.86
Germany (1998)	1.08	1.84
Holland (1998)	1.27	1.74
Italy (1998)	1.64	2.69
New Zealand (1998)	2.00	2.80
Portugal (1998)	1.30	2.58
Sweden (1998)	1.24	1.93
United Kingdom (1998)	0.66	0.95
United States, Bell Atlantic (1997)	2.00	2.00
Average without Argentina	1.46	2.08
Argentina (1999–2000)	3.15	1.15
Argentina (2000+)	2.30 – 2.15	1.00

Source: Chambouleyron (1999).

competitive market.[47] This new order does not include any provisions for local number portability, which would eliminate switching costs for basic telephone service and therefore favor competition from new entrants.

As of the end of 1999, there was still no sign that the new legislation on interconnection agreements had gone into effect. More importantly, there were no formal complaints filed with the Comisión Nacional de Comunicaciones (CNC, which replaced the CNT in 1996). By November 2000, some IOs had made informal protests over the elimination of their subsidy by the LSB-owned long-distance network, prompted mostly by the fact that, in general, such subsidies cannot be fully replaced by universal service fund contributions.

Conclusion

Table 9–5 summarizes the access arrangements for electricity, natural gas, and telecommunications infrastructure in Argentina. With the exception of transportation tariffs in electricity and natural gas, where no price differentiation

[47] It is not clear that this could happen anyway, since promotions by different companies offer free minutes of calling time to encourage switching, offsetting the administered charge. In any case, the general estimates account for a minor charge (less than $5), whereas the minimum permanence of two months was abolished (immediately before long-distance competition was to begin).

is in fact allowed, in all three sectors the general principle is free negotiation between the parties involved, with resort to the regulator's intervention in case of disagreement. Nevertheless, in electricity (since 1996) and in natural gas, there is a regulated default level below which discounts are permitted. In telecommunications, the regulator has set terms for most interconnection tariffs for the next two years. As a result, intervention has occurred more often regarding nonprice conflicts (that is, the permission to perform physical or commercial bypass) than with respect to the determination of access charges following disagreements. However, the latter has been particularly important in the electricity sector, where federal and provincial regulations overlap.

In other words, when differentiation of prices is not allowed (transportation in electricity and natural gas, and overall in telecommunications), access charges are actually cost-determined. By contrast, differentiation exists in access to the distribution facilities in the natural gas sector and discounts are de facto covert in access to the low-voltage network operated by the distribution companies in the electricity sector. In these cases, access prices are also sensitive to demand (elasticity) considerations.

However, none of these cases has had adequate discussions regarding the costs the regulator will include in the computation of access charges or the procedures for arbitrating disputes. In the electricity and natural gas sectors, the regulated default access charges are implemented when the distribution company does not offer a discount, regardless of the offers made by the parties involved. Mediation in telecommunications is not necessary at this point. Thus, there is still plenty of room for advancing regulatory principles for future application in Argentina.

The situations in electricity and natural gas are quite similar regarding the importance of open access in order to perform both physical and commercial bypass to the distribution companies. The main difference is in the degree of competition, which is somewhat more developed in electricity and particularly important in terms of direct access to the distribution network (commercial bypass). In telecommunications, the complexity arises from the diversity of interconnection arrangements. In the past, competition in telecommunications has been applied to complimentary services; in the future, access will serve to connect direct competitors offering substitute services.

Regulatory measures of varied quality have affected the type and degree of competition. The electricity sector has expanded the definition of users allowed to bypass commercial and transportation services provided by the distribution companies, created the compensatory variable charge, and attempted to grant priority over constructed (linear) transportation lines. In natural gas, the creation of the resale market for transportation rights has not shown positive results (perhaps due to some regulatory rigidities therein). The resale market coexists with other restrictions imbedded in the concession contract, and with new regulations that force cross subsidies and distort competition. For example, the

Table 9–5. Summary of Infrastructure Access Arrangements in Argentina

Characteristic	Electricity	Natural gas	Telecommunications
Determination of access charges	Transmission: regulated. Distribution: free negotiation and intervention in case of disagreement, with regulated ceiling.	Transportation: regulated. Distribution: free and confidential negotiation of discounts from default tariff (value added by distribution).	Free negotiation in the future; now tariffs—except long-distance transit—have been set until November 2000 at least (no discrimination allowed). Reduced unbundling required.
Kind and degree of competition	Open access to transmission and distribution facilities. Commercial bypass, 2000 large users in the wholesale market. Physical bypass (limited to short radial lines to the closest connection point with existing network).	Open access to transportation and distribution facilities. Partial commercial bypass (induced by taxes and cross subsidies; not costly to distribution companies). Full commercial bypass. Physical bypass (small but growing).	Until 1999, cellular and fixed telephone service mostly complementary. Since November 1999, long distance is deregulated (four players until November 2000, three more at least then); one year later, basic telephone service also competitive (at least four players).
Relevant regulatory measures adopted	Expanding definition of large users. Resolution 425/98 (variable transition charge for assigned contracts). Resolution 179/98 (priority for radial extensions of transportation network). Resolution 406/96 (maximum default charges for access to distribution network).	Market for resale of transportation capacity (only beginning to work now). Resolutions granting bypass skipping formal arguments against them. Lack of discussion about competition in first revision of price cap in 1997.	Decree 92/97 (interconnection rules, with long-run incremental cost). Decree 266/98 (new interconnection rules, with less unbundling, indirect costs, and fixed access charges). Decree 264/98 ("administrated deregulation").
Desirable regulatory measures in the future	Deeper priority over linear expansion of transportation network. Prepare for generalization of right to choose supplier. Elimination of tax asymmetries. Favor development of contracts and correct allocation of responsibility for failures.	Expanding the definition of large users. Development of spot market and integration of transportation grids. Correct price structure of access charges, including permanence commitment for noninterruptible demands. Stop minor cross subsidies. Elimination of tax asymmetries.	Further deregulation of entry, accepting implied market restructuring of tariffs, explicitly subsidizing targeted users for universal service. Use of best practice references in other countries, or alternatively reduce regulated access charges.
Perception about future developments	Generalization of bypass and right to choose supplier (have to prepare legally for 2007, too difficult before).	Slow progress in furthering bypass. More competitive upstream, conditions facilitate spot market operations and then bypass.	Cross subsidies might not be sustained in the medium run, and further liberalization might be seen. Strong competition, particularly in long-distance and concentrated urban markets, is coming anyway.

first revision of the price cap over the gas industry in 1997 made no consideration of the acceleration of competition or the structure of tariffs. Technical and contractual innovation in the telecommunications industry is such that strong competition should be expected.

All three sectors have an important agenda to deepen competition and its beneficial effects on the general level of tariffs, innovation, and expansion. Legally and technically, the telecommunications industry is the most flexible and will experience the most action in the next few years. In electricity and natural gas, integrating the transportation segment, improving property rights for linear expansions, and increasing flexibility to favor the development of spot and futures markets will make those industries more competitive, not only considering third-party access but also in terms of the behavior of distribution companies.

In all cases, care should be taken with incentives to expand the integrated transportation network, since its development is a necessary vehicle for further competition and open access. In electricity, this has to do with improving the definition of property rights over linear expansions of the transmission network. In natural gas, it has to do with correcting the structure of the access price in order to avoid opportunistic behavior by large users who demand continuous service and then switch to interruptible service.

In comparison with the competition observed 10 years ago or with some other countries today, the degree of competition in these industries is remarkable. Naturally, there are some counter examples that indicate that still more competition is possible. Furthermore, the Argentine experience highlights some problems due to incorrect regulatory measures or just insufficient maturity of the reforms, which might cause a delay in competition.

Nevertheless, as the sectors analyzed show, competition might be excessive in some cases, particularly when it is induced by tax distortions or when it is motivated by the attempt to maintain implicit cross subsidies among different types of final users. Although correcting tax incentives and distortions at lower levels of government is difficult in a federal country, any kind of cross subsidy requires some type of sacrifice of competition. Subsidies for certain users might be deserved, considering externalities or distributive preferences, but they should be explicit in order to judge their merits, minimize their costs, and avoid leaks due to insufficient focus on the intended beneficiaries.

References

Alger, D., and M. Toman. 1990. "Market-based Regulation of Natural Gas Pipelines." *Journal of Regulatory Economics* 2.

Armstrong, M., C. Doyle, and J. Vickers. 1996. "The Access Pricing Problem: A Synthesis." *Journal of Industrial Economics* 94(2) June.

Armstrong, M., and J. Vickers. 1998. "The Access Pricing Problem with Deregulation: A Note." *Journal of Industrial Economics* 96(1) March.

Baumol, W., and J. G. Sidak. 1994. Toward Competition in Local Telephony. Cambridge, MA: MIT Press.

Briceño, A. 1999. *International Comparison Study about Interconnection Charges.* OSIPTEL Preliminary Working Paper. Lima, Peru.

Chambouleyron, A. 1999. "Barreras a la competencia en telecomunicaciones: un estudio comparado." IERAL, Córdoba, Argentina. Unpublished.

Costello, K. 1998. "Fair Competition in Retail Electricity Markets." National Regulatory Research Institute, Ohio State University, Columbus, OH. Unpublished.

ENRE. 1998. Resolution 1726, National Electricity Regulation Agency, Government of Argentina (December).

FIEL. 1999. *La regulación de la competencia y de los servicios públicos: Teoría y experiencia argentina reciente.* Buenos Aires, Argentina: FIEL.

Laffont, J. J., and J. Tirole. 1996. "Creating Competition through Interconnection: Theory and Practice." Journal of Regulatory Economics 10.

Secretaría de Energía. 1998. "Informe de perspectiva." Buenos Aires, Argentina.

Spiller, P., and C. Cardilli. 1997. "The Frontier of Telecommunications Deregulation: Small Countries Leading the Pack." *Journal of Economic Perspectives* 11(4).

Urbiztondo, S. 1999. "Algunas reflexiones iniciales sobre la adquisición de YPF por parte de Repsol." *Indicadores de Coyuntura.* May.

Urbiztondo, Santiago, Sebastián Aguste, and Federico Basañes. 1999. "Access Arrangements in Argentina's Public Utilities: Electricity, Natural Gas, and Telecommunications." Paper presented at conference, Second Generation Issues in the Reform of Public Services, Inter-American Development Bank, Washington, D.C. (October 4–5). Paper available at *http://www.iadb.org/sds/doc/1946end.pdf.*

Waddams Price, C. 1997. "Competition and Regulation in the UK Gas Industry." *Oxford Review of Economic Policy* 13(1) Spring.

Willig, R. D. 1979. "The Theory of Network Access Pricing." In H. Trebing, ed., *Issues in Public Utility Regulation.* East Lansing, MI: Michigan State University.

Part III. Highlights of Second-Generation Reforms in Energy Sectors in Latin America and around the World

CHAPTER 10

The Second Generation of Power Exchanges: Lessons for Latin America

Jaime Millán

Almost two decades ago, Chile and the United Kingdom started experimenting with power sector reform and privatization. Today, many other countries have adopted or are in the process of adopting a model that promotes competition in the wholesale power market that is based partly on the pioneering efforts of those two countries. As often happens, successful pioneers become the most fervent apologists for their innovations, touting their validity for all kinds of situations, regardless of the specific conditions in each case. The Chilean and British models provide the evolutionary basis for two models, which, while having many features in common, reflect special conditions of time and place. Some of the countries that adopted these models have introduced significant improvements, as in the case of Argentina. In particular, Norway stands out as an example of a third way, which carefully considered local conditions with satisfactory results. In addition, "second-generation" reformers, such as Spain, the United States, Australia, and New Zealand have come up with sophisticated innovations. Often the country arrived at these innovations through the support of a group of academics and experts who lent an almost religious air to the discussions.

However, some countries that adopted the British model, but whose systems were dominated by hydroelectric power, found themselves constrained by a structure that did not apply to their particular situation. Furthermore, the United Kingdom and Chile are themselves radically revising their power-trading arrangements. Does this mean that their systems failed and that the countries that adopted them should go on the alert and adjust their models? Or does it mean that the experiment failed, confirming the opinions of the opponents of reform and those who maintained that it was impossible to mount a competitive model in the wholesale electricity market?

This chapter attempts to answer these questions following the approaches of Sioshansi and Morgan (1999) and Henney (1998), among others. These authors seek first to understand the reasons (geography, history, the starting point, or the desired end point) for adopting one model or the other, and then go on to analyze a set of elements that are critical to the behavior of the system and its evaluation. The chapter looks at the purpose and objectives of power markets and discusses the factors that determined the structure of the markets in Chile and the United Kingdom. It compares the characteristics of the systems adopted by the first generation of reformers with an overview of the variations introduced into second-generation markets.

The chapter concludes by setting forth lessons for further modification of first-generation markets and for countries that are just starting to introduce reforms. However, the lessons do not lead to a "correct" model, since there is no such thing. Instead, they lead to a judicious position, which consists of adopting a commitment to follow a process that is guided by certain principles and accompanied by a large dollop of patience and realism.

What Do Power Markets Do?

The countries that have restructured their power systems have similar goals. All of them seek to establish competition in the electricity market to achieve economic efficiency and higher quality services, as well as lower consumer prices for electricity. Yet, there are important differences between developed and developing countries in the immediate objectives of restructuring. In the developed countries, restructuring often responds to the desire to introduce competition into a mature industry in order to make it more transparent, efficient, service-oriented, and self-regulated, as well as to reduce electricity costs. In many developing countries, which have defective infrastructure and a chronic lack of funds, the process is governed by the desire to attract foreign capital to meet growing demand (Sioshansi and Morgan 1999). Developed countries also have a relative abundance of human capital and well-developed market institutions. This introduces an important difference in the path that the reforms take and in the role that can be played by markets in the initial stages.

Power exchanges or wholesale electricity markets, like all organized competitive markets, are primarily vehicles to facilitate transparent transactions in order to contribute to price formation, provide maximum incentives for efficient production, and signal the investments needed in additional capacity. This holds true provided that the nature of technology and demand allows the market to perform these tasks better than an administrative system. However, this does not exempt the market from the need for regulation; it simply alters the nature of regulation to enable it to cope with new problems such as *market power*.

Market power is the capacity of one or more players to raise market prices and reap the ensuing economic benefits. Producers are naturally tempted to wield market power since the objective of the company is to earn profits.

The degree of competitiveness of a market is measured by the speed with which potential or existing competitors and consumers respond to and prevent attempts to exercise a dominant position. Thus, the actions of the regulator should result in lower prices, improved quality, and a larger variety of products, provided that the industry can remain financially viable and make the necessary investments. The two key elements that assure competitiveness in the market structure are the number and size of the participants, and the rules that govern the operation of the market. These two elements interact with each other, since a specific structure demands a set of specific rules and a given rule is not necessarily good for all structures. In turn, the rules can be affected by other factors, such as geography and the primary source of power (hydraulic or thermal). Lastly, the impossibility of storing electricity and the limitations that this imposes on grid operations mean that the electricity market requires special care. A well-designed market, which is the key to competitiveness, becomes the regulator's main task.

Over the last two decades, there has been a veritable avalanche of excellent literature on the subject. The articles by Sioshansi and Morgan (1999) and Henney (1998), as well as the study by Wolak (1997) on the impact of market rules on price formation in restructured electricity markets are excellent sources of information (this chapter is largely inspired by their analyses). Other analysts, such as Ruff (1999), present full descriptions of many aspects of the markets and advocate the need for a centralized compulsory pool. To appreciate the concerns that occupied the attention of the designers of second-generation markets and the solutions they came up with, it is useful to group them into six key issues:

1. Should a centralized compulsory auction, contracts, or both be adopted?
2. Which auctions or offer procedures and which price determination processes work best? How much transparency is needed?
3. What is the best way of balancing supply and demand? What role should demand play in price determination and should prices be decided a priori or a posteriori?
4. How should access to transmission systems with limited capacity be prioritized?
5. How necessary are capacity payments and how can the reliability of the system be guaranteed?
6. Which and how many institutions does the market need to function?

The need for a centralized compulsory auction in the wholesale context is perhaps the most controversial of all the above questions and has been the source of the greatest differences among second-generation markets. The answer to this question determines most of the responses to the others. For some, such as Ruff, the success of competition in the electricity market thus far is mainly due to the development of spot markets integrated with physical dispatch in real time. Ruff argues that this is the only practical method of internalizing the externalities inherent in the real-time operation of electrical grids and that without it many markets are unacceptable, inefficient, and unreliable. This explains why many experts think that an efficient market should reflect short-term marginal costs. By contrast, the proponents of the U.K. pool reform argue that the market should be more like a commodities market, rather than a good imitation of the results of the centralized dispatching that prevailed earlier, which determined the design of the original pool.

The Pioneer Markets

As Green (1998) notes, in spite of British claims that its competitive system was the first in the world, the Chilean model had been in effect for over a decade when the British competitive system was established. However, Chile's system was based on a special form of competition. Curiously, the design of the electricity markets in both countries was affected by similar factors.

Chile

The peculiarities of Chile's political regime and the fact that it was the first country to privatize the power sector allowed for the execution of a gradual transition. The National Power Commission and the establishment of a price system for transactions on the wholesale market took place much earlier than the first privatizations. The need to minimize surprises for potential investors was the dominant concern in designing the Chilean system. While the true cost of that decision would not become evident until the system had been operating for some time, this concern of the system's designers was not unfounded. The private sector was afraid of making the large investments that a system growing at the rate of 6 percent a year demanded. This was compounded by the fear that an eventual return to democracy could reverse the reforms. The result was that the regulator had almost no discretion to make subsequent adjustments. In the opinion of many analysts, this rigidity was the main reason why the limitations would not be addressed for a long time. Another reason may have been the moratorium on criticism that independent analysts and international institutions granted to the Chilean experiment for fear of jeopardizing it.

However, these were not the only factors that influenced the initial design. The designers of the new system were faced with a predominantly hydraulic system with a regulating reservoir, Lake Laja, whose operation was based on a well-tested model. The optimum management model for Lake Laja (GOL) made it possible to determine the cost of water in the reservoir with relative certainty and, hence, to establish short-term prices for efficient trading among power generators. The system adopted for market operation was limited to trade between generating companies and was based on theoretically maximum costs, which, in practice, ended up being the costs used for all transactions among generators. There was no market-clearing price that resulted from the interaction of supply and demand, but rather prices were set by an administrative system. As a result, Chile lacks a true spot electricity market since it is not possible to buy power on a makeshift basis. Although contracts exist with free clients, they are not traded. One of the reasons is that there is no system of charges or tolls for spot transmission, a legacy of the original design that ignored monopolistic aspects.

Despite the fact that apologists of the new system argued that economies of scale were not relevant in Chile and, therefore, that competition could take place in the generating market, most projects in the pipeline were large-scale hydraulic projects that required hefty investments. This conspired against a segmented structure that would promote competition. The Chilean system was structurally flawed from the beginning. Moreover, these flaws were not compensated for in the design of market rules, thereby creating the opportunity for the main players to seek and establish market power.

The United Kingdom

Although the form and fundamental nature of the Chilean and British systems are quite different, the starting conditions that affected the design of the systems were similar. In both cases, the main objectives were to break the government monopoly over power generation and transmission, to create a competitive market, and to privatize the industry. Although democratic, the third Thatcher government enjoyed a large parliamentary majority that gave it de facto control over legislation. However, as in Chile, in order to sell the industry, the government needed a complete project to ensure that the system could function on a commercial basis while maintaining the continuity of supply.

The tradition was centralized management of the sector and there was centralized dispatching by order of merit, which the government had agreed to maintain to calm the fears of the Central Electricity Generating Board engineers. Their fears regarding economical dispatching and the stability of the system led to the adoption of a compulsory pool model. The model was called GOAL, which sounds like a British version of Chile's GOL, although in this case it represented a chiefly thermal system and marginal prices were used instead of marginal costs. As in the case of Chile, the initial design of the U.K. system had flaws that limited the number of participants. In this case, the flaws resulted from the government's commitment to play a leading role in promoting nuclear power (see Henney 1998). This flaw was the source of most of the opportunities for exercising market power that plagued the U.K. system in subsequent years. Again, as in the case of Chile, the United Kingdom adopted an inflexible system of governance that made it difficult to introduce changes. For example, there was a need for consensus among all the participants in the pool. Unlike the Chilean case, however, the existence of a single regional tariff made it impossible to establish price discrimination by zone, which would have made it easier to deal with congestion problems.

Criticism of the U.K. pool, particularly of its lack of competition, could fill a number of volumes. In addition to the works already mentioned, interested readers can refer to the studies by Green (1998) and to those included by OFFER, the U.K. regulator, in its Review of Electricity Trading Arrangements (RETA). The criticisms presented in the final RETA document are summarized below (OFFER 1999).

1. Bids into the pool by generators do not reflect costs. Movements in pool prices have not matched reductions in generating costs in the past. Although market power has been a factor in maintaining high prices, the present trading arrangements have facilitated the exercise of market power.
2. Limited demand-side involvement within the pool leads to higher overall prices and taller price spikes.
3. The complexity and lack of transparency of the pool's price-setting processes have inhibited the development of derivatives markets and reduced liquidity in the contract market.
4. Capacity payments do not provide effective short-term signals to encourage generation and demand to respond to rapidly changing circumstances. In addition, these complex and administered payments provide a poor long-term signal for the need for capacity.
5. Generators and suppliers do not face the full costs and consequences of their actions because neither group makes firm commitments to generate or consume electricity. This will lead to inefficiencies as interaction between the gas and electricity markets increases.
6. Pool governance procedures are inflexible and have precluded change or delayed reform.

Norway

In 1996, the Norwegian model was extended to Sweden and the other Scandinavian countries through the creation of Nord Pool. In sharp contrast to the U.K. system, it does not involve compulsory offers in a centrally dispatched pool, but rather sales through bilateral contracts between consumers and producers. The pool serves as a wholesale market for marginal power supplies. In this case, generators and consumers decide voluntarily whether they want to sell or buy electricity through this market. Nord Pool is actually composed of two markets that operate simultaneously with the bilateral contract market. At any given time of day, transactions are conducted on each of these markets and through bilateral contracts. There is also a futures market on which weekly financial futures contracts are negotiated for periods ranging from one week to three years. The "Daily Power Market," or spot market, trades in fixed volumes of power at prices set one day ahead for each of the 24 hours in the day. To reconcile the differences between programmed and real demand and to maintain the integrity of the system, there is also a balancing market called the "Power Regulation Market."

The designers of Nord Pool opted for a long-term contract system, instead of a pool as in the United Kingdom, because of the system's starting conditions. Most generation in Norway (and, to a lesser extent, in the other Scandinavian countries) is hydraulic. This means that power can be stored and long-term contracts make more sense than in the case of the United Kingdom, where a thermal system is more appropriate for the day-to-day operation of a centralized pool. Furthermore, Nord Pool is highly decentralized. Sixty percent of the power generated in the Norwegian system is produced by small companies mainly belonging to municipalities: Statkraft SF produces about 30 percent and the remaining 10 percent is produced by a subsidiary of Norsk Hydro. In Sweden generation is also decentralized (although less so than in Norway), which makes a contract system more desirable than a compulsory pool. Another interesting aspect of Nord Pool is its use of price zones as a tool for addressing problems of congestion in the grids.

Paradoxically, despite its relative success and the lessons that many countries in similar situations could learn from it, the Norwegian experience is not widely known or used as a reference by Latin American countries. However, it has served as an example for the second-generation wholesale markets, including the proposal for the U.K. system.

First-Generation Markets in Latin America

Argentina, Peru, and Bolivia

Chile's success in privatizing its electricity system without jeopardizing the continuity of service led a number of countries in the region to follow in its footsteps. The adoption of a competitive model by the United Kingdom, the exhaustion of the traditional model in most countries, and the rise of a new economic development model also contributed to this outcome. The multilateral banks welcomed and pondered the Chilean experiment. The original designers became the most sought-after consultants by countries considering reforming their systems. However, the experience was not accepted in its entirety in all countries.

The lesson that Argentina took from Chile's experience was the need to ensure broader competition by unbundling the sector's structure both vertically and horizontally. At the same time, changes in generating technology (namely, the advent of the gas turbine and combined cycles) lessened the importance of economies of scale and permitted the potential number of participants to rise. Several countries complemented these measures by establishing limits on the percentages that a given agent could own in a given business and in other complementary businesses in the sector. Yet international mergers and acquisitions demonstrated that not all the loopholes had been closed tightly enough to prevent collusion of interests and the attainment of market power by certain actors. However, the shortcomings of the market rules in the Chilean model were not sufficiently rectified, with the partial exception of Argentina. The Peruvian wholesale market and, to a lesser extent, the Bolivian market are almost perfect clones of Chile's with regard to their rules, differing only in certain details. In these two countries, the marginal value of water in plants with reservoirs is determined by a market administrator through centralized optimization of operations, using ad hoc mathematical models. In Peru the wholesale market is also a club of generators, like in Chile.

The wholesale electricity market model in Argentina (CAMMESA) differs somewhat from the Chilean model in makeup and details. CAMMESA is not a club restricted exclusively to generators, but includes all the market agents, making it less vulnerable to capture. Dispatching continues to be based on costs, but the basis is the generators' semiannual statements of costs, including hydraulic power. Spot prices are used for trade between generators and between distributors (at a stabilized price) and large users can buy on the wholesale market. Other innovations include the introduction of payments for auxiliary services and procedures to deal with congestion. However, not all the changes are improvements; in some cases, such as capacity charges, they have given the wrong signals. In short, the main innovations of the Argentine model are improvements in the structure of the sector, which make it more competitive, and in wholesale market governance, which make it more independent. Changes in the market rules also facilitate participation, but they are limited in scope. Argentine authorities are currently studying changes to modernize the wholesale power market and adapt it to new trends. The goals are to allow generators more flexibility in preparing their offers, a day-ahead market, more options for different types of contracts, replacement of the capacity payment with auctions of available capacity, changes in the transmission rules, and the involvement of demand in spot market auctions.

Colombia

The Colombian case shares many characteristics with Chile, such as a predominantly hydraulic system and tested management models for trading. Paradoxically, Colombia moved farthest away from the model by adopting a system of centralized auctions and a pool similar to the U.K. pool. Although bilateral contracts are permitted, they are financial in nature, similar to contracts for differences, and use the pool price for reconciliation. Therefore, there is no liquidity in the contract market. The price formation process is similar to that of the U.K. system, with identical bid patterns for hydraulic and thermal generators. Nevertheless, the fundamentally hydraulic and decentralized nature of the system, as well as its earlier experience with contracts and opportunity trading, would lead one to recommend the adoption of a procedure similar to Norway's. The type of market adopted in Colombia was no accident. The selection of Coopers & Lybrand as the consultant to design the market rules came replete with the type of model. However, the Colombian model was novel for the region. Today it is still the only market that sets the price based on auctions of offers to the participants and not on costs. Colombia was also the first market to include suppliers as participants.

Several authors, including Pérez Arriaga (1999) and Benavides (1999), extensively document the problems experienced in the Colombian power market. Apart from the well-known problems of market power and lack of transparency that plagued the U.K. model, there are also the problems of complexity in the offers and inadequate treatment of volatility stemming from the large hydroelectric generation component. The administrative measures to solve the problems of reliability of supply, reservoir levels, and capacity payments have become a continuing headache and the source of opportunities for undue interference by the legislature.

Brazil

Although Coopers & Lybrand, the consultants for Brazil, sought to impose the same model they had recommended for Colombia, local experts succeeded in convincing them that Brazilian conditions required different solutions. The Brazilian power system is over 95 percent hydraulic, it has a large storage capacity, and it is made up of groups of physically interdependent reservoirs and plants that are located in the same river basin (Veiga Pereira 1999). Coordinated operation of the system could account for close to 20 percent of the additional firm power that would be obtained if producers were to make their offers individually. Interdependent decisionmaking by the generators means that it is virtually impossible for them to know the cost of water for each individual. This stands in the way of daily auctions such as those used in the U.K. pool. The system adopted in Brazil involves a long-term contract market and a spot market for the balances administered by the system operator with the help of a complex mathematical model. Some observers, such as Estache and Pardinas (1998), affirm that surprises may crop up during implementation because of the complexity of the proposed design. However, Brazilians have demonstrated a capacity for innovation that can be useful for other countries with similar systems. As noted by Veiga Pereira (1999), for example, some problems may be solved by means of firm power certificates that can be traded in the market.

Second-Generation Markets

The countries that launched reforms in their systems in the mid 1990s, including Australia, Spain, New Zealand, and the United States, had more time to study the practical behavior of the different models used by the original reformers. More importantly, they were able to benefit from the academic debate over the initial models. However, the form and function of markets were dictated by starting conditions. This section is limited to a discussion of the experiences of Australia, Spain, California, and the Pennsylvania-New Jersey-Maryland (PJM) pool in the United States as well as the proposed new structure for the U.K. market (herein referred to as the U.K. II market).[1]

Table 10–1 compares the features of all the markets selected, including Nord Pool. It should be emphasized that, with the exception of the initial period of Nord Pool (in Norway), none of these markets has been operating for more than two years and the U.K. II market is still in the design stage.

Centralized Compulsory Auctions, Contracts, or Both?

The crux of the discussion lies in the convenience of continuing to employ the system of centralized compulsory auctions typical of the U.K. market and most of the first-generation markets (except for Norway). The apparent success of Norway and the problems of lack of competition that plagued the U.K. market led most of the countries (the United States, the U.K. II market, and Spain) to follow the Norwegian experience, at least in part, by allowing physical contracts.[2] The general trend is toward what Pérez Arriaga (1999) calls "successive markets." That is, it is more desirable for the market, rather than a model, to resolve trade in successive rounds ranging from long-term contracts to operations in real time, including the old daily auctions. The main characteristic of the new organization

[1] An excellent comparison of trading arrangements can be found in OFFER (1999) and in RETA (1998).

[2] The Australian market remains centralized and compulsory.

Table 10–1. Characteristics of Second-Generation Markets

Category/system	Australia	California	Pennsylvania, New Jersey, and Maryland	United Kingdom II[a]	Spain	Nord Pool
Type of pool	Compulsory	Voluntary	Mixed	Voluntary	Centralized Voluntary	Voluntary
Reconciliation of supply/demand	System operator	Balancing market	System operator	Balancing market	Successive markets	Balancing market
Type of offers	Volume and price Volumes can be adjusted up to one hour beforehand	Volume and price Portfolio Offers are firm for each market round	Volume and price	Volume and price Offers are firm for each market round	Volume and price Offers are firm for each market round	Volume and price Offers are firm for each market round
Participation by demand	Negative generation	On the hourly and balancing markets	On the daily market	On the successive markets	On the successive markets	On the successive markets
Congestion management	Zonal	Zonal	Nodal		Zonal	Zonal
Security of supply	Reserve contract by the system operator		Reserve market Shared capacity			
Institutions	System operator	Over 30 market exchanges, system operator	System operator	Market exchanges	Market exchange, system operator	Market exchanges, system operator

[a] This new market is still in the design stage.

is that it includes several very simple markets that permit transparency, trade in only one of the market's products, employ firm transactions, and permit additional subsequent transactions for fine-tuning.

The complete organized market would include a succession of different kinds of markets. Starting with the long term, there would be organized futures and forward markets to negotiate standardized long-term contracts with a horizon ranging from several years to one week. The contract periods could be blocks of similar hours (for example, peak, flat, and trough hours) for different kinds of days (for example, weekdays and holidays). The daily physical market (where all demands not already contracted would be fulfilled and where all participating agents should be backed by available physical capacity to produce or consume) is the core of the entire set of transactions and its price serves as a reference for others. There would also be shorter-term markets to negotiate adjustments, as well as markets for other products, such as management of restrictions or operating reserves. A weekly market could have a shorter horizon than the futures market, followed by a daily physical market.

Figure 10–1 illustrates this concept as applied in Spain, but the details vary with each market, as is clear from the earlier discussion of Nord Pool and as can be seen by comparing the information in table 10–1. Figure 10–2 illustrates the various markets in the Spanish system.

A comparison of the designs adopted in two different systems in the United States (California and PJM) illustrates the differences that can exist. While the California design is closer to the generalized scheme presented above, the PJM pool is more of a mixture between a pure pool and the California design. Although physical contracts can exist in PJM (since all generators have the option of supplying bilateral contracts), there is also the option of participating in the pool auction. The system operator proceeds to dispatch to everyone who has not presented individual scheduling. The PJM system operator has much more power than the one in California, where the "System Operator" and the "Power Exchange" are separate and independent. In practice, there are about 30 power exchanges called scheduling coordinators. Cameron and Cramton (1999), in an instructive comparison between the two systems and the results of the first year of operation, conclude that both appear to be functioning reasonably well. They also note that both systems are undergoing adjustments and modifications to fine-tune their operations. In fact, California's intra-day (hourly) markets were quickly dismissed because of lack of liquidity.

Auctions, Price Determination, and Transparency

The main concern with regard to auctions or offers has been flexibility in the proceedings and transparency in price formation. In the search for transparent mechanisms, most of the markets described in table 10–1 have opted for

Figure 10-1. Successive Markets in the Spanish Wholesale Electricity Market

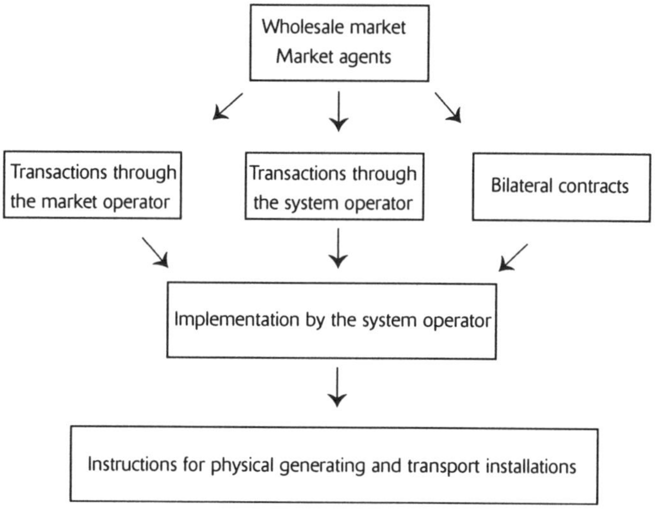

Figure 10-2. The Wholesale Electricity Market in Spain

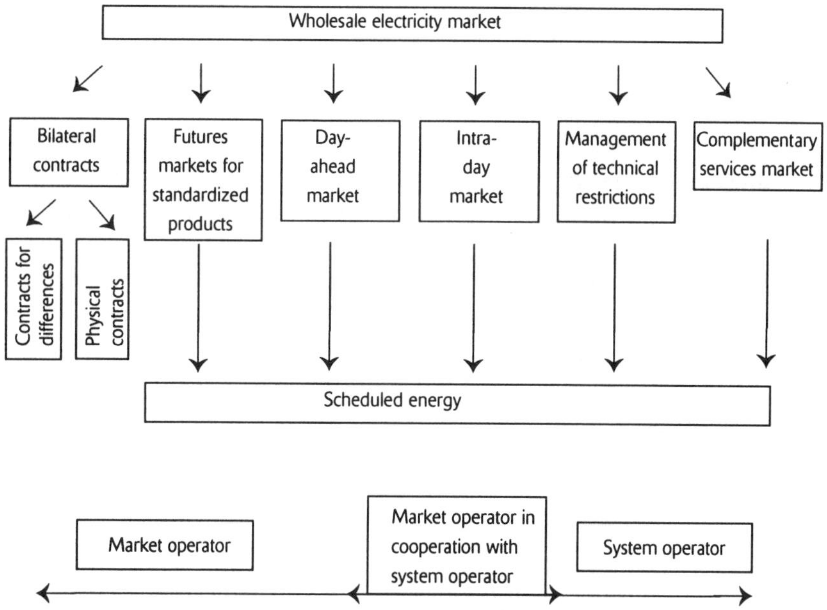

procedures in which each hour of the day is auctioned independently, and in which technical and economic conditions that agents can express in their offers are simplified as much as possible. Offers by generating plants can only be expressed in the total volume of power to be sold or bought in each hour and the corresponding prices (dollars/kWh). In this way, the generators are forced to internalize in their simple offers the variety of costs they could incur in a series of possible situations. Markets based on simple offers have the advantage of lending greater transparency to the dispatching process. However, they introduce risks into the process of offers by the generators, which must be compensated by suitable management mechanisms. The creation of a series of successive markets offers a solution to this problem. In contract markets, the trend is toward transparency by requiring that all transactions be made in the market, like Nord Pool. However, California permits confidential bilateral contracts.

Balancing Supply and Demand and Price Determination

The Norwegian system of establishing a balancing market and its extension in Spain to the system of successive markets offer a solution to the problem of supply and demand equilibrium. In general, all the markets studied can revise their positions in something very close to real time. In some markets, such as in Australia, volumes can be revised, but not prices. The PJM pool allows adjustments to be made. In all the other markets, adjustments are made through new transactions on shorter-term markets or are subject to rescheduling. Remuneration in balancing systems is paid at very short intervals; in California, it is paid every 10 minutes and in the others the maximum term for making offers on the balancing markets is very close to real time. In all cases, the final settlements are paid at the prices prevailing on one of the markets and are not determined by administrative measures. In systems with very volatile markets or when the goal is to prevent speculation, a dual settlement system has been used to encourage most transactions to be conducted on longer-term markets. According to Sioshansi and Morgan (1999), the California system in which generators make last minute offers means that the system operator is involved in the market, with dubious results. Sioshansi and Morgan contend that the Australian system avoids the problem completely by defining the prices *a posteriori* and appears to have functioned well.

There is full agreement in all the markets regarding the need to include demand on an equal footing with supply. Where this rule has been introduced, demand has generally played a small part, but the experience of Nord Pool is encouraging.

Prioritizing Access to Limited-Capacity Transmission Systems

In this case, second-generation reforms provide solutions that originate in the starting conditions. Following Norway's example, some solutions favor the establishment of price zones to resolve congestion problems. This is the case in England and Wales, California, and Australia. New Zealand and the PJM pool favor a solution using nodal prices, which in the case of New Zealand, where generation is remote from consumption, appears to be well thought out. The controversy has been very heated between the proponents of the nodal system, led by Hogan (1998), and the rest of the reformers, who continue to be skeptical that such a sophisticated system is justified in cases with a meshed network and generation very close to load, as in PJM. Henney (1998) argues that the starting conditions played a large part in this decision and that sophistication jeopardizes the transparency of the process and creates more problems than it helps to solve. Although in theory the nodal system offers a more exact solution, the advantages of obtaining it can sometimes be small in comparison with the volume of transactions at stake.

Capacity Payments and the Reliability of the System

Reliability of supply depends on adequate generating capacity to cover long-term demand and accommodate short-term fluctuations in supply and demand. There are two systems for achieving this outcome in the countries studied. The first is based on spot prices and futures to provide long-term investment and short-term availability signals. These systems permit clients and suppliers to determine the maximum price they are willing to pay for secure supplies. California, the Scandinavian countries, Australia, and the U.K. II market have adopted this solution.[3] Spain retains a capacity payment but argues that its main function is to compensate for sunk costs. The second system uses centralized planning procedures to determine the reserve levels required for the entire system and establishes a capacity market that permits suppliers to optimize their reserve levels. This is the case in the PJM pool and New York.

As table 10–1 shows, capacity payments are not very popular in second-generation markets. Continuity of supply does not appear to be a very worrisome problem, but it should be noted that none of the countries studied has a market that is growing at rates comparable to those in Latin America.

Market Institutions

Can the system operator carry out the dual function of operating the system and the electricity market? Is an independent institution such as a market operator necessary? With the exception of Australia and the PJM pool, where the system operator also operates the market, the trend is to have two different types of

[3] The system operator in Australia also buys auxiliary services to maintain reliability.

operators. In California, in addition to the power market itself, there are scheduling coordinators who act as market operators. In cases where several institutions exist, their functions vary. In California the independent system operator administers three markets: a competitive market for purchasing auxiliary services, a real-time market, and a congestion management market. The "Power Exchange" administers another three: a daily auction for each hour of the following day, an intra-day market, and a contract market.

Lessons

Although it is always possible to learn from the experience of others, the lessons will only be truly useful if we are also willing to study the context in which the experiences took place. This chapter shows that the model adopted for each country or system depends on historical, geographical, and political circumstances, in addition to purely technical ones. Moreover, it shows that, despite questions about their efficiency, the original reformers and the first generation carried out an important, if not crucial, task in developing competitive electricity markets. The experiment has not failed in any country so far. Current adjustments to the systems are intended to improve competition rather than return to centralized systems.

The following list describes lessons that the countries of Latin America can learn from the second generation of power markets:

1. *The design of new power markets is a highly dynamic process* in which adjustments are continually being made to incorporate experiences and fine-tune details. This demands a great deal of flexibility. However, experience has also shown that the market is not afraid of these adjustments, provided they are intended to ensure that the power exchanges perform their function, which is serving as a forum for the operation of a competitive market. The original reformers and some of the subsequent generation feared that a credible system would require very rigid schemes. These fears have been proven groundless by the many experiments in progress that are being tracked closely by the market.
2. Contrary to prevailing concerns at the time of the adoption of the California and PJM models, *experience has shown that a centralized, compulsory market is not necessary.* This and other differences of opinion can be resolved by comparing the results of the many experiments under way. The trend appears to be moving away from centralized, compulsory markets toward systems that permit the market to resolve problems in successive rounds, but with firm commitments that can only be altered with new contracts. The first-

generation markets in Colombia and Argentina are considering some of these modifications; their adoption could lead to substantial improvements in present operations.

3. It is also clear that generators cannot be expected to make offers to the pool in a way that mimics centralized dispatching and that *the problems of simple offers can be solved through balancing or successive markets.* Experience also confirms the first lesson learned from the Chilean experiment, which is that you can't have it both ways. No matter how sophisticated the system of offers, only broad competition prevents a dominant market position. As in all competitive markets, transparency is crucial. This is particularly important for small markets, such as those of the Central American countries, where participation in larger regional markets is key to competitive operations.
4. Administrative market management measures, such as the capacity payment, which are common in all the region's systems, and restrictions on the operation of reservoirs used in Colombia to guarantee the reliability of supply are dangerous tools that often produce perverse incentives. However, *designers must carefully examine the implications of all the market procedures they seek to introduce.* This recommendation is particularly important when adopting mechanisms to increase demand participation in the formation of prices, which is indispensable if the market is to be truly competitive.
5. The mechanisms used by the countries for rationalizing access to the system vary, but experience indicates it is fundamental to *bear in mind the relative magnitude of the distortions they are attempting to solve with models that are often complicated and not transparent.*
6. *The type and number of institutions required for the operation of the market are vitally important.* This is the case in the countries of Latin America and the Caribbean where basic institutions (such as the courts, oversight agencies, and the rule of law) are often weak. Institutions specific to the electricity market are especially important, particularly where the opportunity cost of human resources is high. Although institutions are paramount for the proper functioning of markets, the simpler their functions, the greater their chances of success.

References

Benavides, Juan, and Israel Fainboim. 1999. *Private Participation in Infrastructure in Colombia: Renegotiations and Disputes.* Working Paper, Inter-American Development Bank, Washington, D.C.

Cameron, Lisa, and Peter Cramton. 1999. "The Role of the ISO in U.S. Electricity Markets: A Review of Restructuring in California and PJM." *Electricity Journal* 12 (4) April.

Estache, Antonio, and Martin Pardinas. 1998. "Light and Lightning at the End of the Public Tunnel: The Reform of the Electricity Sector in the Southern Cone." The World Bank, Washington, D.C. Unpublished.

Green, Richard. 1998. *England and Wales–A Competitive Electricity Market?* Working Paper. University of California, Berkeley, CA.

Henney, Alex. 1998. "Contrast in Restructuring Wholesale Electric Markets: England/Wales, California and the PJM." *Electricity Journal* 11(7) August/ September).

Hogan, William. 1998. "Getting the Price Right at PJM." *Electricity Journal* 11(7, August/September).

OFFER. 1998. *Electricity Trading Arrangements in other Countries.* Background Paper no. 2, Office of Electricity Regulation, Birmingham, U.K.

———. 1999. "The New Electricity Trading Arrangements". Office of Electricity Regulation, Birmingham, U.K.

Pérez Arriaga, J. Ignacio, et al. 1999. "Formación de precios en generación y diseño del mercado mayorista en el sistema eléctrico colombiano." Study prepared for the Colombian Association of Power Producers, ACOLGEN, Bogotá, Colombia.

Ruff, Larry E. 1999. "Comparative Electricity Markets: Why Are They Working and How to Improve Them." *Electricity Journal* 12(5) May/June.

Sioshansi, Fereidon P., and Cheryl Morgan. 1999. "Where Function Follows Form: International Comparison of Restructured Electricity Markets." *Electricity Journal* 12(4) April.

Veiga Pereira, Mario. 1999. "Perspectivas y escenarios en los mercados de energía SPOT." *Revista CIER* VIII(29): September.

Wolak, Frank. 1997. *Market Design and Price Behavior in Restructured Electricity Markets: An International Comparison.* Working Paper no. PWP-051. University of California Energy Institute, Berkeley, CA.

CHAPTER 11

Retail Competition in Electricity

Paulina Beato and Carmen Fuente

Traditionally, the electricity sector was organized based both on integrated monopolies and a tight regulation that left no room for market forces. This type of organization was founded on the natural monopoly character of the sector. This meant that power generation, transmission, and distribution were less costly when carried out by one integrated firm than when performed by several firms. In other words, scale and scope economies supported the organization of the electricity sector around franchised and vertically integrated utilities.

In the mid 1980s, a new consensus emerged, which questioned the natural monopoly character of the electricity sector. It acknowledged that increasing returns might mean that only one firm should provide transmission and distribution services, but that a reduced optimum size for power generating plants would allow for the participation of various firms without a loss of profits derived from scale economies. This holds even in small countries. As for scope economies among the different electricity service activities, the new consensus states that, due to technological developments, transaction costs arising from the unbundling of generation, transmission, and distribution are minor compared with the efficiency costs involved in an integrated monopoly. As a consequence, there seems to be no reason to support the vertical integration of generation, transmission, and distribution activities.

Electricity markets are being radically transformed throughout the world. Over the past 16 years, most countries have undertaken reform processes leading to the liberalization of generation. Recently, some countries have introduced competition in the retail segment of the industry.

The paradigm pushing reform in Latin American countries has five main features. First, large customers, generators, and distribution companies enjoy free access to transmission and distribution networks. Second, a pool or spot market for power is established and futures markets for power are also at work in some countries. Nevertheless, in most countries, large consumers, distribution companies, and generators may undertake transactions directly without using the organized spot or futures markets. Third, wholesale power prices and prices paid by large customers are deregulated. Fourth, a franchise distribution company provides electricity to small and medium consumers. Customers are captives of the franchise distribution company and are, therefore, not free to switch providers in cases of poor quality service. Fifth, the lack of retail competition and free choice for small and medium consumers mean that regulation is needed to protect them.

Although reforms have resulted in a reduction in wholesale prices, the final outcome may be poor customer service for small and medium consumers, and regulations that disregard customer preferences in terms of price/quality ratios. Retail competition that gives consumers choices for satisfying their power needs may promote efficiency in supplying small and medium-sized customers and reduce the regulatory burden. The challenge is to introduce retail competition without losing the scale economies that are inherent to a sole distribution network. In order to do so, most proposals for introducing retail competition usually give consumers and independent retail companies direct access to wholesale markets, but they usually maintain a legal or de facto distribution monopoly. As do retailers in other sectors, power retailers buy electricity in the wholesale market and package it to meet consumer demand. The survival and profits of retailers depend on their ability to satisfy consumer preferences; that ability fosters lower prices and the development of new products to increase efficiency and consumer welfare. In this way, consumers instead of regulators decide the appropriate combination of price and quality. By introducing choice at the retail stage through retail companies or direct access by consumers to wholesale markets, market competition would ensure quality and appropriate pricing at the same time that consumers profit from a single distribution network. Regulators only have to establish rules for the retail market and will not need to set quality standards and prices.

This chapter analyzes the issues involved when introducing consumer choice into the power sector. The approaches used by several countries to introduce retail competition illustrate several trends. First, forces pushing for consumer choice in the power sector are growing and will soon become a social demand that regulators and utilities in many countries should not ignore. Second, the costs and advantages of free choice can be evaluated only through theoretical approaches, by extending the results from other sectors or pilot experiences. This is because choice in the power sector has only recently been introduced and, in most cases, remains experimental. In addition, the benefits of choice schemes should not be measured by the number of consumers that actually change suppliers, but by the actual benefits, in terms of quality and prices, that arise from consumer choice. Third, although the relative merits of schemes for introducing consumer choice should be evaluated case by case, some degree of unbundling between distribution and retailing services is necessary in order to ensure competition at the retail level. Separation may refer to companies selling services, that is, those that provide wire services may not be the power provider. Or it may refer to pricing, so that the pricing of wires should be an independent and transparent portion of consumer payments for the provision of wires and other services. Fourth, although a condition for establishing a successful consumer choice system is the existence of a wholesale market, introducing competition in the retail segment would improve the functioning and increase the competitiveness of the wholesale market. By so doing, retail competition may increase the efficiency of the whole system.

Forces Pushing Consumer Choice and Retail Competition

Although actual consumer choice is limited in the power sector, social pressures for looser regulations and more consumer freedom have increased and become more widespread in recent years. For instance, in the United States, most states are implementing reforms to allow consumers to choose their power supplier. New Zealand has recently introduced new regulations to extend the benefits of competition to all consumers.[1] In October 1997, the structure of distribution tariffs in Colombia was modified to separate power services from wire services in order to promote retail competition. The same forces that transformed the banking, telecommunications, and airlines industries in the recent past also propel this transformation process. However, change in the power sector is expected to take place faster, within a few years, rather than over two decades, and to be pushed by forces from within the sector.

One such force is the general claim that regulation has failed to deliver low electricity prices. This claim is grounded in large differences in average prices across countries and across regions or states of the same country, and in estimates of so-called stranded costs. For example, in 1993, average prices in the United States ranged from 3.7 cents per kWh in Washington State to 10.8 cents per kWh in New York and New Hampshire. In Europe, the purchasing power parity index of prices for domestic power consumers ranges from 100 in Norway to 411 in Portugal (International Energy Agency 1997). Estimates of stranded costs for the U.S. power industry range between $100 billion and $200 billion.[2] In Spain, a country with 39 million people, stranded costs have been estimated at $17 billion.

Ando and Palmer (1998) confirm the hypothesis that regulatory failure to minimize costs is a driving force in the process toward retail competition in the

[1] See New Zealand New Regulatory Framework (1998).

[2] Values are in U.S. dollars.

United States. Their work points out that the Energy Policy Act of 1992 marks the starting point for introducing retail competition in the states, and seeks to understand why some states are moving quickly toward full retail competition while others are moving more slowly. The hypothesis that economic considerations are the driving force in the process toward retail competition seems to be confirmed. Specifically, high average prices and high stranded cost burdens, both indicators of potentially large welfare gains from competition, have a positive influence on the propensity of U.S. state legislatures to introduce initiatives for increasing competition.

A second driving force is that consumers have become aware of the implications of cross-subsidy practices. Until recently, despite the fact that electricity is a top consumption item, consumers (commercial, industrial, or residential) have had little say in the purchase of electricity and have had no price information. For decades, electric power has been delivered to consumers by a patchwork of utility monopolies. When small-scale energy generation became viable, the existing monopolies began to lose their large consumers because, by using combined cycle and gas turbines, they could generate electricity more cheaply. In an effort to woo those large customers back, utilities began to discriminate in prices, charging industrial consumers lower rates than residential and commercial consumers. At the same time, social pressures may cause regulators in some countries to set special tariffs for low-income consumers. As a result, medium-sized domestic and residential consumers find themselves subsidizing industrial and low-income consumers. The former might begin to look for a fair framework and to demand the freedom to choose providers. Yet, the presence of cross subsidies may also be a retarding factor.

In the power sector, freedom of choice for consumers is usually implemented progressively. In the first phase, only large consumers are permitted to choose their power providers. However, if a significant portion of them receives power at prices below cost from the franchise power company, they will not be willing to switch providers. This may be interpreted by regulators and utilities as a lack of interest on the part of all consumers for choosing providers. As a result, the political forces lobbying for increased competition may lose interest in the process.

Retail competition would, sooner or later, eliminate cross subsidies to low-income consumers. A transparent system for directly subsidizing low-income consumers should be implemented. The whole process of introducing retail competition may be stymied if public authorities are reluctant to use public funds for direct subsidies. Higher power prices for low-income consumers have been presented in the literature as a major problem of introducing retail competition in the United States (Fox-Penner 1997).

A third force pushing the transformation process in the power sector is the reduction in the optimal size of power plants, which encourages large consumers to generate their own power, giving rise to a new type of power company. Combined-cycle natural gas turbines of 50 to 100MW can generate electricity at lower cost (around three cents per kilowatt hour) than large coal-powered plants, the traditional low-cost producers. The new, smaller units are mobile and can be plugged into existing transmission systems, making it possible for substations to conduct the flow of high-voltage energy from generating plants to groups of electricity users. In addition, the easy integration into transmission networks enables the sale of electricity between new firms and final consumers. The ease with which small-scale generators can be integrated in the transmission network and price competitiveness with larger-scale units make competition in generation economically feasible.

The fourth force is the fact that the reduction of metering, communication, and computational costs should facilitate the implementation of large-scale consumer choice. In a retail competition scheme, metering by time of use is no longer merely a way of promoting efficient usage; it has become a commercial necessity and a unique source of information. Each customer needs to be metered according to the settlement period, on a half-hour or hour basis. Since power prices change 48 or 24 times per day, it is necessary to know how much each competing retailer's customers used in each settlement period, in order to be able to bill the right customers and settle accounts properly. Therefore, if settlement periods are short, retail competition increases not only the needs for metering but also the communication and computational requirements.

Although the costs of metering power consumption for one-hour periods have been reduced in the last decade (prices range from one-quarter to one-ninth of the old prices), metering may be a major problem for widening the scope of retail competition. However, the problem seems to be not the cost of metering, but regulation. For instance, regulations in the United Kingdom require that the flow of information provision take place in real time. Such a settlements system does not seem to increase the efficiency of retail markets, but it does retard the introduction of choice for small and medium-sized consumers.

The fifth driving force is that the experience with the transmission grid used as a common carrier in wholesale markets led to the notion that the distribution network could also be used as a common carrier in selling and physically delivering energy to individual consumers. After electricity has been transmitted to a geographic area, the distribution process consists of converting the high voltages into lower voltages and then physically delivering them to all sorts of users. Like transmission, the physical distribution of electricity involves large fixed equipment costs, whereas its marketing involves little cost. Wholesale power markets became possible when regulations established open access to transmission networks to all generators, large consumers, and distribution companies. In most countries, open access to transmission networks was carried out by legally or financially separating integrated utilities into three different companies: generation, transmission, and distribution. As in the wholesale markets, the sales segment of the distribution business can also be unbundled; distribution companies can sell wire services as a monopoly, and retail services may become a competitive enterprise.

These forces have increased the desire of consumers to manage and understand their power purchases. Beato (1997) concludes that there are no technical or economic reasons for preventing consumers from purchasing power from their preferred retail company and abandoning their captive status. Skilling (1997) emphatically expresses the desire of consumers:

> "Imagine the elderly and the poor having a fixed energy bill rolled into their mortgage or rent. Imagine an electric service that could let consumers choose how much of their home power is generated by renewable resources. Imagine farmers negotiating an agreement that ties their electric bill to the prices for their crop. Imagine a business with offices in ten states, receiving a single monthly bill that consolidates all its energy costs. Imagine a meter you can read."

The media has also welcomed the process of introducing retail competition into electricity supply as a way of giving "power to the people" (*The Economist* 1998).

The Basic Retail Competition Model

The basic retail competition model is characterized by the fact that it allows all customers to choose their generator, either directly or through their choice of retailer.[3] In this model, generation is deregulated with free entry and exit, and regulation does not impose capacity requirements on generators. The retail segment is also deregulated and competing retailers can perform the same roles as they do in other markets. Franchise companies provide transportation and distribution services in order to take advantage of economies of scale in these segments. However, the companies must provide open access or common carriage to all consumers, and are regulated to avoid monopolistic behavior.

The main differences between retail competition and wholesale competition models are the following. First, all consumers may choose a generator in the retail competition model, while only distribution companies and large consumers do so in wholesale models. Second, retailing, a specific function of the retail

[3] For more on the basic retail competition model, see Hunt and Shuttleworth (1996) and Bohi and Palmer (1996).

competition model, is a merchant function, which does not require ownership of the distribution wires (although in many cases the owner of the wires also competes as a retailer). Third, distribution companies have open access to transportation services in wholesale models, but consumers do not have access to distribution facilities. In the retail competition model, both consumers and retailers have open access to both distribution and transportation facilities.

Open Access to Distribution Wires

The retail model needs open access to both high-voltage wires (transmission) and low-voltage wires (distribution). The model separates the provision of wires from power service. Customers may purchase their power either directly from the spot market or from one or several competing power retailers. The transportation and distribution companies supply wire services to market agents. Therefore, rules for open access to wires need to be established.

Wholesale models establish rules for distribution companies and large consumers to gain access to high-voltage transmission wires. However, no such rules are required in wholesale models for low-voltage wires. Thus, a distribution company continues being a monopoly in its own area and needs to be regulated. In retail models, retail companies compete within the service territory formerly served by the local distribution company, which remains the exclusive provider of wire services but is not allowed to compete with retail companies in supplying other services.[4]

In the retail competition model, therefore, both the upstream generation and the downstream retail functions are deregulated and open to competition. Generating companies sell power to electricity retailers or directly to customers, instead of to a local distributor with a monopoly selling franchise. Power retailers or marketers buy power from generators and sometimes resell it to retail customers, bundled with energy management services. The transmission function (bringing electricity from generators to local distributors) operates and is regulated the same as under wholesale competition, except that power retailers, generators, or customers (not only local distributors) also arrange for transmission services. The local distributor, or line company, sells its services as a regulated distributor, but it is not the actual retailer of electricity.

Trading Arrangements

In the basic retail competition model, generators and consumers are free to enter into contracts for electric power. Consumers may buy electricity from

[4] In real-world competition models, distribution companies compete with retail companies in providing power services.

generators, retailers, or organized markets. Although market rules and trading arrangements may be different across countries, most systems include a market operator and a spot market.

The retail model needs a spot market to facilitate bilateral and multilateral trading.[5] The reason for this is that carrying out contracts from multiple agents through a third-party network requires rules for solving the following issues: (1) settling imbalances between expected and actual power flows; (2) dispatching the plants in the order of their short-run costs; (3) determining the spot price at each half hour; (4) collecting money from the purchaser and distributing it to the seller; (5) ensuring contract fulfillment; and (6) providing inter-area payment schemes when different parts of a network are operated separately.

The market operator is the institution in charge of developing the spot market and ensuring that it functions appropriately. However, the existence of a market operator does not imply that there is a single buyer of power that resells it to final consumers. Market operators are not purchasing agencies; they are only market makers. They do not own the power and they never bear the market risk. As Hunt and Shuttleworth (1996, pp. 65–66) point out, "The expressions 'selling to the pool' and 'buying from the pool' misrepresent the role of the pool, since producers and retailers sell to each other and not to the pool."

The spot markets generate prices that approximate marginal cost in real time; therefore, spot prices are variable over time. Consumers and producers may be willing to pay a premium to reduce price variability and enter into contracts that dampen price fluctuations. In these contracts, prices may be fixed for all times and volumes or they may vary according to variables that make the parties share in the spot market risk. As a result, long-term contracts between sellers and buyers are usually developed. A wide range of contracts has been implemented.[6]

Distribution and Transmission Prices

Competitive retail requires open access to distribution and transmission systems. This, in turn, requires that prices be set for transmission and distribution services. Prices for access to both high and low-voltage wires must provide the correct short and long-term economic incentives. In the short term, they must give signals for dispatching the cheapest plants without creating congestion problems. In the long run, they must also provide sufficient revenues to the owners of the wires and promote efficient location of plants. The problem is finding prices that meet these conditions.

---

[5] Since there are relatively few regulated customers in the wholesale model, a spot market is useful but not essential.

[6] An analysis of contracts for managing price risk is beyond the scope of this chapter.

According to economic theory, transportation prices should equal the marginal cost that each transaction imposes on the system. However, marginal cost pricing does not guarantee adequate revenue to cover total network cost in systems with economies of scale. Additional constraints should be added to ensure that transportation companies do not suffer losses. Ramsey (1927) proposes discriminating among consumers and setting prices in inverse proportion to the elasticity of demand so that second-best efficiency is achieved and revenues cover full costs. Although Ramsey's proposal is theoretically correct, its implementation is difficult because it requires a central organization to solve a large optimization problem that needs detailed information on each consumer's elasticity and on the technical properties of the network. Ramsey pricing also involves discrimination among consumers, which may be prohibited.

It should be noted that, due to increasing returns and externalities in the transmission and distribution network, prices that give the right signals in the short and long runs cannot be achieved through markets or other decentralized approaches (Calsamiglia 1977). Theoretically, the right prices can be achieved through centralized mechanisms. These solutions are hardly ever applied because the central agent needs too much information about consumer and network features. The required information would be difficult to gather either because it is not available or because consumers will not reveal their preferences or demand elasticity.[7] Therefore, a tradeoff needs to be made between the efficiency properties of prices and the degree of decentralization in the process of calculating them. The final result is that transportation prices become, in real-world systems, a crude approximation of marginal costs.

Metering

In retail competition models, metering each consumer by the length of time of use is a commercial necessity and the sole source of information for billing. Each customer needs to be metered according to the settlement period, on the hour or half-hour. Independent of the type of contract between the retailer and the generator, the actual amount of money that the retailer has to pay to the generator depends on the actual consumption of the retailer's customers. Therefore, in order to bill a retailer, it is necessary to know the amount of power used in each settlement period by the retailer's customers. Of course, metering at each settlement period is required to bill customers if prices are to reflect actual costs to consumers.

[7] Assume that a central agent wishes to calculate Ramsey prices and tries to obtain consumer elasticities by making consumer surveys. Because Ramsey prices are inversely proportional to the elasticity of demand of consumers, who want low prices, the consumer will reveal high demand elasticity.

In wholesale competition models, since the franchise distribution company provides power to all consumers within the distribution area, metering actual consumer consumption only requires metering the power that flows in the distribution areas. That, in turn, requires metering at only a few points. Therefore, billing a power distribution company does not represent a problem, despite the fact that the largest consumers within the franchise area are free to choose their providers. By contrast, in retail competition models, all consumers need to be measured in order to ascertain the actual consumption for which each retailer is responsible.

Logistical problems emerge when metering must be extended to smaller customers. These logistical problems may be worsened, as happened in the United Kingdom, by the specifications of the settlements system that requires that the flow of information be provided in real time, a measure that does not seem necessary for the proper working of the system. To avoid these types of problems in markets open to retail competition, countries introduce measures for ensuring metering capacity before the market is liberalized. For instance, in California (in the United States) and the United Kingdom, measures have been introduced before the date for full retail access. This allows customers with loads between 20kW and 50kW in California and less than 100kW in the United Kingdom to rely on load profiling during a fixed transition period. In California, the May 1997 Unbundling Decision allows retail companies to provide their customers with meters other than those commonly furnished by the distribution company.

Unbundled Services

The vision of the electric services industry that emerges under retail competition schemes is one of great diversity in customer services and in service providers. The achievement of this diversity is based on the unbundling of services traditionally supplied by a vertically integrated utility. Unbundling results in the provision of opportunities for new entry, new rivalry among existing suppliers, and new services to consumers. Thus, from the standpoint of market structure, the unbundling of electric services has been identified as a condition for the attainment of a more open market for suppliers and customers. Unbundling can also provide welfare improvements by allowing customers to better align their preferences with available service options (Oren and Ray 1997).

Unbundling electricity activities is not a benign decision from the standpoint of either efficiency or equity. Moreover, in certain circumstances, it is not an achievable objective due to economic and technical constraints. Although unbundling is instrumental in increasing competition in the electric services industry, it may also raise short-term concerns about undesirable outcomes, such as facilitating the exercise of market power or increasing the cost of service. On the cost side, there are several circumstances in which unbundled supply could be disadvantageous. For example, high fixed or start-up costs or production and delivery economies associated with unbundling could harm profits and social welfare. In addition, metering costs for the separate unbundled goods would be higher than for the bundled ones. However, even with these shortcomings, unbundling is an essential element for electricity markets in which end-users wish to tailor their service purchases to their service needs by choosing the sellers that are most able to provide those services.

Unbundling is frequently taken to mean the provision of services by many suppliers (in particular the separation between market and monopoly activities) and bundled service is interpreted as being provided by a sole supplier. From a broader perspective, unbundling simply means giving customers the right to assemble their own service bundles. Separating structural issues (involving who provides the services) from service selection issues is important because, broadly speaking, unbundling gives consumers additional rights; more narrowly, unbundling limits producer alternatives.

Separation between Generation and Retail

A potential self-dealing conflict exists in the wholesale competition model when a company is both a generator and a distributor. When purchasing self-generated power, the distribution company, which is the sole retailer in the franchise area, will show little interest in minimizing costs that can be passed on to captive customers. In the retail competition model, this is no longer a problem because competition in generation and retail allows customers to choose other generators or retailers.

Hunt and Shuttleworth (1996) find that the integration of generation and sales to final customers is reasonable based on the little value added in retailing electricity. Their argument is that retailers in other trades perform various functions, such as displaying goods, making choices among manufacturers, and unbundling large shipments for sale as smaller bundles. These are value-added activities that earn the retailer a return. The electricity retailer can perform the same activities: taking risks and unbundling services, and buying bulk electricity and repackaging it. Generators can also perform these useful functions, according to Hunt and Shuttleworth. They conclude that retailing, as an independent activity, appears to be a high-risk and low-return business, although the presence of independent retailers introduces discipline into the market. However, that presence could be curtailed if generation companies controlled the retail market because market contestability would be affected and effective competition hampered.

Separation between Transmission and Distribution

Distribution (low voltage) and transmission (high voltage) are similar functions at different levels of voltage. Hunt and Shuttleworth (1996) point out that there are no efficiency reasons for separating them. However, separate companies provide these services in real-world electrical systems even after the introduction of retail competition. This is because reform of electrical systems started with the introduction of wholesale competition, which required open access to transmission, but not to distribution. Therefore, vertically integrated utilities were separated into three segments: generation, transmission, and distribution. In most countries, all transmission assets were pooled in one company or at least managed by a unique agent. Distribution assets were assigned to different companies for the provision of distribution and retail services.

There are no strong efficiency reasons for separating distribution from transmission, and there is no clear distinction between the two functions other than an arbitrary level of voltage. However, separating them seems appropriate because the operation of the transmission network by a unique agent seems to facilitate open access to generators and consumers because network capacity may depend on the manner of network operation. Distribution wires that have little interrelation with transmission networks may be better operated in small loops. In addition, several distribution firms may allow yardstick competition and provide information to regulators.

Separation between Distribution and Retail Services

The basic retail competition model assumes that distribution wires are operated separately from retail activity. They are separate because the wire service remains a monopolized activity, whereas the sales segment is open to competition.

Retailers and distribution companies bill separately to customers. They may enter billing agreements and send only one bill on behalf of both. For instance, in California, the range of options offered to a consumer is even wider. If a customer chooses to purchase energy from a retailer, three billing options are available: (1) retailer consolidated billing in which the customer receives one bill from the retailer that includes charges from the distribution company; (2) consolidated distribution company billing, in which the customer receives one bill from the distribution company that includes the charges of the retailers; and (3) dual billing, in which the customer receives separate bills from the nonutility electric service provider and the utility distribution company.

Allowing distribution companies to perform retailing may reduce market competition because distribution companies may subsidize their retail customers by imposing a wire tariff that is larger than the cost to their captive customers, all within the same distribution territory. The distribution company may also discriminate between both classes of customers. For instance, in cases of wire damage, the distribution company will have a greater incentive to repair service to its own customers first. Regulators should handle this sort of situation in order to prevent a failure of competition. Nevertheless, most of the companies being restructured own the wires and sell the electricity at the retail level. This may be

Box 11–1. Entry Barriers for Power Retailers in California

Around 300 new energy service providers (retailers) entered the market when it opened in April 1998. By mid May, of the nearly 10 million California customers of the three incumbent or investor-owned utilities, approximately 40,000 changed supplier. Although it is still too soon to gain some hindsight on the matter, early evidence shows that several important players are already leaving the market due to the scarce numbers of customers ready to switch suppliers. Customers are reluctant to switch for the following reasons:

- Consumers are automatically entitled to a mandated 10 percent reduction in prices if they do not change supplier.
- A direct result of the restructuring legislation is that all customers, regardless of their energy supplier, have to pay the competition transition charge, a nonbypassable tax to pay off stranded costs of the investor-owned utilities.
- Only 25 percent of consumer charges are subject to competitive pricing. As stipulated under (AB) 1890, roughly half of that bill will go to the incumbent utility for charges on poles and wires; another 25 percent will pay for competition transition charges.

the reason that only a few customers seek retailers other than their distribution companies. Box 11–1 provides information on the number of California consumers that have switched electricity suppliers.

Distribution Companies: Providers of Last Resort

The unbundling of distribution and retail functions could have consequences for the distribution companies in their role as default providers of power. For such an essential commodity as electricity, a purveyor of last resort may be needed, such as the local distribution companies or another company. It would be obligated to offer service to any customer, irrespective of load characteristics or payment record. Regulators have tackled this complex issue in different ways. In the United Kingdom, the distribution companies in each area hold first-tier supply licenses that allow them to supply both the franchise and the nonfranchise market; competing retailers get second-tier licenses that enable them to supply only the nonfranchise market. In California, local distribution companies are default providers whenever a retailer fails to comply with supply obligations.

Box 11–2. Local Authorities Establish the Eligibility Path

In the United States, the Energy Policy Act of 1992 prohibited the Federal Energy Regulatory Commission from ordering a utility to provide open access to its transmission grid for the purpose of completing a retail transaction. The Act implicitly reserves for the states the capacity for establishing the eligibility path.

In the European Union, the 1996 Electricity Services Directive allows member country governments to decide on the path of retail choice eligibility. However, a six-year calendar sets minimum compulsory eligibility thresholds from 40GWh/year for the first year to 9GWh/year for the sixth year.

Designing Retail Competition Mechanisms for the Real World

Regulations set a minimum level of consumption for a consumer to be able to buy electricity from retailers or generators. The scope of eligibility plays a fundamental role in the dynamism of the market and is the key element through which consumers are able to obtain their share of the efficiency gains resulting from bulk electricity markets. However, the process toward full customer choice encompasses not only increased efficiency in the allocation of resources, but also an income redistribution process that might affect consumers and producers in unpredictable ways. Therefore, the introduction of retail competition usually involves a transition period based on gradual market opening, starting with the largest consumers and progressively lowering eligibility thresholds down to full consumer choice after a few years (see boxes 11–2 and 11–3).[8] Although transition schemes are relevant, here we assume that the transition periods have ended and all consumers have several choices for buying electricity.

Most proposals for introducing retail competition result from the combination of three features: retail arrangements, the market mechanism, and transmission pricing. The organization and relationships between consumers, retail companies, and distribution companies define the retail arrangements of a proposal. The market mechanism is delimited by the choice of trading through power pool or bilateral contracts; the scope of consumer options is delimited in terms of access to bulk markets. An extreme transmission pricing option is to set optimal local prices at each node for both power and transmission. An alternative

[8] CSEN (1997) points out that countries where restructuring has started at a later date, and where electricity prices are higher, seem to be opening their retail markets at a faster pace.

Box 11–3. The Transition Period to Full Eligibility in Selected Countries

Less than two years	Two to four years	More than four years
Norway (1991)	Finland (1995–97)	United Kingdom (1990–97)
United States (California, 1998)	Australia (Victoria, 1994–98)	Spain (1998–2007)
New Zealand (1993–94)		

option consists of separating generation and transmission prices. Most real-world arrangements separate transmission and power prices. However, transmission prices are not usually fixed through markets.

Retail Arrangements

Power retail and distribution are two separate functions. The first refers to the activity of buying power directly from generators or in the wholesale markets and selling it to final consumers. Distribution refers to the activity of carrying electricity from the transmission network to the consumer. Other services in the provision of electricity include metering, financing, and billing.

Arrangements for providing distribution and retail services differ among the various retail competition proposals. The most important difference is the degree of separation between companies providing these services because distribution service is provided under monopoly, while retail services are competitive. The welfare and competition approaches demand complete separation between distribution and retailing companies. However, historical and institutional reasons justify a weaker separation.

Complete Separation between Retail and Distribution Companies

This option means that a company may not offer both distribution and retailing services. Proponents of this option argue that because of the monopolistic nature of distribution networks, distribution companies should be allowed to sell only wire services. The reason is that a company providing both services may easily cross subsidize them and discriminate between customers purchasing only wires and customers purchasing both power and wires. Although that argument is solid (Fox-Penner 1997; Bohi and Palmer 1996), all real-world distribution companies are allowed to sell both wires and power services and to serve customers unbundled as well as bundled services.

Failure to separate retail and distribution may occur for several reasons. One reason is the resistance of traditional distribution companies to reducing the scope of their business. Another is that consumer transaction costs may be sizeable and consumers may be reluctant to accept a forced shift from their traditional supplier to a new one. Legislators will not force consumers to abandon their traditional supplier when the point is to give consumers freedom of choice.

Separation may be legal and financial. Legal separation means that one company may not provide both services, but legally independent companies within the same economic group (holdings or firms under common ownership providing different service, such as distribution or retail) may provide both services. Legal separation makes it more difficult to subsidize bundled consumers at the expense of unbundled ones, thus making the regulation of distribution companies more efficient than without any separation at all. However, economic and financial incentives for discrimination remain as in the nonseparation arrangement. Spain's regulatory framework establishes that retailing and distribution companies should be legally independent. The law does not require economic and financial independence for providing both services. The transitory period for legal separation is so long (10 years), that the unbundling may never take place.

Nonmandatory Separation between Retail and Distribution

If separation between retail and distribution is not mandatory, one company may provide both services and independent retail companies may offer retailing services. Distribution companies may offer bundled and unbundled services. Thus, a distribution company may provide wire service and power to some customers and only wire service to others. If distribution companies sell wire service as well as power, the incentive for cross subsidizing and quality discrimination is large because small consumers prefer bundled services to avoid transaction costs. If wire prices are over marginal costs, the distribution company may sell below cost to final consumers in order to retain them, thus hampering the development of retail companies. Distribution companies in Australia, Colombia, New Zealand, and the United Kingdom may sell both services; retailers in those countries also offer retail services. Lobbying by electricity companies and consumer reluctance to enter into contracts with two companies may explain this model.

A setting in which pure retail companies have to compete with companies that perform both retailing and distribution restricts the growth of retailing companies. The market share of pure retailers is negligible in most countries where this arrangement prevails; their customers are all large industrial ones. For pure retailers to compete, companies providing both wire services and power should abide by two separation rules. First, the accounting information of each activity should be separated in order to allow regulators to fix the price of distribution equal to its marginal cost and avoid cross subsidization. Second, distribution companies should separate billing for wires and retail services.

In Colombia, since 1994, the regulatory framework has permitted the establishment of retailers for power services. Consumer choice and free entry are allowed for all activities that are not explicitly restricted in the Colombian constitution. In addition, the 1994 Electricity Service Act and later resolutions of the Energy Regulatory Commission ratified and built on this principle. Nevertheless, pure retailers have not been established. Distribution companies are publicly owned and their losses are absorbed by national or municipal budgets, making it impossible for a private for-profit firm to compete with them. Consumers purchasing only wire service from a distribution company pay a higher price than those requiring both wire and power services. In 1997, two reforms were enacted to make competition fair for retail companies in Colombia. On the institutional side, distribution companies will be sold to the private sector. On the regulatory side, a new resolution establishes that distribution companies shall bill each service independently, in an itemized fashion.

Provision of Retail Services Limited to Distribution Companies

When the provision of retail services is limited to distribution companies, they continue to offer both wire and power services. However, distribution companies may buy electricity in the wholesale market on behalf of consumers. In these schemes, consumers do not negotiate with generators. Consumers may choose to buy bundled wires and power, or to purchase power on a real-time price basis, as in the efficient direct access model (Hogan 1994).

Unbundled Services

Faruqui and Kirsch (1998) analyze the experience of unbundled services in Argentina, Australia, Canada, Chile, Norway, and the United Kingdom. Argentina, Canada, and Norway do not have unbundled distribution and other retail services. Those nations that have unbundled services have done so only very recently, and those services account for only a small share of distribution costs. The utilities are reluctant to unbundle distribution and retailing services because of the difficulty in identifying sensible schemes for separating them and the fear of imposing huge costs on consumers. The unbundling initiatives generally originate from governments and regulators. In fact, representatives of utilities in Australia and the United Kingdom report that technological problems do not pose insurmountable barriers to unbundling distribution, but they do add to cost and time requirements. Those representatives are concerned with metering, billing, and information-handling technologies. They indicate that the introduction of competition is smoother if it is staged to allow sufficient time to implement the new information systems and build the infrastructure necessary for handling competitive market transactions.

The set of potentially unbundled distribution services comprises facility services, revenue cycle services, and energy services. Facility services (corresponding approximately to wire services) comprise connections, line drops, transformers, and power factor corrections. They are provided by equipment throughout the distribution network, but these services sometimes are unbundled when provided by equipment on or near a customer site. Connections and line-drop services connect the customer load to the power system either through a standard single connection path or through an enhanced double path that reduces the chances of customer outages. Transformers, power factor corrections, and premium power-quality services control the quality of the power received by the customer and also control the effects of the customer load on the power system. Meter installation service provides the equipment that measures the use of power. Revenue cycle services include monthly meter reading and billing services, as well as less regular customer contact services. Energy services (supply, audits, analysis and reporting, and equipment financing) are debatably not a part of the distribution function at all. In Australia, for example, these services are offered in an unbundled competitive fashion, as are most facility and revenue cycle services. In the United Kingdom, the latter are also offered unbundled and competitively.

Country practices show that unbundling may occur with or without opening services to competition. The relationship between unbundling services and opening them to competition is different among countries and between services. For instance, in Canada and Norway, some services once offered as part of bundled distribution, such as energy audits or extra transformers, must now be purchased separately by the customer on a competitive basis. Customers in Argentina and Chile must purchase line maintenance, meter reading, customer connection, and billing services separately but through their local distribution monopolies. However, to better control costs, these monopolies have adopted the practice of purchasing the services from subcontractors through competitive processes. The United Kingdom has a mixed arrangement with competitive installation of new assets; but once installed, maintenance of the equipment becomes the responsibility of the distribution monopolist.

Trade Mechanism

In the retail competition model, consumers can buy power either directly from the spot market run by an independent agent, or from one or several competing retailers. However, in practice, going directly to the spot market is feasible only for large consumers that can obtain the information required and afford the transaction costs involved. Small and medium-size consumers are more likely to either aggregate their demand, if the system allows for this option, or use the services of a retail firm.

The alternatives are as follows: (1) consumers may access wholesale markets directly or through retailers or marketers; (2) consumers are not allowed to use intermediaries to access the wholesale market; (3) consumers may not buy directly from the wholesale market, but must use retailers or marketers; and (4) consumers may not buy wholesale electricity. The fourth scheme is a wholesale scheme whereas the others involve retail competition. While the first alternative provides consumers with more options, in the real world, individual consumers face several constraints (such as minimum volume and payment guarantees) in accessing wholesale markets. Although their purpose is not to restrict competition but to ensure market security, these practices may be used for preventing access to wholesale markets by medium-size consumers.

In New Zealand and Norway, regardless of size, consumers may buy power in the wholesale market. However, small consumers have to resort to retailers in order to profit from competition because barriers to entry into the wholesale market for residential consumers are large in terms of operator fees and metering practices. In the United Kingdom, nonfranchise customers have the option of choosing their supplier from one of the 12 distribution companies or from any of the generating companies.

Distribution and Transmission Pricing

Distribution and transmission pricing are necessary for open access to wires. However, available pricing schemes are not satisfactory either because they require centralizing too much information or because they do not meet appropriate efficiency requirements. The lack of efficient and decentralized models for pricing transportation (distribution and transmission) is not due to lack of research, but because electrical networks present both economies of scale and externalities.

Here we discuss the main options for addressing distribution and transmission pricing in retail competition models. The discussion assumes that independent companies provide distribution and transmission services. Thus, it does not address the cherry-picking problem (a major concern of distribution utilities selling retail services) and the ability to institute cross subsidies (a major concern of pure retail companies). Nevertheless, the results extend to cases with bundled retail and distribution services.[9] The analysis also assumes that a unique company provides all distribution and transmission services so that competition is not feasible and transportation prices remain regulated. Nevertheless, results may be extended to the case of several companies holding monopoly power within their franchise territory.

---

[9] For a discussion of access prices in the case of integrated firms, see Laffont and Tirole (1996).

Most pricing schemes use two transportation prices. One price, the access fee, covers the cost of having the network available, and may be considered the right to use the existing network. The second price, the cost of energy, should reflect the marginal cost of transporting power through the existing network. This cost, in turn, is often broken down into two components: the cost of power losses and the cost of dispatching expensive plants due to network restrictions.

The Access Fee

The problem of setting access fees for consumers and generators may be solved in two steps. The first step determines the revenue that the company that owns the network should receive for allowing market agents to use it. The second step assigns payments to market agents.

Regarding the first step, a distinction should be made between the existing network and new additions. For the existing network, traditional methods estimate the operational cost, excluding power losses, and the capital cost for a specific period of time (usually a year).[10] Although the calculation appears simple, there are serious problems of incentives and regulation. Regulations should ensure that if a company is efficient in managing assets, it could earn an appropriate rate of return on its investment. It should be noted that the regulated company would have incentives to exaggerate costs because the regulator will assign revenues based on its assessment of company costs. Several alternatives–including standard costs and yardstick competition–may be used to mitigate this risk.

The construction and operation of new lines is often assigned through a public bid process. The winning proposal is the one requiring the smallest payments.[11] This procedure means that regulators do not have to calculate operational capital costs every year because company revenues would be included in the bid proposal. If there are several proposals, competition for the line drives bidders to minimize cost. However, the optimal expansion of the network requires that a new line should be undertaken only if the payments of the winning proposal are larger than the expected value of power cost reductions resulting from the new line.

The assignment of payments among consumers is the second step. Most systems distribute payments as a function of the power provided to the grid independent of the source, destination, or contract. The price per unit is calculated by dividing the network total cost by the number of power units that the systems are expected to deliver. Expected demand for transmission and distribution during a year may be relatively easy to forecast from current usage patterns. Although errors may be

---

[10] Losses are taken into account through the so-called "short-run transportation price."

[11] Payments may be established in terms of a price per unit of transported power, annual fees, or a combination.

expected, differences in the revenues of the transportation company due to demand errors in forecasting may be compensated for in the next regulatory period.

Other approaches have been used for assigning payments among consumers. For instance, Spain uses several prices, one for each group of consumers. The price for each consumer group is inversely related to demand elasticity. In Germany, the distance between the production and consumption locations is taken into account to figure out the cost of the transmission network. For bilateral contracts, the relevant distance is that between the power plant and consumer locations. For trading through the pool, the pool is assumed to be located in a specific node of the network and a transportation price is assigned to pool power. Consumer transportation prices result from summing up the pool transportation cost plus the transportation cost from the pool to consumer locations. Another proposal assigns network cost as a proportion of the profits received by each relevant group (Bosch and Escribano 1988). These nonlinear approaches try to avoid the inefficiency problems inherent in the simple linear scheme. However, if common costs are small in relation to power costs, the distortion from more theoretically efficient and complicated price schemes may be larger than the distortion from simple linear prices. Distortions in complicated schemes come from gathering information, computational requirements, and the lack of social acceptance of price schemes that are discriminatory and difficult to understand.

Nodal Prices versus Prices for Congestion and Power Loss

If network users have already paid an access fee that covers the fixed cost of the existing network, a price for covering the short-term energy cost associated with the use of the network should promote optimal dispatching. The price needs to ensure balance between payments and power costs.

An optimal dispatch system minimizes the generation cost of satisfying the demand at each node of the network. In such an environment, the marginal cost of generation at each network node may diverge as a consequence of network restrictions. If the network has excess capacity, the marginal cost of generation at each node will be similar. If the network has restrictions, then the marginal cost of generation at each node will differ. Therefore, the short-run marginal cost of transportation from one node to another will be the difference between the marginal cost of generation in both nodes.

Applying this rule requires estimating the marginal cost of generation at each node. One approach for doing this is an optimization approach that would use complicated models for estimating optimal generation and nodal generation prices. The transportation cost would be calculated as a difference of optimal nodal prices. Another approach is the market approach, which proposes a market at each node, resulting in a market price at each node. Again, the difference between two market nodal prices would be the transportation cost. The market approach may be useful for some specific nodes, where many buyers and sellers are willing to trade. For instance, for trading electricity in a node at the border of the country, the market power of each agent is small and the resulting prices would be competitive. However, lack of competition at most nodes of a network, where only a few agents are willing to trade, means that the market approach to nodal and transportation prices is not useful.

Solution through Nodal Prices

Calculating the short-term marginal cost of transportation becomes redundant for two reasons. One is that calculating short-term marginal cost is equivalent to calculating power nodal prices. The other is that nodal prices give more correct signals for minimizing generation costs than transmission prices. The analysis indicates that nodal spot prices should be used instead of transportation prices. In this environment, generators choose the quantity that they are willing to sell at each node by maximizing profits. Similarly, consumers and retailers choose the quantity that they are willing to buy at each node. When the market clears at each node, the production at each plant is optimal.

This approach is theoretically correct. However, estimation of optimal nodal prices through markets is not feasible due to lack of competition at most nodes. Competitive power markets can be established only at nodes with particular commercial features. If nodal prices cannot be calculated through markets, they should be calculated through optimization models. This, in turn, raises two questions. First, could a centralized agent gather the huge amount of information required for calculating optimal prices? That is, will generators and consumers be willing to reveal the correct information? Second, if optimal prices are calculated by using mathematical models, why is retail competition needed? Hunt and Shuttleworth (1996, p. 85) point out the following:

> "The transmission system may be complex and difficult to operate, and energy may flow in all directions, but it has the same economic characteristics as other transport systems. The price of the electricity at two locations will differ by the price of transport. If the price is badly set, by poor regulation, then the amount of transport will be suboptimal. If it is set at marginal cost including the shadow prices of constraints, and if the system is expanded when the cost of constraints exceeds the cost of relieving them, then the transport system will be optimal. This is the job of the regulator of the monopoly transmission system."

Solutions through Prices for Congestion and Power Loss

Most systems solve the problem of distribution and transmission pricing by dividing it into two partial problems. One partial problem is the calculation of the additional power losses in the network that result from an increase in consumption at a network node. The other problem is the cost incurred due to an increase in consumption at a node that provokes congestion and prevents use of the cheapest plant.

Regarding the first problem, each transportation customer should be responsible for the marginal losses associated with its specific transaction. These assignments are usually calculated from the penalty factors that electric power systems use for generator dispatch. However, some systems, for instance the U.S. power industry, hold each customer responsible for losses that are set equal to the average loss rate of the power system. This approach encourages costly transportation transactions and discourages transactions that are cheap or contribute to loss reduction.

Regarding the second problem, two basic mechanisms are used. In the centralized approach, a central agent calculates transmission prices, in real time or some hours in advance, in accord with the bids of all market agents. The transmission price is the difference between power prices at different nodes. This centralized mechanism is feasible because it is based on optimal dispatching programs that already exist. The market mechanism gives the right of power transmission to those market agents offering the highest prices for transmission rights.

Optimization versus Market Approaches

Hunt and Shuttleworth (1996) discuss the market and optimization approaches for selecting the following features of a scheme for retail competition: trading arrangements, pricing schemes, and retail arrangements. In the market approach, the goal is to ensure that electricity markets work as any other market. In the optimization approach, the goal is to ensure optimal resource allocation.[12]

The market approach results from observing normal markets, where producers, wholesalers, and retailers own a physical product and transport it from one place to another in different ways. The retailer purchases electricity from the pool, repackages it into contracts, and tariffs and sells it to customers. A market model for retailing (that is, a model designed using the market approach)

[12] Economists have used these two approaches extensively to discuss mechanisms for resource allocation. For example, Lange (1938) derives his proposals from an optimization approach, while Hayek (1989) derives his from a market approach.

requires a large amount of settlement software to clear central accounts. Those who use this approach observe that, if the trading system is set up to accommodate bilateral energy transactions, competition will ensure that arbitrage and contestability will push the market price to the competitive level.

Under the alternative approach, electricity is not like other commodities because buyers and sellers do not arrange their trading price and quantity directly, but through a central auctioneer. The auctioneer receives bids from buyers and sellers and sets a price that clears the market, and all trading proceeds at that price. The generation or distribution company delivers power to the final customer, charging the spot price. Final consumers pay the same price, the optimal price, regardless of who is the electricity provider. Therefore, the distribution company could do the job and cumbersome settlement procedures could be avoided. Under this approach, the customer is free to make arrangements for insurance and hedging against the spot price.

If models derived from both approaches work well, their results are similar. However, mechanisms derived from the market approach seem to work better than those derived from the optimization approach for two reasons. One is that the optimization approach rests on central auctioneer calculations that, due to large computational requirements, may be wrong. The other is that the central auctioneer lacks the incentive to perform well. As Black (1994, p. 58) puts it, "the central economic lesson of this century is that imperfect markets work a lot better than imperfect central planning."

Retail Arrangements

The bundled provision of wires and power services can be readily associated with optimization paradigms, whereas unbundling them seems to be an inherent condition for the proper working of any market scheme. First, unbundling wires and other services is a necessary condition for consumer choice. If these services are bundled, consumers do not have a choice. Second, unbundling improves economic welfare in the consumption of end-use services, insofar as it allows consumers to receive and pay for the particular service attributes that they desire. Third, unbundling reduces price discrimination by motivating more detailed service-specific cost analyses. Fourth, unbundling constrains market power arising from tie-in sales. Tying can be used to raise entry barriers by reducing customer choice and the potential market share for entrants, and also by forcing new entrants to offer similar bundles. If bundling can be used to extend market power, then unbundling may prevent the leverage of market power from one market to another, so as to facilitate an increase in competitive pressures within the industry. Fifth, unbundling provides information about the cost of each service that facilitates rational consumer decision-making and helps alternative suppliers to identify opportunities for entry.

Trade Mechanism

Under the market paradigm, consumer access amounts to the consumer's ability to purchase electricity through bilateral contracts with generators or at spot prices. Independent from distribution companies, retailers are also allowed to supply power to customers choosing an energy services provider for the energy portion of their demand. Under the optimization paradigm, customers cannot enter directly into commercial arrangements with generators (this allows wholesale competition for commodity electricity), and there are no independent retailers. Therefore, consumers do not have direct retail choice. Distribution companies supply power and wires to captive, franchised customers who are only able to choose between traditional rates or real-time rates for the power portion of their bills.

Distribution and Transmission Pricing

Proponents of nodal prices are regarded as favoring an optimization approach, whereas proponents of pricing the distribution and transmission services explicitly are taken to have a market approach. However, for distribution and transmission prices, the marginal cost of losses and the cost of congestion are calculated through optimization models. The reasons for such characterizations are the following. First, for market prices at each node to represent marginal cost, some competition is required at each node. However, real-world networks do not have many traders at each node. Therefore, it is not feasible to calculate nodal prices through markets; they must be calculated through centralized optimization models. Second, explicit separation between prices for generation and those for distribution and transmission leaves room for markets regardless of what the regulator determined.

Examples of the Optimization and Market Approaches

The efficient direct access model proposed by Hogan (1994) follows an optimization approach, whereas the basic retail model is an example of the market approach. Hogan's proposal rests on three features. First, there are exclusive retail sales franchises for distribution utilities, which means that consumers do not have retail choice. Second, a competitive wholesale market provides a readily available spot price. Third, distribution companies offer real-time pricing to all customers who want it. This, in turn, requires the market to have an efficient pool for pricing electricity for final consumers.

Advocates of the efficient direct access model argue that a wholesale market could be correctly set up to produce accurate hourly prices, which could be available through traditional franchised monopoly distribution companies (in place of the simple retail tariffs they use today). If this happens, then every retail customer will be able to achieve the equivalent level of efficiency as in a robust competitive retail marketplace, without the hassle of shopping and contracting for suppliers. According to Hogan (1994, p. 30), "faced with the uncertainty and volatility of the spot price, customers may look for longer-term arrangements that would reduce or fully eliminate the risk. Generators, selling into the same market for the spot price, would have the complementary interest and would be the source of long-term contracts for those customers who felt the need."

The efficient direct access model eliminates retail competition and forces the existence of a pool for fixing power prices. These are two marks of the optimization approach. By assuming optimal wholesale markets, consumers may attain all the benefits of competitive markets without their costs. However, if wholesale markets are not optimal, distribution companies do not have an incentive to make them work because their profits are independent of wholesale prices. Arms-length spot prices may guarantee optimal prices if wholesale markets are efficient. However, when they are not, there is no mechanism to drive the wholesale markets toward optimality.

Under the retail competition model, unregulated retailers and consumer free choice are essential for the model to work adequately. A wholesale market is required, but it can be developed through bilateral contracts or by a pool. In this model, regulators are concerned with transportation prices, but they do not worry about power prices. These characteristics correspond to market approaches. Fox-Penner (1997) concludes that the retail choice model is the one that more closely replicates the conventional modes of buying and selling products in other markets, which is the goal of market approaches.

Evaluation of the Retail Competition Model

This section analyzes the advantages and problems of electricity retail competition schemes from different perspectives: conventional economic theory, risk management, lessons from other industries, and less visible effects of competition. This type of analysis may be useful insofar as there is scarce evidence about how retail competition schemes work in real life. Once the retail competition models become widely adopted and enough time elapses, more robust evaluation exercises may be performed.

Conventional Economic Approach

Benefits of Retail Competition

Retail competition models introduce competition on the demand side and complete the liberalization of electricity systems. For the sake of coherence, after large consumers and utilities are able to profit from wholesale market opening, full retail choice allows benefits to all customers. Competing retailers put an end to the old idea of franchised, captive customers that are unable to choose and, therefore, are forced to abide by monopoly conditions, in terms of both prices and quality. Nevertheless, high prices and low quality would not be a unique outcome of a monopoly scenario. Equally frustrating outcomes would be for consumers to receive bundles of products that they did not choose, or to be unable to choose a provider and a preferred combination of services.

Retailing is transforming the stodgy utility culture into a normal business culture. Therefore, the expected benefits from retail competition are similar to those expected when introducing competition in any other industrial sector. These benefits include the following:

- efficient pricing
- diversity of products and services
- new technology and innovation
- greater attention to consumers
- reduction of the regulatory burden
- sector reform.

Retailing allows price arbitrage when costs are not properly reflected in prices, therefore favoring efficient pricing. Arbitrage consists of taking advantage of the differences in prices and margins among different demand segments by offering lower prices to high-price and high-margin segments in order to attract that demand and obtain a profit. If arbitrage is feasible, the final outcome will consist of prices that are adjusted to the costs prevailing in each demand segment, up to the point where no more profit can be achieved. Competitive retailers will be instrumental in introducing price arbitrage by means of price differentiation in terms of the different consumption patterns of their customers. Competition among retailers will replace tariff regulation by delivering cost-adjusted prices with no cross subsidies or excessive margins. Even in systems where retailing coexists with centralized tariffs, consumers can get better terms than under the tariff regime. Incumbent utilities will do what is necessary to keep their customers by means of standard offers (as in New England in the United States) and plain rate reductions (as in California). However, the mere existence of retailers benefits all consumers because arbitrage provides useful information to regulators and consumers, even those who decide not to change providers.

Retail competition mechanisms are expected to increase the diversity of products and services, enhancing consumer welfare and economic efficiency. In contrast to regulated distribution companies, unregulated retailers can profit from selling power or other products to consumers. Moreover, competition will prompt retailers to differentiate their energy services. Some may choose to specialize, for instance, in renewable energy to be sold to environmentally conscious customers willing to pay higher prices to protect the environment.

In retail competition schemes, economic agents face the appropriate incentives to develop new technologies that will lower the costs of supplying or using electricity or expand the range of productive uses of electricity. The incentives for innovations in power supply are likely to be similar because the status of generating companies does not differ between retail competition and wholesale schemes. This includes more efficient generation technologies, new methods of monitoring the use of the transmission system and electricity consumption, and new methods of metering and storage. Incentives for demand-side innovations such as new energy-efficient appliances and equipment, new uses of electricity such as electric vehicles, and new ways to shift load from high-cost to low-cost periods are strong in the retail competition models. A competitive environment requires new products for satisfying consumers and increasing market share.

Utilities holding a monopoly in the sector have traditionally paid scant attention to customer service. The presence of retailers or the mere possibility of future competition has forced existing distributors to establish appropriate customer service and commercial divisions. This is in response to the forthcoming scenario where clients became more sophisticated in a diversified and dynamic retail market.[13] These clients will be allowed to exercise their options to select their preferred quality-price-service mix. Even partial retail competition will mean improved customer service.

Market mechanisms operating under full retail choice schemes are expected to progressively replace regulators in many fields. The pace and scope of that replacement process will depend, among other factors, on the political will of the regulatory authorities and on the technological and institutional features of the different restructuring experiences. One clear outcome of all unfolding retail competition models appears to be increasing customer freedom in terms of moving away from expensive, low-quality power providers. The ability of consumers to choose electricity retailers constitutes the most efficient regulatory mechanism when it comes to striking a suitable balance of quality and price for each customer.

Introducing wholesale competition requires the separation of generation and transmission, as well as separation between retail and generation due to the potential conflicts that could arise from self-dealing. Retailers owning some generation capacity would not represent an obstacle for the proper working of a retail competition model. When purchasing from its own generation, the

[13] A headline in *The Wall Street Journal* (1998)—"As Spain Opens Up Electricity, Iberdrola and Others Aim to Please"—shows the change in corporate culture within the incumbent utilities.

distribution company (sole franchise retailer in wholesale models) will show little interest in minimizing costs that can be passed on to captive customers. In the retail competition model, this is no longer a problem because customers can choose other generators or retailers.

Objections to Retail Competition

Objections to retail competition are based on the fear that it will do the following:

- reduce the reliability of electricity services
- encourage customers to leave the utility system
- facilitate cherry-picking
- diminish the public interest programs sponsored by utility companies
- cause underinvestment in transmission capacity.

Retail competition opponents maintain that a fully competitive market will reduce the reliability of electricity service. They argue that if the utility loses its monopoly, capacity reserves will be at risk. However, making service available when other power sources are already being used is a market service like any other, and suppliers will provide service at peak hours if there is demand for it. Moreover, competition seems likely to improve reliability because it would increase the number of consumers choosing interruptible service and provide an incentive for good maintenance. In a competitive environment, more customers will choose interruptible service in return for lower rates, which will improve reliability for customers choosing noninterruptible service. In addition, power plant outages should be less common in a competitive market because an unregulated producer cannot earn a return on out-of-service assets or keep its customers if it provides poor service. Evidence does not show that regulated monopolies are more reliable than deregulated ones. For instance, the deregulated natural gas industry in the United States successfully faced harsh weather conditions during the winter of 1993, whereas many electricity utilities suffered important shortages.

A second complaint raised by opponents of competition is that some customers will leave the utility system when it becomes less expensive for them to be served by the incumbent utility. This type of bypass is economically implausible; it can occur only in specialized factual settings and, therefore, is unlikely to be economically significant. If it were significant, the need for more deregulation would become all the more apparent. In fact, given the prevailing inefficiency of utilities, reflected in above-market rates, situations of uneconomic bypass are surely swamped by situations where bypass would be efficient because the new producers have lower costs. There are also examples of sensible uneconomic bypass, based on green or renewable options from ecologically-minded customers who are willing to pay higher rates for preservation of the environment. The only worrying option, therefore, is that of uneconomic nonbypass by ill-informed customers who are fearful of exercising their right to choose.

A further complaint against retail competition is that new producers will pick the best customers. Actually, what will happen is that competition will eliminate cross subsidies. No customer, regardless of size, will be supplied at below-cost prices because this would cause the business to lose money. The elimination of cross subsidies is not a shortcoming; it is an advantage of competition.

In the past, electricity utilities have played a key role in providing a variety of public goods, including universal service, protection of low-income customers, protecting the environment, and serving various national energy policy objectives. With few exceptions, the legal obligation to provide these goods was imposed on utilities that either owned generation or sold at retail. Retail choice makes the allocation of responsibilities like these more difficult. Discussions of retail regulation have raised the question of which segment of the new industry, if any, should bear future public interest obligations. Because of the nature of these obligations, the principles that guide efficiency in private goods markets offer only limited insight. Moreover, because the physical, economic, and political natures of these public goods are different, generalized solutions are essentially impossible.

In competitive models, the impetus for expanding capacity will come from the parties that will benefit from the expansion, and they will be expected to pay for it. The problem is that the benefits from investment in transmission capacity cannot be fully appropriated by those bearing the cost of the investment, since all parties connected to the grid will benefit. Market incentives will generally lead to underinvestment in transmission capacity. The possibility of underinvestment is less serious in the wholesale than in the retail model because the cost of additions to transmission capacity will likely be a smaller share of the total cost of power transactions. The parties involved would be less inclined to risk losing the transaction by resorting to free riding. By contrast, in the retail model, the smaller marketing companies will not be able to exploit the scale economies in transmission and the incentive to free ride will be stronger.

Risk Management Approach

Consumers and producers may be willing to pay a premium to reduce spot market price variability and engage in contracts that mitigate price fluctuations. An evaluation of retail competition models from a risk management standpoint requires analyzing whether contracts for mitigating and managing price risks are expected to work better under retail competition than under other trading arrangements.

Bohi and Palmer (1996) compare the performance of market contracts in wholesale and retail competition schemes and conclude that, from a risk management perspective, retail competition schemes are better than wholesale ones. They argue that the tradeoff between premium and risk and the allocation of risk are more efficient in retail competition than in wholesale models. They also point out that in the retail competition model, risk is borne by consumers who are able to manage it better than generators.

According to Bohi and Palmer (1996), the incentive to enter into contracts and the relationship between the spot price and the contract price depend on the risk preferences of buyers and sellers. If both parties were risk-neutral regarding spot price variability, they would be indifferent between buying at the variable spot price or at a fixed contract price that equaled the mean value of spot prices. Risk-averse buyers would be willing to pay more than the average spot price for a contract that smoothed the acquisition cost of electricity, and risk-averse sellers would be willing to take a fixed contract price at less than the average spot price. A contract is efficient if it achieves an optimum tradeoff between risk bearing and the cost of shifting risk to another party. The tradeoff between risk and price will vary across customers and generators, so that the market model that best represents the diverse interests of customers will likely achieve the highest efficiency level.

To best represent the preferences of consumers and generators, the model should have final customers enter into contracts directly with generators. Direct contracts will represent their interests better than if they use a noncompetitive intermediary, such as a regulated distribution company. Therefore, retail competition models that allow this direct relationship among consumers and producers are expected to perform better than wholesale models. However, the transaction cost is large because individual consumers and producers need to accumulate and manage too much information.

Retail competition models with retail companies may not do a good job representing the preferences of consumers. However, competitive pressure will force retailers to improve their knowledge of consumer preferences. By contrast, distribution companies will not feel the same competitive pressures, and will not be as responsive to changes in consumer preferences. The result is that retailers will obtain a better tradeoff between price and risk than distribution companies. Therefore, a superior tradeoff is likely to occur in retail competition models where consumers engage in contracts through competitive retailers.

Bohi and Palmer (1996) argue that contract efficiency requires that risk be borne by the party that is most able to manage it. The primary sources of price risk are variations in consumption and in the marginal cost of generation. In addition, consumers have much more flexibility in altering consumption patterns. Therefore, the retail model is more likely to encourage efficient responses from consumers.

Transaction costs involved in creating and enforcing contracts are relevant in evaluating the capacity for undertaking efficient contracts for risk management. Transaction costs will increase directly with the number and variety of transactions that take place, which may be expected to be higher in the retail model than in the wholesale model. However, retail companies may specialize and reduce the transaction costs of gathering information on consumer preferences. Therefore, specialized retailers are expected to appear, offering a few contracts appropriate for different groups of consumers, thus reducing transaction costs.

Lessons from Other Industries

Companies have had more than a decade of experience with regulatory reform in a variety of industries that share some similarities with electricity. Natural gas, telecommunications, airlines, railroads, and trucking are all industries in which competing producers use a network of wires, pipe, roads, or rails to reach their customers. Economists have analyzed the effects of deregulation and restructuring on these industries in great detail, aided by a wealth of data collected by regulators and trade associations. An overwhelming consensus emerges from these scholarly studies, namely that real-world competition, although not necessarily perfect, is far better for consumers than economic regulation.

Reforming Analogous Industries

From an economist's perspective, these five network industries share a number of similarities with electricity. Like the electricity industry, all five have a production, transmission, and distribution stage. Gas wells, telephone equipment, trains, airplanes, and trucks are, at the production stage, analogous to power plants. Interstate gas pipelines, long-distance phone lines, railroad trunk lines, airways and air traffic control, and interstate highways offer long-distance transportation similar to high-voltage transmission lines. And local gas pipes, local telephone lines, rail sidings, airports, and local streets are economically similar to electricity distribution lines.

The production side of the other network industries was deregulated in the late 1970s and early 1980s in the United States.[14] Most natural gas wellhead prices were deregulated between 1978 and 1984. Competition in telephone equipment came in the late 1970s. Airline route and rate regulations were phased out beginning in 1978, and surface freight companies were partially or fully deregulated in 1980. Large segments of these industries are also subject to some

[14] In economic terminology, deregulation means the partial or complete elimination of governmental restrictions on prices and entry.

form of open access regulation. Interstate natural gas pipelines became open access transporters in the late 1980s. When AT&T was broken up in 1984, local phone companies were required to allow competing long-distance companies to use their lines to reach customers. The U.S. federal government has long had authority to impose open access on a railroad in specific cases. Airlines and trucking companies, meanwhile, both use publicly owned infrastructure that is generally open to all competitors.

Customer Benefits

In the United States, in all five industries, regulatory reform produced significant customer benefits that grew over time. Inflation-adjusted prices fell within two years after regulatory reform, often by 10 percent or more. Within 10 years, prices were at least 25 percent lower and, in some cases, 50 percent lower.

Although regulatory reform did not cause all of these price reductions, it is worth noting that most predictions of price reductions from electricity restructuring fall comfortably within this range. In an August 1997 report, the U.S. Energy Information Administration estimated that in the next two to three years, competition would lower the average retail price of electricity by between 6 and 22 percent; by 2010, the price would be roughly 11 to 28 percent lower than it is today. Citizens for a Sound Economy Foundation (1995) projects that retail competition in the United States will reduce the price of electricity by 13 percent in the short run and by 42 percent in the long run.

Statistical studies of transportation industries in the United States that control for other factors affecting prices have consistently shown that regulatory reform produced more than $50 billion annually in price reductions and other consumer benefits (Crandall and Ellig 1997). A significant portion of these benefits comes in the form of improved quality of service. In the airline industry, for example, one study found that increased flight frequency accounted for more than half the value of consumer benefits. Surface freight deregulation also generated billions of dollars in shipper savings due to the improved reliability of rail and truck transportation.

Distribution of Benefits among Consumers

Another major fear about regulatory reform in electricity is that lower prices for some consumers will come at the expense of higher prices for others. The experience of other industries demonstrates that relief for high-cost customers does not come at the expense of low-cost customers. Rather, all customers gain as increased efficiency and productivity make it possible to reduce rates for all. Crandall and Ellig (1997) show that the reforms of natural gas, airlines, and rail in the United States reduced prices for most consumers. In the gas sector, the average wellhead price fell by $2.32 per million cubic feet in the 10 years following 1985, when most wellhead prices were deregulated. Prices paid by every customer class fell by even more: $2.93/mmcf for residential customers; $3.13/mmcf for commercial customers; $3.53/mmcf for industrial customers; and $3.41/mmcf for electricity utilities. The additional price reductions came largely out of the margins earned by interstate pipelines for transporting gas.

Despite such figures, the general notion is that large industrial customers got most of the benefits of wellhead regulation. This misperception survives because the savings are often expressed as percentages of previous bills and these percentages are larger for industrial consumers than for residential and commercial ones.[15] This pattern stems from the fact that the share of residential and commercial gas bills is much greater than the share of industrial bills. Distribution, metering, and billing expenses per unit are higher for residential and commercial customers, and thus the total cost per unit is higher. As a result, even an equal price reduction for all customers would amount to a smaller percentage for residential and commercial bills.

Airlines provide another example of widespread benefits. Few people dispute that deregulation lowered airfares on average. It is less known that even captive markets enjoy lower fares than those under regulation. For example, in hub cities dominated by one carrier, real fares were 19 percent lower in 1995 than they were in 1979 in the United States (Crandall and Ellig 1997). On routes dominated by a single carrier, fares were 27 percent lower. Fares for small, medium, and large cities were all lower in 1995 than in 1979. It is true that fares for some cities and routes dominated by one carrier are generally higher than for other cities and routes, but most of these fares are still lower than they would have been under continued regulation.

In the United States prior to 1980, the Interstate Commerce Commission dictated that bulk commodities, like coal and farm products, would pay relatively low rail rates compared with high-value products like automobiles and other manufactured goods. It seemed that deregulation would lead to lower rail rates for manufactured products and higher rates for bulk commodities. In reality, all rates fell. Within two years after deregulation, average inflation-adjusted rail rates had fallen by 4 percent, coal rates had fallen by 1 percent, and rates for farm products had fallen by 18 percent. Within 10 years, coal and farm rates had fallen by 38 and 50 percent, respectively. Low-cost and high-cost shippers alike got lower rates because railroad productivity more than doubled in the 10 years following deregulation, after a decade of stagnation (Association of American Railroads 1997).

[15] Residential customers saved 32 percent and industrial customers 57 percent of previous bills (Crandall and Ellig 1997).

Trucking provides a similar example. Less-than-truckload shipments are more expensive to haul than truckload shipments, but the cost of both fell following trucking deregulation in the United States. Between 1977 and 1993, the inflation-adjusted operating cost per mile for less-than-truckload shipments fell by 35 percent, while the cost of truckload shipments fell by 75 percent (Crandall and Ellig 1997).

Less Visible Effects of Competition

A great deal of the electricity debate focuses on how an existing pool of costs will be divided among arbitrarily-defined groups of customers: industrial, residential, captive, low-cost, high-cost, and so forth. From a consumer perspective, this debate is misleading for two reasons. First, even if some big customers receive the lion's share of deregulation benefits, this does not mean that the rest do not benefit at all. If big consumers receive lower utility bills, they do not keep all of those savings as profits. Their competitors will also save money as a result of deregulation, and competition will force them to pass some or all of their savings on to their customers. For this reason, consumer advocates who focus only on residential electricity rates overlook many of the more significant consumer benefits deregulation can produce.

Second, experience shows that regulatory reform does not simply redistribute costs from one group of customers to another. Instead, competition unleashes processes of efficiency gains and innovation across the board. Exposed to both increased competition and greater risk, gas pipelines increased their operating efficiency, railroads doubled their productivity, and truckers found ways to move more freight with fewer resources. Airlines not only reduced costs, but also created a new corporate culture that propelled change in the nature of the product. Such innovations were difficult, if not impossible, to predict in advance (Crandall and Ellig 1997). We are just starting to see the way in which the introduction of competition in electricity retail sets in motion a "virtuous circle" that enhances technological creativity and customer welfare.

Challenges for the Power Companies

The electricity industry is being transformed into a competitive industry, with open access for all customers to electricity providers and new entrants in the field of electricity retailing. Many uncertainties surround any attempt at figuring out what electricity retailers will look like in the future. Will utility firms dominate the retail electricity market? What will be the role played by outsiders from other service sectors? Will any pure retailers survive?

The Role of Utilities

Incumbent utilities, whether generators or distribution companies, are reluctant to lose control over their traditional, integrated business. These utilities are ready to use all of their lobbying and financial power in order to slow down any cultural or institutional change that endangers their position. Horner (1997) shows that in all areas related to competitive retailing, brand marketing, sales, billing, meter reading, collections, trading, logistics, and risk management, utility rates range from weak to very weak. However, financial service companies, telecommunication and oil firms, outsourcers, and logistic specialists are world-class firms in their areas and should, therefore, be well placed in the competitive race for controlling the retail segment of the electricity business.

The Electric Power Research Institute surveys conducted in 1995, 1996, and 1997 provide some evidence that electricity utilities could keep many more of their customers under deregulation by improving the quality of customer service. Many customers would not change suppliers only for reasons of lower price, although the results do not indicate any strong loyalty to current energy providers.

The retail consumer makes three broad buying decisions: planned, spontaneous, and imposed. The first kind applies to homes, cars, or longer vacations. The second governs most small transactions, like entertainment, books, and gifts. The third applies largely to purchases from monopolies, such as energy utilities and governments. With retail competition, the buying decisions of the energy consumer will shift from imposed to a combination of planned and spontaneous. Product positioning will drive this shift, along with promotional inducements and discounting plans. According to Dar (1996), "within the next decade, the emerging infrastructure anchored by an evolved multimedianet will transform energy retailing into a high-volume, high-selection, superb-quality, and relatively low-margin business, conducted by a few with great sophistication and intimidating knowledge."

The Role of the Customer

The heart of second-generation regulatory reforms is giving the customer free choice for buying electricity services. Therefore, the fortunes of electricity retailers will largely be determined by how well they understand their customers and respond to their needs and preferences in terms of prices, services, products, and expectations.

The old business model emphasized industrial technology and quantitative increases in the consumption of energy commodities. The new model will accentuate information technology and qualitative increases in the consumption of energy services. Exploiting new service opportunities in restructured energy markets will become a first priority in all deregulated markets (Rabl 1997). The new strategy focuses on the role of the customer at the center of the entire process as the utilities endeavor to meet the challenges of the new market structure.

The new customer is able to choose and, hence, is willing to demand greater value in exchange for loyalty. In this situation, the provision of top-quality customer service and the supply of innovative products that anticipate or meet customer demands will be key factors in the competitive race. But the race will prove to be especially difficult because, as the Electric Power Research Institute's market research demonstrates, electricity customers have a variety of different needs and priorities (Rabl 1997). There seems to be no way to design a single product or service that can meet the needs of a substantial fraction of the market. Sophisticated market segmentation techniques must be applied to retail offerings, just as they are for other consumer products.

Dar (1996) points out that the gas and electricity industries in the United States control about $900 billion in assets, which they employ to serve about 150 million customers. But they manage to offer only two rudimentary products, molecules and electrons, and at only two levels of service: continuous and interruptible. Such a poor consumer content stands without precedent in the history of world business. Retail competition will bring this game to an end.

Within a few years, retail competition in the gas and electricity industries will create great shifts in revenue and capital. By itself, electricity as a commodity may do few things for the consumer. However, electricity plus technology plus knowledge about consumer needs lead to a variety of services designed to satisfy customer preferences. Real spending on energy commodities will fall noticeably over the next couple of decades as the real prices of molecules and electrons decrease. However, real spending on energy services may rise sharply. Corporate growth in the energy enterprise will reflect ideas, not things; quality, not quantity; and packaging, not unbundling.

Retail Company Bundles

Retailers will strive to develop new services and products in accordance with the new environment in a historic transition to a competitive, market-driven approach to the customer. However, since these new offerings have to be profitable, marketing methods that are well developed in other competitive industries must be adopted by retail agents in the power industry. Since electricity utilities are no longer the only players in the electricity markets, many potential competitors are seeking the most profitable opportunities to enter these markets. Therefore, the successful 21st century energy and services provider will be radically different from its predecessors. The modern provider will focus on speedy innovation, economy, and aggressive marketing to newly discerning customers in a highly competitive environment.

Marketing managers in the power industry indicate that the market segmentation goal of new retail companies should be to provide the whole range of electrical services to their customers. The range of electricity products and services goes from technical services to pricing and billing, and from information services to financing and logistics. Retailers can provide assistance to their customers in the following areas:

- consulting and installation of energy equipment
- equipment service repairs and warranty programs
- energy and environment audits
- waste management solutions
- cogeneration assessment and assistance
- power quality investigations and engineering diagnosis and solutions
- plant operations and maintenance optimization
- energy management services.

Competitive provision of services will require a wide variety of pricing and billing options. Some of the concepts now being developed include the following:

- consolidated billing for multiple meters and locations
- custom billing and data analysis, and reliability and power quality options
- energy service package pricing
- end-use billing and commodity bundling
- electronic billing and collection
- real-time pricing.

Retailers are well placed for offering data and information on process and appliance technology options, local economic conditions, customer energy management, real-time pricing communications, home automation and related services, and telecommunications and computer-based network services. Major innovations are expected in the area of financing as energy service providers try to identify and meet a wider range of customer needs. Examples of financial activities are equipment financing and leasing, buyout-sellback equipment options, build-own-operate contracts, and service contracts. Some energy service providers offer shared savings options. They secure the initial financing and get paid by the customer on the basis of energy savings generated by the new equipment and services.

Will today's utilities survive information technology? How many truly national energy retailers survive mass customization? Imaginative thinkers suggest transforming existing power retailing firms into entities that create alliances with various companies and broker supplies and services from a host of competitive providers, that is, *virtual utilities* (Hirsch 1997).

References

Ando, A., and K. Palmer. 1998. *Getting on the Map: The Political Economy of State Competition.* Discussion Paper 98–19. Resources for the Future, Washington, D.C.

Association of American Railroads. 1997. Industry Reference Files, Washington, D.C.

Beato, P. 1997. "América Latina: la electricidad, opción de futuro." Paper presented at the seminar organized on the occasion of the IDB Governors, Annual Meeting, March, Barcelona, Spain.

Black, B. 1994. "A Proposal for Implementing Retail Competition in the Electricity Industry." *The Electricity Journal* (October).

Bohi, D., and K. Palmer. 1996. "The Efficiency of Wholesale vs. Retail Competition in Electricity." *The Electricity Journal* (October).

Bosch, A., and C. Escribano. 1988. "Aplicaciones de la teoría de juegos al reparto de costes." *Cuadernos Económicos del I. C. E.* 40(1988/3): 163–194.

Brennan, T., and K. Palmer. 1996. *A Shock to the System: Restructuring the American Electricity Industry.* Washington, D.C.: Resources for the Future.

Calsamiglia, J. 1977. "Decentralized Resource Allocations and Increasing Returns." *Journal of Economic Theory* 14: 262–285.

Citizens for a Sound Economy Foundation. 1995. *Customer Choice, Consumer Value: An Analysis of Retail Competition in America Electric Industry.* Department of Economics Working Paper, The University of Clemson, Clemson, S.C.

Comisión del Sistema Eléctrico Nacional (CSEN). 1997. *Documentos sobre el Proyecto de Ley del Sector Eléctrico.* Comisión Reguladora del Sistema Eléctrico de España. Madrid: CSEN.

———. 1996. "The Search for Consumer Content in Energy Marketing and Retailing." *Public Utilities Fortnightly* 134(17): 24–29.

Crandall, R., and J. Ellig. 1997. *Economic Deregulation and Customer Choice: Lesson for the Electric Industry.* Center for Market Processes Working Paper, George Mason University, Fairfax, VA.

The Economist. 1998. "Power to the People," March 16.

Faruqui, A., and L. Kirsch. 1998. "Unbundling Electric Discos Overseas and at Home." *Public Utilities Fortnightly* (April).

Fox Penner, P. 1997. *Electric Utility Restructuring: A Guide to the Competitive Era.* Vienna, VA: Public Utilities Reports.

Hayek, F. A. 1989. *The Fatal Conceit: The Errors of Socialism.* Chicago, IL: Chicago University Press.

Hirsch, R. 1997. "Consensus, Confrontation and Control in the American Electric Utility System: An Interpretative Framework for the Virtual Utility Conference." In S. Awerbuch, ed., *The Virtual Utility: Accounting, Technology*

& Competitive Aspects of the Emerging Industry (Topics in Regulatory Economics and Policy Series). New York: Allstair Preston.

Hogan, W. 1994. "Efficient Direct Access: Comments on the California Blue Book Proposals." *The Electricity Journal* (September).

Horner, J. 1997. "Identifying the Practicalities and Cost of Outsourcing the Metering, Billing, and Data Collection Function." Presentation given at Metering, Billing and Customer Data Management, 22–23 September, London, England.

Hunt, S., and G. Shuttleworth. 1996. *Competition and Choice in Electricity*. Chichester, England: John Wiley & Sons.

International Energy Agency (IEA). 1997. *Energy Statistics of OECD Countries 1997 Edition*. Paris: IEA.

Laffont, J. J., and J. Tirole. 1996. "Creating Competition through Interconnection: Theory and Practice." *Journal of Regulatory Economics* 10: 227–256.

Lange, O. 1938. "On the Economic Theory of Socialism." In O. Lange, F. M. Taylor, and Benjamin E. Lippincott, eds., *On the Economic Theory of Socialism*. Minneapolis, MN: University of Minnesota Press.

Oren, S., and D. Ray. 1997. "Services in an Unbundled and Open Electricity Services Marketplace." In S. Awerbuch, ed., *The Virtual Utility: Accounting, Technology & Competitive Aspects of the Emerging Industry (Topics in Regulatory Economics and Policy Series)*. New York: Allstair Preston.

Rabl, V. 1997. *Exploiting New Service Opportunities in Restructured Energy Markets*. Palo Alto, CA: Electric Power Research Institute.

Ramsey, F. P. 1927. "A Contribution to the Theory of Taxation." *Economic Journal* 37: 47–61.

Skilling, J. 1997. "Testimony before the Committee on Energy and Natural Gas." Hearing on Competitive Change in the Electric Power Industry, U.S. Senate, Washington, D.C.

The Wall Street Journal. 1998. "As Spain Opens Up Electricity, Iberdrola and Others Aim to Please," May 15.

CHAPTER 12

Liberalization of the Gas Sector in Argentina, Colombia, and Mexico

Paulina Beato and Carmen Fuente

Natural gas was not a significant energy input in Latin America until the 1990s. Lack of transportation and distribution infrastructure, unsound industrial development, and the recession of the 1980s explain the low level of natural gas use in the past. However, since the early 1990s, significant reserves in several countries and the discovery of major new gas fields have taken the volume of reserves to unprecedented levels.

Renewed economic growth and liberalization of the region's markets have driven this shift.[1] Since 1990, economic expansion has been behind the sizeable increase in energy demand. Rapid growth in the demand for energy and environmental concerns led to the development of natural gas infrastructure that was initially intended to cater to industry and power generation. Significant increases in investment were necessary to meet the rising demand for natural gas. As a consequence, governments promoted regulatory reforms aimed at paving the way for private sector participation and attracting foreign capital. Gas-producing countries have progressively opened their markets in order to attract private capital and achieve greater efficiency and competitiveness. Thus, the gas industry has undergone a process of deregulation and restructuring, resulting in the development of new markets and new ownership patterns. Although private sector interest was initially concentrated on the use of natural gas as an input in power generation (by means of combined cycle gas turbine plants that offer great efficiency and a quick return on investment), natural gas has become important to the transportation, commercial, and residential sectors as well.

[1] Although an exact evaluation of the role of environmental protection in increased natural gas consumption is difficult to make, environmental regulations are also responsible.

At present, the region is self-sufficient in natural gas. Argentina, Mexico, and Venezuela account for roughly 75 percent of total natural gas production. Production in Bolivia and Colombia amounts to a sizeable portion of the remaining 25 percent. All of these countries, with the exception of Venezuela, have implemented reforms aimed at introducing competition and obtaining the funds needed for the expansion of natural gas infrastructure. This chapter examines the scope, outcomes, and shortcomings of the reforms in Argentina, Colombia, and Mexico.[2]

The Monopoly Model

Although the structures and regulations of the gas sector before and after the reforms are not uniform across countries, we use two stylized models—the monopoly model and the competition model—to describe two extreme structures of the sector. The monopoly model describes schemes in the United States and in most Latin American countries before the reforms.[3] Gas sectors in countries such as Spain and France, which have yet to undertake reforms, are close to the monopoly model. The competition model describes the current structure of the gas sector in the United Kingdom and the United States. In Latin America, Argentina and Colombia have gas sectors akin to the competition model. Mexico's gas sector remains close to the monopoly model despite the reforms of 1996.

The main features of the monopoly model are that gas exploration, production, transportation, and distribution are partially vertically integrated and fully regulated. The industry's development is planned, with no room for market forces to operate. Economic authorities, regulators, or public companies set rates, and prices serve as cost-recovery devices for each industry segment.

Such an environment hampers economic decisionmaking by gas producers or consumers. Ignorance of market realities has led to all sorts of evils in the form of shortages, outages, lack of customer choice, investment incentives, cost cutting, and innovation. Although gas consumption increased in the 1970s as a result of higher oil prices, regulation (in the form of capped prices) kept the industry from accommodating that increase in demand and resulted in an increasingly unbridgeable gap between demand and production.

A monopoly model may work efficiently in theory. However, in practice, the model is doomed to inefficiency because regulators lack information about market conditions and producers lack incentives for minimizing costs. The

---

[2] The appendixes provide more detailed descriptions of the gas sector in Argentina, Colombia, and Mexico.

[3] This model was determined by reserve localization, the length of the pipelines, associated political risks, and lack of appropriate financial tools for risk diversification.

monopoly model seems appropriate when the costs of these inefficiencies are offset by the economies of scale of concentrating services.

Production and Transportation

Although exploration and production take place before transportation in the provision of natural gas, discussing transportation first makes it easier to understand how the organization of production and the interaction between the two segments result in a fully regulated model with no room for markets.

Regulation of the transportation of gas has historically been justified on the grounds that it is a natural monopoly and that economies of scale and heavy sunk costs may discourage investment in the presence of free entry. Limits on market entry were supposed to decrease total and average pipeline costs by reducing risks and ensuring that pipelines were put to heavy use. Cost-based price regulation would protect consumers and service regulation would maintain adequate quality standards. Therefore, traditional transport regulation was supposed to create a social contract benefiting pipelines and consumers (Ellig and Kalt 1996). This notion led to the monopolistic structure of the transportation segment, with only one state-owned company controlling the entire network in many countries. In others, one or several private companies own the pipelines. However, these companies enjoy franchise protection that prevents free entry and consolidates monopolistic control in the corresponding areas. The monopolistic character of the transportation segment permeates the production segment, and prevents market forces from operating even in the presence of a large number of potential competitors within the exploration and production segment.

There are two main patterns in exploration and production activities: one single company controls exploration and production, or several companies make up these segments without any one of them holding individual monopoly power. In spite of the fact that these seem to be two different models, market control of the transportation company makes the resource allocation mechanism similar in both cases.

The first pattern (one company controlling production and exploration) results when exploration and production are considered strategic activities that the public sector should own and control. The company also owns the transportation pipelines, but it does not own the distribution network. The company is the sole seller of gas to the distribution companies and may set prices greater than marginal cost. The company should be regulated to avoid this behavior. However, in many cases, regulation and service provision are the responsibility of the same institution. Since the production and transportation segments are integrated, the rate of return of the monopoly can be controlled by fixing a unique price, the price of a bundle of transportation services and gas supply. Under that scheme, regulators do not need reliable information about transportation costs; they need only aggregated information about production and transportation costs.

The second pattern does not consider exploration and production to be strategic activities. As a result, the market is made up of many private firms, leaving room for market forces to drive production and exploration. However, lack of competition in transportation and the practice of bundling transportation and gas supply transform the transportation company into a two-sided monopoly: a demand and supply monopoly (see figure 12–1). The transportation company is also the sole buyer of gas from independent producers and the sole seller of gas to the distribution companies and, thus, provides transportation services bundled with gas supply. Under this pattern, regulation has to set wellhead prices and prices at the city gate in order to reduce the monopolistic power of the transportation company. The aim of regulation is to establish a fair rate of return for independent producers and providers of transportation services. Therefore, regulators need reliable and separate information about transportation and production costs.

Distribution

Regulation of distribution has historically been justified on the grounds that it is a natural monopoly and that economies of scale and heavy sunk costs may discourage investment in the presence of free entry. As a consequence, only one enterprise owns the distribution network in a geographic area and holds a franchise for supplying and distributing gas to all consumers in that area. The municipality often owns the distribution company. Alternatively, distribution companies can be private firms or subsidiaries of the monopoly that produces and transports gas. In all cases, the local distribution company offers a bundle of services related to gas provision, such as transportation within the city, gas supply, or metering.

Given the monopolistic character of the distribution company, regulation is required. Yet, regulations do not distinguish between gas supply and its transport from the city gate to households. Therefore, regulators set a global price for a bundle of services. The distribution margin, the difference between prices at the city gate and consumer prices, is set to provide distribution companies with a fair rate of return.

The Competition Model

The natural gas industry has changed radically over the past two decades as a consequence of economic and regulatory factors. The core elements for transforming a fully regulated monopolistic gas sector into a modern and

Figure 12–1. Regulated Monopoly Model for Natural Gas

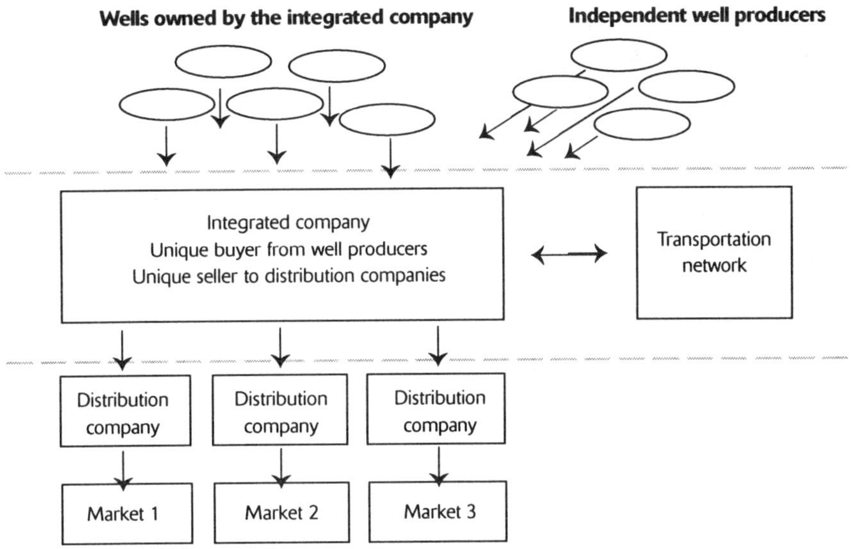

competitive one differ among sector segments. Privatization, free entry, and wellhead price deregulation are the core competitive reforms in the production segment. Free entry, full separation of transportation and supply, and the ability to freely sell transportation rights are the forces pushing the transportation segment toward greater competition. The introduction of retail competition requires open access to distribution networks and regulations to avoid price discrimination.

Markets for gas and transportation should result from implementation of these reforms. However, the degree of market competitiveness depends on the sector structure and the behavior of market participants. The main features of the natural gas market are the following:

- Trading takes place by means of decentralized bilateral transactions among producers, marketers, local distribution companies, and end users.
- Deregulation of the gas industry has permitted the separation of physical and financial trading.
- Participants in the natural gas market manage supply risks by means of short and long-term supply contracts and may enter into financial risk management contracts in order to counteract price risk.
- Buyers purchase gas and transportation services from different suppliers.
- Pipeline transport prices remain fully or partially regulated in the primary market, but competition operates in the secondary market for pipeline capacity.

The competition model features incentives for reducing costs. In addition, the information that each market participant requires to make decisions is decentralized and the allocation of resources that results from a competition model is, in theory, efficient. However, in practice, some flaws may become apparent. The most important is the tendency of producers to increase their market share in an attempt to take advantage of increasing returns in most segment services, in particular, in transportation. This means that some producers could gain control of the market and hamper efficiency. In situations such as these, antitrust regulation and laws governing competition are a must.

Production

Free entry at the exploration and production stages and price deregulation at the wellhead lead to increased competition and improved price signals, thus transforming the supply environment from one of shortages to one with adequate gas supply.[4] When production is concentrated in one state-owned enterprise, free entry is not possible because the existing company wields sufficient market power to prevent other participants from entering the market. In order to remedy the situation, three additional measures are needed: (1) a reduction in the market share of the company; (2) privatization; and (3) the separation of production and transportation activities.

The size of the monopolistic company has to be reduced in order to diminish its market power and allow for the entry of new firms. Privatization is required in order to ensure a level playing field for all market participants.[5] It is recommended that the company be restructured before it is privatized in order to avoid conflicts between the government and the new private shareholders. However, governments are reluctant to undertake such actions because the market value of a company with monopolistic control is higher than the market value of several companies with the same market share but without individual market power. Separation of activities allows competition in gas supply even when a few firms control the transportation segment.

Transportation

Capacity and transportation services are traded in natural gas transportation markets. The supply side of the market consists of pipeline companies, while the demand

---

[4] Without a market to facilitate the sale of reserve and exploration rights, it is not possible for new participants to enter the sector. If no reserves are available, free entry cannot increase the number of market participants.

[5] Although the rules governing state-owned enterprises may be similar to those governing private businesses, in most cases state-owned enterprises enjoy more government protection than private ones.

side is made up of producers, suppliers, local distribution companies, and retailers or large end users. Transactions take place by means of contracts that define the conditions under which natural gas will be transported and delivered.

Two markets, primary and secondary, may arise in this segment. In the primary market, pipeline companies sell transportation contracts to marketers, local distribution companies, or end users. The primary market is often regulated to avoid market control by pipeline companies. In the secondary market, pipeline companies and holders of transportation contracts resell unused capacity in an environment of free negotiation with no threat of market control by pipeline companies (see figure 12–2).

Although the introduction of open access means restricting the scope of utility regulation and leaving room for other agents to participate, it is not sufficient for promoting competitive gas markets. Free entry and unbundling of transportation and gas supply services are the two key requirements of competitive markets. When market participants are able to resell their transportation rights, the efficiency of transportation markets increases.[6]

Liberalization of entry for agents willing to assume financial risks represents the first major step toward an open gas transportation system. In a liberalized environment, pipelines are neither protected from competitors nor awarded franchise privileges. By the same token, most gas transport rates are negotiated. Rates for large customers, retailers, and distribution companies are negotiated in a competitive market. However, no real-world gas transportation sector has yet arrived at that stage, even in countries where free entry prevails, because there are large sunk costs. This means that the number of participants is small, and each one maintains a certain degree of market power. Therefore, other reforms need to be introduced in order to avoid monopolistic behavior and to promote competition.

The second major step, unbundling gas supply and pipeline transportation, reduces the scope of market control by pipeline owners because even if the companies control transportation services, they cannot control gas supply. Thus, if regulations are necessary, they only have to cover transportation. Some countries, such as the United States, introduced unbundling when large users began to profit in the face of decreasing wellhead prices by purchasing their own gas and using the pipelines just for transport, thus breaking the pipeline monopoly over gas sales. Nevertheless, regulators also play an important role establishing open access and revoking take-or-pay contracts. In other countries, such as Argentina, the regulatory authorities introduced unbundling of transportation and gas sales without pressure from large consumers. In Colombia, transport unbundling is a main feature of a wider reform process.

---

[6] Secondary markets mitigate inefficiencies in the allocation of resources when the regulations of primary markets provoke imbalances between the supply of and demand for transportation services (Juris 1998, pp. 40–43).

Figure 12–2. Competition Model for Natural Gas

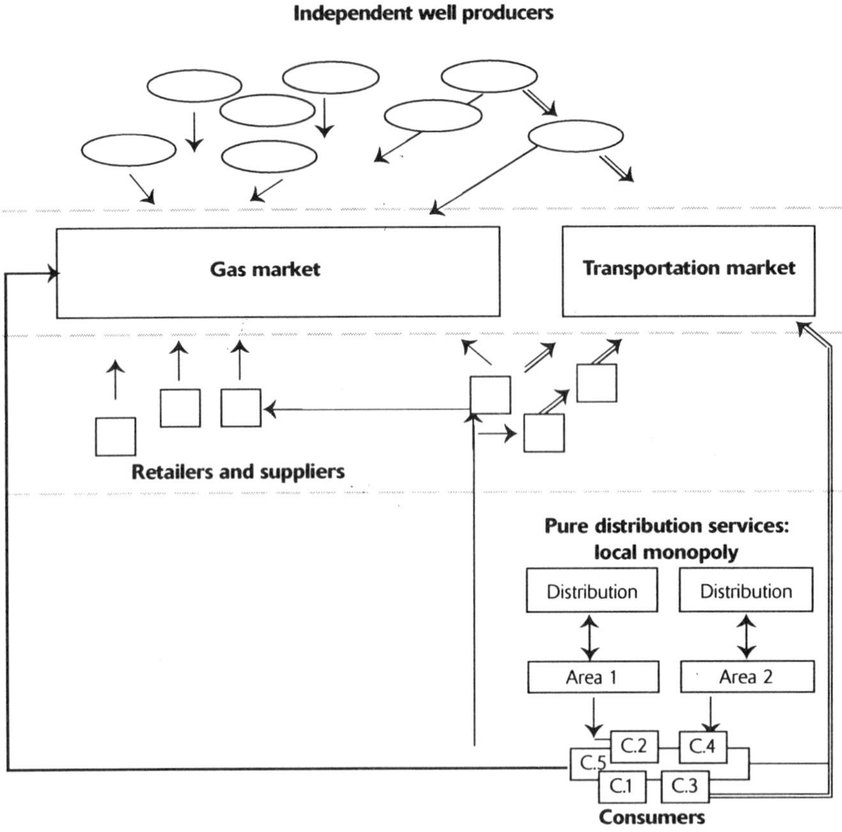

When pipeline companies do not offer supply services, the regulator does not require common carriage or contract carriage. In that context, some service terms can be freely negotiated and tailored to the needs of pipelines, shippers, and users. Some cases require rules for distributing capacity among users, leading to the establishment of price caps for transportation services. These regulatory measures are needed because the small number of distribution companies participating in the sector is able to acquire market power. Competition is also fostered when holders of transportation capacity contracts are permitted to sell them in secondary markets.[7] The interaction between regulation in primary markets and competition in secondary markets dilutes the market power of pipeline companies and reduces regulatory distortions.

---

[7] Transportation companies should not participate in secondary markets to avoid monopolistic behavior.

Distribution

In spite of similarities between the transportation and distribution of natural gas, the key elements of reform in each market segment are very different. While free entry and full unbundling are key in transportation, the same is not true in distribution for two reasons. First, economies of scale are larger in distribution than in transportation. Second, technical and urban restrictions make it difficult to develop a new distribution network in urban areas. Measures other than free entry are necessary to enhance competition in distribution. This is achieved by allowing consumers, suppliers, and retailers open access to distribution networks and by unbundling gas distribution activities, retail, and supply. Open access allows some consumers to enter into separate contracts with suppliers and distributors. When distribution companies provide both transportation and retail services, they may have an incentive to charge higher prices to those consumers entitled to choose a retailer other than the distribution company. However, no country has established a separation of ownership between distribution and retail activities similar to the unbundling established between transportation and supply activities. In the United Kingdom, where consumers may choose their suppliers, distribution companies provide both transportation and retail services. Given that ownership separation does not seem to be a real option, regulations should be established in order to avoid discriminatory behavior.

If open access for all consumers and nondiscriminatory treatment were established, price regulations would not need to cover gas supply; they would need to cover only the rates for transporting gas from the city gates to the consumers. All consumers would be able to buy gas in competitive markets with a large number of participants, but they could not buy transportation services only from the distribution company. However, gas retail competition has not yet arrived at the stage where most small consumers bypass the distribution company. In most countries, the regulation of distribution prices covers gas supply as well as distribution services.

The Role of International Trade

Multinational pipelines and free trade complete the competition model. International transactions increase the scope of choice for consumers, marketers, and distributors, but such transactions are limited by the availability of pipelines with open access. Multinational as well as domestic pipelines require regulations to establish access conditions and prices because competition is poor among pipelines joining two countries and monopolistic behavior may arise. While open access is a must for national pipelines in competition models, regulations in countries with a competitive environment do not require open access to multinational pipelines. Nevertheless, these countries do impose restrictions on companies or economic groups that participate in production and transportation activities.

Gas Production and Wholesale Markets

Sector Structure

The structure of the production sector in Argentina, Colombia, and Mexico is characterized by significant market control by a few participants. This is a consequence of nationalization policies pursued across the region during the 1950s, 1960s, and 1970s due to the strategic character attributed to energy resources. Although reforms in Argentina and Colombia allowed the entry of new production companies, a few large companies retained control of the market. Public sector companies control over 50 percent of the gas produced in Colombia. In Argentina, a former state-owned enterprise that was privatized controls more than 50 percent of the market. Mexico allows no entry into the production sector. These concentrated sector structures do not favor competition; they result in monopolistic prices that require regulation.

Argentina privatized its oil and gas industry in 1993, becoming the first country in the region to do so. Although the formerly state-owned company Yacimientos Petrolíferos Fiscales (YPF) still controls more than one-third of gas production and more than two-thirds of the wholesale market, more than one hundred other firms operate in the market. Moreover, transactions for distributors and large consumers were liberalized and prices are now set, in principle, through the interaction of supply and demand. However, wellhead gas prices do not seem to reflect competition. Action should be taken to remedy that lack of competitive drive among wellheads by gradually reducing YPF's market share.

In Colombia, in spite of reforms, Ecopetrol still holds close to 50 percent of the upstream market share. The country's tough association contract terms have hampered the development of gas reserves by private companies. Unusually high tax levels, royalties, and Ecopetrol's 50-percent mandatory stake in all successful exploration contracts deter foreign investment. A recent reduction in the mandatory share of Ecopetrol in exploration activities apparently prompted a sizeable number of private firms to enter the market.[8]

In Mexico, PEMEX still controls close to 100 percent of domestic gas production. Liberalized imports, amounting to 10 percent of total supply, represent the only opportunity for introducing competition into an otherwise highly

---

[8] According to Ecopetrol, 12 new association contracts with foreign and Colombian private firms were signed in January 2000.

monopolistic upstream segment. That narrow opportunity is further limited by PEMEX's control of pipelines and its capacity to sell commercial services to large consumers. PEMEX's dominant position in the wholesale market determines the need for some sort of price regulation.

Market concentration is the main stumbling block in the way of effective wholesale competition in the three countries. In Argentina, the foundations for progress lie in the YPF announcement in September 1999 that it would take measures aimed at reducing its market share to 35 percent by May 2003. In Colombia, the path to liberalization is clearly established by regulation and it seems that the process will be completed in the next three to five years. In Mexico, no competitive scenario can be envisaged.

Wholesale Gas Prices

Production prices in Argentina are set competitively by various producers. However, YPF (which was recently acquired by Spain's Repsol) sells more than 60 percent of the gas produced, thus hampering the effective development of competition. Since 1993, prices at the wellhead have increased by about 17 percent in real terms, an increase that can be explained either as a natural competitive development or as a consequence of dominant position abuse by YPF (Urbiztondo, August, and Basañes 1999).[9]

In 1996, the Colombian government established regulations that will lead to fully deregulated natural gas wholesale prices by 2005. Once deregulation is complete, regulators will set a maximum reference price and producers, industry, distribution companies, and electric utilities will be free to negotiate wholesale prices. At present, prices are partially regulated. Some producers may sell at regulated prices according to a formula, while others may sell their output at negotiated prices. So far, producers choosing to sell at the formula-determined regulated price have obtained lower prices than those selling at market prices.

Although PEMEX still holds its dominant market position in Mexico, wholesale prices (or "first-hand sales prices") are set in a maximum price system. The regulatory commission has established a methodology for calculating prices that uses 1996 as a reference point. The adjustment mechanism is based on indicators that reflect gas prices in the United States and transport prices from the border to PEMEX City. In order to ascertain compliance with maximum price regulations, Pemex has to disclose the difference between gas sales prices and transportation costs. The regulatory commission can eliminate the regulatory mechanism when effective competition is judged to be working.[10]

---

[9] ENARGAS is considering presenting the case before the regulatory commission.

[10] In January 2000, the regulatory commission issued new regulations for determining these prices.

Transportation

Free Entry

All three countries allow private sector participation in gas transportation. Participation is implemented through concession agreements that may or may not entail exclusive rights. This means that entry of new transportation companies is controlled and limited by the government through its ability to grant concessions.

In Argentina, the government grants transportation licenses with exclusive rights for 35 years (renewable for 10 additional years). Only two gas transportation companies operate in the country.

The Colombian concession regime does not grant exclusive rights and allows for the maximum degree of free entry of the three countries. Several pipelines were built and financed with private foreign capital through build-operate-transfer concessions awarded for 15 or 20-year terms. As a result, two of the country's main pipelines (with a length of 1,510 kilometers) represent 30 percent of the total network and are in private hands.

While PEMEX controls the greater part (10,000 kilometers) of Mexico's gas transport facilities, private participation has been allowed since 1995. Private participation is conferred by a direct award that does not bestow exclusivity. Recent government approval of the construction of 2,000 additional kilometers of pipeline boosted private participation (yet it remains small).

Unbundling

Transportation services and gas supply are fully unbundled in Argentina and Colombia, but not in Mexico, which requires only an accounting separation between the two activities.

In Argentina, the gas industry was vertically separated in order to favor the development of competition wherever it was economically and technically feasible. However, restrictions were imposed on the ownership of gas transport, production, and distribution. No owner may control more than 20 percent of the market.

Colombian regulation considers unbundling a must for guaranteeing open access to the transport system. Gas transport has to be performed independently from gas distribution, supply, or retail. Production, distribution, and retail firms are not permitted to hold more than a 25-percent interest in transportation firms.

Given that unbundling is not required in Mexico, PEMEX engages in supply and transportation activities despite the fact that it controls a large portion of the pipelines.

Open Access

Although open access regulations may seem unnecessary in an environment with free entry and full separation of transportation from retail and supply activities, most countries do include it.

Argentina's regulatory framework prohibits transporters from engaging in acts involving unfair competition or abuses of controlling market positions. Transporters are also required to allow access to transport facilities to other market participants as long as this does not endanger their ability to meet contracted commitments. Colombian regulations require transporters to allow access to their networks and storage facilities to any supplier, retailer, or distributor, and, in general, to any user applying for access. In addition, owners of existing networks must permit the building of new pipeline connections in compliance with technical codes and the rules of the regulatory commission. Third-party access to existing networks (whenever there is available capacity) is established by law in Mexico. Therefore, concessionaires are required to provide equal treatment on demand to all users.

Sale of Transportation Rights

Argentina's regulators have recently established a resale market for unused transportation capacity. Although so far only a small number of operations have taken place, the proper working of this market will prove instrumental in further enhancing competition.

Colombian regulations permit suppliers, retailers, large users, and distributors to resell unused contracted capacity to third parties, subject to nondiscrimination. The regulation requires that advanced notice be provided to the transporter and other interested users about the availability of unused capacity volume and dates when there is capacity available. Notice must be published in a public venue so that all interested parties can be informed simultaneously and be able to present their bids to the assignor. Regulatory bodies guarantee fair competition throughout the process.

Mexico's gas transportation regulations also establish the possibility for the transfer of surplus capacity. However, secondary markets lack information.

Transportation Prices

Price cap mechanisms prevail in the three countries. This means that the regulating authorities set maximum prices and transportation companies may negotiate a price with customers subject to the cap.

In Argentina, the regulatory commission, ENARGAS, determines transportation tariffs on the basis of the cost of providing service plus a reasonable rate of return on assets, taking into account the efficiency levels of concessionaires.

Cross subsidies are not allowed. ENARGAS sets price caps, which are adjusted for inflation semiannually and every five years to take into consideration improvements in efficiency and additional investments. The efficiency adjustment factor allows for efficiency gains to be shared between consumers and producers. The investment factor is intended to compensate shippers for investments planned for the subsequent five-year period. Transport companies are free to charge rates lower than cap levels. Transportation companies can make inflationary adjustments to their rates every six months, using changes in the U.S. producer price index for industrial commodities as a reference.

Colombian transportation is divided into three systems (integrated, interior, and Atlantic) with different rates. The regulatory commission sets the rates for the integrated system. Producers and consumers pay according to their location in the network, regardless of contracts between consumers and producers within each market. In the interior system, entry charges are calculated as a function of the cost of transporting gas from the production fields to a reference node. Exit charges are given by the cost of transporting gas from the reference node to exit nodes. Entry and exit charges consist of two components: a capacity charge, which is applied on contracted capacity, and a use charge, which is applied on the volume of gas transported. To enter Atlantic Coast pipelines, shippers pay a stamp fee regardless of the distance traveled.

Transport rates in Mexico are set in accordance with a price cap scheme or incentive based on a five-year revision mechanism. Departure prices, which are used as the basis for further revisions, are based on the cost of service. Inflation adjustments are based on an inflation index that takes into account changes in consumer prices in Mexico and the United States, as well as movements in exchange rates. An efficiency factor is also included; however, it is currently set at zero in an attempt to attract investment. Mexican transport rates include a cost factor as well, which enables the transfer to users of costs related to taxes and the system's balance. A correction factor, applied when earned income is less than maximum income, is intended as a guarantee or floor on the earnings of concessionaires. Users and concessionaires can negotiate prices freely, subject to these constraints.

Distribution

Open Access

All three countries have legally established open access to distribution networks for consumers and retailers. The scope of competition, as measured by the percentage of consumption that bypasses the distribution company, is relevant in Argentina and Colombia, but not in Mexico.[11] The scope of competition as measured by the number of small consumers that choose to buy gas directly in the wholesale market is limited in Argentina and Colombia.

Distribution companies in Argentina are assigned specific geographic zones and, in principle, any consumer may legally purchase natural gas directly from the producer or marketer and freely negotiate transaction conditions. In such cases, consumers must notify the regulatory commission and the distribution company of their intentions six months in advance, and must also finance the required metering equipment. However, the concession contracts of distribution companies limit eligibility for bypassing the distribution company to retailers and large users (that is, those who use over 10,000 cubic meters per day). In spite of this limitation, 40 percent of the gas consumed in the country is contracted for bypassing the distribution companies. This figure has increased sharply since 1993.

In Colombia, distribution concessions are awarded through a bidding process for 15-year periods. The law establishes open access of distribution networks to producers, retailers, and consumers. However, only large consumers may effectively choose the gas retailer. Distribution and ancillary activities are conceptually unbundled, but distribution companies may undertake both distribution and retail activities. Nevertheless, distributors performing retail activities within their service area need to hold separate accounts for each activity in order to avoid discriminating against consumers who choose a retailer different from the distribution company.

In Mexico, distribution companies are awarded franchises by means of concession arrangements entered into through a bidding process. Mexican regulations allow all customers to freely choose their supplier, and enable retailers other than the distribution companies to operate. However, the monopoly character of the production segment hampers putting into practice such regulations. In fact, no evidence of the existence of independent retailers has been found.

Retail Gas Prices

A distinction should be made between retail prices of bundled gas services—transportation, gas, distribution, and retail services—and retail distribution prices that refer only to charges for transporting gas from the city gates to consumers. In all three countries, regulators cap both prices, setting an upper limit on the ability of market participants to negotiate prices.

Retail prices in Argentina consist of charges for gas, transportation, and distribution. The regulatory commission fixes a price cap for each component

[11] About 60 percent of gas consumption in Argentina bypasses distribution companies. Official figures were not available for Colombia, but some specialists estimate that around 30 percent of gas consumption is negotiated excluding distribution companies. No effective bypass has been reported in Mexico.

and distribution companies may offer lower prices to customers. The price cap for gas charges depends on the effective price paid by the distribution companies. However, since 1998, the regulatory commission establishes a reference price as an incentive for distribution companies to minimize their gas costs. Thus, if the price paid by distributors is higher than the reference price, only half of the difference can be transferred to final consumers through prices (see table 12–1). Price caps may be revised on a periodic as well as an extraordinary basis. Periodic revisions take into consideration gas prices paid by the distribution companies and transportation charges.

Prices received by Colombian distributors and retailers are established by considering several variables. Three components make up the maximum price that distributors and retailers may charge consumers when the distributor provides gas, transportation, and distribution services: the price of gas, the transport and connection price cap, and the distribution price cap. The gas price is negotiated between the distribution company and the supplier subject to the wellhead price set by the regulatory commission. (Wellhead prices will be fully deregulated after 2005.) The regulatory commission establishes price caps for connection, transportation, and distribution prices. When the distributors only provide distribution services, just connection and distribution prices are collected. Similarly, charges for bundled services must fall below the relevant caps. Distributors and retailers can also offer bundles of services to large consumers at prices below the maximum. However, prices paid by large consumers have to be publicized.

In Mexico, the retail price structure is based on price caps and minimum prices. Gas prices, transport and connection charges, and charges for the distribution component are capped. Price caps apply to residential and commercial consumers, while industrial customers may negotiate the actual price of each service separately. Minimum prices are established to avoid predatory competition. Discounts offered to large consumers have yet to be analyzed because of a lack of information on bypass consumers.

Regulatory Issues

The soundness of a regulatory setting depends on three pivotal features. The first is the degree of separation between regulatory authorities and institutions providing services. The second refers to the capacity of regulatory commissions to make transparent and independent decisions. The third feature relates to the suitability of the regulatory framework to the sector structure.

Argentina separates and differentiates between policymakers and service providers. It welcomes private service providers in both monopolistic and competitive segments of the gas chain. However, energy policymaking is in the

Table 12–1. Consumer Discounts on Natural Gas in Argentina

Consumer type	Discount (percentage over price cap)
Nonbypass customers	13.7
Power plants	11.2
Others	9.5
Bypass customers	17.7
Power plants	18.5
Others	15.5
Total customers	15.6
Power plants	15.3
Others	12.8

Source: Authors' calculations using ENARGAS data.

hands of the government. Colombia formally separates policymaking and service provision, but public ownership of large segments of the gas industry may prevent effective separation. Ecopetrol holds a sizeable share of production, and plans to privatize Ecogas have not materialized. Given that the government is the sole shareholder in Ecopetrol, full separation between policymaking and service provision does not occur. Mexico has limited separation between service providers and the government. The government controls gas production and transport through PEMEX and private sector shares of natural gas production and transportation are scant, making separation even weaker than in Colombia.

The independence of the regulatory commission is reflected in the degree of independence from political control enjoyed by board members and in the commission's financial autonomy. In Colombia, the regulatory commission includes a government representative among its members. The board is made up of the ministers of energy and finance, the director of national planning, and five energy experts appointed by the president for four-year renewable terms. The commission appoints an executive director, selected from among the experts. However, there are no legally established grounds for removing a board member. The Colombian commission has a low degree of regulatory independence from policymakers.

The regulatory commission in Argentina consists of five board members selected by the government from among experts with a solid professional and technical background. Provincial governors propose two candidates and a congressional commission is required to report on the proposed appointments. Board members are appointed for five years and their appointment can be renewed indefinitely. Resignations occur in an alternate manner on a yearly basis, as specified on the occasion of the first board appointment. Removals must be based on solid grounds and require government action.

In Mexico, the president appoints the chairman of the board of the regulatory commission and its four commissioners for five-year alternate terms. Reasons for removal are legally specified.

Financial autonomy varies in the three countries. In Argentina, the resources of the regulatory commission include inspection fees paid by storage agents, transporters, retailers, and distributors; subsidies and donations; proceeds from tickets and seizures; and interest and profits. Each year, the regulatory commission sets its budget, which is published before being presented to the government for approval. Once approved, it becomes part of the national budget bill. In Colombia, all regulated entities make a special contribution to fund the regulatory commission's activities. The commission's budget is managed through a trust merchant contract between the Ministry of Energy and a trust entity. The regulatory commission's budget is processed through the Ministry of Finance in accordance with the by-laws on the national budget. In Mexico, each year the government allocates resources for financing the regulatory commission.

Operating transparency can be ascertained by means of the frequency of public hearings or other public involvement in the regulator's activities. Regulators in Argentina hold frequent public hearings, which promote the participation of interested parties in the decision-making process. Regulatory transparency is further enhanced by legal provisions requiring that the commission's decisions (as well as the background information on which the decisions were based) be publicized. Colombia's regulatory commission holds public hearings whenever the board of commissioners deems it appropriate. The same holds true for publicizing decisions made by the board. In Mexico, the Energy Regulatory Commission Law establishes that general administrative provisions, such as general criteria and methodological matters linked with regulated activities, can be dispatched through public hearing procedures. In principle, the measure seems to shrink the scope of public hearings as a source of transparency. That law also requires that records of the commission's resolutions on regulated activities be kept for purposes of making the information public.

Compatibility between the regulatory framework and the structure of the sector is instrumental for effective reforms. The stated aim of the regulatory frameworks of the three countries is to promote a competitive environment. However, competitive markets are not achieved by legally imposing free entry, in particular, when incumbent firms hold sizeable market shares and bear large sunk costs. Under these circumstances, entry threats are not credible and incumbent firms may continue to behave in a monopolistic manner. Authorities have three options: restructuring the gas sector and reducing the market power of large incumbent firms; recognizing the lack of competition and making the regulatory framework coherent with such an environment; or maintaining regulations designed for a competitive environment.

Some lack of compatibility between the regulatory framework and the sector structure can be found in all three countries. For example, wellhead prices in Argentina are fully unregulated, although some production companies have large market power. However, in the transportation sector, the regulatory framework recognizes the lack of competition and regulates it accordingly by setting maximum prices and establishing rules for assigning capacity. In Colombia, Ecopetrol and Ecogas control over 50 percent of the production and transportation segments. The regulatory framework recognizes that poor competition exists and has established a deregulation plan. In the meantime, regulators set maximum prices. The lack of compatibility between the regulatory framework and the structure of the sector seems to be wider in Mexico than in the other two countries. Although free entry is allowed in the transportation segment in order to foster some degree of competition, it is difficult because PEMEX controls the production segment and, although imports are allowed, they remain insignificant and have no impact on the monopolistic environment.

Lessons Learned

The gas sector in Argentina, Colombia, and Mexico has undergone profound changes as a result of the regulatory and structural reforms begun during the 1990s. The reforms were part of overall economic restructuring programs aimed at improving economic efficiency and increasing investment through greater reliance on market forces and the participation of private capital.

A common feature of the reforms has been the unbundling of the different segments involved in the process of providing gas. The separation of production and exploration, transportation, distribution, and retail has been implemented in the three countries by identifying and regulating them as different activities. However, Argentina established restrictions on the participation of a firm or an economic group in production and transportation. In Colombia, one firm cannot participate in both production and transportation activities. However, the separation is more formal than real, given that Ecopetrol and Ecogas, two state-owned enterprises, are involved in production and transportation activities, respectively. In Mexico, there are no restrictions on undertaking production and transportation activities. In fact, PEMEX participates in both. Moreover, gas production and exploration are legal monopolies.

A common feature of the three countries is the stated objective of making the wholesale gas market competitive in the presence of firms with large market shares. Nevertheless, the degree of compatibility between the aim of the reforms and the structure of the sector differs in the three countries. In Argentina, competition in the wholesale market is partially limited by the large share of production controlled by one privatized firm. Although that private firm has proposed some measures to reduce its own market power, they may not be sufficient for encouraging more participants to enter the production segment and for promoting competition in the wholesale market. The experience of Argentina seems to show that measures to reduce market control of firms after privatization have to be adopted with extreme caution in order to avoid eroding the credibility of the regulatory framework. In Colombia, Ecopetrol, a state-owned enterprise, controls a large share of the production segment, but gas production by other private firms is growing. In Mexico, gas imports are the open window to wholesale competition because production is a legal monopoly.

In Argentina, the ownership of transportation pipelines is concentrated in a few firms. The legal framework supports this concentration by preventing free entry in the transportation segment. However, free entry in transportation prevails in Colombia and Mexico. Nevertheless, the three regulatory frameworks acknowledge the lack of effective competition and include measures to improve efficiency. Thus, the monopolistic power of the transportation companies has been reduced by forcing them to give open access and nondiscriminatory treatment to all market participants. In Colombia and Argentina, these measures have been strengthened by separating transportation activities from production and retail activities.

In all three countries, the distribution sector is made up of companies that enjoy a distribution monopoly within a geographic area. In order to increase efficiency and introduce some competition in the distribution sector, consumers have the right to choose a gas supplier that is different from the distribution company. However, consumer choice is limited in practice. For instance, in Argentina, distribution concession contracts state that only large consumers (those consuming more than 10,000 cubic meters/day) have the effective capacity for choosing a retailer. In Mexico, we found no instances of consumers buying gas directly from independent retailers.

Reforms in the three countries place great value on the political independence of the regulatory commission and transparency in the decision-making process. However, in all cases, the government appoints board members. To enhance political independence, the countries rely on fixed terms of office for the commissioners and limits on the reasons for their removal from office. Transparency is increased by means of public hearings and by publicizing regulatory decisions.

Finally, although it is too early to evaluate the impact of transnational pipelines on competitiveness, they are expected to push competition and efficiency. However, transnational pipelines may also be a way for restoring some vertical integration in the gas industry. This may happen to the extent that production companies own transnational pipelines, although restrictions on participating in production and transportation within a country may exist. Promoting transnational pipelines without giving attention to regulatory and market structure issues should be avoided. Restructuring ownership of international pipelines already constructed and in operation would be a difficult task and would likely erode the credibility of any government proposing such measures.

Appendix 12–1. The Gas Sector in Argentina[12]

During the 1990s, Argentina's natural gas sector underwent profound structural and regulatory changes to introduce competition and attract private investment. Argentina produces 102.8 million m^3 of natural gas per day and imports 4.8 million m^3. Daily industrial consumption of natural gas is 27 million m^3, power plants consume 23 million m^3 per day, daily residential consumption reaches 16 million m^3, and exports total 5.2 million m^3. The structure of consumption has changed markedly since the 1992 reform. Total average growth since then has been 24 percent, but the rate of growth of power plant consumption has reached 43 percent, while industrial consumption has risen by 27 percent and residential consumption has increased by only 4 percent as of 1998. Exports accounted for more than 5 million m^3 per day in 1998, 7.7 percent of total demand, a figure that is expected to increase with the construction of the pipeline that will connect Argentina with Chile and Brazil.

Sector Structure

The 1992 law vertically separated the industry to foster competition. The legislation also imposed cross-ownership restrictions on gas production, transport, retail, marketing, and distribution companies. Companies in one segment of the gas industry are not allowed to own more than 20 percent of the equity of a company in another segment.

Production

Argentina accounts for 1.5 percent of total world production of natural gas. In 1998, production was close to 30 billion m^3, ranking Argentina as the region's second largest producer. Argentina's production potential is enormous: in 1998, gas reserves totaled 23 years, three times higher than in the United States, whose gas reserves are eight years.

The most important production area is the Neuquen basin, which produces more than 20 million m^3 per day and has the largest reserves in the country, 341 billion m^3. The Austral area ranks second in production, with nearly eight million m^3 per day and estimates of 155 billion m^3 in reserves. The third in importance is the northwest, which produces 3.5 billion m^3 per day and has an estimated 174 billion m^3 in reserves.

Despite the fact that free entry is allowed in the exploration and production segments of the sector, activity is concentrated in only a few companies. YPF

[12] This appendix is based on Fernández-Ordóñez (1999a).

Appendix Table 12–1. Producer Shares of Wholesale Gas Transactions in Argentina

Producer	Share (percent)
YPF	59.1
Astra/Bridas	2.4
Chauvco	0.8
Bridas/Chauvco	5.0
Pluspetrol	1.7
CNPC/Astra	11.2
Glacco	0.7
Quintana/CGC	2.6
Total/Bridas/Deminex	3.1
Plusp./Tecpetrol/Astra	1.4
ROCH	0.7
OEA	0.7
PCR	0.6
Santa Fe	4.0
CGC	1.2
Tecp./Ampolex/CGC	1.7
Capex	2.9
Others	0.2

Source: Authors' calculations using ENARGAS data.

accounts for 59.1 percent of total gas production and CNPC/Astra accounts for 11 percent (appendix table 12–1). Wholesale activity is even more concentrated because YPF purchases around 25 percent of the gas it sells from other producers and, therefore, accounts for about 60 percent of total sales. Imports of natural gas from Bolivia account for less than 5 percent of production and are smaller than exports.

Transportation

Argentina's regulated transportation segment has four basic features. First, the government grants pipeline transport rights by means of concessions. Second, concessionaires hold exclusive rights over a given geographic area but must give access to the pipelines to consumers, retailers, producers, and distribution companies. Third, the price mechanism incorporates a price cap, but shippers may negotiate rates freely up to the cap. To avoid discrimination, the regulation requires the disclosure of prices and discounts. Fourth, transportation users may resell their transportation rights in the secondary markets free of limitations on negotiating prices.

Transportation is organized around two large companies: Transportadora de Gas del Norte and Transportadora de Gas del Sur. Transportadora de Gas del Norte covers the northern part of the country and controls 4,900 km of pipelines that have access to the areas of Cuyo and Neuquén, as well as imports from Bolivia. These pipelines are connected to the following distribution companies: Cuyana, Litoral, Centro, Noroeste, Buenos Aires Norte, and part of the Pampeana. The Canadian company Nova Corporation operates Transportadora de Gas del Norte and controls 20 percent of Transportadora del Norte's capital. Other shareholders are Trancopas, Inversoras Catalinas, and Petronas Argentina. Transportadora de Gas del Sur covers the southern part of the country and controls 6,000 km of pipeline. This company transports gas from the Austral area and also from Neuquén, and serves the southern distribution companies. The operator is the U.S. company Enron, which controls 37 percent of the equity. There are two important shareholders, each with 25 percent of the equity.

In the past few years, international interconnection has increased significantly. The extension of several pipelines was authorized in 1998 and new pipelines connecting with Brazil, Chile, and Uruguay are currently being studied. Regional integration projects are important for Argentina's natural gas industry because they increase the size of the market and introduce more competition.

Distribution

The distribution segment is also organized geographically into nine areas (appendix table 12–2). Each area is assigned to a distribution company that has exclusive rights to develop the distribution network. Concession contracts establish investment requirements for the distribution companies. The investments fall under three categories: compulsory investments related to the security and integrity of the system, noncompulsory investments related to expected increases in demand, and noncompulsory investments to increase the efficiency of the system.

Metrogas, which covers most of the Buenos Aires metropolitan area, is one of the top three companies, distributing more than 13 billion m^3 per day. Metrogas and Gas Pampeana, another one of the top three distribution companies, are operated by Camuzzi, an Italian distributor. Gas Pampeana covers southern Buenos Aires, a considerable part of the province of Buenos Aires, Mar del Plata, and the northernmost area of La Pampa up to the Colorado River. The third largest distributor is Gas Natural Ban, which covers the northern part of Buenos Aires. It is operated by Gas Natural of Spain and delivers eight billion m^3 per day.

Distribution companies have exclusive rights for developing the network over a geographic area. However, the regulatory framework allows users who consume more than 10,000 m^3 per day to choose a supplier and bypass the distribution company. Nevertheless, the distribution company maintains the obligation of delivering gas from the city gate to all consumers.

Appendix Table 12–2. Expansion of the Distribution Network by Concessionaire, Argentina, 1990s

Concessionaire	Pipeline stock, December 1998 (kilometers)	Increase, 1992–98	
		Kilometers	Percent
Metrogas	13,951	2,760	24.7
BAN	18,821	4,879	35.0
Pampeana	19,470	6,513	50.3
Litoral	7,862	3,115	65.6
Sur	11,920	3,822	47.2
Centro	10,161	4,106	67.8
Cuyana	7,978	2,648	49.7
Gasnor	6,025	1,580	35.5
Nea	591	591	–
Country total	96,779	30,014	45.0

– Not available.
Source: ENARGAS.

Between 1994 and 1998, the number of large gas users (mainly industries and power stations) who chose to buy gas through direct contracts with producers and shippers increased by almost 32 percent (appendix table 12–3). By the end of 1998, 100 large consumers were purchasing gas directly and entering into contracts with the distribution and transportation companies. In addition, 14 companies chose direct connections to the transportation pipelines, bypassing the distribution network. Finally, users who are located at the wellhead are also able to sidestep the transportation and distribution companies. As a result, distribution companies negotiated roughly 60 percent of the gas sold to final consumers in 1998.

Regulatory Framework

Reform legislation (Ley 24076, enacted in 1992) established the regulatory framework for the natural gas sector and the privatization of state-owned gas companies (as well as some other temporary and complementary provisions). A decree-law (1020/95) introduced changes in prices to end users. The legislation declared that private sector companies could participate in all sector activities (exploration and production, transportation, and distribution), but kept for the government the responsibility of establishing sector policies and regulations (but not service provision).

An autonomous body, ENARGAS, was established to regulate transport and distribution activities. The law also separates sector activities into those that will require regulation (transportation and distribution) and those that will operate

Appendix Table 12–3. Supply Methods, Argentina, 1994 and 1998

Supply method	1994 (percent)	1998 Million m^3 per day	1998 Percent
Distribution company	84.0	43.5	58.4
Bypass of the distribution companies	16.0	31.0	31.6
Commercial bypass	6.0	19.5	26.2
Physical bypass	2.5	3.6	4.8
Other	7.5	7.9	10.6
Country total	100.0	74.5	100.0

Source: ENARGAS.

within a competitive framework (gas supply, retail, and marketing). To ensure the separation of activities, transportation companies are not allowed to provide supply services and are required to provide transportation services to all clients (retailers, end users, and distributors) on a nondiscriminatory basis. In the same manner, gas producers and retailers cannot control distribution or transportation companies.

The Regulatory Body: ENARGAS

The mandate of ENARGAS (Article 2 of 24.076 Law of 1992) is to adequately protect consumer rights, support competition, promote efficient and reliable operation, and encourage investment to ensure long-term supply. ENARGAS has regulatory and supervisory functions as well as dispute resolution powers.

The regulator sets safety rules, technical procedures, and quality standards, and approves rate schedules. Its supervisory tasks include inspection and auditing (ENARGAS has the capacity to request the necessary information to perform these responsibilities). In addition, the regulatory body is authorized to issue sanctions. The regulator has decision powers related to the resolution of conflicts and controversies among agents and between agents and third parties. Consultation and attention to users' complaints are particularly important; in 1998, ENARGAS responded to 58,000 consultations and more than 6,000 complaints.

ENARGAS has autonomy and independence from the government and has sufficient resources to carry out its job. Its five board members are appointed by the government for five-year terms that can be renewed indefinitely. Board member terms end on alternate years. Budgetary resources stem from the inspection and control fee paid by transporters, distributors, retailers, and storage companies; subsidies, donations, and legally assigned resources; revenues from fines and seizures; and interest and profits accruing from its resources. This regulatory body operates through public hearings where different associations of users, service providers, and others are invited to participate. The administrative decisions made by ENARGAS can be appealed. Of the 57 cases appealed up to 1998, 47 were favorable, four were unfavorable, and six were rejected.

Quality Control

ENARGAS is also involved in activities to improve quality standards. A resolution issued in 1998 (resolution 891/98) put into effect a provisional reference framework for the control system based on quality indicators. A penalty scheme ensures compliance with these regulations.

Price Mechanisms

Production

Transactions carried out in the gas wholesale market (that is, gas purchases from producers or marketers by distribution licensees and large users) were liberalized when the market was deregulated. Therefore, natural gas prices are determined through the interaction of supply and demand. However, YPF controls nearly 60 percent of the supply of natural gas and, as a result, wholesale competition is less robust than it could be and prices may be set above competitive levels.

In September 1999, during the public hearing organized by ENARGAS for the seasonal adjustments of rate schedules due to price variations at the wellhead, YPF announced measures to reduce prices and increase competition. It announced a 3-percent reduction in the wellhead price; a reduction in YPF sales to final consumers in order to eliminate them completely by 2003; removal of restrictive clauses from sales contracts; and reduction in YPF's market share to 35 percent by 2003. The impact of these measures is difficult to predict.

Transportation

Regulation establishes that ENARGAS has to set transportation rates on the basis of the cost of the service plus a reasonable rate of return on assets. It also has to consider the degree of efficiency that can be reached by the companies; however, cross subsidies are not allowed. It is a price cap or incentive rate type of system with semiannual inflation, efficiency, and investment adjustments. Distribution and transportation companies can adjust their rates every six months to take inflation into consideration. The adjustment is based on changes in the U.S. producer price index (PPI) for industrial commodities. Efficiency improvements are factored into the rates and are kept fixed for five years, serving as a mechanism for consumers and producers to share efficiency gains. The rate is also adjusted by a factor, also fixed for five years to compensate companies for the investments planned for the following five years. Apart from these adjustments, ENARGAS can make rate changes to reflect unusual costs such as, for example, tax changes.

Transportation companies can set their prices subject to the cap fixed by ENARGAS. However, in order to ensure transparency and nondiscriminatory treatment, companies have to disclose their rates for continuous and interrupted transportation services.

Distribution

The price cap distribution system is similar to the transportation pricing system just described. Prices are adjusted every six months to take into consideration changes in inflation, efficiency, and investment. Two different sets of prices need to be examined in distribution. One is the bundled gas rate paid by final consumers who are unable to choose a supplier. These customers pay a rate that includes transportation and distribution services as well as natural gas supply. The other is the distribution price paid by consumers who are able to choose their supplier and pay only for the shipment of gas from the city gate to their home or place of business.

Bundled rates are made up of three elements: the price of gas at the point it enters into the transportation system, transportation charges, and distribution rates. ENARGAS determines distribution rates based on the distance from production centers, whether the service is continuous or interrupted (continuous services are more expensive), and the actual volume of gas consumed (the cost per m^3 decreases as consumption increases). Distribution companies might provide gas at prices below caps, but they are obligated to disclose standard distribution rates for the different categories of consumers. The mechanism for transferring gas costs to consumers resulted in frequent disputes. The mechanism in use prior to 1995 incorporated actual costs paid by distributors into the consumer price cap. In order to promote the development of a short-term natural gas market, the decree that followed the reform establishes an optional regime for calculating distribution caps. The new system is based on a reference price fixed by ENARGAS. Thus, if actual prices paid by distributors are below reference prices, rate caps are not modified and distribution companies may profit from buying gas at favorable prices. This mechanism allows distributors to minimize their wholesale gas costs.

Although the system of fixing the retail price cap does not envisage cross subsidies, it must be noted that residential users in Patagonia do enjoy relatively subsidized rates. The subsidies increased until 1997, when they began to decrease.

Final Observations

The structure and regulation of Argentina's natural gas sector are close to the competitive model. The main differences are related more to the sector's structure than to the regulatory framework. Those differences can be grouped into three categories. The first category is lack of competition in the wholesale market resulting from YPF's market power. The large share of production controlled by YPF pushes wholesale prices well above competitive prices. The measures that YPF proposed voluntarily may not be sufficient to allow additional participants to enter the production segment or to promote competition in the wholesale market. Despite this shortcoming, however, any measures taken after privatization, even those intended to promote competition, have to be adopted with extreme caution in order to avoid eroding private investor credibility in the regulatory framework.

The second category is differences that facilitate entry to promote competition in the transportation segment. To achieve this goal, the 30-year exclusivity rights now allowed in the concession mechanism should be modified. The capacity resale market should also be overhauled to improve competitiveness in natural gas transportation. Due consideration should be given to regulatory risk issues when devising new measures for gas transport.

The third category is retail competition, which is hampered by the height of the consumption threshold for consumers to be able to bypass distribution companies. Broadening consumer freedom to choose a supplier (which is now limited to those consuming more than 10,000 cubic meters/day) would promote the appearance of retail companies capable of grouping different consumers and increasing their ability to negotiate favorable natural gas rates with producers and wholesale suppliers. It may not be easy to effectively implement consumer choice, but it increases consumer awareness of business operations and helps regulators to gather opinions that are different from those of distributors. However, this measure is not easy to put into effect because distribution licensees could argue that it involves a change in the conditions of the concession contract. In order to move forward on this issue, it will be necessary to enter into negotiations with these companies.

Appendix 12–2. The Gas Sector in Colombia

A program to expand the natural gas sector in Colombia was drafted in 1986. It had three main objectives: to foster the use of natural gas, to promote exploration given the shortage of existing reserves, and to offer an alternative to gas integration with Venezuela. The discovery of the large reserves of natural gas in the Cusiana field in 1989 was a major breakthrough in the history of natural gas exploration in Colombia. The development of the Cusiana reserves by Ecopetrol and British Petroleum (BP) doubled the country's gas reserves and proved instrumental in prompting the industry's expansion. That process was further reinforced by the subsequent discovery of the Guajira fields in the early 1990s. In December 1998, reserves in these two fields amounted to nearly 90 percent of total reserves (see appendix table 12–4).

In 1991, the government launched a new program, which encompassed the development of several new gas transportation pipelines, the expansion of existing distribution areas in the main cities, and an increase in distribution concessions in rural areas. These measures were aimed at developing a nationwide gas market and industry, and replacing other costlier and more polluting sources of energy. The plan involved spending US$3 billion on gas transportation and distribution pipelines, compressed natural gas stations, and customer equipment conversions between 1993 and 2012. The plan was expected to lead to a doubling of total gas demand in the country by 2000, and to require 1,400 km of trunk lines and 1,000 km of distribution lines, as well as the conversion of 900 km of oil pipelines to natural gas. Recent figures update investment plans up to 2002, showing that the lion's share of that investment effort goes to consolidation of the pipeline network (see appendix table 12–5).

Sector Structure

The gas industry in Colombia is made up of a large number of companies in each industry segment (10 firms in production, nine in transport, and 24 in distribution and retail). Public and private ownership coexist; and ownership of the public segment is shared by the central and local governments. Foreign companies hold important positions in the sector. There are also a number of companies with cross ownership and differences in vertical integration.

Vertical and horizontal integration are restricted by various regulations. Resolution 57, enacted in 1996, provides for the unbundling of the industry's regulated and competitive activities, establishes safeguards for competition, and defines economic interest (appendix table 12–6 provides data on consumption of natural gas by sector). To guarantee open access to the national transportation system, gas supply, retail, and distribution activities are independent of transportation. As a consequence, transport contracts, rates, charges, and related

Appendix Table 12–4. Gas Reserves by Field in Colombia, December 1998

Field	Billions of cubic feet	Percent
Guajira	2,975	44.1
Guapaje	49	0.7
Opon	46	0.7
Other Interior	313	4.6
Cusiana	2,984	44.2
Piedemonte	380	6.5
Total	6,747	100.0

Source: Asociación Colombiana de Gas Natural (Naturgas).

Appendix Table 12–5. Gas Transport, Distribution, and Retail Investments in Colombia, Projections for 1999–2002

(Billions of U.S. dollars)

Sector	1999	2000	2001	2002	Total
Transportation	88.2	64.0	14.0	13.3	478.0
Distribution	16.3	19.4	14.0	1.0	80.9
Retail	61.8	56.7	64.5	43.2	283.7
Total	166.5	140.7	218.5	188.0	842.6

Source: Asociación Colombiana de Gas Natural (Naturgas).

Appendix Table 12–6. Increase in Natural Gas Consumption by Sector, Colombia, 1990s

(Percent)

Sector	Sector share, 1998	Growth rate	
		1997/96	1996/95
Ecopetrol	19	7.3	–1.3
Petrochemical	2	–4.6	–25.0
Industry	10	–3.0	4.8
Households	10	24.5	23.4
Thermoelectric	50	58.9	6.1

Source: Asociación Colombiana de Gas Natural (Naturgas), using Ecopetrol data.

prices are negotiated independently of purchase or distribution contracts. Gas transporters are barred from being directly involved in gas production, supply, retail, or distribution activities, and from holding economic interest in firms that perform these functions. Suppliers, distributors, and retailers are excluded from performing transport functions or holding an economic interest in gas transport companies.[13]

Another regulation (Resolution 71, May 1998) limits the ability of gas operators to control the market by requiring that by January 2015, no single distributor will service more than 30 percent of users. Firms that hold more than 30 percent of market shares at the time the regulation goes into effect are not allowed to expand their control in existing or future firms. The regulation limits gas retailers to 25 percent of the shares of the market and prohibits joint retailing. Beginning on September 12, 2000, gas firms were required to provide the regulatory commission (CREG) with information about shareholder participation and relationships between parent and subsidiary firms.

Historically, the sector has been dominated by Ecopetrol, which was created in 1948 as a state industrial and commercial company attached to the Ministry of Mines and Energy. Ecopetrol's responsibilities covered exploration, extraction, processing, transportation, and marketing hydrocarbon resources. Ecopetrol has since participated in the sector as a shareholder of producers and transporters or as a distributor in areas lacking private investors. The natural gas industry was gradually opened to private participation beginning in 1994.

Production

Although private firms may participate in production and exploration, all new entrants must enter into a contract with Ecopetrol. As a result, Ecopetrol remains the main player in the industry, owning 50 percent of all commercial production activity in Colombia. Other upstream production companies are AIPC, Amoco, BP, Shell, Texaco, and Triton.

In order to create the conditions necessary for long-term self-sufficiency and to solidify Colombia's position as a key player in the hemisphere's energy sector, Ecopetrol's participation in newly discovered commercial fields was reduced to 30 percent (that is, Ecopetrol will assume 30 percent of the investment and receive 30 percent of the hydrocarbons produced). The contracts between new entrants and Ecopetrol have been modified, making them more attractive to private investors.

---

[13] Economic interest is defined as ownership of 25 percent or more of another firm's capital.

Transportation

Natural gas transport is subject to regulations that establish rights, duties, and prices. Pipeline capacity rights are granted by the government by means of concessions. Concessionaires have exclusive rights over a given geographical area, but they must give consumers, retailers, producers, and distributors access to the pipelines. Shippers are free to negotiate transport rates subject to a price cap; however, prices must be disclosed to avoid discrimination. Transportation rights may be resold in secondary markets with no price limitations. To avoid discrimination, regulations require that priority be given in accordance with contract terms and regulatory conditions. As a consequence, lowest priority is accorded to interruptible contracts, while firm and peak contracts have first priority for access and transport service. The transporter is responsible for ensuring that contract terms are fulfilled and guaranteeing capacity.

Colombia's natural gas transportation system (which integrates the Atlantic coast, center, interior, and southern transportation systems) has been managed by Empresa Colombiana del Gas (Ecogas) since 1977. Ecogas is a public body within the Ministry of Mines and Energy, organized as an industrial and commercial company with its own legal and financial standing. The company is accountable to CREG and the public services superintendency (SSP). Its mission consists of guaranteeing natural gas shipping services to producers, distributors, power generators, industries, and commercial interests in an efficient and freely accessible manner. Ecogas is charged with offering transportation services to all producers and/or consumers; operating and administering the pipeline network; developing pipeline infrastructure; and organizing and operating the Center for Gas Transmission and Coordination and transportation services for contract users. Colombia's president appoints all seven members of the Ecogas board of directors.

Ecogas operates a network of pipelines that is 3,233 km. A large part of the network was built over existing oil pipelines, which were adapted for natural gas use. Ecogas will have the option of acquiring the pipeline being built by Ecopetrol under build-operate-transfer (BOT) arrangements. The first project developed under this scheme was the Ballena-Barrancabermeja pipeline. A 15-year BOT contract was signed in 1994 between Ecopetrol and Centragas (owned by Enron) for a 578km pipeline that reaches 31 towns. Transgas de Occidente has operated the 340km Mariquita-Cali pipeline, which caters to 48 municipalities and two electricity plants, under a similar scheme since 1998.

Promigas, based in Barranquilla, operates an independent transportation network along the Caribbean coast and owns about 25 percent of most distribution companies. In 1996, Ecopetrol sold its 39 percent participation in Promigas to Enron. The company is now privately owned and listed on the Bogotá stock exchange. Its shareholders are Enron (38.9 percent) and IFC (11.8 percent); 49.4 percent is privately held.

Distribution

In some cases, local distribution companies are granted concessions, with exclusive rights for a particular geographic area.[14] Local distributors will operate as natural monopolies until 2014, and will be regulated in a way that allows efficient distributors to achieve a reasonable rate of return.

The largest distributor is Gas Natural de Bogotá. Its majority public stake was auctioned in 1997 and acquired by a group led by Gas Natural of Spain, which manages the company. Two remaining distribution concessions north of Bogotá (Tolima and Boyacá) were awarded in 1998 to a consortium led by Gas Natural of Spain. They cater to 25 municipalities in the department of Cundinamarca, 28 in Boyacá, and three in Santander. Potential growth estimates for these companies indicate an expected increase in customers from 768,293 in 1998 to 1,300,000 in 2001. There are four distribution companies operating on the North Coast: Gases de la Guajira, Gases del Caribe, Surtigas, and Gas Natural del César.

In 1997, concessions were awarded for 15-year periods to build and operate gas distribution facilities in the four coffee-growing areas of Valle del Cauca, Quindío, Caldas, and Risaralda. The area's population totals two million people and the number of potential users is estimated at 500,000. A consortium consisting of all the major gas companies operating in Colombia and Noram (Texas) as a foreign partner won all these distribution concessions. Empresas Públicas de Medellín, owned by the local authority, is constructing its own gas distribution network.

Consumers are free to choose a supplier and all market participants have open access to distribution networks. Regulation prevents discrimination between consumers who buy gas directly and those who bypass the distribution company.

Regulatory Framework

Liberalization of the gas sector began in the mid 1990s with the enactment of the Residential Public Services Law (Ley 142) in 1994 and additional regulations summarized (Resolution 057) in 1996. The relevant regulations establish the general criteria for contracting exclusive service areas for gas distribution and marketing; assert the need for using the contractual method of exclusive service areas in several zones; establish general definitions of the gas network transportation service and methodology; establish general service provisions that regulate the selling, marketing, transporting, and distribution of gas through the

[14] Resolution 57 establishes that exclusive service areas for gas distribution and marketing are the exception when large investments are required to increase gas coverage.

network system; provide for open access to the transport system for any supplier, retailer, distributor, or any other user; and open access to the distribution networks to fuel gas producers, retailers, and large users.

Residential Public Services Law

The residential public services law sets the stage for private sector participation in the provision of residential public services: electricity and gas, sewerage and water, and basic and mobile telephone service. It defines the legal framework for the provision of residential public services by the state, municipal entities, or private agents. The legislation establishes that firms providing these services must be incorporated as shareholding corporations or as industrial and commercial state companies. And it specifically bans practices that restrict competition, such as the following: charging rates that do not cover operating costs; providing services free of charge, or charging prices or rates that are insufficient to cover the cost of additional services not contemplated in the initial rate; reaching agreements with other firms to share market quotas, set rates, restrict supply, or raise rates above competition levels; any agreement with competitors for the purpose of modifying the outcomes of the competitive process; and the abuse of a dominant position.

Title VI of the legislation establishes the general criteria for the rate regime in terms of economic efficiency, neutrality, solidarity, redistribution, financial self-sufficiency, simplicity, and transparency. Economic efficiency means that rates should replicate competitive market prices. Neutrality means that each consumer is entitled to the same treatment as any other consumer. Solidarity and redistribution funds are created in order to enable commercial, industrial, and high-strata users to help lower-strata users pay for their basic needs.[15] Financial self-sufficiency implies that rate formulas guarantee adequate cost recovery, shareholder compensation equivalent to that provided by an efficient firm operating within a sector of comparable risk, and the use of technologies able to guarantee the best quality services.

The law also establishes three regulatory commissions: water and sewerage; telecommunications; and CREG for energy and gas. The agency's functions are to regulate monopolies involved in the provision of gas and electricity in cases where competition is not feasible. In other cases, the commission should promote competition among public service providers in order to ensure economic efficiency, no abuses of dominant market positions, and good quality services. The regulatory body establishes rates for electricity and gas supply or delegates

[15] Municipalities shall classify residential buildings, for public service provision purposes, in a maximum of six socioeconomic strata: (1) low-low; (2) low; (3) medium-low; (4) medium; (5) medium-high; and (6) high.

rate-setting authority to the distribution companies, subject to guidelines established by the regulator.

The board of the regulatory commission is made up of the ministers of Mines and Energy, Finance, and Economic Planning. The departmental aims and objectives of these ministries may at times conflict, giving rise to the opportunity for direct ministerial interference in the commission's work. The turnover of regulatory commission presidents, concomitant with the turnover of ministers, accelerated during 1998 and 1999. However, regulatory attempts at conveying further capacities on technical commissioners are apparent in Resolution 120 of December 1998 and Resolution 029 of July 1999.

Resolution 057 of 1996

Resolution 057 of 1996 summarized and clarified some aspects of most natural gas resolutions issued by the regulatory commission up to July 30, 1996. The resolution established a sector structure with four main features. First, five categories of independent agents are identified: producers, retailers, transporters, distributors, and large consumers. Limitations on market share and vertical and horizontal unbundling are established to ensure that competition is the rule for relationships among agents. Second, transport, distribution, and retail prices can be negotiated, subject to the maximum prices established by Resolution 057, except when free retail prices are stipulated. Wholesale prices are either free or subject to a transition scheme. Third, all agents have open access to distribution and transportation networks. Fourth, exclusive service areas for gas distribution and marketing are the exception, which is applicable when large investments are required to increase gas coverage.

Price Mechanisms

Production Prices

Producers are free to negotiate prices with their counterparts provided that equal users are awarded equal treatment, that is, industries in the same sector deserve the same treatment. Nevertheless, the regulatory commission sets maximum prices for wellhead gas. Resolution 057 of 1996 established the basis for a deregulated wholesale market subject to maximum prices and also determined a transition scheme.

The transition scheme gives producers the choice of negotiating prices or relying on a formula. Prices for reserves discovered in contracts signed after September 1995 are freely determined. In the case of reserves discovered in contracts signed prior to that date, producers may negotiate prices or rely on the formula that sets gas prices as a function of fuel prices. Beginning in 2005, prices

Appendix Table 12–7. Wellhead Gas Prices in Colombia, 1996–97
(U.S. dollars/MBTU)

Period	Regulated prices	Market prices
First semester 1996	1.04	1.30
Second semester 1996	1.20	1.39
First semester 1997	1.31	1.49

Source: Asociación Colombiana de Gas Natural, Naturgas (1999).

will be fully deregulated with one maximum reference price. It should be pointed out that most producers that have opted for formulas (regulated prices), established by the Resolution of 1983, obtained lower prices than those who chose market prices (see appendix table 12–7).

Resolution 057 permits different types of agreements in order to introduce a certain degree of flexibility on the maximum price-setting mechanism. One type of agreement is to calculate an average weighted maximum price for a period of time lasting up to two years. This means that, at a point in time, prices or rates can exceed the established maximum, provided that by the end of the period the average price or rate does not exceed the maximum. Second, Resolution 057 establishes the possibility of signing peak, interruptible, availability premium, variable price, and occasional spot contracts. Third, the resolution also allows for interruptible contracts in which the availability charge may not be linked to the whole volume supplied, but only to the noninterruptible one.

Transportation Rates

The regulator sets transportation rates for the integrated gas system. Producers and consumers pay according to their location in the network, regardless of the contracts between consumers and producers within each market. Resolution 057 establishes a new system of charges for entry in the Atlantic coast pipelines and in the interior system. To facilitate coordination with the interior system, entry into the Atlantic coast pipelines requires a unique charge or *estampilla* regardless of the distance involved. Entry charges to the interior system are calculated as a function of the cost of transporting gas from the producing fields to a reference node.[16] Exit charges are given by the cost of transporting gas from the reference node to exit nodes. Entry and exit charges are made up of two components, a capacity and a use charge. The capacity charge is applied on effectively contracted capacity and the use charge is applied on the volume of gas transported.

[16] The node selected as the reference center is located in Vasconia.

Distribution Rates

Resolution 057 also regulates distributors, that is, agents operating urban fuel gas distribution networks. According to the resolution, distributors must present studies of costs and rates to the regulatory commission, which then establishes an average maximum distribution charge. Distribution companies must then establish a rate structure so that average charges are below the average maximum. The average maximum distribution charge is calculated based on average long-term cost methodology, using the information presented by each firm. Accordingly, distribution costs factor in operating or projected investment in fixed assets (main pipelines, distribution networks, regulating stations, and other fixed assets), operating expenses, and return on investment. Each one of the preceding items is projected for a 20-year period, discounted by an opportunity rate representing the present value of the firm's profitability. Consumption items are also discounted by the same opportunity rate. The maximum average distribution charge is calculated by dividing the present value of executed costs by the present value of expected consumption. Rates calculated according to this method are approved for a five-year term unless, prior to expiration, the regulator and the distribution firm agree to modify it or extend the term or period, or for other reasons specified in the legislation.

Distribution companies have to set natural gas tariffs for small consumers by calculating the maximum unit average cost in dollars per cubic meter of natural gas purchases and per cubic meter of main pipeline transport. This is done on the basis of the agreed purchase and transport contracts, as indicated in the resolution. Distribution companies have the obligation to inform the public about rate adjustments resulting from variations in the formula's price indexes.

Contributions and Subsidies

Law 142 of 1994 requires that the local authority establish six categories of consumers, each with a different rate. Consumers in the highest categories (5 and 6) face rates that are above long-term marginal cost, while those in categories 1 through 3 face rates that are below long-term marginal cost. A consumer category is defined by the neighborhood where the consumer lives, rather than by consumer income. The maximum contribution from consumers in categories 5 and 6 to consumers in categories 1 through 3 is 20 percent. Likewise, the maximum subsidy received by categories 1 and 2 is 50 percent and 40 percent, respectively. However, Law 286 of 1996 establishes a transition period for public service firms to reach the limits established by Law 142.

Studies carried out by the regulatory commission to establish the transition period found that in 1996, the national average contribution was 60 percent for category 5 and 68 percent for category 6. The regulator, therefore, required firms to adjust the contributions of category 5 and 6 consumers and the subsidies received by category 1 and 2 consumers according to a defined path, reaching the maximum contributions and subsidies established in the law in 2001.

Final Observations

Beginning in 1994, Colombia took steps to gradually increase competition in the gas sector. There are still some obstacles to a fully competitive industry. The major obstacle to competition in the wholesale gas market is the size of Ecopetrol's share of production. Competition is restricted in a market where a state-owned enterprise holds a production share larger than 50 percent because this enterprise may effectively control the market and prevent the entry of new participants. Several measures have been taken recently to reduce Ecopetrol's market control. First, Ecopetrol's share in the exploitation of new gas fields has been reduced. Second, beginning in September 2000, natural gas producers will be prohibited from jointly retailing their production with other partners in the association contract. Third, producers and/or transporters of natural gas cannot directly generate electricity with natural gas. However, they will be allowed to hold up to a 25-percent stake in a firm involved in these activities. Exempted from that rule are transporters participating in electricity generation with gas in plants located outside their operating area.

The most important obstacle to competition in transportation seems to be lack of full unbundling that, in practice, might hamper open access because the transport company will be naturally prone to favor its participating agents. In addition, if after 15 years in private hands, Centragas and Gasoducto de Occidente are absorbed by Ecogas, competition would be set back.

In spite of the large number of distributors, distribution networks and consumer retail are controlled by a few related companies. In order to reduce the degree of concentration, several measures in the areas of distribution and retailing will be put in place in what seems a quite distant future. Beginning in 2015, no single firm will be permitted to cater, directly or indirectly, to over 30 percent of users (this will be estimated by dividing the number of a firm's users by the total number of users in the country). Firms with a market share of over 30 percent in 2015 will not be permitted to expand their distribution systems by acquiring participation in other existing or future companies. In addition, no firm will be permitted to provide over 25 percent of the gas of regulated or nonregulated final users, excluding gas sold for electricity generation, the petrochemical industry, or producer consumption. The resolution will be reviewed after five years to assess whether more than 25 percent of the national market is jointly managed.

Appendix 12-3. The Gas Sector in Mexico[17]

Mexico is the largest natural gas producer in Latin America; its production reached 32 billion cubic meters in 1998. It is estimated that Mexico's ratio of reserves to production is similar to Canada's, a country that produced 170 billion cubic meters in 1998. However, as appendix table 12–8 shows, production stagnated until the sector underwent a period of reform.

Petroleum represents 60 percent of the country's energy consumption. Natural gas ranks second, accounting for 20 percent of consumption. Gas consumption began to increase following the 1994 reform, and increased by 980 million m^3 per year to 1.4 billion m^3 per year in 1998. PEMEX accounts for approximately half of total consumption. PEMEX is a leader in the petrochemical industry and uses gas as an input in the production of oil. Industrial consumption accounts for 29 percent of total consumption, power plants represent 18 percent, and residential consumption remains insignificant at approximately 3 percent. As expected, consumption by power generation plants is the fastest-growing source of demand.

Sector Structure

The regulatory framework considers transportation, distribution, and gas supply to be different activities. However, one company may undertake all these activities subject to two limitations. First, distribution companies cannot carry out transportation services in the same geographic area, except when the regulatory commission authorizes it. Regulatory authorization takes place when vertical integration results in efficiency gains, the transportation infrastructure is lacking, and no other party is interested in the transportation project. Second, transportation, storage, and distribution concessionaires are required to maintain separate accounting and financial information related to each activity.

Consumers are free to purchase natural gas from a distributor other than the one assigned to their geographic area. Distribution and gas companies must provide third parties with access to the network. Concessionaires must provide services to all customers under similar conditions.

Production

Domestic output is concentrated in PEMEX, which enjoys a monopoly in exploration, production, and wholesale supply of domestic output. Reform has led to the liberalization of imports; however, imports are less than 10 percent of domestic sales.

[17] This appendix is based on Fernández-Ordóñez (1999b).

Appendix Table 12–8. Natural Gas Production and Dry Gas Domestic Sales in Mexico, 1980–99
(Millions of cubic feet per day)

Year	Production (1)	Sales (2)	Share (percent) (2)/(1)
1980	3,548.0	1,373.6	38.7
1981	4,060.8	1,423.4	35.1
1982	4,246.4	1,430.7	33.7
1983	4,053.6	1,398.7	34.5
1984	3,752.6	1,314.3	35.0
1985	3,603.8	1,296.9	36.0
1986	3,431.1	1,170.5	34.1
1987	3,498.4	1,176.5	33.6
1988	3,478.3	1,142.8	32.9
1989	3,571.7	1,192.7	33.4
1990	3,651.5	1,343.2	36.8
1991	3,633.5	1,467.0	40.4
1992	3,583.6	1,447.1	40.4
1993	3,576.5	1,379.9	38.6
1994	3,624.6	1,450.5	40.0
1995	3,759.2	1,551.2	41.3
1996	4,194.9	1,633.2	38.9
1997	4,467.1	1,717.0	38.4
1998	4,790.7	1,896.1	39.6
1999	4,924.3	2,105.6	42.8

Source: PEMEX.

Transportation

With its approximately 10,000 km of pipeline, PEMEX also controls the transport of natural gas. However, the reform allows private investors to enter the market and, as a result, the construction of 500 km of pipeline for private use was authorized between 1996 and 1998. During the same period, the construction of 1,600 km for public service was also approved.

The regulatory commission grants transportation licenses and permits to individuals and companies for periods of 30 years, renewable for 15 more. However, concessions do not entail exclusive rights over a geographic area because the regulatory framework establishes open access to transportation pipelines for all consumers and suppliers. Yet, PEMEX's control of production and transportation means that third-party use of pipelines has not been significant.

Distribution

Distribution concessions, granted through bids, give exclusivity rights over a geographic area. Coverage is expected to grow from 604,000 in 1997 to 952,000 in 2000, 1.3 million in 2001, 1.6 million in 2002, and 2.0 million in 2003. Since consumers have the right to choose suppliers, both suppliers and consumers have open access to the distribution and transportation networks. However, open access and free choice have seldom been implemented.

Regulatory Framework

Ley Reglamentaria, Article 27 of the Constitution, approved in May 1995, makes private participation possible in the construction and operation of natural gas transportation, storage, and distribution systems, activities previously reserved for PEMEX. The regulation of natural gas was approved in November 1995. The legal framework for creating the regulatory commission was established in 1994 in the Comisión Reguladora de Energía (CRE) legislation. The CRE was originally created in 1993 as a consultative body within the Energy Secretariat. In 1994, it was established as an autonomous body separate from the Energy Secretariat. The CRE has issued several norms regulating technical aspects of gas provision.[18] Norma Medio Ambiental 085 (Environmental Regulation 085) went into effect in January 1998. Although it does not refer to natural gas regulation, it introduces requirements that favor the use of natural gas on environmental grounds.

The regulatory commission is an independent body. The chairman of the board and four commissioners are appointed by the president for five-year alternate terms. The law specifies the specific reasons for removal of the commissioners from their posts. However, the commission is financed through annual budgetary allocations. This financial dependency may reduce the autonomy of the regulatory commission.

The commission relies on public hearing procedures to attend to general administrative issues (such as criteria and methodological matters) linked with regulated activities. That measure, in principle, seems to shrink the scope of public hearings as a source of transparency. The law also requires that records of the commission's resolutions be kept and made public.

---

[18] Regulation 001 (NOM-001-SECRE-1997) on the quality of natural gas; Regulation 002 (NOM-002-SECRE-1997) on the system/facilities for the exploitation/better use of natural gas; Regulation 003 (NOM-003-SECRE-1997) on the distribution of natural gas; Regulation 006 (NOM-006-SECRE-1998) on gas odorizing (which makes it possible to smell gas and prevents risks); Regulation 007 (NOM-007-SECRE-1998) on gas transportation; Regulation 008 (NOM-008-SECRE-1998) on protection for the steel pipelines for gas transportation.

The commission's functions are broad. It is charged with regulating and supervising various aspects of the provision of gas service. The regulatory commission approves the methodology for calculating rates and adjustments, approves and determines the rates that concessionaires charge users, carries out rate adjustments for each concessionaire every five years, approves the methodology that distributors should use to calculate natural gas acquisition prices, and verifies natural gas acquisition prices charged by distributors to end users. The regulatory commission also grants transportation, storage, and distribution permits; evaluates the technical feasibility of concessionaire proposals; defines the geographic distribution areas; organizes and carries out the procedures to issue permits in the geographic area; evaluates proposals; authorizes transfers, renovations, modifications, and early termination of concessions; and revokes permits within the limits established by law.[19] The commission regulates third-party access to the network and approves the rates, conditions, rights, and obligations of concessionaires and procedures for conflict resolution. It keeps a public registry of all regulated activities and also defines the rules for separating the accounting systems of production, transportation, retail, and distribution activities. It can also request information from import companies, export companies, concessionaires, and PEMEX on their natural gas activities. The commission is also capable of resolving conflicts between different agents and establishing sanctions within the framework and limits of the law.

Price Mechanisms

Production

As long as PEMEX holds a dominant position in the wholesale market, wholesale prices have to be capped by a maximum price system. To that end, the regulatory framework establishes rules for determining the price cap on PEMEX sales. The methodology for calculating the price cap is more a system for revising a given initial price than a product cost calculation. The initial price is PEMEX's 1996 price.[20] Adjustments are based on indicators that refer to gas prices in the United States as well as transportation price indicators from border to city. PEMEX must disclose the sales prices of the product and the transportation components in order to avoid discriminatory treatment in the case of consumers wishing to import gas instead of buying it from PEMEX.

The regulatory commission sets a price cap for transportation services that are reviewed every five years. The initial price cap for new pipelines is determined

[19] Ley de Regulación de Petróleo.

[20] A new regulation was issued in January 2000.

by the proposals that new sponsors present to the regulatory agency when requesting authorization. Distribution companies and consumers may sell their transportation rights. The secondary market that could exist as a result has yet to develop because of PEMEX's vertical control and the lack of independent suppliers.

Distribution

The regulatory commission also caps final consumer prices. The price caps are reviewed every five years. The initial price is the one included in the proposal when the concession is granted. Adjustment mechanisms include several adjustment factors, among them inflation (the most important) as well as efficiency and fiscal and concessionaire revenues. The inflation adjustment factor takes into account changes in producer prices in Mexico and the United States, as well as exchange rate fluctuations. The efficiency factor aims at stimulating and attracting investment in this initial phase, but it has not been used. The fiscal factor transfers tax costs related to users. The concessionaire factor aims to ensure a minimum income for the concessionaire. However, this factor is applied only during the fourth and sixth year after initial prices have been set.

In addition, to encourage network use by consumers, the regulatory commission requires that rates be broken down into two components: a capacity charge and a variable charge for use. Fixed transportation costs are included in the capacity charge and variable costs in the charge for use. Distribution costs are assigned 50 percent to capacity charges and 50 percent to use charges.

Final Observations

Despite recent reforms designed to increase competition in the sector, Mexico's natural gas industry remains monopolistic. This model has several shortcomings. The most important impediment to the development of competitive markets in Mexico is PEMEX's control of production and transportation. This control and the lack of adequate separation between regulated and nonregulated activities mean that the liberalization of imports has not had much of an impact on competition.

PEMEX's production and exploration monopoly is difficult to eliminate because it is enshrined in the Constitution. Without changing this, other reforms would have only a marginal impact on promoting competition. However, PEMEX's control of the transportation sector can be reduced through the divestiture of assets and separation of regulated and nonregulated activities. This would better facilitate competition from imports.

The distribution features of the Mexican gas sector are similar to those in the competition model. For instance, consumers may choose a supplier, transportation concessions do not grant exclusivity, and the possibility of a secondary market in transport capacity exists. Nevertheless, PEMEX's control over exploration, transportation, and production has prevented effective competition.

Policymaking, regulation, and service provision functions have been assigned, respectively, to the government, the regulatory commission, and the companies. This separation is an initial step in the right direction; however, the weight of publicly owned enterprises in the market may render this separation ineffective.

References

Asociación Colombiana de Gas Natural. 1999. *El gas natural en Colombia.* Bogotá, Colombia: Naturgas.

Ellig, J., and J. P. Kalt. 1996. *New Horizons in Natural Gas Deregulation.* Westport, CT: Praeger Publishers.

Fernández-Ordóñez, M. A. 1999a. "El gas natural en Argentina." Inter-American Development Bank, Washington, D.C. Unpublished.

———. 1999b. "El gas natural en México." Inter-American Development Bank, Washington, D.C. Unpublished.

Juris, A. 1998. *The Emergence of Markets in the Natural Gas Industry.* Private Participation in Infrastructure Group Working Paper, Private Sector Development Department, The World Bank, Washington, D.C.

Urbiztondo, S., S. August, and F. Basañes. 1999. "Access Arrangements in Argentina's Public Utilities: Electricity, Natural Gas and Telecommunications." Inter-American Development Bank, Washington, D.C. Unpublished.